CAMBRIDGE
UNIVERSITY PRESS

CAMBRIDGE ENGLISH
Language Assessment
Part of the University of Cambridge

CAMBRIDGE OFFICIAL PREPARATION MATERIAL

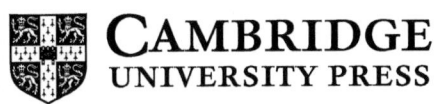

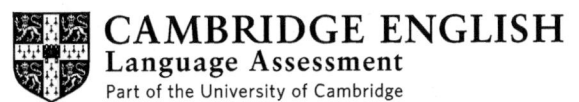

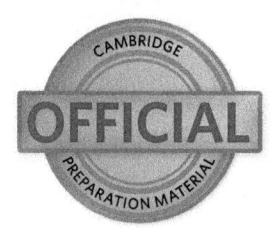

Kid's Box

Updated Second Edition

Teacher's Book 4

British English

Lucy Frino and Melanie Williams
with Caroline Nixon & Michael Tomlinson

Cambridge University Press
www.cambridge.org/elt

Cambridge English Language Assessment
www.cambridgeenglish.org

Information on this title: www.cambridge.org/9781316627921

© Cambridge University Press 2009, 2015, 2017

It is normally necessary for written permission for copying to be obtained *in advance* from a publisher. The worksheets, role-play cards, tests, and audioscripts at the back of this book are designed to be copied and distributed in class. The normal requirements are waived here and it is not necessary to write to Cambridge University Press for permission for an individual teacher to make copies for use within his or her own classroom. Only those pages that carry the wording '© Cambridge University Press' may be copied.

First published 2009
Second edition 2015
Updated Second edition 2017
20 19 18 17 16 15 14 13 12 11 10 9 8 7 6 5 4

Printed in Great Britain by CPI Group (UK) Ltd, Croydon CR0 4YY

A catalogue record for this publication is available from the British Library

ISBN 978-1-316-62792-1 Teacher's Book 4
ISBN 978-1-316-62769-3 Pupil's Book 4
ISBN 978-1-316-62877-5 Activity Book with Online Resources 4
ISBN 978-1-316-62899-7 Class Audio CDs 4 (3 CDs)
ISBN 978-1-316-62946-8 Teacher's Resource Book with Online Audio 4
ISBN 978-1-316-62865-2 Flashcards 4 (pack of 103)
ISBN 978-1-316-62979-6 Interactive DVD with Teacher's Booklet 4 (PAL/NTSC)
ISBN 978-1-316-62802-7 Presentation Plus 4
ISBN 978-1-316-62855-3 Language Portfolio 4
ISBN 978-1-316-62870-6 Posters 4

Additional resources for this publication at www.cambridge.org/kidsbox

Cambridge University Press has no responsibility for the persistence or accuracy of URLs for external or third-party internet websites referred to in this publication, and does not guarantee that any content on such websites is, or will remain, accurate or appropriate. Information regarding prices, travel timetables, and other factual information given in this work is correct at the time of first printing but Cambridge University Press does not guarantee the accuracy of such information thereafter.

Contents

Language summary	iv
Introduction	vi
Hello there!	4
1 Back to school	10
Maths: Measuring	16
2 Good sports	18
Sport: Ball games	24
Review 1 and 2	26
3 Health matters	28
Music: Body percussion	34
4 After school club	36
English literature: Poems, plays and novels	42
Review 3 and 4	44
5 Exploring our world	46
Science: Endangered animals	52
6 Technology	54
Technology: Robots	60
Review 5 and 6	62
7 At the zoo	64
Science: Skeletons	70
8 Let's party!	72
Science: Food	78
Review 7 and 8	80
Values 1 and 2 Value others	82
Values 3 and 4 Be kind	83
Values 5 and 6 Be safe	84
Values 7 and 8 Recycle	85
Grammar reference	T86
Movers practice test audioscript and key	T88
Movers practice test	88
Photocopiable activities	T90
Extra activities	T108
Extra project ideas	T121
Irregular verbs	T125

Language summary

	Key vocabulary	Key grammar and functions	Phonics	Revision
Hello there! page 4	Character names Personal descriptions **Jobs**: *farmer, dentist, detective, driver, doctor, teacher*	Comparative adjectives Present simple Frequency adverbs: *always, sometimes, never* *have to* *like / love* + *-ing* *want to be*	short vowel sound 'a' (m<u>a</u>n) and long vowel sounds 'ai' and 'ar' (s<u>ay</u> and c<u>ar</u>)	adjectives, numbers, personal information, hobbies, comparative adjectives, character names, actions, jobs, days of the week, daily routines, *was / were*
1 Back to school page 10	**Adjectives**: *boring, busy, careful, difficult, easy, exciting, quick, slow, terrible*	Relative clauses with *who*	short vowel sound 'i' (qu<u>i</u>ck) and long vowel sounds 'ee' and 'ie' (<u>ea</u>sy and fl<u>y</u>)	school, school subjects, comparative adjectives, colours, *like, have got,* prepositions, relative clauses with *who*, present continuous, actions and activities, clothes, food and drink, question forms, numbers, classroom objects, measurements

Maths **Measuring** page 16

	Key vocabulary	Key grammar and functions	Phonics	Revision
2 Good sports page 18	*inside, outside* **Activities**: *climb, dance, fish, ride, run, sail, sing, skate, skip, swim* **Adverbs of manner**: *badly, carefully, easily, happily, quickly, quietly, slowly, well*	Relative clauses with *where* *learn to do* (something) Adverbs of manner	silent consonants (i<u>s</u>land)	weather, prepositions, present continuous, adjectives, *can, have got*, sports and activities, jobs, sports equipment, *want to, must, have to, need,* question forms, present simple, action verbs, impersonal *you*, adverbs

Sport **Ball games** page 24   **Review** 1 and 2 page 26

	Key vocabulary	Key grammar and functions	Phonics	Revision
3 Health matters page 28	**Health**: *dentist, have a dream, have an eye test, hospital, ill, nurse, see the doctor, take some medicine*	Past simple irregular verbs: affirmative, negative, interrogative and short answers Clauses with *because*	Consonant sounds 'b', 'f' and 'v' (<u>b</u>all, <u>ph</u>one and <u>v</u>illage)	days of the week, *was / were*, school subjects, illnesses, food, time, town, family, prepositions, adjectives, countable and uncountable nouns, sports and activities, past simple, *have got*, physical descriptions, parts of the body

Music **Body percussion** page 34

	Key vocabulary	Key grammar and functions	Phonics	Revision
4 After school club page 36	**Activities**: *do a musical, play chess / table tennis* **Ordinal numbers**: *first–twentieth*	Past simple regular verbs: affirmative, negative, interrogative and short answers Spelling of *-ed* endings	*-ed* endings 'd', 'id' and 't' (call<u>ed</u>, want<u>ed</u>, kick<u>ed</u>)	*can / can't, have to, want,* activities and actions, houses and flats, adjectives, sports, past simple, animals, food, clothes, prepositions, weather, descriptions

English literature **Poems, plays and novels** page 42   **Review** 3 and 4 page 44

	Key vocabulary	Key grammar and functions	Phonics	Revision
5 Exploring our world page 46	**Exploring**: Antarctica, continents, exhibition, expedition, explorer, ice, make a camp, museum, school trip, ship	Past simple irregular verbs could / couldn't: ability and short answers Clauses with so Comparative of two- and three-syllable adjectives Comparative adverbs Possessive pronouns	long vowel sound 'er' (n<u>ur</u>se)	actions, weather, animals, adjectives, prepositions, connectors, numbers (years), past simple, question forms, days of the week, must, need, Let's … , comparatives

| Science | Endangered animals | page 52 |

	Key vocabulary	Key grammar and functions	Phonics	Revision
6 Technology page 54	**Technology**: button, computer, DVD, email, the internet, mobile phone, mouse, MP3 player, screen, text message, turn on, video	Past simple irregular verbs	long vowel sound 'or' (d<u>au</u>ghter)	have to, present simple, comparative adjectives, questions, technology, numbers, have got, daily routines, prepositions, clothes, past simple, household chores, relative clauses with which, parts of the body

| Technology | Robots | page 60 | | Review 5 and 6 page 62 |

	Key vocabulary	Key grammar and functions	Phonics	Revision
7 At the zoo page 64	**Animals**: bat, bear, bird, blue whale, crocodile, dolphin, elephant, giraffe, kangaroo, lion, lizard, monkey, panda, parrot, polar bear, rabbit, shark, snake, tiger	Superlative of two- and three-syllable adjectives Past simple irregular verbs Prepositions: behind, between, in, in front of, into, next to, on, opposite, out of, under, round	the short vowel sound 'oo' and the long vowel sound 'oo' (l<u>oo</u>k and t<u>oo</u>th)	animals, prepositions, adjectives, size, weight, distance, questions, family, can / can't, wild animals, definitions, past simple, town, country, have to, superlative adjectives, parts of the body, numbers, action verbs

| Science | Skeletons | page 70 |

	Key vocabulary	Key grammar and functions	Phonics	Revision
8 Let's party! page 72	**Containers**: bag, bowl, bottle, box, cup, glass **Food**: cheese, pasta, sandwich, salad, soup, vegetables	Expressions of quantity: a cup / bag / bowl / glass / bottle / box of Superlative adverbs: the most quickly want someone to do (something)	one-, two- and three-syllable words	food and drink, Would you like … ?, polite requests, containers, parties, colours, adverbs, adjectives, present continuous, question forms, jobs, have to, need, should, must, weights and measures, sequencing, relative clauses, describing people, sports and activities, superlative adjectives, present continuous, past tense

| Science | Food | page 78 | | Review and page 80 |

Values 1 & 2	Value others	page 82
Values 3 & 4	Be kind	page 83
Values 5 & 6	Be safe	page 84
Values 7 & 8	Recycle	page 85
Grammar reference	page T86

Introduction

Kid's Box introduces pupils to the pleasures of learning English and enables them to consistently improve throughout the seven books in the series. All seven levels develop pupils' abilities in the four skills – listening, speaking, reading and writing – as well as challenging them cognitively and helping them to feel a real sense of achievement in learning. As experienced teachers ourselves, we are aware of the demands and difficulties involved in managing a diverse and mixed ability classroom. Teaching younger learners can be at once the most rewarding and the most soul-destroying of pursuits! Sometimes we can have very bad days, but it's the good days that give us an exhilarating sense of achievement, a sense of being part of a child's future development.

Plutarch reminds us that **'The mind is not a vessel to be filled, but a fire to be ignited'** and this concept of learning underpins *Kid's Box*. Pupils learn when they are interested and involved: when they want to find something out, when they are playing a game, when they are listening to a story, when they are doing craft activities. Learning is an active process in every way and *Kid's Box* makes sure that pupils are physically and mentally active and that they are encouraged to make sense of the language themselves. **'The art of teaching is the art of assisting discovery'**, Mark Van Doren.

The language syllabus of *Kid's Box* has been carefully selected and graded to suit the age and level of the pupils. Language is introduced in context and in manageable chunks, giving pupils plenty of opportunities to practise and become familiar with the meanings and the sounds. Language is recycled throughout the units and pupils can practise the language in different contexts. They can also personalise it. Recycling is particularly important for young learners, who tend to forget quite quickly and who do not have the study skills of older learners. For this reason, there is constant revision and recycling throughout the units and course.

The units are based around the Star family and their friends. Characters give pupils a way of contextualising the language and help them to make it meaningful and purposeful. The characters develop throughout the books so as to sustain the pupils' interest and motivation.

Cambridge English: Young Learners

In *Kid's Box* we have followed the syllabus for the Young Learners tests so that each cycle of two levels corresponds to one of the tests. Thus the material covered in the first cycle coincides with that which is required for Starters, cycle 2 with Movers, and cycle 3 with Flyers. *Kid's Box* covers all the relevant language structures, presents and practises the vocabulary and includes examples of the task types from the tests. Where certain topics include a vocabulary list which is too comprehensive to include all of the lexical items in the Pupil's Book, additional activities have been offered in the Teacher's Resource Book.

Each *Cambridge English: Young Learners* test consists of three papers: Listening, Reading and Writing, and Speaking. These tests are child-friendly and motivating, and have been specially written for primary learners. They are taken by pupils all over the world, have international recognition and are backed by the reputation and research of Cambridge English Language Assessment. They provide a gentle introduction to public exams, and research shows that children find the tests highly motivating. The tests can act as a stepping stone to other Cambridge English exams, as the highest level, *Cambridge English: Flyers*, is roughly equivalent in language level to *Cambridge English: Key for Schools*.

The *Cambridge English: Young Learners* tests are an incentive; however, they should at no stage be seen as obligatory. For further information on the component papers for each test, visit: www.cambridgeenglish.org/exams

Common European Framework of Reference for Languages – Learning, Teaching, Assessment

Kid's Box has been written taking into account the proposals included in the Common European Framework of Reference (CEFR). The CEFR has been designed for language teachers and material developers to be able to define different levels of competence and performance. These objectives coincide with those of *Cambridge English: Young Learners tests*.

Flyers	(at around Level A2 of the CEFR)
Movers	(at Level A1)
Starters	(below Level A1)

The framework places emphasis on values such as pupil autonomy, proposing a task-based methodology with functional evaluation criteria. Although large parts of the CEFR are more relevant to older learners and have not been designed specifically for the primary classroom, it includes two particularly useful parts which are the Common Reference Levels and the English Language Portfolio.

The Common Reference Levels offer a description of what a language learner 'can do' at different stages of the learning process. These levels can be consulted separately, but they have been mirrored here in the self-evaluation sections.

The Language Portfolio is designed as a compendium of skills acquired and work done which incorporates the 'can do' checklists for self-assessment. This is important for pupil motivation and can also be shown to parents to inform them of the syllabus and objectives set for their children.

Course components

Levels one to six of *Kid's Box* include a Pupil's Book, Activity Book, Class Audio CDs, Teacher's Book, Teacher's Resource Book, Presentation Plus, Online Resources, Interactive DVD, Language Portfolio, Tests and Posters. There are also Flashcards for Levels 1 to 4. The new Starter Level offers a Class Book with CD-ROM, Class Audio CDs, Flashcards, Teacher's Book, Teacher's Resource Book, Presentation Plus, Interactive DVD and Posters.

Pupil's Book

This 104-page full-colour book consists of nine units. Each unit is six pages in length, with each page providing sufficient material for one lesson. After each unit there is a Content and Language Integrated Learning (CLIL) spread to learn about other subjects through English. The Review sections cover language from the previous two units. There is a phonics section within every unit. There are four Values pages at the end of the book to develop pupils' social awareness. Lessons include a variety of interesting and motivating activities such as pair work, role plays, craft activities, guessing games, songs and chants. The series' strong cast of characters appears throughout the book. The antics of the popular Lock and Key are played out in a picture story at the end of each unit. At the end of the book there is a *Cambridge English: Movers*-style practice test covering the Listening and the Reading and Writing papers.

Activity Book
This 88-page book is designed to give pupils further practice with the new language and to help them consolidate their understanding. The pupils will have fun doing the activities and you will find that they stimulate their creativity too. The Activity Book materials are designed to be integrated into the lessons and there is guidance in the Teacher's Book as to how this works. This edition also features a full-page *Cambridge English: Young Learners* practice activity for each unit.

Class Audio CDs
The Class Audio CDs contain all of the listening material for the Pupil's Book and Activity Book, including all of the songs and stories. The songs are available in both sung and karaoke versions.

Teacher's Resource Book with Online Audio
The Teacher's Resource Book contains a wealth of photocopiable activities to help with mixed ability classes. There are two reinforcement and two extension worksheets for every unit, as well as song and topic worksheets for further exploitation. The Teacher's Resource Book also includes extra *Cambridge English: Young Learners*-type tests with listening content online. The book also features word cards to reinforce target vocabulary.

Language Portfolio
In accordance with CEFR guidelines, there is a Language Portfolio of individual competencies to lead the pupil to self-evaluation and to record the learning experience of each pupil throughout the primary school years.

Interactive DVD
As you navigate your way through the Star family house on our interactive DVD, you will find animated versions of the stories in Suzy's room, the songs with animation and video in Mr Star's music room, video documentaries in the living room, interactive games in Simon's room and a quiz in Stella's room.

Teacher's Book
This 232-page interleaved Pupil's and Teacher's Book provides teaching notes for each lesson, which include recording scripts for all listening activities and answer keys for all activities, an overview of the syllabus for each level, extra activities, photocopiable pages and extra project ideas.

Teaching notes
The teaching notes provide step-by-step guidelines for each page. Lesson objectives are clearly described and the materials needed for each lesson are specified. Each lesson starts with a *Warmer* and finishes with an *Ending the lesson* activity. Activities from the Activity Book are integrated with the Pupil's Book activities to provide a balanced range of appropriate activities. There are two *Extra activities* provided for each lesson for times when you need even more material. These Extra activities only appear in the Teacher's Book and there are suggestions in the teaching notes as to when each activity should be used in the lesson. They are not designed only for the end of the lesson.

[M] towards these activities introduce children to the Movers test tasks to gain confidence in aspects of the task types.
[M] these activities are closer in format and content to the Movers test tasks.

Photocopiable pages
There is at least one photocopiable page for each unit in the back of the Teacher's Book. These pages provide you with a range of manual activities to use with your pupils: for example, there are crosswords, a survey and an information-gap activity. There are full instructions in the teaching notes on how to prepare the materials and when and how to use them in class.

Presentation Plus
Presentation Plus includes Interactive Whiteboard tools, a fully interactive Pupil's Book and Activity Book, digital versions of the Teacher's Book and Teacher's Resource Book, a multimedia library including video from the DVD, Class Audio and access to online teacher training support. This pack enables you to plan and deliver your lessons 'paper-free' from a tablet or a computer.

Online Resources
The online platform includes games and extra grammar, vocabulary and writing activities for every single unit, providing plenty of extra practice. All the pupils' online work can be tracked and reviewed by the teacher.

Tests
The Level 3 and 4 Tests and Audio allow you to regularly assess your pupils in different ways. You can choose the unit tests, review tests and end-of-level tests, as customisable Microsoft Word documents. If you are preparing pupils for the *Cambridge English: Young Learners* tests, you can additionally select the *Cambridge English: Young Learners* style unit tests, review tests and end-of-level tests, as Adobe PDFs. Visit cambridge.org/kidsbox/tests

Posters
These colourful and appealing posters aid revision by giving pupils the chance to practise unit language in a different and fun context. They can be added to the classroom wall as you progress through the course to aid revision. This pack includes eight posters with clear teaching notes available online.

Flashcards
There are 103 flashcards to accompany level 4. These colourful flashcards illustrate the key vocabulary items of each unit on one side and have the words on the other. They are large enough for all pupils to see and there are numerous ideas of how to use them in the Teacher's Book for each lesson.

What does Kid's Box offer?
'To awaken interest and kindle enthusiasm is the sure way to teach easily and successfully', Tyron Edwards.
Once pupils are interested, and ready and eager to learn, then the job of teaching them becomes so much easier. The materials in *Kid's Box* have been designed to do just that. Here's how and why it works:

- **Humour through the characters and the stories**
  'The important thing is not so much that every child should be taught, as that every child should be given the wish to learn', John Lubbock.

  For younger pupils, motivation is vital if the language acquisition process is to be successful. We have tried to include an element of humour in the presentations and, more particularly, in the story which rounds off each of the units. This story is designed to revise what pupils have been studying and galvanise them to study more because they want to follow the adventures of the characters.

- **Creativity and learning through action and activity**
'I hear and I forget. I see and I remember. I do and I understand', Chinese proverb.

Young learners need a lot of meaningful, contextualised practice if they are to become successful language learners. In *Kid's Box* there is plenty of 'hands on' practice. Drawing, colouring, 'make and do', songs, games and chants are all activity types which form an integral part of the learning process. These enable pupils to be creative and they help to anchor knowledge more effectively. It's only through repeated practice that skills, awareness and understanding can be developed.

- **Connecting to the world outside the classroom**
'A child educated only at school is an uneducated child', George Santayana.

The CLIL sections bring the outside world into the classroom so that pupils learn about the world around them as they learn English. This helps them understand that English is more than a classroom subject and lets them realise ways in which English can be used as a tool for knowledge.

'I like a teacher who gives you something to take home to think about besides homework', Lilly Tomlin (Edith Ann).

- **Discovery and the development of learner autonomy**
'The object of teaching a child is to enable him to get along without his teacher', Elbert Hubbard.

For pupils to be able to learn effectively and to continue to learn, they need to be encouraged and enabled to find things out for themselves. *Kid's Box* includes self-correction and other activities to develop learner autonomy. Communicative activities, such as pair work, group work and role play, give pupils the opportunity to work independently of the teacher. In these types of activities, the teacher's role is as a guide and facilitator. In this instance we should stand back a little from the activity and monitor and assist when necessary.

- **Promoting tolerance and respect**
'The highest result of education is tolerance', Helen Keller.

The material and activities in the book help pupils to appreciate cultural diversity, respect differences and develop human values. Respect for and protection of the natural environment goes hand in hand with the respecting of other human beings. This theme runs throughout the whole of *Kid's Box* and in particular in the Values sections of the Pupil's Book and the Activity Book.

Learning styles / Multiple intelligences

'If a child can't learn the way we teach, maybe we should teach the way they learn', Ignacio Estrada.

We now understand that people learn in different ways. We don't talk about 'intelligence' any more, we talk about 'intelligences'. The activities in *Kid's Box* are designed to stimulate these different intelligences. This means there will always be something to appeal to every learner.

- **Linguistic intelligence:** sensitivity to the written and spoken word and the ability to learn languages.

  It is a core element of any language course, and in *Kid's Box* this is exploited in combination with the other intelligences.

- **Interpersonal intelligence:** effective communication with others.

  Communication activities have been incorporated from the Starter Level onwards. It is a vital aspect of language learning and is essential in making younger learners aware that language is a tool for communication and not just another school subject. Communication activities help interpersonal skills, encouraging children to work together and develop important communication strategies.

- **Intrapersonal intelligence:** expression of inner thoughts and feelings.

  Throughout the course there are various reflective activities. For example, 'Do you remember?' and 'Can do' sections help pupils become more aware of themselves.

- **Musical intelligence:** appreciation of rhythm and music.

  This intelligence runs almost parallel to linguistic intelligence, as Howard Gardner points out. Each unit of *Kid's Box* includes a song as well as occasional raps, rhymes and chants.

- **Bodily-kinaesthetic intelligence:** coordination and connection with the whole body.

  This is extremely important for the developing minds and bodies of younger learners, as there is a significant relation between mental and physical activity. In *Kid's Box* there are plenty of action songs and rhymes, which can help develop bodily-kinaesthetic intelligence at the same time as offering a change of rhythm and activity to the ever-restless young learner.

- **Logical-mathematical intelligence:** problem solving and logical thought.

  There is a range of different activity types for this intelligence in *Kid's Box*. These activities help develop logical reasoning, problem solving and the detection of patterns. We feel they are vital and extremely motivating.

- **Visual-spatial intelligence:** expression and understanding through the visual world.

  This intelligence is one of the key ways that children learn. In *Kid's Box* there is a range of ways in which pupils' visual-spatial intelligence is supported and developed, such as the full colour illustrations in the Pupil's Books, the flashcards, the colouring activities and the content from the interactive DVD.

Tips for teachers

Preparation

- In order to guarantee a positive learning experience, pupils need to be properly prepared before doing any task. Ensure they have the language they need to carry out an activity and that they know exactly how to do it.
- Before starting an activity, demonstrate it. For pairwork activities, choose an individual pupil to help you. Do the first question of the pairwork task with the pupil for the class to get an idea. You can follow this up with an open pair demonstration, choosing two pupils from the class to do another question and answer for the whole class.
- When you divide the class into pairs or groups, point to each pupil and say, for example, A–B, A–B, A–B and so on, so they are in no doubt what their role is. You can follow this up with *As, put up your hands. Bs, put up your hands* as a further check. Try to give simple, clear instructions in English. Say, for example, *As ask the question and Bs answer the question: A–B,*

A–B, A–B. Then Bs ask the question and As answer the question: B–A, B–A, B–A.
- Always bring a few extra copies of the photocopiable worksheets to avoid tears if any pupils do it wrong and want to start again.

Classroom dynamics
'**A good teacher, like a good entertainer, first must hold his audience's attention, then he can teach his lesson**', John Henrik Clarke.
- Try to move around the classroom while explaining or doing the activities. Circulating among the pupils enables you more effectively to supervise and monitor those who may need more attention at times.
- In the same way that it is a good idea for teachers to move around, it is also advisable to move the pupils themselves around occasionally. By periodically changing seating arrangements, you can help group dynamics and break up potentially disruptive pupils. For example, weaker pupils could be put next to stronger ones, and more hard-working pupils next to disruptive ones. Pupils might benefit from working with learners they may not usually associate with.
- When forming pairs or groups, we suggest that, whenever possible, pupils just move their chairs. For group work, they can bring chairs around one or two tables, allowing them an easy environment for discussion and written work. For pair work, they can position their two chairs to face each other. This allows a more realistic eye-to-eye communication situation. This change of seating prepares them for the oral work they are about to begin.

Noise
- While speaking activities which involve movement around the classroom can make the class more lively and dynamic, they will also generate a lot of excitement. When pupils are excited, they can become noisy and may even use their first language to talk about or discuss some aspect of the activity. Although it can be difficult to get used to it at first, noise in the classroom is tolerable if it is related directly to the activity and is an expression of interest or enthusiasm for the task in hand. You should ensure, however, that only English is used for the completion of tasks and for correction at the end of the activity.

Teaching and learning
'**Mistakes are the portals of discovery**', James Joyce.
- Making mistakes is a vital part of the learning process, so when pupils are asked to invent their own sentences, stories, chants, etc we should not expect these to be perfect. Sometimes accuracy should be forfeited for the sake of creativity, enthusiastic participation and learning.
- Activities that pupils traditionally find engaging include: moving about, singing, playing games, doing puzzles and colouring in. Wherever possible, use these as effective teaching tools. In this way, young learners can use language to practise English, and work very hard, without being conscious of it. By setting them in meaningful contexts, the diverse disciplines of language learning such as grammar, reading, pronunciation and communication can be taught with a dynamic and child-friendly approach.

- The Extra activities for each lesson can be used when you feel that pupils need more practice with some of the language, or when you think you will finish the lesson material before the end of the lesson.
- Try to avoid the immediate repetition of an activity simply because it has worked well in class and your pupils have enjoyed it. If you do this, the novelty will quickly wear off and pupils will become bored. Save it for a later occasion and they will come back to it with fresh enthusiasm.
- When pupils are doing listening activities, it is usual for them to listen to the material twice. After the first listening, it is a good idea for pupils to check their answers with each other. This makes them feel more confident if they have the same answers, and is less intimidating if they don't. This approach also gives them a purpose for listening the second time: to confirm or to check again. When checking answers with the whole class, try to include as many pupils as you can and encourage them to say longer phrases rather than single words.
- Pupils are sometimes shy to speak out. They say the answer quietly to the teacher and then the teacher repeats it for the class. This is effective – but it does not help the pupils develop their speaking or listening skills. Whenever possible, you should encourage pupils to speak loudly and clearly and, if the rest of the class didn't hear what the pupil said, you should ask the pupil to repeat, rather than repeat it yourself.

'**A teacher is a person who never says anything once**', Howard Nemerov.
- Recycling is an important part of the learning process. Don't expect pupils to remember everything from a previous lesson in the next one. They will only absorb what attracts or interests them, and what they are ready to learn. *Kid's Box* builds in regular recycling and, as the pupils get older, they will come to realise that they can investigate something further by themselves if it really interests them.
- Be flexible within teaching. It is important to take time to listen to pupils and to connect with them. You should try to familiarise yourself with their likes and dislikes and identify both their learning and their emotional needs. If you can do this, then you will be better able to support them in their learning.

Assessment and evaluation
- With pupils of this age, it is best to use continuous assessment. This means we monitor their progress in the classroom and use this information to help us with our teaching. For example, we may find that we need to review language previously taught, or that we can add more challenging activities because pupils are ready for these.
- Children do not develop at the same rate and they do not learn in the same way. So we need to assess each pupil as an individual and not compare them with the other pupils in the class. We should look for progress and development in every pupil. With young children, we should assess and monitor their social and emotional development, as well as their learning of English. This means we should praise effort, and encourage them to share and to work in pairs and groups, as well as giving them feedback on their English.

Discipline

'No life ever grows great until it is focused, dedicated, disciplined', Harry Emerson Fosdick.

- One of the most challenging aspects of teaching young learners is holding their interest in the classroom. Pupils have limitless energy, combined with an extremely limited attention span. We have to juggle these factors to try to avoid boredom, restlessness and demotivation, all of which lead to problems with discipline. By channelling pupils' innate energy to the good, we can often avoid unruliness and indiscipline. A lot of discipline problems arise when pupils are underchallenged and bored, or when activities are too repetitive. *Kid's Box* has been written by experienced teachers who at all times have borne in mind the needs and requirements of pupils and have included a variety of activities for them to enjoy.
- It is important that you establish a context of discipline in your class. Make sure pupils know what is acceptable and what is not and make sure you treat all pupils in the same way. Pupils are very aware when we are not 'fair'. Clear and fair discipline parameters create a 'safe' classroom environment in which pupils can work confidently and freely. This makes for an ordered, busy classroom, rather than an anarchic one.

Songs, rhymes and chants

- For the activities based around songs, rhymes and chants, it is not always necessary for pupils to understand every word outside the key words being practised. In these activities, we are more interested in pupils understanding the gist, and we are using the rhyme as a means with which to practise language, rhythm and pronunciation. The visuals that accompany the rhymes, songs and chants, and the actions included in some, should provide pupils with sufficient information to be able to understand the overall concept. It is important then, at this stage, not to spend precious class time on lengthy and complicated explanations of specific words.
- Get pupils to stand up when performing the songs, rhymes or chants. It can make a tremendous difference to their performance and enjoyment.
- Songs, rhymes and chants can be presented in different ways to make them more interesting and challenging. These techniques are especially useful if you want to go back to previously-used material for revision or further exploitation and want to avoid your pupils' reaction of 'We've already done this!'
  - Whisper the rhyme or phrase while clicking your fingers. Repeat the rhyme, getting gradually louder each time and then reverse the process.
  - Say a rhyme or chant whilst clapping hands and tapping your foot in time to the rhythm.
  - Divide the class into groups and ask them to repeat the rhyme or chant in rounds. To do this, the first group starts to say the rhyme and then, at a suitable point, usually one or two lines into it, the second group starts to say the rhyme from the beginning.
  - With your class audio or video recorder, record the class performing. Be sure to give them a round of applause and encourage the rest of the class to do the same. Let your pupils listen to themselves. If they feel that they could improve on a second attempt, record them again.
- It can be extremely motivating for children to watch their own performances on video, but if you video or photograph your pupils, make sure you get written permission from parents or guardians first.

Competition

- An element of competition can make many pupils try harder. However, while a competition can be a good incentive for an otherwise unenthusiastic pupil, it can sometimes be demotivating for a less able but ordinarily hard-working one. Before playing a competitive game, it may be useful to explain to pupils that this is only a means of learning. Although they may not win the game, all pupils are 'winners' if they know more English at the end than they knew at the beginning. Help pupils to understand that when they play a game they can practise and learn more English, so they each win a prize and that prize is knowledge.

  Nonetheless, it is always a good idea to balance competitive games with cooperative ones and to include other activities so that you can reward and praise individuals according to their own needs and performance.

Display

- Pupils find it extremely motivating to have their work displayed and will generally work hard to produce work to the best of their ability if they know it is going to be seen by others. So try to arrange to display pupils' work around the classroom or school whenever possible. Don't forget to include work by all the pupils (not in every display, but over a period of time) and to change the displays regularly.

Craft activities: storage of material

- It is useful to keep supplies for craft activities, for example scissors, glue, wool, crayons, in a large box in the classroom. Then when it is time for craft activities, you can put the box on a table and pupils can come and collect what they need.
- Make sure pupils always clear up at the end of craft activities; that they put materials back in the box and that they put rubbish in the bin. You will need to supply each pupil with an envelope for photocopiable activities, such as game cards. At the end of the activity, pupils write their name on their envelope and put their cards inside. With younger pupils, it is best if you look after the envelopes until the next time you want to use the cards.

A final word

We've had a lot of fun writing this course and sincerely hope that you and your pupils have as much fun using it.

Caroline Nixon and Michael Tomlinson, Murcia 2017.

Hello there!

1 Look, think and answer.
1. What does Stella want to be?
2. Who's a farmer?
3. What's Simon reading?
4. Who's riding Suzy's bike?

2 🎧 Listen and check.

3 Listen again. Choose the right words.
1. Stella's **twelve** / **twenty** / **ten**. — Stella's ten.
2. Simon's older than **Suzy** / **Stella** / **May**.
3. Fred is Simon's **father** / **brother** / **uncle**.
4. Simon wants to be a **farmer** / **detective** / **dentist**.
5. Grandpa Star's **funny** / **young** / **sad**.
6. Aunt May's **younger** / **older** / **smaller** than Suzy.

LOOK
Stella's **older than** Simon.
Simon's **younger than** Stella.

OBJECTIVES: By the end of the lesson, pupils will have reviewed introductions and how to ask for and give personal information.

● TARGET LANGUAGE
Key language: greetings, jobs (*teacher, doctor, dentist, farmer, detective*), family, comparative adjectives (*older than*), *want to be*
Additional language: character names
Revision: adjectives, numbers, personal information, hobbies (*go fishing, play table tennis*)

● MATERIALS REQUIRED
Warmer: Star family flashcards (1–9) and nine sticky labels with the names of the Star family characters, sticky tack and flashcards of Lock and Key (13–14)
Extra activity 1: The following scrambled questions written on a large piece of paper:
name your what's?   old you how are?   you where do live?
got pet you have a?   want be to you dentist a do?
your food what's favourite?
Extra activity 2: CD of quiet music
Optional: *Kid's Box Teacher's Resource Book 4* Hello there! Unit Reinforcement worksheet 1 (page 9), *Kid's Box 4 Language Portfolio* pages 1 and 2

Warmer
- Introduce yourself and greet the class. Show the Star family flashcards (1–9) and say the names. Hand out the flashcards and the name labels. Say each character, e.g. *Suzy*. The two pupils with Suzy's picture and her name label stick them on the wall. Repeat for the other characters.

PB4. ACTIVITY 1. *Look, think and answer.*
- Tell pupils to open their Pupil's Books at page 4 and to look at the picture. Elicit where the characters are. Ask a pupil to read the activity instruction and others to read the four questions. Pupils compare their predictions in pairs, looking for clues in the picture.
- Ask pupils to point out the *grown-ups* and the *children* in the picture.
- Ask pupils to say yes or no. *Mrs Star's the cook. Suzy's younger than Simon. Simon wants to be a dentist. Uncle Fred's a farmer. Aunt May's a detective. Stella wants to be a doctor.*

PB4. ACTIVITY 2. *Listen and check.*
- Play the CD for pupils to listen and check. Elicit complete sentences for the answers. Let pupils provide more information if they can, e.g. about Lock and Key. Use flashcards 13 and 14 to present / revise the characters.
Key: 1 Stella wants to be a doctor. 2 Uncle Fred's a farmer. 3 Simon's reading a comic (*Lock and Key*). 4 Grandpa Star's riding Suzy's bike.

CD 1, 02
MR STAR: Hello there, everybody. We're the Stars.
STELLA: Hello. I'm Stella and I'm ten. This is my Aunt May. She's a doctor, and I want to be a doctor too.
SIMON: Hi. I'm Simon and I'm nine. This is my Uncle Fred. He's my mum's brother. He's a farmer. This is my favourite comic, *Lock and Key*. It's about two detectives. I want to be a detective.
SUZY: Hello. I'm Suzy. I'm six. This is my grandfather, Grandpa Star. He's funny. He knows lots of good games. I want to be funny too!

PB4. ACTIVITY 3. *Listen again. Choose the right words.*
- Focus pupils on Activity 3. Play the first part of the CD and go through the example. Play the rest of the CD. Pupils work individually and then check in pairs. Play the CD again. Check with the class. Check understanding of question 2 by asking how old Suzy is (six), and of question 5 by asking why Grandpa Star is funny (he's riding Suzy's bike). Check understanding of *dentist*. Focus pupils on the Look box and use it to review comparative adjectives.
- In pairs, pupils write two more sentences with options. They swap with another pair, answer each other's and then check together.
Key: 2 Suzy, 3 uncle, 4 detective, 5 funny, 6 older

AB4. ACTIVITY 1. *Read and circle.*
- Tell pupils to open their Activity Book at page 4. Focus on Activity 1. They read the instruction. Check they know what to do, using the example. Pupils do the activity individually and then check in pairs. Check with the class.
Key: 2 older, 3 taller, 4 longer, 5 bigger, 6 happier

AB4. ACTIVITY 2. *Complete the sentences.*
- Focus pupils on the pictures. Elicit the sports / hobbies and tell pupils to choose *go / play*. Go through the example. Make sure pupils realise they need to provide more parts of the sentences as they go along. They complete the sentences individually and then compare in pairs. Check with the class.
Key: 2 fishing, 3 go cycling / go for a bike ride, 4 play hockey, 5 to fly a kite, 6 want to play table tennis, 6 wants to go swimming / wants to swim

Extra activities: see page T108 (if time)

Optional activity
- Hello there! Unit Reinforcement worksheet 1 from *Kid's Box Teacher's Resource Book 4* (pages 8 and 9).

Language Portfolio
- Pupils complete the cover and pages 1 and 2 of *Kid's Box 4 Language Portfolio* (*About me* and *My English language skills*).

Ending the lesson
- Say *Goodbye* or *Bye* to different pupils. Add *See you on* (day of next lesson). Pupils do the same to you and say *Goodbye* to each other.

OBJECTIVES: By the end of the lesson, pupils will have reviewed personal descriptions.

● TARGET LANGUAGE
Key language: personal descriptions, *have got*, *wear*, adjectives, definitions
Revision: comparative adjectives, adjectives, character names, personal information

● MATERIALS REQUIRED
Star family flashcards (1–9)
Extra activity 1: The following adjectives, each written on a small piece of card / paper: *funny, hungry, thirsty, loud, quiet, happy, clever, tired, young, old, beautiful, sad*
Extra activity 2: A blank sticker or piece of paper and safety pin for each pupil, CD of quiet music
Optional: *Kid's Box Teacher's Resource Book 4* Hello there! Unit Reinforcement worksheet 2 (page 10)

Warmer
- Revise personal descriptions. Describe someone in the class using the language in Pupil's Book page 5 Activity 4. The other pupils guess who it is. Repeat for another two or three pupils.

PB5. ACTIVITY 4. *Read and match.*
- Tell pupils to open their Pupil's Books at page 5. Elicit who the people are in the pictures by asking, e.g. *Who's c?* Use the Star family flashcards to review some of the names if necessary. Check pupils have read and understand the activity instruction. Do number 1 as in the example with the class. Pupils work in pairs. They take turns to read the sentences quietly to each other and match them with the person. They say the name of the person. Elicit answers from pairs. They read the sentences and then say the letter and who it is. Check understanding of the final adjectives by eliciting an appropriate mime / definition.
- Ask, *Is Suzy big or little?* to elicit *little*. Explain that *little* is the same as *small*. Continue, *Is a panda big or little? Is a bat big or little?* Ask pupils to tell you the names of animals/insects that are little. Do number 1 as an example with the class.

Key: 2 c, 3 f, 4 i, 5 g, 6 b, 7 e, 8 a, 9 d

PB5. ACTIVITY 5. *Listen and say the name.*
- Focus pupils on the activity instruction and the example and check understanding. Review the character names again. Tell pupils to whisper the name to their partner the first time they listen. Before listening, pupils make sure they remember the names of all the characters in the pictures. Play the CD. Pupils listen and whisper. Play the CD again. Pause after each question to elicit the answer from the class.

Key: 2 Simon, 3 Mrs Star, 4 Mr Star, 5 Suzy, 6 Grandpa, 7 Aunt May, 8 Grandma, 9 Stella

CD 1, 03
1. Who smiles a lot?
2. Who's happy?
3. Who's quiet?
4. Who's hungry?
5. Who's loud?
6. Who's funny?
7. Who's tired?
8. Who's thirsty?
9. Who's clever?

PB5. ACTIVITY 6. *Play the game.*
- Focus pupils on Activity 6 and tell them this is a game. Demonstrate the activity first. Tell pupils you're thinking of one of the characters. They ask questions like the ones in the speech bubbles to try to guess. They can only ask three questions. Pupils then play the game in pairs. Pupil A writes a letter from *a* to *i* in a secret place (the letter of the person). Pupil B then asks three questions to guess. Help with appropriate questions.

AB5. ACTIVITY 3. *Sort and write the words.*
- Focus pupils on Activity 3 and elicit what this is (a crossword) and that the words are anagrams. Point out the example answer written below the picture of the clever girl. First pupils solve the anagrams and write the words correctly underneath the pictures. Elicit answers. Then, in pairs, pupils work out where the words go (point out the example answer in the grid). Check with the class.

Key:

			c	l	e	v	e	r
			h	u	n	g	r	y
	q	u	i	e	t			
	+	c	o	l	d			
l	o	u	d					
t	h	i	r	s	t	y		
t	i	r	e	d				
	n	a	u	g	h	t	y	

AB5. ACTIVITY 4. *Kid's Box File.*
- Focus pupils on the Kid's Box File. Elicit words to complete the first two or three lines of the file. Remind pupils that they need to complete the sentences with information about themselves. Pupils write in pencil first. Check around the class as they are doing this and help / suggest / prompt if there are problems. Supply English words if pupils need them. Pupils complete the fact file. They then draw a picture in the box to illustrate one piece of information in the fact file. They make groups of four and take turns to read out their fact files. The other pupils listen for two things they have in common with the reader, e.g. age / number of people in the family.

Extra activities: see page T108 (if time)

Optional activity
- Hello there! Unit Reinforcement worksheet 2 from *Teacher's Resource Book 4* (pages 8 and 10).

Ending the lesson
- Pupils open their Pupil's Books and cover the page with paper so that they can see only the pictures of the characters at the top. Say, e.g. *Tell me about Suzy*. Pupils describe her from the picture.

4 Read and match.

1 His hair is white and curly. He's funny.
2 He's got short black hair and he's wearing sunglasses. He's hungry.
3 She's got straight grey hair. She's thirsty.
4 She's got short brown hair and she's young. She's little, but loud.
5 She's got very long blonde hair and she's beautiful. She's quiet.
6 He's got short straight red hair. He's happy.
7 She's got straight blonde hair and she wears glasses. She's clever.
8 He's got curly red hair, a beard and a moustache. He smiles a lot.
9 She's got straight black hair. She's tired.

5 Listen and say the name.

6 Play the game.

7 Read and answer.

1 Where does Aunt May work?
2 What does she like doing?
3 Where does Uncle Fred live?
4 What time does he get up?

Aunt May's a doctor. She works in a big hospital in the city. She sometimes works during the day and she sometimes has to work at night. She doesn't like working at the weekend. She likes listening to music and taking photos.

Uncle Fred's a farmer. He lives on a farm in the country. He's got twenty-seven cows and forty-three sheep. He always gets up at five o'clock. Uncle Fred has to work in the morning, the afternoon and the evening. He sometimes works at night too. He loves working on his farm, and driving his lorry!

8 Correct the sentences.

Aunt May's a doctor.

1 Aunt May's a bus driver.
2 She works in a big school.
3 She never works at night.
4 She likes working at the weekend.
5 Uncle Fred lives in a flat in the city.
6 He's got forty-three cows.
7 He never gets up at five o'clock.
8 He always works at night.

 **LOOK**

She **always** wears a white coat at work.
He **sometimes** works at night.
He **never** gets up at ten o'clock.

OBJECTIVES: By the end of the lesson, pupils will have reviewed using the present simple to talk about daily routines.

● **TARGET LANGUAGE**
Key language: present simple, adverbs of frequency: *always, sometimes, never, like / love + -ing,* routine activities
Revision: actions, jobs, *during the day, at night, in the morning / afternoon / evening, at work, white coat, hospital,* days of the week, *weekend, work, wear, listen to music, take photos, get up, farm, cow, sheep, flat, city, country*

● **MATERIALS REQUIRED**
Extra activity 2: 15 pieces of paper, each with one of the following phrases written on it: *get up, wake up, get dressed, have a shower, have breakfast, go to school, do homework, have lunch, play in the playground, come home, have supper, watch TV, go to bed, go to the park, go to sleep*
Optional: *Kid's Box Teacher's Resource Book 4* Hello there! Unit Extension worksheet 1 (page 11), *Kid's Box 4 Language Portfolio* page 7

Warmer
● Draw a circle on the board and write *Jobs* in the centre. Elicit the jobs pupils know and build up a mind map. Ask which job(s) they want to do. Leave the mind map on the board (see *Ending the lesson*).

PB6. ACTIVITY 7. *Read and answer.*
● Tell pupils to open their Pupil's Books at page 6 and to look at Activity 7. Use the pictures to elicit Aunt May's and Uncle Fred's jobs (doctor and farmer). Ask a pupil to read the instruction aloud and two others to read the questions. Pupils read silently and find the answers. They check in pairs. Check with the class. Pupils take turns to read the texts aloud around the class. Ask other questions about the texts to check understanding, e.g. Aunt May: *Does she always work at night?* Uncle Fred: *When does he have to work?* Review *always, sometimes* and *never* using the Look box at the bottom of the page.
Key: 1 She works in a hospital. 2 She likes listening to music and taking photos. 3 He lives on a farm in the country. 4 He gets up at five o'clock.

PB6. ACTIVITY 8. *Correct the sentences.*
● Focus pupils on Activity 8 and on the activity instruction. Check understanding, particularly of *bus driver.* They do the task orally first in pairs. Check with the class. Pupils write the corrected sentences in their books, following the model.
Key: 2 She works in a big hospital. 3 She sometimes works at night. 4 She doesn't like working at the weekend. 5 Uncle Fred lives on a farm in the country. 6 He's got twenty-seven cows. / He's got forty-three sheep. 7 He always gets up at five o'clock. 8 He sometimes works at night.

AB6. ACTIVITY 5. *Ask your friend. Complete the questionnaire.*
● Tell pupils to open their Activity Book at page 6. Focus them on the questionnaire and on the instructions. They take turns to ask and answer and to mark the correct box with their friend's answer.

AB6. ACTIVITY 6. *Write about your friend.*
● Focus pupils on Activity 6. Elicit sentences from pupils about their friends. Tell them to refer to the completed questionnaire from Activity 5. Write a few examples on the board, writing the third person *s* in a different colour to remind pupils to use it. Elicit why they need to write the *s*. Draw a square around each adverb too to highlight to pupils where it goes in the sentence. Pupils write five sentences about their partner using the information from Activity 5.

AB6. ACTIVITY 7. *Read and match.*
● Ask two pupils to read the example question and answer. Pupils work individually to complete the activity. Check with the class.
Key: 2 e, 3 f, 4 b, 5 a, 6 d

Extra activities: see page T108 (if time)

Optional activity
● Hello there! Unit Extension worksheet 1 from *Teacher's Resource Book 4* (pages 8 and 11).

Language Portfolio
● Pupils complete page 7 of *Kid's Box 4 Language Portfolio* (*Learning English*). Help with new language and elicit sentences (e.g. *I sometimes like working in pairs and groups. I don't like doing tests*). Pupils compare their completed pages in pairs.

Ending the lesson
● Go back to the jobs elicited at the beginning of the lesson. Elicit some ideas from pupils about the jobs, using sentences like the ones in the texts about May and Fred, e.g. (Detective) *He works in an office. He sometimes works at night. He wears a hat and always carries a magnifying glass.* (Dentist) *She wears a white coat and a mask. She looks at our teeth.*

OBJECTIVES: By the end of the lesson, pupils will have written about their daily routines using *before* and *after* and sung a song.

● **TARGET LANGUAGE**
Key language: present simple, *must*, imperatives, routine, *before / after*
Additional language: *no time to lose*
Revision: daily routines, word families

● **MATERIALS REQUIRED**
Warmer: Cards with the following actions written on them (large enough to be read by the class): *wake up, get up, have a wash, get dressed, run to the kitchen, sit on a chair, eat your breakfast, comb your hair, get your bag*
Optional: *Kid's Box Teacher's Resource Book 4* Hello there! Unit Song worksheet (page 13), *Kid's Box Interactive DVD 4* booklet (pages 28–33), *Kid's Box Interactive DVD 4: Simon's room* 'The Memory Game'

Warmer

- Display the word cards on the board. Point to each one and elicit / say the instruction, e.g. *Run to the kitchen*. Write a number under each one. Mime one of the actions. Pupils answer with the number and the verb and then say, e.g. *It's number 1. Sit on a chair*.

Note: Make sure pupils don't use the present continuous.

PB7. ACTIVITY 9. *Look at the song and order the pictures. Listen and check.*

- Tell pupils to open their Pupil's Book at page 7. Ask what they can see in some of the pictures. Focus on picture 'e' and ask: *What are they doing?* to elicit *They're cleaning their teeth*. Ask *What do we use to clean our teeth?* to elicit (explain if necessary) *toothbrush* and *toothpaste*. Ask further questions: *What colour is your toothpaste? What colour is the boy's/girl's toothbrush? Can you eat toothpaste?* Ask a pupil to read the activity instructions aloud. Focus on the example speech bubble and check pupils know what to do. Pupils work in pairs to try to order the activities. Remind them to check in the song text. Point out that there isn't a picture for every phrase in the text. Monitor pupils and prompt them to think (e.g. point to a picture), but don't tell them the answers.
- Play the CD for pupils to check their answers. Elicit answers. Explain any new vocabulary in the song text. Check understanding of the different actions. Ask pupils which ones they do in the morning.

Key: 2 i, 3 f, 4 j, 5 c, 6 g, 7 e, 8 d, 9 a, 10 h

CD 1, 04
As in Pupil's Book

PB7. ACTIVITY 10. *Sing the song.*

- Play the CD. Pupils listen. Play the CD again. Pupils join in with the song, miming the actions if they want to. They can clap their hands or click their fingers in time with the rhythm of the rap if they prefer. Divide the class into 12 groups. Each group sings a pair of lines and mimes as they sing.

CD 1, 04
As in Pupil's Book

CD 1, 05
Now sing the song again. (Karaoke version)

- Ask questions about the song using *before* and *after*, e.g. *What do we do before we eat breakfast? What do we do after we get up?* Check pupils understand the sequence. Use the word cards to help. Place two word cards next to each other on the board and make two sentences, one with *before* and one with *after*. Write the two model sentences underneath. Personalise the activity by asking pupils, e.g. *What do you do after you eat breakfast? What do you do before you have a shower?*

PB7. ACTIVITY 11. *Write about your day.*

- Focus pupils on the activity instruction and the model text. Pupils work individually to write sentences about their daily routine in their notebooks using *before / after*. Monitor and support if necessary. This activity can be completed for homework.

AB7. ACTIVITY 8. *Look. Write 'before' or 'after'. Match.*

- Tell pupils to open their Activity Book at page 7. Ask a pupil to read the activity instruction aloud. Go through the example. Pupils work individually and complete the activity. Check the activity carefully with the class, making sure pupils understand the sequence of the actions.

Key: 2 before d, 3 after c, 4 before a, 5 before f, 6 after e

AB7. ACTIVITY 9. *Circle the odd one out.* [M] *towards*

- Focus pupils on Activity 9. Ask what they can see in some of the pictures. Ask a pupil to read aloud the activity instructions and the first line. Elicit from pupils why *trousers* is different (clothes). Pupils complete the activity individually and then check in pairs. Check with the class, eliciting reasons for the answer each time.

Key: 2 bus, 3 lorry, 4 rock, 5 blanket, 6 cook, 7 driver, 8 island, 9 comic, 10 dentist

Extra activities: see page T108 (if time)

Optional activities

- Hello there! Unit Song worksheet from *Kid's Box Teacher's Resource Book 4* (see pages 8 and 13)
- Extra activity for Hello there! Unit Song and / or karaoke worksheet. See pages 28–33 of the Teacher's Booklet for the Interactive DVD.
- Play 'The Memory Game' from the *Simon's room* section of the *Kid's Box Interactive DVD 4*. See page 34 of the Teacher's Booklet for the Interactive DVD.

Ending the lesson

- Sing the song from the Pupil's Book again.

9 **Look at the song and order the pictures. Listen and check.**

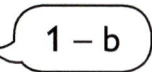
1 – b

The morning rap,
We do it every day.
The same routine,
Now listen and say.

It's seven o'clock,
Wake up, wake up!
You must get up
And have a wash.

Come on, come on,
It's time to go.
Get dressed, get dressed!
Put on your clothes.

Run to the kitchen,
Sit on a chair.
Eat your breakfast,
Comb your hair.

The morning rap …

It's seven o'clock …

Clean your teeth.
No time to lose.
Get your bag,
Put on your shoes.

Goodbye to Mum,
Goodbye to Dad.
My friends are at school,
So I'm not sad.

The morning rap.
The morning rap.

10 Sing the song.

11 Write about your day.

I wake up at seven o'clock.
I get dressed after I get up …

12 Stella's phonics

A c**a**t in a b**a**g.

A sn**a**ke and a sn**ai**l in the r**ai**n.

A f**ar**mer in his c**ar**.

The f**ar**mer's parking the c**ar** in the c**ar** p**ar**k.

13 Make questions. Ask and answer.

- have / got / younger cousin
- like / snails
- can / play basketball
- catch / bus / school
- can / swim
- have / got / older brother
- wake up / eight o'clock
- have / got a pet
- want to be / doctor

Have you got a younger cousin?
Yes, I have.

Do you like snails?
No, I don't.

Can you play basketball?
Yes, I can.

OBJECTIVES: By the end of the lesson, pupils will have practised identifying the phonemes /æ/, /eɪ/ and /ɑː/ and recognising alternative spellings for these sounds. They will also have completed a communication activity.

● **TARGET LANGUAGE**
Key language: words with the phonemes /æ/, /eɪ/ and /ɑː/ (e.g. *cat, snake, farmer*), family, routines, questions and short answers
Revision: pronunciation of words with the target phonemes from *Kid's Box* Levels 1–3

Warmer
- Say *Look and think. Make three groups.* Write these words on the board: *sad, last, dad, name, dance, say, make, bag, start*. Say the words aloud, emphasising the vowel sounds. If pupils still can't do it, write down one of the groups (*sad, dad, bag*). Elicit the other groups and write them on the board (*last, dance, start* and *name, say, make*). Say the words in groups. Pupils repeat.

PB8. ACTIVITY 12. *Stella's phonics*
- Tell pupils to open their Pupil's Book at page 8. Elicit Stella's name. Explain that the Stella's phonics activities help with pronunciation. Focus on the smaller pictures. Elicit *cat, bag, snake, rain, farmer* and *car*. Focus on the larger picture and ask, e.g. *What animals can you see?* Review *market*.
- Point to the sentences. Say *Listen and read.* Play the CD for pupils to listen only. Play the CD again. Pupils repeat the sentences.

Note: Distinguishing between the /æ/ and /ɑː/ phoneme can be difficult when words with the /ɑː/ phoneme don't follow the spelling pattern (e.g. *father* and *aunt* in this unit).

Pupils need help recognising spelling patterns for the /eɪ/ phoneme (*ay* and *a_e*), as well as irregular spellings (e.g. *eight, straight*).

CD 1, 07

STELLA: Hi, I'm Stella! Repeat after me!
/æ/, /æ/, cat
/eɪ/, /eɪ/, snake
/ɑː/, /ɑː/, farmer
A cat in a bag.
A cat in a bag.
A snake and a snail in the rain.
A snake and a snail in the rain.
A farmer in his car.
A farmer in his car.
The farmer's parking the car in the car park.
The farmer's parking the car in the car park.

PB8. ACTIVITY 13. *Make questions. Ask and answer.*
- Focus pupils on Activity 13. Practise the questions and answers in the speech bubbles. Check pupils know how to form questions, as in the examples, and to give the short answers. If necessary, write all the questions on the board. Pupils work in pairs. A asks all the questions for B to answer, and then they swap. Pupils tell the class about their partner, e.g. *Claude doesn't catch the bus to school.*

AB8. ACTIVITY 10. *Write. Listen, check and say.*
- Tell pupils to open their Activity Book at page 8. Check they know the meaning of all the words in the box. Point out the words at the top of each column. Say the words, emphasising the vowel sounds. Pupils repeat. Draw attention to the example answer. Elicit an example for the other two columns if necessary. Pupils complete the activity in pencil. Tell them to say the words aloud again to help.
- Play the CD for pupils to listen and check. They compare answers in pairs. Check with the class. Play the CD again for pupils to listen and repeat.

Key:

s<u>a</u>d	r<u>ai</u>n	c<u>ar</u>
bag	name	start
stand	play	farmer
have	straight	dance
catch	grey	father
man	take	aunt

CD 1, 07
/æ/, bag, stand, have, catch, man
/eɪ/, name, play, straight, grey, take
/ɑː/, start, farmer, dance, father, aunt

AB8. ACTIVITY 11. *Change one letter to make new words.*
- Write *book, boot, foot* on the board. Show pupils how only one letter has changed each time. Point out the two examples and solve the second with the class. Pupils do the activity in pairs. Check on the board.

Key: 2 bed, 3 bad, 4 bat, 5 cat, 6 car, 7 ear, 8 eat

Extra activities: see page T108 (if time)

Ending the lesson
- Write the long sentence from Pupil's Book Activity 12 on the board. Say it as a tongue twister. Pupils repeat and then practise in pairs.

OBJECTIVES: By the end of the lesson, pupils will have read a story and reviewed numbers.

● **TARGET LANGUAGE**
Key language: language in the story, numbers, *joke box*
Revision: functional language, *was / were, Lock and Key, magnifying glass*

● **MATERIALS REQUIRED**
A simple but striking poster which reads:
Lock and Key Detective Agency.
We're here to help you, night and day.
Call us on 01449 228000. Email: lockandkey@detectives.com
Flashcards of Lock and Key (13–14)
Word cards from *Kid's Box Teacher's Resource Book 4* pages 88–89
Optional: *Kid's Box Teacher's Resource Book 4* Hello there! Unit Extension worksheet 2 and Topic worksheet (pages 12 and 14), animated version of the Hello there! Unit story from *Kid's Box Interactive DVD 4* (*Suzy's room* section)

Warmer

- Display the Lock and Key poster you have made on the wall and the flashcards of Lock and Key. Ask pupils to read the poster and to tell you what it is (an advert for the Lock and Key Detective Agency). Check understanding of *detective agency*. Ask who Lock and Key are (pupils point to the flashcards) and for examples of the things they do. If pupils didn't study *Kid's Box 3*, use these examples: *look for lost cats, find lost paintings, find car thieves*. Ask pupils how you can contact the detectives (by phone / email). Ask pupils if they think Lock and Key use a magnifying glass. Check comprehension by drawing one on the board.

Story

PB9. LOCK AND KEY.

- Tell pupils to open their Pupil's Book at page 9. Elicit who the story is about (Lock and Key). Tell pupils to point to Lock and then to Key in the pictures (using the flashcards as reference). Set the gist listening / reading questions: *What's today's problem for Lock and Key? Do they find the answer?* Play the CD. Pupils listen and read. They don't shout out the answers, but check quietly with their partner at the end of the CD. Check with the class (a picnic thief; yes, it's a bird). Play the CD again. Pupils listen and repeat. Encourage them to say the words with intonation and feeling relevant to each character.
- Check comprehension by holding up your book and asking, e.g. *What's the little boy's name?* (Peter). *Who's the woman with him?* (His aunt). *Are Lock and Key in their car?* (No, on a motorbike). *Where are they?* (In the park). *What's Key holding?* (A magnifying glass).
- Elicit Key's favourite phrase (No problem).

CD 1, 08
As in Pupil's Book

AB9. ACTIVITY 12. *Write the numbers and join the dots.*

- If time, revise numbers with the word cards on Teacher's Resource Book pages 88 and 89. Cut out the cards and hand out one to each pupil randomly (make sure you hand out matching pairs of numbers and words). Pupils stand up and walk around the class. Clap your hands. Pupils find a partner and say their number. When they find a classmate with the same number as themselves, they come and show you. Stick the matching cards on the board. Repeat until all the cards have been matched.
- Tell pupils to open their Activity Book at page 9. Ask a pupil to read the activity instructions aloud and check understanding. Pupils do the task individually and then check in pairs. Check with the class, asking what the numbers are each time and what they found to link the pictures. Elicit what they drew when they joined the dots (shark).

Key: 39 tree 74, 74 balcony 53, 53 bike 95, 95 cloud 47, 47 rainbow 21, 21 blanket 82, 82 trainers 19, 19 scarf 33, 33 rock 15, 15 cave 98

Extra activities: see page T108 (if time)

Optional activities

- Hello there! Unit Extension worksheet 2 and Topic worksheet from *Teacher's Resource Book 4* (pages 8, 12 and 14).
- The animated version of the story from *Kid's Box Interactive DVD 4* (*Suzy's room* section). See pages 38–45 of the Teacher's Booklet for the Interactive DVD.

Ending the lesson

- Ask pupils which chant / song they'd like to do again from the unit. Do it together to end the lesson.

1 Back to school

1 Look, think and answer.
1 Where are the children?
2 Which class are Alex and Simon in?
3 Who likes Maths?
4 What's Meera doing?

Simon   Alex
Art

Stella   Lenny
Maths

Meera
Sport

boring   busy   careful   difficult   easy   exciting   quick   slow   terrible

2 Listen and check.

3 Listen and match.

1 Be careful with those glasses, Sally!
I am being careful!

e

a

b

c

d

e

f

g

h

i

OBJECTIVES: By the end of the lesson, pupils will have used adjectives to talk about school and people's feelings and reactions.

● TARGET LANGUAGE
Key language: *boring, brave, quick, exciting, busy, careful, difficult, easy, slow, terrible*
Additional language: *pottery, bowl, grownup*
Revision: *school, school subjects*

● MATERIALS REQUIRED
Character flashcards (Stella (5), Simon (6), Lenny (10), Alex (11), Meera (12))
Adjective flashcards (15–23)

Warmer
- Ask pupils what subjects they have on their timetable today. Ask which their favourites are. Ask pupils if they have started any new subjects this year. Build a mind map on the board of the school subjects.

PB10. ACTIVITY 1. *Look, think and answer.*
- Tell pupils to open their Pupil's Book at page 10. Elicit who they can see (Simon and Stella). Introduce Alex, Lenny and Meera using the flashcards. Review all five character names by sticking the flashcards on the board, pointing to the cards in turn and saying, e.g. *Hello, Alex*. Point to the flashcards again. Pupils say *Hello, (name)* for each one.
- Pupils read the activity instruction and the four questions. They discuss their answers / predictions in pairs. Don't give the new vocabulary at this stage.

PB10. ACTIVITY 2. *Listen and check.*
- Play the CD for pupils to listen and check. Elicit complete sentences.
- Play the first part of the CD (the Art class). Elicit what Simon says (*My bowl's terrible*) and what the narrator says about Alex (*Alex is careful and slow*). Check understanding of the adjectives. Repeat for the other sections.
- Focus pupils on the adjectives in the box in Activity 1. Elicit words that link to them in the listening, e.g. *What's boring?* (basketball). Check understanding of the adjectives as you do the activity.

Key: 1 The children are at school. 2 Alex and Simon are in the Art class. 3 Stella likes Maths. 4 Meera's playing basketball.

CD 1, 09
NARRATOR: Simon and Alex are in their Art class. They're making bowls and they can't stop. They're busy.
SIMON: Oooh. My bowl's terrible!
NARRATOR: Alex is careful and slow. His bowl's good.
NARRATOR: Stella and Lenny are in their Maths lesson. Stella's very happy because she loves Maths and thinks it's easy. Lenny doesn't think Maths is easy. He thinks it's difficult.
LENNY: I can't do this Maths problem. It's difficult.
STELLA: Come on, Lenny. You can do it. It's easy.
NARRATOR: … It's 73–72. What an exciting game! Meera's got the ball and she's running with it. Meera's quick. The boy's slow.
GIRL: This is really boring. I don't like basketball.

PB10. ACTIVITY 3. *Listen and match.*
- Focus pupils on Activity 3. Pupils work in pairs and try to do the matching. Play the CD for them to listen and match. Check with the class.

Key: 2 a, 3 f, 4 c, 5 h, 6 g, 7 d, 8 b, 9 i

CD 1, 10
1. Be careful with those glasses, Sally! / I **am** being careful.
2. What was the film like? / It was really boring.
3. What's 397 and 79? / Oh, I don't know. That's difficult.
4. What was the football match like? / It was really exciting!
5. Come on, Mary. Don't be so slow. / I'm not slow!
6. What's 2 and 2? / That's easy. It's 4.
7. Can I talk to you? / No, sorry. I'm busy.
8. The bus is coming. Be quick!
9. The weather's terrible! / Oh, no! Look at our food.

AB10. ACTIVITY 1. *Find the words.*
- Pre-teach *brave*. Write *brave* on the board and read it aloud for pupils to repeat. Say *Firefighters are brave. They get people out of dangerous places. Can you think of brave people?* (e.g. police officers, climbers, etc.)
- Tell pupils to open their Activity Book at page 10. Check they know what to do. Pupils do the task individually, checking in pairs. Check with the class.

Key:

d	z	e	s	s	b	r	a	v	e	a
i	p	h	c	u	f	b	m	e	v	r
f	w	w	a	r	j	i	m	x	c	e
f	z	a	r	p	j	n	f	c	r	k
i	n	l	e	r	e	s	p	i	n	p
c	q	h	f	i	k	l	q	t	p	e
u	u	b	u	s	y	o	h	i	g	u
l	i	j	l	e	i	w	l	n	f	h
t	c	g	b	o	r	i	n	g	d	k
u	k	r	t	e	r	r	i	b	l	e

AB10. ACTIVITY 2. *Look at the pictures. Complete the sentences.*
- Focus pupils on Activity 2 and on the activity instructions. Check they realise they need to look at the pictures in Activity 1, using the example. Pupils complete the sentences and then check in pairs. Check with the class.

Key: 2 boring, 3 difficult, 4 careful, 5 terrible, 6 slow, 7 quick, 8 exciting, 9 busy

Extra activities: see page T109 (if time)

Ending the lesson
- Stick the adjective flashcards on the board. Number them 1 to 9. Elicit the words. Say, e.g. *I have a lot to do. I'm very …* Pupils say the correct number flashcard and the word. Repeat for the other adjectives.

OBJECTIVES: By the end of the lesson, pupils will have written a text about a teacher and completed a questionnaire with a friend.

- **TARGET LANGUAGE**
Key language: adjectives, present simple, descriptions
Revision: comparative adjectives, colours, school subjects, *like, have got, very*

- **MATERIALS REQUIRED**
Adjective flashcards (15–23)
Adjective word cards from *Kid's Box Teacher's Resource Book 4* (page 80)
Optional: *Kid's Box Teacher's Resource Book 4* Unit 1 Reinforcement worksheet 1 (page 16)

Warmer
- Write some school subjects as anagrams on the board. Pupils race to unscramble the words and write them correctly. Take a vote for the pupils' favourite subject.

PB11. ACTIVITY 4. *Read and correct the text.*
- Tell pupils to open their Pupil's Book at page 11. Focus them on Activity 4 and elicit what they can see (a photograph of a teacher at work and a child's piece of writing about a teacher). Elicit the name of the teacher (Mr Newton) and the subject he teaches (Maths). Ask a pupil to read the activity instruction aloud and check understanding. Do the first one as an example with the class.
- Pupils work individually and unscramble the words. Set three reading questions: *Where is the school? Are his lessons boring? Why do the children like his lessons?* Pupils read to find the answers. Check with the class (in a big city; no, they're exciting; because they're not difficult). Pupils write the corrected text in their notebooks.

Key: busy, slow, boring, exciting, difficult, easy, careful

PB11. ACTIVITY 5. *Write about one of your teachers.*
- Using the list of subjects from the warmer, help pupils choose a teacher to write about. Make sure it's a teacher they like. Remind them to use the model in Activity 4 to help them and to use the adjectives to talk about the lessons and their work. Monitor pupils as they write their drafts. When you have checked their work, they can write a final version on paper.

PB11. ACTIVITY 6. *Read and say their names.*
- Focus pupils on Activity 6. Ask a pupil to read the activity instruction and do the first one as an example. In pairs, pupils take turns to read the descriptions aloud and to say the names of the children. Check with the class using open pairs.

Key: 2 Paul, 3 Mary, 4 Daisy, 5 Fred

PB11. ACTIVITY 7. *Make sentences for your friend. Say and answer 'true' or 'false.'*
- Pupils use the example speech bubble on the left to write four sentences about the children in Activity 6. They include some false information. They take turns to read their sentences and to say *True* or *False*.

AB11. ACTIVITY 3. *Complete the questionnaire.*
- Tell pupils to open their Activity Book at page 11. Elicit what this is (a questionnaire). Pupils complete it about themselves by ticking the best adjective. They can only tick one in each line.

AB11. ACTIVITY 4. *Ask your friend. Write the answers.*
- Make new pairs. Pupils take turns to ask and answer and to note the information about their partner.

Extra activities: see page T109 (if time)

Optional activity
- Unit 1 Reinforcement worksheet 1 from *Teacher's Resource Book 4* (pages 15 and 16).

Ending the lesson
- Stick the adjective flashcards and the word cards on the board. Call volunteers to come to the board and match them.
- Pupils group the adjectives according to the number of syllables (do this as a class if necessary).

Key: 1 syllable = quick, slow, 2 syllables = easy, boring, careful, busy 3 syllables = exciting, terrible, difficult

4 Read and correct the text.

My teacher.
This is Mr Newton. He's my Maths teacher. He works in a school in a big city. He's very sbyu because he's got a lot of work. There are 28 children in my class. His lessons aren't wols or grinbo, they're very ecgitxin. We like his lessons because they're not ftlcudfii. It's yase to learn lots of new things with him.
Mr Newton's very fclareu when he writes, but I'm not!

5 Write about one of your teachers.

6 Read and say their names.

Daisy   Fred   Mary   Johnny   Paul

1 This child likes being busy with lots of homework. — Johnny
   His hair is straight and black and he's got glasses.
2 This child loves Art and is careful at painting.
   He's got short, brown curly hair.
3 The child with straight blonde hair is very brave.
   She loves reading to her class!
4 This child with glasses thinks Maths is exciting.
   Her hair is black and curly.
5 This child with short curly blonde hair thinks Music's difficult.

7 Make sentences for your friend. Say and answer 'true' or 'false'.

The child with glasses thinks Maths is boring.   False.

8 Look, think and answer.
1 Where are the Star family?
2 Who's Mrs Star talking to?
3 Who's the Art teacher?
4 Who's the Music teacher?

9 Listen and check.

10 Play the game.

He's the teacher who's talking to Mrs Star.

Mr Newton.

LOOK
She's the woman **who's** wearing the long green skirt.
He's the man **who's** carrying the lorry.

OBJECTIVES: By the end of the lesson, pupils will have used relative clauses with *who*.

• TARGET LANGUAGE
Key language: relative clauses with *who*, descriptions
Revision: adjectives, school subjects, prepositions, *school show, He's / she's called ... , over there, He's / she's the one ...*

• MATERIALS REQUIRED
Warmer: Four large pictures of people (two men, two women) showing clothes / appearance
Coloured pencils (one set per pupil)
Optional: *Kid's Box Teacher's Resource Book 4* Unit 1 Reinforcement worksheet 2 (page 17)

Warmer
- Put the four pictures on the board. Number them 1 to 4. Review descriptions by playing a guessing game, e.g. *Who's got long, dark hair? Who's wearing a black jacket? Who's carrying a newspaper?*

PB12. ACTIVITY 8. *Look, think and answer.*
- Tell pupils to open their Pupil's Books at page 12. Elicit who they can see and where they are. Ask a pupil to read the activity instruction aloud and others to take turns to read the four questions. Pupils compare their answers / predictions in pairs, looking for clues in the picture.

PB12. ACTIVITY 9. *Listen and check.*
- Play the CD for pupils to listen and check. Elicit complete sentences. Write the teachers' names on the board. Elicit the subject each one teaches and what they're doing. Play the CD again if necessary. Focus on the target structure, e.g. *Mr Burke is the man who's singing. He's the Sports teacher.* Elicit other sentences from pupils. They copy them into their notebooks.

Key: 1 They are at the school show. 2 She's talking to Mr Newton, the Maths teacher. 3 Mr Turner is the Art teacher. 4 Miss Flower is the Music teacher.

CD 1, 11
SIMON: Hey! The school show's really exciting, Dad.
MR STAR: Yes, it is ... and it's good to see your teachers. Who are they all?
SIMON: Well, the man who's talking to Mum is my Maths teacher. He's called Mr Newton.
MR STAR: Right. Is the man who's singing your Music teacher?
SIMON: No, he's Mr Burke, our Sports teacher. Miss Flower's our Music teacher. She's the woman who's wearing the long green skirt. They do the 'After school club'.
MR STAR: The 'After school club'? What's that?
SIMON: It's a new club where we can do lots of exciting things on Thursday afternoons. ... And can you guess who my Art teacher is?
MR STAR: Ooh, Simon, that's difficult. Is it the woman who's playing the guitar?
SIMON: Very funny, Dad. No, that's Mrs Robinson, our English teacher. Our Art teacher's over there. He's the one who's carrying the lorry.
MR STAR: Is his name Mr Strong? Ha ha ha.
SIMON: No, Dad. His name's Mr Turner.

PB12. ACTIVITY 10. *Play the game.*
- Clean the board. Focus pupils on Activity 10, the Look box and the example speech bubbles. They play the game in pairs. A looks at the picture, and B closes his / her book. A makes statements to test B's memory, as in the example. After one or two minutes, pupils swap roles.

AB12. ACTIVITY 5. *Listen and draw lines. Colour.* [M] towards
- Tell pupils to open their Activity Book at page 12. Play the CD. Pause after each dialogue for pupils to draw lines. They check in pairs. Play the CD again. Pause after each one to give pupils time to place coloured dots in the right place. Pupils check in pairs. Play the CD a final time. Pause after each one to elicit, e.g. *Paul's the one who's reading a book. He's wearing a red T-shirt ...*

CD 1, 12
1. Who's Mr Edison? / He's the man who's writing on the board. / What's he wearing? / He's wearing a green sweater, grey trousers and blue shoes.
2. Who's Paul? / He's the boy who's reading a book. He's wearing a red T-shirt and blue trousers.
3. Who's Mary? / She's the girl who's got long blonde curly hair. She's wearing a pink dress. She's talking to Peter.
4. Who's Jane? / She's the girl who's drawing a beautiful picture. She's wearing an orange skirt and a purple jacket.
5. Who's Jim? / He's the boy who's sharpening his pencil. He's wearing a brown shirt and grey trousers.

AB12. ACTIVITY 6. *Read and circle the correct answer.*
- Focus pupils on Activity 6. Pupils work individually and choose the correct words. They check in pairs. Check with the class.

Key: 2 are, 3 who, 4 who, 5 on, 6 who, 7 to, 8 must

Extra activity: see page T109 (if time)

Optional activity
- Unit 1 Reinforcement worksheet 2 from *Teacher's Resource Book 4* (pages 15 and 17).

Ending the lesson
- See if pupils remember the pictures from the Warmer. They say, e.g. *Number 1's the woman who's carrying a handbag. She's wearing red shoes.* Show the pictures to check.

OBJECTIVES: By the end of the lesson, pupils will have had further practice with relative clauses using *who* and sung a song.

● TARGET LANGUAGE
Key language: relative clauses with *who*, present continuous question forms
Additional language: *playground*
Revision: relative clauses with *who*, present continuous, actions and activities, clothes, adjectives, school subjects, food and drink

● MATERIALS REQUIRED
Extra activity 2: 12 small pieces of paper / card for each group of four
Optional: *Kid's Box Teacher's Resource Book 4* Unit 1 Extension worksheet 1 and / or Song worksheet (pages 18 and 20), *Kid's Box Interactive DVD 4* booklet (pages 28–33)

Warmer
- Write the names of about six pupils on the board and write a piece of unique information about each one, e.g. *He's wearing black trousers.* Say *Tell me about* (name) to elicit, e.g. *(Name)'s the boy who's wearing black trousers.* Repeat for the other names on the board.

PB13. ACTIVITY 11. *Read and find.*
- Tell pupils to open their Pupil's Book at page 13. Elicit what they can see (a playground) and what some of the children are doing. Ask a pupil to read the activity instruction aloud. Check understanding using the example. Pupils work in pairs, taking turns to read the statements and find the child / children in the picture. Check with the class, using open pairs: one pupil reads a statement aloud, and another says the letter.
- Focus on the use of *They're ... who are ...* by eliciting examples in the classroom, e.g. Teacher: *Tell me something about* (name) *and* (name). Pupils: *They're the girls who are sitting at the front.* Make other similar statements. Pupils then make statements for the class to answer.

Key: 2 f, 3 a, 4 c, 5 e, 6 b

PB13. ACTIVITY 12. *Choose a child. Ask and answer.*
- Turn the activity into a guessing game. Say *I'm looking at a boy in the picture. Can you guess?* Pupils ask questions as in the speech bubble on the left. Repeat for *girl*. Practise two or three more times. Pupils do the activity in pairs, taking turns to guess.

PB13. ACTIVITY 13. *Read and say the letter. Listen and check.*
- Focus pupils on Activity 13. Ask a pupil to read the instruction aloud. Check understanding. Pupils read the text and match who's speaking with one of the pictures, as in the example. They check in pairs. Play the CD. Pause after each teacher's section and elicit the letter and the name.

Key: 2 d, 3 c, 4 b

CD 1, 13
As in Pupil's Book

PB13. ACTIVITY 14. *Sing the song.*
- Play the CD again for pupils to join in with the song. They sing as a whole class first and then as the teachers (make four groups). They do an appropriate mime for each school subject as they sing.

CD 1, 13
As in Pupil's Book

CD 1, 14
Now sing the song again. (Karaoke version)

AB13. ACTIVITY 7. *Look at the pictures. Read and correct.*
- Tell pupils to open their Activity Book at page 13. Go through the example to check they know what to correct.
- Pupils work individually and correct each sentence. They check in pairs. Check with the class. Pupils write the correct sentences in their notebooks.

Key: 2 The man who's throwing a ball has got a little black dog. 3 The woman who teaches Music lives in a little house. 4 The man who's got a moustache rides his bike to school. 5 The woman who likes books gets up at 7 o'clock.

AB13. ACTIVITY 8. *Read and complete the table.*
- Focus pupils on Activity 8 and check they know what to do. They work in pairs to read and complete the table. Check with the class by drawing the table (with gaps) on the board. Elicit the missing information.

Key:

Name	Description	Age	Subject	Hobby
Mr Brown	black beard	42	English	playing tennis
Miss Stone	long fair hair	30	Maths	horse riding
Mr Kelly	brown moustache	28	Sport	playing the guitar
Mrs Bird	grey curly hair	57	Music	reading

Extra activities: see page T109 (if time)

Optional activities
- Unit 1 Extension worksheet 1 from *Teacher's Resource Book 4* (pages 15 and 18).
- Unit 1 Song worksheet from *Teacher's Resource Book 4* (pages 15 and 20).
- Extra activity for Unit 1 Song and / or karaoke worksheet. See pages 28–33 of the Teacher's Booklet for the Interactive DVD.

Ending the lesson
- Pupils sing the song again.

11 Read and find.
1 They're the boys who are laughing.   d
2 She's the girl who's drinking orange juice.
3 He's the boy who's wearing a red sweater.
4 They're the girls who are wearing pink dresses.
5 She's the girl who's skipping.
6 He's the boy who's throwing a ball.

12 Choose a child. Ask and answer.

Is it the boy who's reading a comic?   No, it isn't.

13 Read and say the letter. Listen and check.   1 – a

The classroom's where you learn,   **a**
The classroom's where we teach,
Lots of exciting things,
To do in our school week …

1 I teach Sport,
It's quick, not slow,
Run, jump and skip,
Go, go, go!

2 I teach English,
All I need,
Are lots of words,
And books to read.

3 I teach Maths,
It's easy to add,
But if it's wrong,
Don't be sad.

4 I teach Art,
We can paint and draw,
Careful with the paint,
Don't drop it on the floor!

The classroom's where you learn,
The classroom's where we teach,
Lots of exciting things,
To do in our school week …

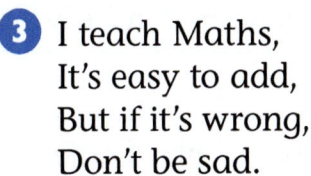

14 Sing the song.

15 Stella's phonics

Six busy insects.

A smiling crocodile.

Sixteen teeth.

It's easy to clean a smiling crocodile's teeth.

16 Make questions. Ask and answer.

Do you think Maths is exciting?

No, I don't.

Maths   Art   English   difficult   exciting   easy

Find two people who …		name 1	name 2
… think Maths is exciting	Do you think Maths is exciting?		
… think Art is easy	Do you think _____ ?		
… think English is difficult	Do you _____ ?		

OBJECTIVES: By the end of the lesson, pupils will have revised and contrasted the phonemes /ɪ/, /iː/ and /aɪ/. They will be able to recognise alternative spellings of these sounds.

- **TARGET LANGUAGE**
Key language: words with the phonemes /ɪ/, /iː/ and /aɪ/ (e.g. *quick, easy, exciting*)
Revision: school subjects, adjectives, question forms, definitions with *who*

Warmer

- Write these words on the board: *be, my, sit, tree, easy, right, quick, time, bin.* Say *Think about the sound. Make three groups.* Help by saying two of the words with the vowel sound /ɪ/, e.g. *sit, bin.* Write these words in a group on one side. Elicit the other word with the same sound (*quick*). Elicit the other groups in the same way (*be, tree, easy* and *my, right, time*). Elicit the word *little* on the board.

PB14. ACTIVITY 15. *Stella's phonics*

- Tell pupils to open their Pupil's Book at page 14. Elicit what they can see in the pictures (insects, a crocodile who is smiling, teeth). Play the CD. Pupils listen and repeat. Play the CD again for pupils to repeat once more.

Note: Language learners often have difficulty hearing the difference between the short /ɪ/ and long /iː/ phonemes. In this lesson there are both regular and irregular spellings for the long /iː/ phoneme (e.g. *teeth* and *easy*).

CD 1, 15

STELLA: Hi, I'm Stella! Repeat after me!
/ɪ/, /ɪ/, insects
/aɪ/, /aɪ/, crocodile
/iː/, /iː/, teeth
Six busy insects.
Six busy insects.
A smiling crocodile.
A smiling crocodile.
Sixteen teeth.
Sixteen teeth.
It's easy to clean a smiling crocodile's teeth.
It's easy to clean a smiling crocodile's teeth.

PB14. ACTIVITY 16. *Make questions. Ask and answer.*

- Tell pupils today's communication activity is about school subjects. Focus them on the information on the page and elicit the questions for the second and third examples. Pupils copy the table into their notebooks and complete the second and third questions. Pupils each ask the three questions of two other pupils. They move around the classroom. Clap your hands. They make pairs and ask and answer. Repeat. Pupils report back to the class. Provide prompts on the board, e.g. *(Paula) thinks Maths is exciting, but she thinks English is difficult.*

AB14. ACTIVITY 9. *Write. Listen, check and say.*

- Tell pupils to open their Activity Book at page 14. Check pupils know the meaning of all the words in the box. Say the words at the top of each column, emphasising the vowel sounds. Pupils repeat. Draw attention to the example answer. Elicit an example for the other two columns if necessary. Pupils complete the table individually. Tell them to say the words aloud again to help. Give them time to think about the way the words sound.
- Play the CD for pupils to listen and check. Pupils compare answers in pairs. Check with the class. Play the CD again for pupils to listen and repeat.

Key:

s<u>i</u>t	s<u>ee</u>	f<u>i</u>ve
quick	easy	time
busy	teach	night
give	me	fly
think	key	buy
finish	need	smile

CD 1, 16

/ɪ/, quick, busy, give, think, finish
/iː/, easy, teach, me, key, need
/aɪ/ time, night, fly, buy, smile

AB14. ACTIVITY 10. *Read and write the words.*

- Focus pupils on Activity 10 and on the instruction. Go through the example. They work in pairs and discuss the answers. Pairs check with pairs. Check with the class.

Key: 2 doctor, 3 never, 4 dentist, 5 trees, 6 easy, 7 snail

AB14. ACTIVITY 11. *Cross out the words from Activity 10.*

- After pupils have completed Activity 10, tell them that the words for Activity 10 are in the grid in Activity 11. Focus pupils on the words in the grid. They cross out the words they wrote in Activity 10. They write a sentence with the other words. They work in pairs. Check with the class.

Key: Lenny likes his new teacher.

Joke box

- Focus pupils on the Joke box. Ask a pupil to read the joke to the class. They guess / find the answer. Explain the joke if necessary by explaining the different meanings of the word *problems*.

Extra activities: see page T109 (if time)

Ending the lesson

- Write the sentence *It's easy to clean a smiling crocodile's teeth* on the board. Say the sentence. Pupils repeat. Pupils practise saying the sentence as a tongue twister in pairs. Ask volunteers to say the tongue twister.

OBJECTIVES: By the end of the lesson, pupils will have read a story and reviewed language from the unit.

- **TARGET LANGUAGE**
Key language: language in the story
Revision: language from the unit

- **MATERIALS REQUIRED**
Flashcards of Lock and Key (13–14)
Adjective flashcards (15–23)
Optional: *Kid's Box Teacher's Resource Book 4* Unit 1 Extension worksheet 2 (page 19) and / or animated version of the Unit 1 story from *Kid's Box Interactive DVD 4* (*Suzy's room* section)

Warmer
- Show the Lock and Key flashcards and review what pupils remember about the characters. Pupils say, e.g. *They're the detectives who always do silly things.* Review who Peter is. Tell pupils that Lock and Key are going to Peter's school to talk about their job. Elicit what they think happens.

Story

PB15. LOCK AND KEY.
- Tell pupils to open their Pupil's Book at page 15. Focus on the first small frame and elicit who they can see (Peter) and what day he's talking about (Thursday). Play the CD. Pupils listen and read for what happens and to see if anything they predicted in the warmer happens. They check in pairs. Check with the class (Lock scares the children, Key spills some sauce, they play basketball and get told off by the teacher).
- Play the CD again. Pause after each frame for pupils to repeat. Check general comprehension by asking, e.g. *Who are Lock and Key eating lunch with? What does she ask them? Is it Key who sees the basketball? What does the teacher say when she finds them? Are they naughty?*

CD 1, 17
As in Pupil's Book

AB15. DO YOU REMEMBER?
- Write the word *Adjectives* in the centre of the board. Use the flashcards to elicit the adjectives from the unit and write them as a mind map on the board (you could also use the word cards from *Teacher's Resource Book 4* page 80).
- Tell pupils to open their Activity Book at page 15. Clean the board. Ask a pupil to read the activity instructions aloud and check they know what to do. Pupils study the words on the right in silence, using the pictures to help. Then they fold the page down the middle so that they can only see the pictures and the lines to write the words. Without looking, they write the words in pencil, using the pictures to help. They check in pairs, asking, e.g. *What's this one? How do you spell 'terrible'?* They don't look at the words on the right. When pupils have finished, they can either correct their own work or swap books and check their partner's.

AB15. CAN DO.
- Focus pupils on the *Can do* section of the page. Say *Let's read the sentences together.* Read the first sentence. Elicit what this means with examples and elicit / remind pupils of the activities they did in this unit when they described people. Review what the three faces mean (not very well / OK / very well). Remind pupils they circle the one they think is true for them.
- Repeat for the second sentence, eliciting / reminding pupils of things they described (e.g. *slow car, terrible weather, quick motorbike*). Pupils circle the appropriate face. Repeat for the third sentence, reminding pupils of the communication activity. Pupils circle the appropriate face.
- Say *Now show and tell your friends.* Pupils work in groups of three and take turns to show their work for / talk about each one.

Extra activities: see page T109 (if time)

Optional activities
- Unit 1 Extension worksheet 2 from *Teacher's Resource Book 4* (pages 15 and 19).
- The animated version of the story from *Kid's Box Interactive DVD 4* (*Suzy's room* section). See pages 38–45 of the Teacher's Booklet for the Interactive DVD.

Ending the lesson
- Ask pupils which chant / song they'd like to do again from the unit. Do it together to end the lesson.

Maths Measuring

Fact
The smallest house in the UK is only three metres high!

1 Read and look.

length · height

We measure length and height in metres (m), centimetres (cm) and millimetres (mm). There are ten millimetres (10 mm) in a centimetre and a hundred centimetres (100 cm) in a metre.

2 🎧 CD1 18 Listen and say the letter.

1 Sixty-four centimetres. —  f

- **a** 17 mm
- **b** 38 cm
- **c** 39.67 m
- **d** 83 m
- **e** 75.12 m
- **f** 64 cm
- **g** 62 mm
- **h** 93.56 m

3 Read and choose the answer.

1 How high is it?
  a 9.6 m
  b 96 cm
  c 96 m

2 How long is it?
  a 76.3 m
  b 42.8 m
  c 72 mm

3 How tall is it?
  a 95 cm
  b 5.9 m
  c 9.5 m

4 How tall is he?
  a 2.31 m
  b 1.8 m
  c 3.9 m

LOOK

2.45 m   two metres forty-five centimetres

OBJECTIVES: By the end of the lesson, pupils will have read about measuring and practised talking about height and length.

● TARGET LANGUAGE
Key language: measurements with decimal points, *measure, measurement, metre, centimetre, millimetre, height, length, How high / long is it? How tall is he / are you?*
Revision: numbers, classroom objects, comparatives

● MATERIALS REQUIRED
Warmer: Photocopies of the number cards from *Kid's Box Teacher's Resource Book 4* pages 88 and 89 (two pages per pair of pupils), scissors, envelopes (for collecting cards)
A tape measure or metre rule

Warmer
- Ask what pupils are learning in Maths. Review numbers by writing figures between 1 and 100 on the board. Pupils say them chorally and individually.
- Hand out the photocopies from the Teacher's Resource Book. Pairs cut them into cards. They turn them over and mix them up. Then they turn them back and match the figures and the words in pairs. Monitor and check, asking individuals to say some of the numbers.

PB16. ACTIVITY 1. *Read and look.*
- Tell pupils to open their Pupil's Book at page 16. Focus on the Fact. Read it with the class and ask them how long three metres is. Show the pupils on a tape measure. Point to the lines and elicit what they mean in L1 (centimetres, millimetres). Present *measure*. Point to the lesson title. Focus on the photo and on the arrows for *length* and *height*. Elicit translations.
- Say *Read and look*. Pupils read the text individually. Check comprehension by writing the abbreviations *m, cm* and *mm* on the board. Elicit the words in English. Practise pronunciation of *metre, centimetre* and *millimetre* (note that the last syllable is pronounced as a schwa (/ə/).

PB16. ACTIVITY 2. *Listen and say the letter.*
- Explain the English use and pronunciation of *point* (your pupils may use a comma to separate decimals from hundredths). Write examples of measurements with decimal points on the board, e.g. *43.15 m, 10.1 cm, 28.75 m*. Point and say the numbers (*forty-three metres fifteen centimetres, ten centimetres one millimetre, twenty-eight metres seventy-five centimetres*, etc). Pupils repeat chorally.
- Focus pupils on the Look box. Point out that if there are numbers after the whole metres, pupils should say the word *centimetres* at the end.
- Read the activity instruction and play the example. Play the CD. Pupils listen and number. They check in pairs. Play the CD again for them to check. Elicit answers. Practise saying the measurements with the class.

Key: 2 c, 3 e, 4 a, 5 h, 6 g, 7 b, 8 d

CD 1, 18
1. sixty-four centimetres
2. thirty-nine metres sixty-seven centimetres
3. seventy-five metres twelve centimetres
4. seventeen millimetres
5. ninety-three metres fifty-six centimetres
6. sixty-two millimetres
7. thirty-eight centimetres
8. eighty-three metres

PB16. ACTIVITY 3. *Read and choose the answer.*
- Pre-teach *How long, How high* and *How tall*, explaining the difference between *high* (for a thing) and *tall* (for a person).
- Focus on Activity 3 and on the four photographs. Elicit what pupils can see (Big Ben clock tower in London, an aeroplane, a giraffe, a basketball player). Read the questions aloud. Pupils repeat. Explain that while we refer to a person or animal's 'height', we ask *How tall is he / she / it?*
- Ask a pupil *How tall are you?* Write the answer on the board. Ask the class *What's his / her height?* Repeat with three or four more pupils.
- Pupils work in pairs to work out the answers. Check with the class.

Note: The plane length is a typical length for a Boeing 747-8 and the giraffe height is the typical height for an adult giraffe. Explain that, of course, other types of planes and female / young giraffes will be different in length / height. The basketball player is Paul Sturgess, also known as 'Tiny'.

Key: 1 c, 2 a, 3 b, 4 a

AB16. ACTIVITY 1. *Look and write the number.*
- Tell pupils to open their Activity Book at page 16. Focus on Activity 1. Practise some numbers first. Pupils work in pairs, writing the numbers. Check by asking pupils to come and write the numbers on the board.

Key: 2 twenty metres forty-seven centimetres, 3 thirty-five metres sixty-nine centimetres, 4 forty-one metres fifty-four centimetres, 5 seventy-eight metres ten centimetres, 6 ninety-two metres fifteen centimetres, 7 eighty-three metres twelve centimetres, 8 sixty-four metres twenty-seven centimetres

AB16. ACTIVITY 2. *Read and answer.*
- Focus pupils on Activity 2. Go through the example, showing pupils the addition on the board (1.25 + 0.19 = 1.44). Point out that when they are adding or subtracting, pupils need to make sure that both lengths are in the same units (either metres or centimetres). Do number 2 together if necessary. Pupils work in pairs to solve the rest. Check with the class.

Key: 2 She's one metre seventy-four centimetres. 3 She's three metres ninety-six centimetres. 4 It's fifteen metres seventy-three centimetres. 5 It's six metres ninety-one centimetres.

Extra activities: see pages T109–110 (if time)

Ending the lesson
- Review with pupils what they learnt about in today's lesson.

OBJECTIVES: By the end of the lesson, pupils will have carried out practical measuring tasks and completed a project involving comparing the heights of the members of their class.

• TARGET LANGUAGE
Key language: comparatives, numbers, classroom objects, *How long is your … ?*
Revision: pronouncing measurements (length and height), *How high / long is it? How tall is he / are you?*

• MATERIALS REQUIRED
Warmer: Two board pens
Project: Rulers and tape measures / a wall chart for pupils to measure their height
Photocopiable 1 (pages T93 and T94), one copy of page A and one copy of page B for each pair of pupils (Optional: a completed crossword from Photocopiable 1, photocopied so that each pair has one copy for checking answers)
Optional: *Kid's Box Teacher's Resource Book 4* Unit 1 Topic worksheet (page 21)

Warmer
- Write a selection of 10 to 12 measurements in metres in figures on the board. Make two teams. One pupil from each team comes to the front. Give him / her a board pen. Say one of the measurements (e.g. *Sixty-two metres thirty-five centimetres*). The first pupil to circle the correct figures on the board wins a point for their team. The two pupils hand the board pens to different members of their teams. The two new pupils come to the front. Repeat until all numbers have been circled.

PB17. ACTIVITY 4. *Measure the things in your classroom.*
- Tell pupils to open their Pupil's Book at page 17. Focus on Activity 4.
- Ask a pupil to read the activity instruction. Hand out the tape measures. Pupils copy the chart into their notebooks, perform the measuring tasks and write the answers. Make sure they measure different pencils, erasers, pens, etc. so they don't all have the same answers.
- Make new pairs. Pupils take turns to ask and answer about the information in their charts, guessing what each length represents. Pupils do not look at one another's charts as they do the activity.
- Pupils think of three more things to measure in their classroom. How long / high are they?

PB17. PROJECT. *Do a class survey. Draw a graph.*
- Focus pupils on the speech bubbles at the top of the activity. Remind them this is the project. Ask a pupil to read the project instructions aloud and check they remember how to do a survey. Pupils take turns to read the questions aloud. Check understanding. Brainstorm other questions pupils will need to ask when they are working, e.g. *How long is your little finger? How long is your hair?* Make groups of five. In the groups, pupils measure each other and record the information. They share the information in their groups. They copy the bar chart from the Pupil's Book page onto a large piece of paper (with question letters a–e along the bottom horizontal axis and *Number of children* and numbers 1–5 up the left-hand vertical axis) and fill in their information. Display the posters around the class. Groups discuss and compare the results.

Photocopiable 1 (see pages T90, T93 and T94)
AB17. ACTIVITY 3. MOVERS Reading and Writing, Part 3
Read the story. Choose a word from the box. Write the correct word next to numbers 1–6. There is one example. [M] towards
- Tell pupils to open their Activity Book at page 17. Focus them on the activity instruction and check understanding. Make sure they read the instruction for number 7 at the bottom of the page. Check comprehension of the words below the pictures. Pupils complete the text individually. They compare answers in pairs. Check with the class.

Key: 1 sheep, 2 night, 3 teacher, 4 draw, 5 boring, 6 Sally wants to be an Art teacher

Extra activity: see page T110 (if time)

Optional activity
- Unit 1 Topic worksheet from *Teacher's Resource Book 4* (pages 15 and 21).

Ending the lesson
- Review with pupils what they talked about in today's lesson and which activities they liked best from this and the previous lesson and why.

4 Measure the things in your classroom.

pencil	11 cm
desk	
Activity Book	
eraser	
me	

How long is your pencil?
How high is your desk?
How long is your Activity Book?
How long is your eraser?
How tall are you?

Project Do a class survey. Draw a graph.

How tall are you?

One metre thirty centimetres.

How many children in your group …		
a are taller than 1.35 m?	How tall are you?	4
b have got arms which are shorter than 60 cm?	How long are your arms?	
c have got feet which are longer than 28 cm?	How long are your feet?	
d have got little fingers which are shorter than 3 cm?		
e have got hair which is longer than 10 cm?		

2 Good sports

1 Look, think and answer.
1. Who do you think wants to climb?
2. How many water sports can they do?
3. Where can they do water sports?
4. Which activity can they do inside and outside?

2 Listen and check.

3 Listen and say the letter.   1 He's learning to skate.

LOOK

What can I **learn to** do?   You can **learn to** sail and fish.
It's a place **where** you can learn to do lots of exciting sports.

OBJECTIVES: By the end of the lesson, pupils will have talked about the sports children can learn to do.

● TARGET LANGUAGE
Key language: *learn to (swim), climb, sail, It's a place where …, activity centre*
Additional language: *rock climbing, climbing wall, water sports*
Revision: *weather, prepositions, present continuous, adjectives, inside, outside, skate, dance, fish, What does … mean?, can (ability), have got, the girl / boy who … , good at*

● MATERIALS REQUIRED
Sports flashcards (24–33)

Warmer
- Brainstorm sports and make a mind map on the board. Ask pupils which sports they like and which ones they do every week.

PB18. ACTIVITY 1. *Look, think and answer.*
- Tell pupils to open their Pupil's Book at page 18. Elicit the sports in the picture. Practise with flashcards. Confirm the meaning of *inside* and *outside* using the flashcards. Pupils discuss their answers / predictions in pairs.

PB18. ACTIVITY 2. *Listen and check.*
- Play the CD. Pupils listen for the answers. Elicit sentences. Elicit what an *activity centre* is. Say *It's a place where …* Check understanding of *climbing wall, rock climbing, water sports*. Play the CD again.
- **Key:** 1 Simon wants to climb. 2 They can do three water sports: sailing, fishing and swimming. 3 They can do water sports at / on the lake. 4 They can do climbing inside and outside.

CD 1, 19
SIMON: Look, this is the new activity centre which is opening in the village next to ours.
SUZY: What does 'activity centre' mean?
SIMON: It's a place where you can learn to do lots of exciting sports. Look. It's got rock climbing. I'd like to learn to climb.
STELLA: Hmm. It's not nice when it's cold, wet and raining.
SIMON: No, it's OK. They've got a climbing wall inside and outside.
SUZY: Look! There's a lake too.
SIMON: Yes, you can do water sports. You can learn to sail and fish, and you can go swimming there when it's hot.
SUZY: I don't want to sail or climb. What can I learn to do?
STELLA: Hmm. Let's see. You can learn to skate, Suzy.
SUZY: Hmm, skating. That's exciting, but I haven't got any skates.
STELLA: That's OK. They've got skates at the centre. And they do dancing. I can learn to dance.

PB18. ACTIVITY 3. *Listen and say the letter.*
- Focus pupils on Activity 3. Go through the example. Play the rest of the CD. Pupils whisper the letter to a partner. Play the CD again. Elicit answers.
- **Key:** 2 g, 3 f, 4 b, 5 c, 6 d, 7 e, 8 a

CD 1, 20
1. He's learning to skate.
2. She's learning to climb inside.
3. They're learning to dance.
4. He's learning to climb outside.
5. They're learning to skate.
6. He's learning to swim.
7. They're learning to fish.
8. They're learning to sail.

Look box
- Focus pupils on the Look box. Practise the question and answer. Write more sentences with *It's a place where …* on the board. Pupils say the place, e.g. *It's a place where you can learn English.* (school) … *buy food.* (supermarket) … *catch a train.* (station) … *borrow a book.* (library)

AB18. ACTIVITY 1. *Listen and draw lines.* [M] *towards*
- Tell pupils to open their Activity Book at page 18. Elicit what they can see. Point out the example. Play the CD. Pupils check in pairs. Play the CD again. Check with the class. Elicit the name they didn't use (Mary).

CD 1, 21
1. What are you doing? / We're learning to do different sports. Some of us are learning to climb, some are learning to skate and some are learning to fish. / And there are some children over there who are learning to sail. / Yes, the boy who's sitting at the front of the boat is my brother, Jim.
2. Who's that? / Who? / The girl who's helping the boy to skate. / That's Daisy.
3. And who's the boy learning to ride his bike? / The one who's with his older sister? / Yes, that's right. / That's Fred.
4. Who's that climbing up the wall? / The boy who's near the top? / No, the slower girl who's with him. / That's Jane. She's my cousin.
5. So, who's the boy swimming in the lake? / That's Jack. He's a good swimmer. / Yes, he is.
6. Now, there are two children over there fishing. Who are they? / The boy's called Peter. He's good at fishing. He knows you must be quiet to fish.

AB18. ACTIVITY 2. *Write the sentences.*
- Focus on Activity 2. Pupils do the activity individually. Check with the class.
- **Key:** 2 We can learn to sail. 3 She's the girl who likes skating. 4 You can play basketball inside. 5 Do you want to go fishing?

Extra activities: see page T110 (if time)

Ending the lesson
- In pairs, pupils play a mime game with sports. Pupils take turns to mime the sports and to guess.

OBJECTIVES: By the end of the lesson, pupils will have talked more about sports, using *want to learn to* and relative clauses with *where* and *who*.

● **TARGET LANGUAGE**
Key language: relative clauses with *where* and *who*, *want to learn to do (something)*
Additional language: *What do we call people who ... ?, lose, equipment*
Revision: sports and activities, jobs, sports equipment, *want to / doesn't want to, mustn't, need*

● **MATERIALS REQUIRED**
Sports flashcards (24–33)
Sports word cards from *Kid's Box Teacher's Resource Book 4* page 81
Optional: *Kid's Box Teacher's Resource Book 4* Unit 2 Reinforcement worksheet 1 (page 23), *Kid's Box 4 Language Portfolio* page 8

Warmer

- Write the new sports as anagrams on the board. Volunteers come and write them correctly. Check answers using the word cards and the flashcards.
- Say *Which sport do you want to learn to do?* Ask about each in turn, e.g. *Do you want to learn to (sail)?* Take a vote.

Presentation

- Write the question *Do you want to learn to ... ?* on the board. Find a pupil who said *Yes* in the warmer and write *(Name) wants to learn to ...* Find a pupil who said *No* and write *(Name) doesn't want to learn to ...* Write *I want to learn to ... / I don't want to learn to ...* Elicit from pupils the difference between *I* and *he / she* in the negative sentences (*don't* and *doesn't*).

PB19. ACTIVITY 4. *Make five true sentences. Use the words in the boxes.*

- Tell pupils to open their Pupil's Book at page 19. Ask a pupil to read the activity instructions aloud. Explain that pupils will need to ask their classmates *Do you want to learn to ... ?* in order to make five true sentences. They will also need to ask you, if they want to make a sentence with *My teacher ...* They move around the room to ask different pupils. They note down the answers. They then use the chart to help them make sentences. Remind them to include one sentence about themselves. Monitor and check for correct use of *don't / doesn't*. Elicit example sentences.

PB19. ACTIVITY 5. *Say the places.*

- Focus pupils on Activity 5. Go through the example. Check answers. Focus on the use of *a place where ...*

Key: 2 Park, 3 Road, 4 Swimming pool

PB19. ACTIVITY 6. *In pairs guess the place or person. You can only ask four questions.*

- Ask a pupil to read the Activity 6 instructions aloud and check understanding. The pupil who is thinking of a place or person needs to write the name on paper first so that there's no cheating. Remind pupils they can ask only four questions. Demonstrate the game for the class first. They play in pairs.

AB19. ACTIVITY 3. *Read and complete the table.*

- Tell pupils to open their Activity Book at page 19. Review *need* by asking, e.g. *What do you need to play football? What do you need to play tennis?*
- Pupils work individually. Check with the class. Elicit full sentences, e.g. *Sue is ten. She wants to roller skate. She needs some skates and a helmet.*

Key:

Name	Age	Sport	Equipment
Jim	11	volleyball	a big ball
Mary	12	swim	a towel
Sue	10	roller skate	skates, a hat
Paul	12	climb	strong shoes, a hat

AB19. ACTIVITY 4. *Write the words.*

- Focus pupils on Activity 4 and elicit some of the people they can see, e.g. *dancer*. Ask a pupil to read the first question aloud, and another the answer. Say *Teach ... teachers ... Which one is the job?* Help pupils notice this feature of word building. Remind them that the answers are in the plural (*people who ... teachers*). Pupils work in pairs. They take turns to read the questions aloud and work out the answers. Check with the class. Point out that the *b* in *climbers* is silent and the spelling of *swimmers* and *winners*.

Key: 2 dancers, 3 climbers, 4 swimmers, 5 ice skaters, 6 winners, 7 singers

Extra activities: see page T110 (if time)

Optional activity

- Reinforcement worksheet 1 from *Teacher's Resource Book 4* (page 23).

Language Portfolio

- Pupils complete page 8 of *Kid's Box 4 Language Portfolio* (*My interests*). Tell them they can use a photograph or draw a picture in the frame.

Ending the lesson

- Invite five pupils to the front. Whisper one of the sports / activities from Pupil's Book Activity 4 to each one. They quickly line up in alphabetical order, saying their words to the other pupils to work out the order. Repeat with seven more pupils for the jobs in Activity Book Activity 4.

4 Make five true sentences. Use the words in the boxes.

> My teacher wants to learn to climb.

I	wants to	learn to	sail.
My teacher	doesn't want to		dance.
	want to		climb.
My friends	don't want to		ice skate.
			skip.

5 Say the places.

> park ~~lake~~ swimming pool road sea

1 A place where you can go ice skating. — Lake.
2 A place where you mustn't roller skate.
3 A place where you can learn to swim.
4 A place where you can learn to ride a bike.
5 A place where you can learn to sail.

6 In pairs guess the place or person. You can only ask four questions.

Jim   Jack   Sally and Paul

Is it a person? — Yes, it is.
Is it a place? — Yes, it is.
Is it the girl who's learning to swim? — No, it isn't.
Is it the place where you mustn't roller skate? — It's a road. — Yes, it is.

7 Look, think and answer.
1 Where's Mr Star?
2 Who's climbing?
3 Where is Grandpa Star?
4 What's Suzy doing?

badly   carefully   quickly   slowly   well

8 🎧 Listen and check.

9 Read and choose the right words.
1 They're running **quietly** / **quickly** / **slowly**.   *Quickly.*
2 They're shouting **loudly** / **quietly** / **carefully**.
3 He's playing **badly** / **loudly** / **well**.
4 She's riding her bike **carefully** / **quietly** / **quickly**.
5 They're reading **quietly** / **loudly** / **badly**.
6 They're running **quickly** / **well** / **slowly**.
7 He's playing **well** / **loudly** / **badly**.
8 He's riding his bike **carefully** / **loudly** / **quickly**.

OBJECTIVES: By the end of the lesson, pupils will have described sports and activities using adverbs of manner.

• TARGET LANGUAGE
Key language: adverbs of manner: *well, quickly, slowly, carefully, badly, quietly*
Additional language: *roller skating, How's she doing?*
Revision: question forms, activities, actions and sports, present continuous, present simple, *good at, bad at*

• MATERIALS REQUIRED
Warmer: Sports flashcards (24–33)
Extra activity 1: At least ten pieces of card with an action written on each, e.g. *read a book, get dressed, ride a bike, climb, wash your face*, six pieces of card of a different colour with the adverbs from the lesson written on them (*well, quickly, slowly, carefully, badly, quietly*).
Optional: *Kid's Box Teacher's Resource Book 4* Unit 2 Reinforcement worksheet 2 (page 24)

Warmer
- Review sports and activities using the flashcards. Elicit more sports. Write them on the board. Ask volunteers *Who is good at … ? Who is bad at … ?*

Presentation
- Present *well / badly* by writing two examples from the Warmer on the board, e.g. *Juan plays tennis well. Francesca plays tennis badly.* Elicit that the adverbs tell us how people do an activity (they tell us more about the verb). Focus pupils on the word order. Write these adverbs on the board: *quickly, slowly, carefully, quietly*. Use different colours for the letters *ly*.

PB20. ACTIVITY 7. *Look, think and answer.*
- Tell pupils to open their Pupil's Book at page 20. Elicit who and what they can see. Ask a pupil to read the activity instruction aloud and others to read the questions. Pupils discuss their answers / predictions in pairs.
- Focus pupils on the adverbs. Ask about the pictures, e.g. *How is Simon climbing?* (quickly). Check understanding of each adverb using mime.

PB20. ACTIVITY 8. *Listen and check.*
- Play the CD for pupils to listen and check. Elicit complete sentences. Play the CD again in sections. Give pupils practice with the adverbs, e.g. *How are Alex and Simon climbing? Is Simon climbing slowly?*

Key: 1 Mr Star's inside the activity centre. 2 Simon and Alex are climbing. 3 Grandpa Star's outside the activity centre. 4 Suzy's skating.

CD 1, 22

MR STAR: Hello.
GRANDPA: Hello, son. Where are you?
MR STAR: Hi, Dad. I'm inside, watching Simon and Alex. They're climbing really well. Simon's climbing quickly and he's near the top of the wall. Alex is climbing slowly and carefully. Where are you, Dad?
GRANDPA: I'm outside with Suzy. She's learning to skate.
MR STAR: How's she doing?
GRANDPA: Well, she isn't doing badly. She doesn't want to fall, so she's skating slowly.
SUZY: Look at me, Grandpa! I can skate really well now, but I'm tired. Let's go inside and watch Simon.
GRANDPA: Good idea, Suzy. See you in a minute, son. We're coming in now.

PB20. ACTIVITY 9. *Read and choose the right words.*
- Focus pupils on Activity 9. Elicit who they can see (athletes, children, footballers, etc.). Go through the example. Pupils choose the best adverb in pairs. Check by asking pairs to read the sentences aloud.

Key: 2 loudly, 3 badly, 4 quickly, 5 quietly, 6 slowly, 7 well, 8 carefully

AB20. ACTIVITY 5. *Read and circle the correct answer. Match.*
- Tell pupils to open their Activity Books at page 20. Ask a pupil to read the activity instruction aloud and another to read the example. Elicit why *carefully* is correct (because *careful* is an adjective, not an adverb). Pupils complete the activity individually and then check in pairs. Check with the class. Ask why 5 is different (*well* is irregular).

Key: 1 carefully a, 2 quickly b, 3 badly f, 4 slowly e, 5 well c, 6 quietly d

AB20. ACTIVITY 6. *Complete the sentences about you. Use the words in the box.*
- Focus pupils on Activity 6. Ask a pupil to read the activity instructions and others to read the words in the box. Point out the example. Pupils complete sentences about themselves, choosing words that are true if possible.

AB20. ACTIVITY 7. *Now ask a friend.*
- Focus pupils on Activity 7 and on the instruction. Ask a pair of pupils to read the example question and answer. Tell pupils to ask about the activities in Activity 6. They ask and answer in pairs. Monitor and help as necessary.

AB20. ACTIVITY 8. *Read. Sort and write the words.*
- Focus pupils on Activity 8 and on the instructions. They complete the activity individually and then check in pairs. Check with the class.

Key: 2 river, 3 park, 4 lake, 5 forest, 6 beach

Extra activities: see page T110 (if time)

Optional activity
- Reinforcement worksheet 2 from *Teacher's Resource Book 4* (page 24).

Ending the lesson
- Call out actions and adverbs for pupils to follow, e.g. *Stamp loudly. Turn around quickly. Pick up your pencil carefully. Stand up slowly.*

OBJECTIVES: By the end of the lesson, pupils will have had further practice using adverbs of manner and sung a song.

- **TARGET LANGUAGE**
Key language: adverbs, *easily, happily*
Additional language: *round and round, over the ground, lots of fun, up the wall, fall, verse, chorus, drop, very* (+ adverb)
Revision: activities, sports, actions, present continuous, present simple, *activity centre, the person who …*

- **MATERIALS REQUIRED**
Optional: *Kid's Box Teacher's Resource Book 4* Unit 2 Song worksheet (page 27) and / or extra activities from *Kid's Box Interactive DVD 4* booklet (pages 28–33)

Warmer

- Review the adverbs from the previous lesson by giving instructions, e.g. *Please get your books out quickly and quietly. Now write the date slowly at the top of the page. (Name), please hand out the books carefully.*

PB21. ACTIVITY 10. *Listen and say 'yes' or 'no'.*

- Tell pupils to open their Pupil's Book at page 21. Ask a pupil to read the activity instruction aloud. Remind pupils to whisper the word to their partner the first time they listen. Play the CD. Pupils listen and whisper. Play the CD again. Pause after each one and elicit *Yes* or *No*. For 'yes' responses, elicit the statement, and for 'no' responses, elicit a correct statement.

Key: 2 Yes, 3 No, 4 Yes, 5 Yes, 6 No

CD 1, 23

1. They're playing well. [sound of playing football well]
2. She's singing badly. [sound of singing badly]
3. He's walking quickly. [sound of walking slowly]
4. They're talking quietly. [sound of talking quietly]
5. She's walking slowly. [sound of walking slowly]
6. They're playing loudly. [sound of playing music quietly]

PB21. ACTIVITY 11. *Read and say the letter. Listen and check.*

- Focus pupils on the song. They read the song lyrics and match the numbers with the letters in the picture. Play the song for pupils to check their answers.
- Check understanding of the new vocabulary. Focus on *easily* and *happily* and show / elicit how the adverbs are formed from the adjectives.

Key: 2 a, 3 b

CD 1, 24

As in Pupil's Book

PB21. ACTIVITY 12. *Sing the song.*

- Play the CD in sections for pupils to listen and repeat. They sing the song as a class.

CD 1, 24

As in Pupil's Book

CD 1, 25

Now sing the song again. (Karaoke version)

PB21. ACTIVITY 13. *Write another verse. Sing.*

- Focus pupils on the activity instructions and elicit the meaning of *verse*. Elicit / teach *chorus*. Pupils work in groups. They write another verse for the song, using the model. Monitor and help / advise. Pupils perform their new verses for the class: they sing the chorus and then they sing and mime their verse.

AB21. ACTIVITY 9. *Read and match.*

- Tell pupils to open their Activity Books at page 21. Ask a pupil to read the activity instruction aloud and check understanding. Demonstrate, using the example. Pupils work individually and match the sentences. They check in pairs, taking turns to read their correct sentences aloud to each other. Check with the class, again asking pupils to read sentences aloud.

Key: 2 e, 3 d, 4 a, 5 f, 6 b, 7 c

AB21. ACTIVITY 10. *Read and complete the table.*

- Focus pupils on Activity 10 and ask a pupil to read the activity instruction aloud. Elicit that this is a problem-solving activity. Write one of the sentences on the board and show pupils how to decipher it (each sentence includes two pieces of information about each person). Tell pupils to match the actions with the people first.
- Pupils work either individually or in pairs. Monitor and help where necessary. Copy the table from the Activity Book onto the board (or a large piece of paper) with the gaps. Check with the class by asking pupils to read the sentences and then to come and write the relevant information on the table on the board. Give pupils more practice by making false statements about the children and / or asking, e.g. *Tell me about Lenny.*

Key: Alex – play the piano well, climb carefully; Meera – swim quickly, sing quietly; Suzy – sing loudly, write slowly; Simon – climb quickly, draw well; Stella – swim slowly, write well

Extra activities: see page T110 (if time)

Optional activities

- Pupils listen to the song again and complete the Unit 2 Song worksheet from *Teacher's Resource Book 4* (pages 22 and 27).
- Extra activity for Unit 2 Song and / or karaoke worksheet. See pages 28–33 of the Teacher's Booklet for the Interactive DVD.

Ending the lesson

- Pupils sing their new verses of the song again.

10 Listen and say 'yes' or 'no'.

> 1 They're playing well.

> Yes.

11  Read and say the letter. Listen and check.

> 1 – c

Activity centre,
Lots of fun.
A place to skate,
Sail and run.
Activity centre …

1 I'm skating well,
Round and round.
I'm moving quickly,
Over the ground.

Activity centre,
Lots of fun.
A place to skate,
Sail and run.
Activity centre …

2 I'm climbing easily,
Up the wall.
I'm going carefully,
So I don't fall.

Activity centre,
Lots of fun.
A place to skate,
Sail and run.
Activity centre …

3 We're sailing happily,
Our boat's short.
We're going slowly,
What a great sport.

Activity centre,
Lots of fun.
A place to skate,
Sail and run.
Activity centre …

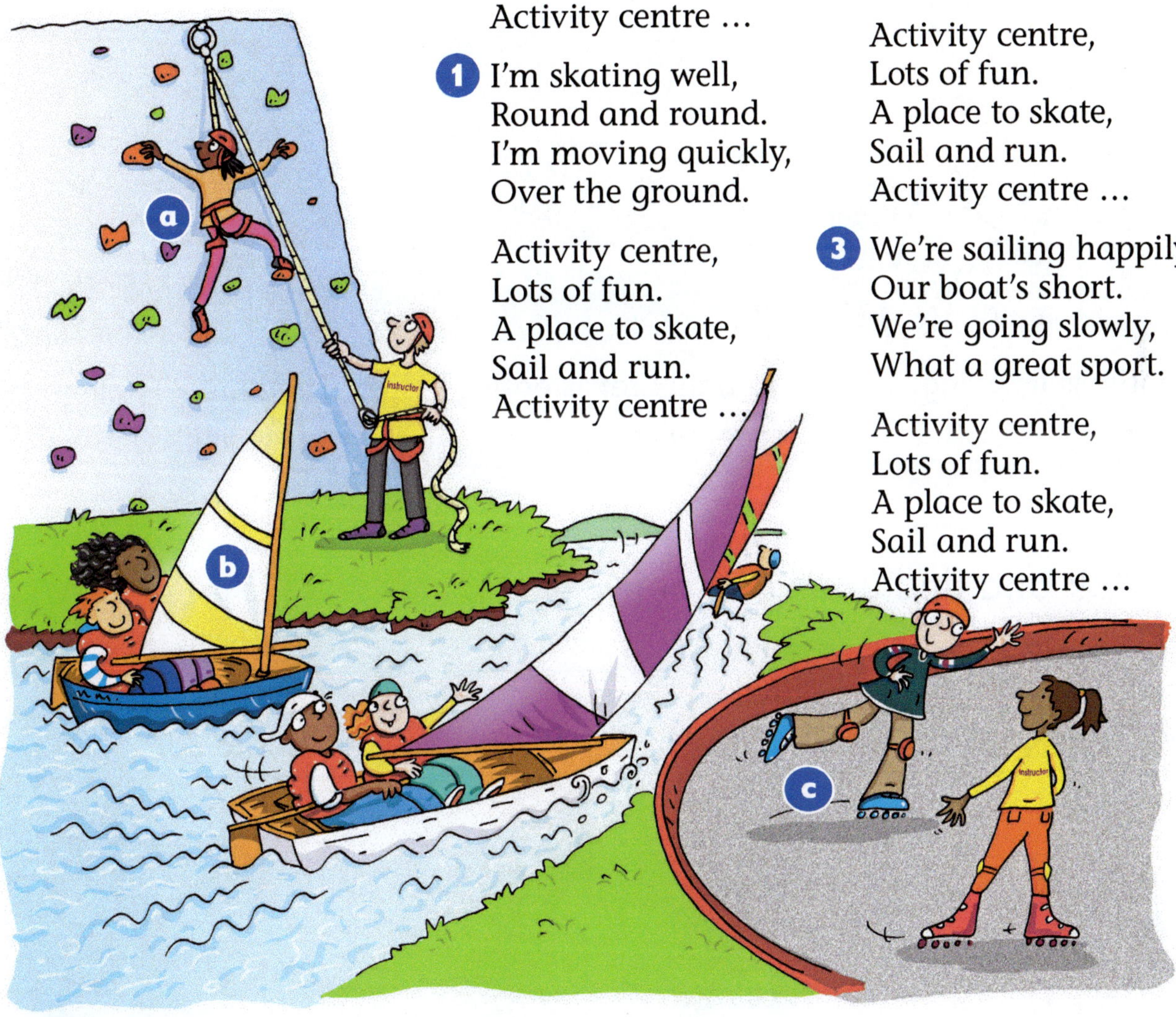

12 Sing the song.

13 Write another verse. Sing.

I'm **running** / **dancing** / **skipping** well,
Look at me.
Doing it **slowly** / **quickly** / **happily**,
Now you can see.

> I'm dancing well,
> Look at me.

14 **Stella's phonics**

A scientist is listening to music.

His daughter is eating a sandwich.

They mustn't climb on this island!

15 Ask and find your partner.

OBJECTIVES: By the end of the lesson, pupils will be able to recognise that there are silent consonants in some words and will be able to identify them in some common words. They will also have completed a communication activity.

- **TARGET LANGUAGE**

Key language: words with silent consonants (e.g. lis*t*en, i*s*land, clim*b*)
Revision: sports and activities, language from previous units, *want to*

- **MATERIALS REQUIRED**

Photocopiable 2a (page T95), copied onto card and cut into cards. Make sure you have at least two copies of each different card. You will need enough cards so that there is one for each pupil in the class (if you have an odd number of pupils, take a card yourself and participate).
Optional: *Kid's Box Teacher's Resource Book 4* Unit 2 Extension worksheet 1 (page 25)

Warmer

- Write the following words on the board: *write, answer, island, knee*. Say *Look and think about the spelling and the sounds. What do they have in common?* Give pupils time to discuss in pairs. Elicit / explain that the words all have silent consonants. Underline them (*write, answer, island, knee*).

PB22. Activity 14. *Stella's phonics*

- Tell pupils to open their Pupil's Book at page 22. Elicit who and what they can see in the pictures. Check comprehension of *scientist, daughter* and *sandwich*. Play the CD. Pupils listen and repeat.

Note: Words with silent consonants are often part of spelling patterns (the letter *b* is silent after *m*: e.g. *climb, thumb*; a *t* after an *s* can be silent: e.g. *listen, fasten*; the *k* is silent in *kn*: e.g. *know, knee*; the *w* is silent in *wr*: e.g. *write, wrong*; the *c* is silent in *sc*: e.g. *scissors*; the *l* is silent in *lk*: e.g. *walk, talk*; and the *h* is silent in *wh*: e.g. *when, where*).
Rhyming words can help students remember irregular pronunciations, e.g. *climb / time* or *daughter / water*.

`CD 1, 26`

STELLA: Hi, I'm Stella! Repeat after me!
A scientist is listening to music.
A scientist is listening to music.
His daughter is eating a sandwich.
His daughter is eating a sandwich.
They mustn't climb on this island!
They mustn't climb on this island!
A scientist is listening to music. His daughter is eating a sandwich. They mustn't climb on this island!

Photocopiable 2a (see pages T90, T95 and the notes below)

PB22. Activity 15. *Ask and find your partner.*

- Ask two pupils to read out the speech bubbles. Tell them you're going to give them all cards with things they want to do. They don't show their card to other pupils. They move around the room taking turns to ask and answer until they find the pupil whose card has the same activities as theirs.
- Hand each pupil a card from Photocopiable 2a (see page T95). They keep it secret. They move around asking *What do you want to do?* and answering, e.g. *I want to go climbing and skating* until they find the pupil who has the matching card.

AB22. Activity 11. *Write. Listen, check and say.*

- Tell pupils to open their Activity Book at page 22. Check pupils know the meaning of the words in the box. Point out the example. Pupils work individually. Tell them to practise saying the words. They compare answers.
- Play the CD for pupils to listen and check. Check with the class. Play the CD again for pupils to listen and repeat.

Key: 2 Science, 3 writing, 4 walk, 5 answer, 6 island, 7 mustn't, 8 climbing, 9 listening, 10 know

`CD 1, 27`

1. We can see whales in the sea.
2. In Science we learn about the heart.
3. Vicky's writing a story about a detective.
4. I always walk to school.
5. What's the answer to that question?
6. I want to go to an island for my next holiday.
7. The teacher says we mustn't talk in the library.
8. I love climbing mountains.
9. John likes listening to pop music.
10. What's her name? I don't know.

AB22. Activity 12. *Complete the crossword.*

- Focus pupils on Activity 12. They write the words in the crossword and check in pairs. When the puzzle is complete, pupils find the sport (tennis).

Key: 2 beard, 3 fishing, 4 sports centre, 5 difficult, 6 artist

Joke box

- Focus pupils on the Joke box. Ask a pupil to read the joke to the class. They guess / find the answer. Explain the joke if necessary by explaining the double meaning of the word *bats*.

Extra activity: see page T110 (if time)

Optional activity

- Unit 2 Extension worksheet 1 from *Teacher's Resource Book 4* (pages 22 and 25).

Ending the lesson

- With books closed, elicit the words with silent letters and call volunteers to write them on the board. The rest of the class check the spelling.

OBJECTIVES: By the end of the lesson, pupils will have read a story and reviewed language from the unit.

- **TARGET LANGUAGE**
Key language: language in the story
Revision: language from the unit

- **MATERIALS REQUIRED**
Sports flashcards (24–33)
Optional: *Kid's Box Teacher's Resource Book 4* Unit 2 Extension worksheet 2 (page 26) and / or animated version of the Unit 2 story from *Kid's Box Interactive DVD 4* (*Suzy's room* section), *Kid's Box Interactive DVD 4: The living room* 'Let's play basketball!' episode

Warmer
- Review the two previous episodes of *Lock and Key* by asking questions, e.g. *Do you remember the episode about the picnic thief? What's the little boy's name? Where do Lock and Key go? Who was the real thief? In the next episode, why do they go to Peter's school?* Ask pupils who they like better, Lock or Key.

Story

PB23. LOCK AND KEY.
- Tell pupils to open their Pupil's Book at page 23. Focus pupils on the first frame and ask where this episode is taking place (the swimming club). Ask a pupil to read aloud the first speech bubble to find out what the problem is (somebody's got the swimming cup). Pre-teach *coach*. Set the gist questions: *What does the note say? Why does the coach shout? What's Mr Sweep doing?* Play the CD. Pupils listen for the answers. They check in pairs. Check with the class ('I've got the swimming cup. T.S.'; because it's difficult to hear in the swimming pool; he's cleaning the cup).
- Check understanding by asking about each frame, e.g. *What's Key doing in frame 2? Why? Why does he fall into the water? What does the coach say in frame 4? Who sees the cup first? What does he say? What does Terry Sweep say at the end? How does he feel?* Play the CD again. Pause after each frame for pupils to repeat.

CD 1, 28
As in Pupil's Book

AB23. DO YOU REMEMBER?
- Review the sports words in the unit, including *inside* and *outside*, using the flashcards. Tell pupils to open their Activity Books at page 23. Ask a pupil to read the activity instructions aloud. They study the words on the right in silence, using the pictures to help. Then they fold the page down the middle so that they can see only the pictures and the lines to write the words. Without looking, they write the words in pencil, using the pictures to help. They check in pairs, asking, e.g. *What's this one? How do you spell 'outside'?* They don't look at the words on the right. When pupils have finished, they can either correct their own work or swap books and check their partner's.

AB23. CAN DO.
- Focus pupils on the *Can do* section of the page. Say *Let's read the sentences together*. Read the first sentence. Elicit what this means with examples and elicit / remind pupils of all the activities they did in this unit when they used action verbs. Review what the three faces mean (not very well / OK / very well). Remind pupils they circle the one they think is true for them. Repeat for the second sentence, eliciting / reminding pupils that adverbs give information about *how*. Talk about the mime games they played. Pupils circle the appropriate face. Repeat for the third sentence, reminding pupils of when they used *I want to …* Pupils circle the face.
- Say *Now show and tell your friends*. Pupils work in groups of three and take turns to show their work for / talk about each one.

Extra activities: see pages T110–111 (if time)

Optional activities
- Unit 2 Extension worksheet 2 from *Teacher's Resource Book 4* (pages 22 and 26).
- The animated version of the story from *Kid's Box Interactive DVD 4* (*Suzy's room* section). See pages 38–45 of the Teacher's Booklet for the Interactive DVD.
- 'Let's play basketball!' episode from *Kid's Box Interactive DVD 4* (*The living room* section). See pages 8–11 of the Teacher's Booklet for the Interactive DVD.

Ending the lesson
- Ask pupils which chant / song they'd like to do again from the unit. Do it together to end the lesson.

Sport | Ball games

Fact
The first basketball was brown.

1 Read and match. 1 – c

baseball

basketball

My favourite sport is baseball. You play baseball on (1)**a field** with (2)**a little white ball**, called a baseball. You hit the ball with (3)**a long bat**. There are two teams with nine players. One team throws and catches the ball. The other team hits the ball.

There are four bases: first base, second base, third base and fourth base. When a player hits the ball they run round the bases. When they arrive at fourth base they get a run. The winning team is the team with more runs at the end of the game.

My favourite sport is basketball. You play basketball with (4)**a big orange ball**. There are two teams with five players. Both teams try to get points by throwing the ball into (5)**a basket**, which is 3 metres above the floor.

You can throw, run and bounce the ball, but you can't run and carry the ball at the same time. The winning team is the team with more points after 40 minutes.

2   Listen and say 'baseball' or 'basketball'.

1 You play with a big ball.   Basketball.

OBJECTIVES: By the end of the lesson, pupils will have read about baseball and basketball and written about football.

● **TARGET LANGUAGE**
Key language: *ball games, pitcher, bat, batter, first / second / third / fourth, base, arrive, run* (n), *basket, basketball court, baseball field*
Revision: *can, can't* (permission), action verbs, impersonal *you*

● **MATERIALS REQUIRED**
Extra activity 2: Reference books on sport / the internet
Optional: *Kid's Box Teacher's Resource Book 4* Unit 2 Topic worksheet (page 28)

Warmer
- Ask pupils what they think the five most popular sports are in the USA. Elicit ideas. Tell them they are: 1 American football, 2 baseball, 3 basketball, 4 hockey, 5 golf. Ask pupils what they know about any of these sports, e.g. players, leagues, rules.

PB24. FACT
- Tell pupils to open their Pupil's Book at page 24. Introduce the topic of the lesson (ball games). Elicit examples of ball games and then tell pupils to look at the Fact box. Read the Fact box aloud and ask pupils what colour a basketball is nowadays.

PB24. ACTIVITY 1. *Read and match.*
- Tell pupils to open their Pupil's Book at page 24 and focus on Activity 1. Elicit what they can see in the photos (a baseball field, a basketball court and some of the equipment players use for these sports). Pupils take turns to read the text about baseball aloud. Help them with any difficult words and, after reading, check understanding of the new vocabulary. Repeat for basketball. Pupils re-read the texts and match the letters of the photos with the numbered words in the text. They check and discuss in pairs. Check with the class, discussing the two texts and the two games.

Key: 2 b, 3 a, 4 e, 5 d

PB24. ACTIVITY 2. *Listen and say 'baseball' or 'basketball'.*
- Focus pupils on Activity 2 and ask a pupil to read the instruction. Play the CD. Pupils listen, think and whisper the name. Play the CD again. Check with the class.

Key: 2 baseball, 3 basketball, 4 baseball, 5 basketball, 6 baseball, 7 basketball, 8 basketball, 9 baseball

CD 1, 29
1. You play with a big ball.
2. You play with a small white ball.
3. There are five players in a team.
4. You hit the ball with a bat.
5. You can throw and bounce the ball.
6. There are nine players in a team.
7. A game is 40 minutes.
8. You must throw the ball into a basket.
9. There are four bases.

AB24. ACTIVITY 1. *Order the sentences.*
- Tell pupils to open their Activity Book at page 24. Ask a pupil to read the activity instruction and check understanding (they sequence the rules). Pupils read the rules silently and try to sequence them. They can look back at the Pupil's Book page. They check in pairs. Check with the class.

Key: 8, 1, 3, 4, 2, 6, 5, 7

AB24. ACTIVITY 2. *Write about football. Use these words.*
- Focus pupils on Activity 2 and ask a pupil to read the instructions aloud. Confirm that this is not American football. If pupils don't know the rules of the game, discuss them first with the class so that everyone knows how the game is played. They can look at the prompts on the page to help them. Pupils work in pairs. They write a first draft of their text on paper. They swap with another pair and check each other's texts. Pupils then write their text on the page, illustrating the text with a key feature / aspect of the game / pitch (as with the baseball text).

Sample answer: In football there are two teams with eleven players each. This is how you play: First the player from one team has to kick the ball. Next the players run to kick the ball. Both teams try to score goals. The winning team is the team with more goals after ninety minutes.

Extra activities: see page T111 (if time)

Optional activity
- Unit 2 Topic worksheet from *Teacher's Resource Book 4* (pages 22 and 28).

Ending the lesson
- Review with pupils what they learnt about in today's lesson.

OBJECTIVES: By the end of the lesson, pupils will have read more about sports and completed a project.

- **TARGET LANGUAGE**
Key language: *have to* (obligation), *balloon*
Additional language: language of instruction, procedural language
Revision: sports, question forms, adverbs, *have to, must, sand, salt, fall out, break, neck (of balloon)*

- **MATERIALS REQUIRED**
Project: Each pupil will need: 200 grams salt or sand, 5 balloons, scissors; make a ball according to the project instructions, as a model
Photocopiable 2b (page T96). One copy, cut in half, for each pair of pupils. (Optional: the text from Photocopiable 2b completed (see page T92), one for each pair of pupils)
Extra activity: A ball

Warmer
- Review what pupils remember about the sports from the previous lesson (baseball, basketball, football).
- Introduce *have to* for obligation, and explain that *have got to* can be used as an alternative.

PB25. ACTIVITY 3. *Do you remember? Read and answer.*
- Tell pupils to open their Pupil's Book at page 25. Ask a pupil to read the activity instructions aloud. Pupils work in pairs. They cover page 24 with paper. They take turns to ask and answer the questions: they can do them in any order. At the end of the activity, they look and check.

Key: Baseball: 2 No, you play with a small white ball. 3 There are nine players in a baseball team. 4 You hit the ball with a bat. 5 There are four bases. 6 They have to arrive at the fourth base. Basketball: 1 There are five players in each team. 2 No, you can't. 3 You get points by throwing the ball into the basket. 4 You play for 40 minutes.

PB25. PROJECT. *Make a ball.*
- Focus pupils on the photos and on the activity. Remind them this is the project. Ask a pupil to read the project title aloud and confirm they are going to make a ball. Show the ball you've made. Read the instructions first with pupils, before handing out any of the materials. Hold up the materials as they are mentioned, pointing to, e.g. the neck of the balloon. Pupils clear their desks and work individually. They follow the instructions to make the ball. Monitor and check.

Photocopiable 2b (see pages T90, T96 and T92)

AB25. ACTIVITY 3. MOVERS Listening, Part 5
Listen and colour and write. There is one example. [M] *towards*

- Tell pupils to open their Activity Book at page 25. Elicit the activities they can see (climbing, skating, fishing, playing with a ball). Check they know what to do. Explain there is an example (the girl who is climbing, whose jacket is coloured grey) and that they will hear the example described first.

- Play the CD. Pupils don't colour or draw the first time. They listen and look. Play the CD again. Pupils put a coloured dot on the relevant part of the picture. They check in pairs. Pupils colour the picture and draw, or listen again if necessary. Show a completed picture for pupils to check their answers or elicit the correct colours / word from the class.

CD 1, 30

Can you see the children climbing? / Yes, I can. The girl is climbing very well and the boy is watching her. / Yes. Now colour the girl's jacket grey, please. / OK.

Can you see the girl's grey jacket? This is an example. Now you listen and colour and write.

1. OK. Look at that boy who's catching the ball. / The boy with the hat? / Yes. Colour his hat red. / OK.

2. What can I do now?/ Do you want to write something?/ Yes, I do. What can I write?/ Look at the boy who's sitting under the tree./ Oh yes. He's reading something./ That's right. Can you write 'comic' on that? Yes, OK. I'm writing that now.

3. Do you want to colour something? / Yes. Can I colour the big ball? / OK. What colour? / Orange. / Fine.

4. OK. Now can you see the woman? / Which one? The one with curly hair or the one with straight hair? / The one with straight hair. Can you colour her hair brown, please? / OK. I can do that now.

5. What do you want to colour now? / I'd like to colour this girl's jacket. / Which girl? / The girl who's learning to skate. She's skating very carefully. / OK. Colour her jacket purple, please. / Fine. Finished.

Extra activity: see page T111 (if time)

Ending the lesson
- Review with pupils what they talked about in today's lesson and what activities they liked best from this and the previous lesson and why.

3 Do you remember? Read and answer.

Baseball
1 Where do you play baseball?   *You play baseball on a field.*
2 Do you have to play with a big orange ball?
3 How many players are there in a baseball team?
4 What do you use to hit the ball?
5 How many bases are there?
6 Which base do the players have to arrive at to get a run?

Basketball
1 How many players are there in a basketball team?
2 Can you run and carry the ball at the same time?
3 How do you get points in basketball?
4 How many minutes do you play?

 **Project**   Make a ball.

You need:
- 200 grams salt or sand
- 5 balloons
- scissors

1 Cut the necks off all the balloons.
2 Put the salt or sand into the first balloon.
3 Open the second balloon and put your ball inside it. Put it over the neck of the first balloon.
4 Open the third balloon and put your ball inside it.
5 Repeat with the fourth balloon.
6 Put the last balloon over the ball. Now you're ready to play.

Review Units 1 and 2

1 Play the game.

Instructions
Red – Whose is it / are they?
Blue – What's this?
Grey – What's he / she doing?

OBJECTIVES: By the end of the lesson, pupils will have reviewed language from Units 1 and 2 and played a game.

● TARGET LANGUAGE
Key language: vocabulary and language from Units 1 and 2
Revision: language for games *It's my / your / his / her turn. Pass the dice, please. I'm / You're / He's / She's (yellow). You should move (five) squares, not (four). I've / You've / He's / She's finished / won.*

● MATERIALS REQUIRED
Warmer: Key vocabulary from Units 1 and 2 written on pieces of paper or the Back to school and Good sports word cards from *Kid's Box Teacher's Resource Book 4* (pages 80–81), one for each pupil
Dice and different coloured counters for each group or pair of pupils
Photocopiable Review 1 and 2 (page T97), copied onto card and cut into cards, one set for each group of three or four pupils

Warmer
- Hand out the pieces of paper with key vocabulary or the word cards. Pupils work in groups of six. They don't show their word to the other people in their group. They take turns to give clues about their word for the others to guess.

PB26. ACTIVITY 1. *Play the game.*
- Pupils open their Pupil's Book at page 26. Elicit what this is (a board game). Demonstrate the game for pupils first, showing them when to use which questions (at the top of the page) according to the colour. Elicit the language pupils will need to play the game, e.g. *It's my / your turn.*
- Pupils play the game in pairs or small groups. They take turns to throw the dice, move and answer the question according to the colour. The other pupil(s) decide(s) if their answer is correct. Monitor and help.
- If time, pupils can play the game again.
- Pupils can check by looking back in their book for answers, especially those about the belongings.

Key: They're Stella's. He's running. It's Simon's. She's climbing. It's Lock's. It's a ruler. She's sailing. It's Lenny's. She's swimming. It's a ball. They're Suzy's. He's skating. It's Lock and Key's. It's a dolphin. It's Uncle Fred's. He's dancing. It's Aunt May's. She's fishing. It's Mrs Star's. It's Stella's. It's an elephant. It's Alex's. It's a bottle. She's singing. It's Suzy's. It's Mrs Star's. It's a glass. She's walking. They're Mr Star's. He's / She's drawing. It's a baseball bat.

Photocopiable Review 1 and 2 (see pages T90 and T97)

AB26. ACTIVITY 1. *Answer the questions.*
- Tell pupils to open their Activity Book at page 26. Ask a pupil to read the instruction aloud and check understanding using the example answer. Pupils work individually and solve the problems. They check in pairs. Check with the class using open pairs.

Key: 2 l (lake), 3 p (skip), 4 h (hat), 5 a (skate), 6 b (badminton), 7 e (tennis), 8 t (football). The word is alphabet.

AB26. ACTIVITY 2. *What's wrong with these pictures? Write the answers.*
- Focus pupils on Activity 2. Ask a pupil to read the instructions aloud and check understanding using the example. Remind pupils to use full sentences. They work in pairs to interpret what's wrong orally and then they write the answers individually. Monitor to check.

Key: 2 The cow's got glasses. 3 They're sailing in a swimming pool. / The boat is in a swimming pool. 4 The girl's wearing a scarf in the sun. 5 The girl's writing with a ruler. 6 He's fishing on a basketball court.

Extra activities: see page T111 (if time)

Ending the lesson
- Play a mime game to end the lesson. Pupils come up in turn. Whisper an activity and adverb, e.g. *Write carefully.* The pupil mimes the activity. Pupils ask questions, e.g. *Are you writing slowly?* Classmates continue asking until one of them guesses correctly. Repeat.

OBJECTIVES: By the end of the lesson, pupils will have reviewed language from Units 1 and 2.

- **TARGET LANGUAGE**

Key language: language and vocabulary from Units 1 and 2
Revision: word families, functional language, offers / suggestions, conversational openers and responses

- **MATERIALS REQUIRED**

The completed crossword for Activity Book Activity 4 copied on a large piece of paper
Optional: *Kid's Box Interactive DVD 4: Stella's room* Quiz 1, *Kid's Box 4 Language Portfolio* page 3

Warmer

- Review games and equipment. Write sports from Units 1 and 2 on the board, e.g. *baseball, basketball, sailing, climbing.* Call out equipment, e.g. *Bat, boat, helmet.* Pupils point to / call out the sport.

PB27. ACTIVITY 2. *Read the text and choose the best answer.* [M] *towards*

- Tell pupils to open their Pupil's Book at page 27. Ask a pupil to read the instruction aloud and focus the class on the example. One pupil reads the opener, and the other the correct answer. Check they know what to do. Pupils complete the activity individually. They check in pairs. Check with the class, but ask pupils to take turns to read the opener and then all three options, before eliciting from the class which one is correct. Ask them how they know each time. Elicit suitable openers for some of the other options.

Key: 1 B, 2 C, 3 B, 4 A, 5 A, 6 C

PB27. *Quiz!*

- Say *Now let's read and remember.* Explain / elicit the meaning of *quiz.* Focus pupils on the questions. Pupils look back through Units 1 and 2 and find the answers. They discuss them in groups of four. Check with the class.
- If time, pupils write two more questions of their own. Pupils close their Pupil's Books. Volunteers ask the class one of their questions.

Key: 1 They're busy in their Art class. 2 Mrs Robinson. 3 In the park (near the lake). 4 She wants to learn to dance. 5 He's climbing well. 6 They go to Peter's school.

AB27. ACTIVITY 3. *Circle the odd one out.* [M] *towards*

- Tell pupils to open their Activity Book at page 27. Ask a pupil to read the activity instruction aloud and go through the example. Pupils work individually. They check in pairs. Check with the class before pupils do the next activity (they will need the answers to Activity 3 to do Activity 4).

Key: 2 quick, 3 tall, 4 holiday, 5 earache, 6 weather, 7 first, 8 shopping, 9 beard, 10 roller skate, 11 climb, 12 bike

AB27. ACTIVITY 4. *Now complete the crossword. Write the message.*

- Focus pupils on Activity 4 and the first part of the activity instruction. Explain that they use the words from Activity 3 to complete the crossword.
- Tell pupils to look and find where their words can fit. Discuss the example (they need to find a word in Activity 3 beginning with 'e' and with five letters). Pupils work in pairs and complete the crossword using the word lengths and the letters given to help them. Display the large copy of the completed crossword so pupils can check their answers.
- Pupils then write the message, using the shaded letters from the crossword (Welcome back!).

Key:

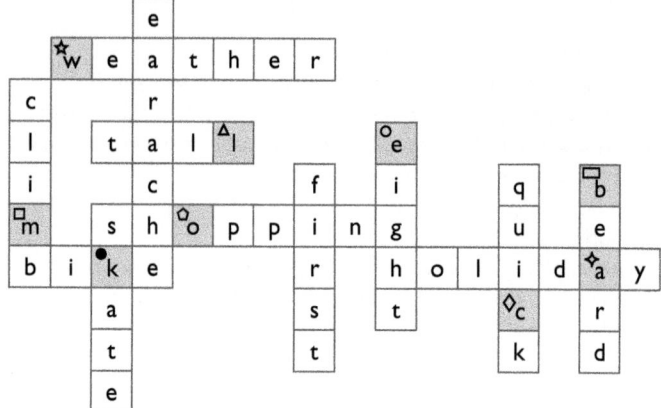

Extra activities: see page T111 (if time)

Optional evaluation

- Quiz 1 from *Kid's Box Interactive DVD 4* (*Stella's room* section). This quiz can be done as a whole-class activity or as a team competition. See pages 36 and 37 of the Teacher's Booklet for the Interactive DVD.

Language Portfolio

- Pupils complete page 3 of *Kid's Box 4 Language Portfolio* (*I can ... Units 1–2*).

Ending the lesson

- Pupils work in groups of four. They need one *Do you remember?* for Unit 1 from the Activity Book (page 15) between four. Two pupils (A) use a book (or paper) to cover the words from Unit 1. The other two pupils (B) take turns to say what each picture is and to spell the word. 'A's look and check. They reverse roles for the words for Unit 2 (Activity Book page 23).
- Talk about the *Can do* statements from Units 1 and 2 with pupils and elicit examples from volunteer pupils for each one.
- Ask pupils which lessons, topics and / or activities were their favourites.

2 Read the text and choose the best answer.

Example
Tony: Hi, Sue. What are you doing?
Sue: A I'm playing badminton.
B I'm playing baseball.
C I'm hitting the ball.

Questions

1 **Tony:** Who are you playing with?
Sue: A She's my Aunt Sue.
B My brother, Alex.
C We're playing well.

2 **Tony:** Is he older than you?
Sue: A No, he's my brother.
B Yes, he's holding the ball.
C No, he's a year younger than me.

3 **Tony:** Are you good at badminton?
Sue: A Yes, I've got three.
B I'm not bad, but Alex is better than me.
C No, thank you.

4 **Sue:** Do you like badminton?
Tony: A Yes, it's my favourite sport.
B Yes, please.
C Yes, let's.

5 **Sue:** Would you like to play badminton with us?
Tony: A I'd like that, thanks.
B Yes, I like board games.
C No, I prefer tennis.

6 **Sue:** Shall I start?
Tony: A Yes, I want to stop.
B No, I want to play.
C Yes, good idea.

Quiz!

1 Which lesson are Alex and Simon busy in?
2 Who's the teacher playing the guitar at the school show?
3 Where do Peter and his friends have their picnic?
4 What does Suzy want to learn?
5 How's Simon climbing?
6 Where do Lock and Key go on Thursday morning?

3 Health matters

1 Look, think and answer.
1 What was Simon's temperature?
2 Where was Simon on Thursday?
3 Why were Simon and his mother at the hospital?
4 When was Simon well again?

Monday
Tuesday
Wednesday
Thursday
Friday

was   were   had   drank   saw   gave   took   went   ate

2 🎧 31 Listen and check.

3 🎧 32 Listen and say the day.

1 The doctor gave him some medicine.   Wednesday.

OBJECTIVES: By the end of the lesson, pupils will have used the past simple to talk about illnesses.

● **TARGET LANGUAGE**

Key language: past simple affirmative irregular verbs: *have, give, see, drink, eat, go, take; What was the matter with you?, ill, sick, tests, exam*

Additional language: *health matters, I was the first to finish, fish and chips, diary*

Revision: *days of the week, was / were, wasn't well, temperature, bad headache, terrible cough, medicine, doctor, hospital, worse, better, before / after, mine, library, school subjects*

● **MATERIALS REQUIRED**

Flashcards 'ill' (34), 'take some medicine' (36), 'see the doctor' (37)
Health matters word cards from *Kid's Box Teacher's Resource Book 4* page 82 (irregular past forms)
Extra activity 1: The script for Pupil's Book Activity 2 written on a large piece of paper
Optional: *Kid's Box Teacher's Resource Book 4* Unit 3 Reinforcement worksheet 1 (page 30)

Warmer

● Present *sick* using the flashcard. Explain that *sick* and *ill* are the same.. Revise these illnesses using mime: *headache, stomach-ache, cough, temperature, cold, backache, toothache*. Pupils come to the front in turn and mime one of the illnesses. Say *What's the matter?* The class says, e.g. *She's got a cough*. Review *doctor's, hospital, medicine*. Ask pupils: *What was Simon's temperature when he was sick?* Elicit who they can see (Simon) and that he's *sick*.

PB28. ACTIVITY 1. *Look, think and answer.*

● Tell pupils to open their Pupil's Book at page 28. Check comprehension of the unit title. Elicit who they can see (Simon) and that he's ill. Tell pupils that this was last week. Remind pupils to read the instruction. Pupils take turns to read the four questions. They discuss possible answers in pairs.

PB28. ACTIVITY 2. *Listen and check.*

● Focus pupils on Activity 2. Present / check the meaning of *have some tests*, and present *see the doctor* and *take some medicine* using the flashcards. Play the CD. Pupils check in pairs. Elicit complete sentences. Play the CD again. Write the days of the week on the board. Say, e.g. *Tell me about Simon on Monday*. Pupils: *He had a temperature*. Write the sentence on the board. Continue for the other days. Check pupils remember this is the past. Focus pupils on the past tense forms. Use the Unit 3 word cards to practise the words.

Key: 1 His temperature was 39 degrees. 2 He was at hospital. 3 They were at the hospital for Simon to have some tests. 4 Simon was well again on Friday afternoon.

CD 1, 31

ALEX: You weren't at school last week, Simon. Where were you?
SIMON: I was at home because I wasn't well.
ALEX: What was the matter?
SIMON: I was ill. Last Monday I had a temperature. It was 39 degrees.
ALEX: Wow. What was the matter?
SIMON: I don't know. I drank lots of water, but on Tuesday I was worse and I had a bad headache too.
ALEX: Were you better on Wednesday?
SIMON: No, I wasn't. I had a terrible cough, so I saw the doctor. He gave me some medicine.
ALEX: Were you better after you took the medicine?
SIMON: No, I wasn't. On Thursday I went to the hospital with Mum and had some tests.
ALEX: So, what was the matter?
SIMON: Er, I had a cold … but I wasn't ill on Friday afternoon. I was fine! I ate a big dinner … and then I had a really good weekend!

PB28. ACTIVITY 3. *Listen and say the day.*

● Clean the board. Tell pupils to read the Activity 3 instruction and look at the example speech bubbles. Play the CD. Pupils whisper the answer to their partner the first time. Play the CD again. Check with the class.

Key: 2 Friday, 3 Monday, 4 Wednesday, 5 Thursday, 6 Monday, 7 Wednesday, 8 Tuesday, 9 Wednesday, 10 Thursday

CD 1, 32

1. The doctor gave him some medicine.
2. He ate a big dinner.
3. He had a temperature.
4. He had a terrible cough.
5. They went to the hospital.
6. He drank a lot of water.
7. He took some medicine.
8. He had a bad headache.
9. He saw the doctor.
10. He had some tests.

AB28. ACTIVITY 1. *Read Stella's diary.*

● Tell pupils to open their Activity Book at page 28 and read the activity instruction. Elicit / teach *diary* and who wrote the diary (Stella). Pupils read.

AB28. *Now look for the past of the verbs.*

● Check pupils know what to do. They check in pairs. Check with the class.

Key: 2 had, 3 ate, 4 drank, 5 went, 6 saw, 7 took, 8 gave, 9 were

AB28. ACTIVITY 2. *Complete the diary. Use the past verbs.*

● Focus pupils on Activity 2. Check they know what to do. Pupils work individually. They check in pairs. Check by asking pupils to read full sentences aloud and showing the word cards for Unit 3.

Key: 2 were, 3 saw, 4 gave, 5 took, 6 was, 7 had, 8 ate, 9 drank

Extra activities: see page T111 (if time)

Optional activity

● Unit 3 Reinforcement worksheet 1 from *Teacher's Resource Book 4* (pages 29 and 30).

Ending the lesson

● Call out the verbs, either past or present. Pupils say the present or past, e.g. Teacher: *Ate*. Pupils: *Eat*. Teacher: *Give*. Pupils: *Gave*.

OBJECTIVES: By the end of the lesson, pupils will have had further practice with the past simple and used *because* to join sentences.

● TARGET LANGUAGE
Key language: present simple irregular verbs, *because*
Additional language: *awake, eye test*
Revision: adjectives, illnesses, food, time, town, family, *nurse, dentist, diary*

● MATERIALS REQUIRED
Flashcards 'have an eye test' (35) and 'see the doctor' (37)
Photocopiable 3 (page T98), copied onto card (one sheet of card per pupil)
Optional: *Kid's Box Teacher's Resource Book 4* Unit 3 Reinforcement worksheet 2 and Extension worksheet 1 (pages 31 and 32)

Warmer
- With books closed, review what pupils can remember about Simon's week from the previous lesson. Join some of the pupils' responses with *because* to review use and meaning, e.g. *He saw the doctor because he had a terrible cough.*

PB29. ACTIVITY 4. *Read and say the letter.*
- Tell pupils to open their Pupil's Book at page 29. Check they have read the activity instruction and know what to do. They look at the pictures, read the sentences and match. They say the answers quietly to their partner. Remind them to look for pronouns when they match. Check with the class.

Key: 2 e, 3 a, 4 c, 5 f, 6 b

PB29. ACTIVITY 5. *Look and answer. Say 'Tom', 'Sue' or 'the nurse'.*
- Focus pupils on Activity 5. Read the activity instructions aloud and point to the pictures. Tell pupils the girl in the pictures is called Sue and the boy is called Tom. Write the names on the board. Use the pictures to review *nurse* and *dentist*. Review *see the doctor* and present *have an eye test* using the flashcards and the pictures. Go through the example and check pupils know what they have to do.
- Pupils work in pairs. They take turns to read a sentence and say *Tom*, *Sue* or *the nurse*. Check with the class.

Key: 2 Sue, 3 Sue, 4 the nurse, 5 Tom, 6 Sue, 7 Tom, 8 Tom

Photocopiable 3 (see pages T90 and T98)

AB29. ACTIVITY 3. *Choose the words.*
- Tell pupils to open their Activity Book at page 29. Elicit what they have to do. Pupils do the activity individually. Make groups of four. Pupils take turns to read a sentence aloud. When they say their choice, e.g. *great*, the other pupils compare it with their answer and say *Same* or *Different*.

AB29. ACTIVITY 4. *Now write about your weekend.*
- Talk with pupils about what they did last weekend, using ideas from Activity 3 as prompts. Pupils write about last weekend using the Activity 3 text as a model. They write a first draft in their notebooks. Monitor and check. Pupils check each other's work in pairs. Pupils write their final copy in their Activity Books.

Extra activities: see page T111 (if time)

Optional activity
- Unit 3 Reinforcement worksheet 2 and Extension worksheet 1 from *Teacher's Resource Book 4* (pages 29, 31 and 32).

Ending the lesson
- Start a chain, e.g. *I went to the doctor because I was ill.* Pupil A says *I was ill because* and completes the sentence (e.g. *I ate a lot of cakes*). Pupil B says *I ate a lot of cakes because* and continues the chain in the same way (e.g. *I was hungry*). Continue with as many pupils as possible.

4 Read and say the letter.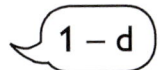

a

b

c

d

e

f

1 He took some medicine because he had a cold.

2 We ate a lot because we were hungry.

3 She went to bed early because she was sick.

4 I drank a lot because I had a temperature.

5 The doctor gave her some medicine because she had a stomach-ache.

6 They saw the dentist because they had a toothache.

5 Look and answer. Say 'Tom', 'Sue' or 'the nurse'.

  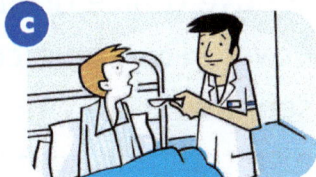 
a b c d

1 Who saw the nurse?
2 Who went to the hospital to see Tom?
3 Who had a headache?
4 Who gave Tom some medicine?
5 Who ate lunch in bed?
6 Who had an eye test?
7 Who drank orange juice?
8 Who took some medicine?

29

6 Look, think and answer.

1 Who's Stella talking to this morning?
2 Where was Stella in her dream?
3 What was Stella's job?
4 What was wrong with the man?

This morning

Last night

7 🎵33 Listen and check.

8 Answer the questions.

1 Did Stella have a nice dream? — No, she didn't. She had a terrible dream.
2 Did she have a long blue coat?
3 Did she see a woman who had a cough?
4 Did she give the man some flowers?
5 Did she see a woman with backache?
6 Did she take a box off the girl's head?

LOOK

have ➔ had
do ➔ did

I **had** a terrible dream.
I **didn't have** time to stop.
How many people **did** you see?

OBJECTIVES: By the end of the lesson, pupils will have used questions and negatives to talk about the past.

• TARGET LANGUAGE

Key language: past simple negatives and questions and short answers: irregular verbs, *have a dream, bowl*
Revision: illnesses, prepositions, *how many, woman, people, head*

• MATERIALS REQUIRED

Flashcard 'have a dream' (38)
Health matters word cards from *Kid's Box Teacher's Resource Book 4* page 82 (irregular past forms)
Extra activity 2: Choose eight sentences / questions from the lesson, including past simple affirmatives, past simple negatives and past simple questions. Write each one in scrambled word order on a large piece of paper.

Warmer

- Show the word cards. Elicit the infinitives. Clap a rhythm. Say, e.g. (Clap, clap) *give*. Pupils clap and say the past form, e.g. (Clap, clap) *gave*.

PB30. ACTIVITY 6. *Look, think and answer.*

- Tell pupils to open their Pupil's Book at page 30. Elicit who pupils can see (Stella) and teach / elicit *have a dream* using the pictures and the flashcard. Pupils read the questions aloud around the class. They discuss their predicted answers in pairs, using the information in the pictures to help.

PB30. ACTIVITY 7. *Listen and check.*

- When pupils are ready, play the CD. Check answers with the class. Check general understanding. Play the CD again, pausing and focusing on Meera's questions. Write the four questions on the board in two columns:
  Were you awake all night?   How many people did you see?
  What was your dream about?   How did you take it off?
- Elicit what pupils notice about how the questions are made: a) *was / were*, and b) *did*. Use colours to highlight / underline the structure.
- Repeat with the negative sentences from the conversation: *I didn't have time to stop. He didn't have a temperature.*

Key: 1 She's talking to Meera. 2 She was in a big hospital. 3 She was a doctor. 4 The man had a cough.

CD 1, 33

STELLA: I'm really tired this morning.
MEERA: Really? Why? Were you awake all night?
STELLA: No, I had a terrible dream.
MEERA: Oooh, what was your dream about?
STELLA: I was a doctor in a big hospital. I had a long white coat … and I had lots of doctor's things, but I didn't have time to stop!
MEERA: Oh? How many people did you see?
STELLA: I saw lots. I saw a man who had a cough, but he didn't have a temperature so I gave him some medicine … And there was a woman with a bad headache. And then, there was a girl who had a bowl on her head!
MEERA: A bowl on her head! How did you take it off?
STELLA: It was really difficult, but in the end I took it off and … do you know who was under the bowl?
MEERA: No.
STELLA: It was Suzy!

PB30. ACTIVITY 8. *Answer the questions.*

- Focus pupils on Activity 8 and on the Look box. Do the activity in open pairs first. Elicit long answers in order to practise the past form of the verbs. Then pupils take turns to ask and answer in closed pairs. After the oral practice, pupils write the answers in their notebooks.

Key: 2 No, she didn't. She had a long white coat. 3 No, she didn't. She saw a man who had a cough. 4 No, she didn't. She gave the man some medicine. 5 No, she didn't. She saw a woman with a bad headache. 6 No, she didn't. She took a bowl off the girl's head.

AB30. ACTIVITY 5. *Read and complete.*

- Tell pupils to open their Activity Book at page 30. Focus them on the wheel and the information. Check they understand the activity instruction. They read the text and complete. They check in pairs. Check with the class.

Key: Clockwise from top: Daisy: went to a party / didn't go to the cinema; Sally: went to the cinema / didn't drink any milk at breakfast; Jack: had a stomach-ache / didn't eat any food all day. Susan: gave her mum some flowers / didn't have lunch at school; Paul: did his homework / didn't see his friends.

AB30. ACTIVITY 6. *Write sentences about the children.*

- Focus pupils on Activity 6 and on the example. They write sentences about the children in Activity 5 using the model. Monitor and check. Remind pupils they can work with a partner if they want.

Key: (in any order) 2 Daisy went to a party in the afternoon. She didn't go to the cinema. 3 Sally went to the cinema. She didn't drink any milk at breakfast. 4 Jack had a stomach-ache. He didn't eat any food all day. 5 Susan gave her mum some flowers. She didn't have lunch at school.

Extra activities: see page T111 (if time)

Ending the lesson

- Review Stella's dream with the class, using prompt questions. Elicit if any pupils remember what they dreamt the previous night.

OBJECTIVES: By the end of the lesson, pupils will have had further practice using the past simple and sung a song.

- **TARGET LANGUAGE**
Key language: past simple: questions and short answers
Revision: illnesses, adjectives, countable and uncountable nouns, word families

- **MATERIALS REQUIRED**
Optional: *Kid's Box Teacher's Resource Book 4* Unit 3 Song worksheet (page 34) and / or extra song activities from *Kid's Box Interactive DVD 4* booklet (pages 28–33)

Warmer

- Write the words *jobs, food, drinks, places*, each in its own circle on the board. Pupils copy the circles and words onto paper and, in pairs, have three minutes to add as many words to the circles as they can. Elicit the words and write them on the board. Add key words from Pupil's Book Activity 9 and Activity Book Activity 7, if they are not included.

PB31. ACTIVITY 9. *Read and say the word. Listen and check.*

- Tell pupils to open their Pupil's Book at page 31. Elicit who is in the large picture (mum, girl, nurse). Ask, *What's the matter with the girl?* Elicit as many different answers as possible, *She's sick., She isn't well., She has a stomachache., She has a temperature.*, etc. Check pupils have read the activity instruction and that they know what to do, using the example. In pairs, they read the song text and match each of the small pictures with a word in the box.
- Play the song for pupils to check their answers. Check understanding of vocabulary (*worse, What's the matter?* etc.). Focus on *easily* and *happily* and show / elicit how the adverbs are formed from the adjectives.

Key: party, burgers, sausages, lemonade, ice cream, chocolate, three, fruit, water

CD 1, 34
As in Pupil's Book

PB31. ACTIVITY 10. *Sing the song.*

- Play the CD again in sections for pupils to listen and repeat. When they are confident, they perform the whole song. Divide the class into three groups: girl, nurse, mum. They sing their parts. Swap roles. Make sure pupils use the correct intonation for different lines (questions / telling off).

CD 1, 34
As in Pupil's Book

CD 1, 35
Now sing the song again. (Karaoke version)

PB31. ACTIVITY 11. *Ask and answer questions about the song.*

- Focus pupils on Activity 11. Demonstrate the activity for the class. Pupils read the two example questions aloud for others to answer. Elicit other questions. Focus on the short answers: *Yes, she did / No, she didn't*. Give pupils five minutes to think of and write some questions about the song. They write the answers in brackets. They take turns to ask and answer in pairs.

AB31. ACTIVITY 7. *Put the words in groups.*

- Tell pupils to open their Activity Book at page 31. Remind them of the word families in the Warmer. Check pupils have read and understood the activity instruction, using the example. They do the activity in pairs. Check with the class.

Key: Places: school, hospital, cinema, park; People: cousin, teacher, mum, nurse; Food: burger, banana, apple; Drink: milk, lemonade, juice, water

AB31. ACTIVITY 8. *Use the words from Activity 7 to complete Meera's day.*

- Demonstrate the activity for pupils. Individually, they choose and write appropriate words from Activity 7 in the table (places in the 'go' column, people in the 'see' column, food in the 'eat' column and drinks in the 'drink' column). They keep their ideas secret.

AB31. ACTIVITY 9. *Ask and answer. Complete the table.*

- Elicit a question word for each column of the table (*where, who, what, what*) and review how to form past simple questions about each thing. Volunteer pupils read out the speech bubbles. Demonstrate with four or five questions and answers, using open pairs.
- Make new pairs. Pupils ask and answer to guess what their partner has written in the table. They write the words from their partner's table in the second table. Monitor and check that pupils are hiding their books and asking complete questions. They compare their tables when the activity is complete.

Extra activities: see pages T111–112 (if time)

Optional activities

- Unit 3 Song worksheet from *Teacher's Resource Book 4* (pages 29 and 34).
- Extra activity for Unit 3 Song and / or karaoke worksheet. See pages 28–33 of the Teacher's Booklet for the Interactive DVD.

Ending the lesson

- Sing the song again with pupils in three groups.

9 Read and say the word. Listen and check.

> lemonade   ice cream   burgers   chocolate
> three   water   party   sausages   ~~nurse~~   fruit

nurse

Mummy, Mummy call the 🧑‍⚕️!
I had a stomach-ache but now it's worse.

What's the matter?

I don't know,
But please be quick,
Don't be slow.

Did you have a 🎉 yesterday?

Yes! There was lots to eat and games to play.

Did you eat 🍔?

Yes, I did.

Did you eat 🌭?

Yes, I did.

Did you drink 🧴?

Yes, I did.

Did you have 🍨 and 🍫 too?
I think I know what's the matter with you!
Take this medicine 3 times a day,
When you are better, go out and play!

No more chocolate cake for you my daughter.
Vegetables, 🍎🍌 and a drink of 🥛!

10 Sing the song.

11 Ask and answer questions about the song.

> Did she eat ice cream?

> Yes, she did.

> Did she drink orange juice?

> No, she didn't.

12 Stella's phonics

A **f**rog with a **ph**one.

A **v**ery small **v**olley**b**all.

The **f**rog and her **f**riends are playing **v**olley**b**all at the **b**each.

13 Ask and answer.

Did you have a temperature last week? *No, I didn't.*

Health matters

1 **Did you have** a temperature last week?
2 _____ to hospital last year?
3 _____ milk for breakfast?
4 _____ a cough last year?
5 _____ an apple yesterday?
6 _____ to bed early last night?
7 _____ any medicine last week?
8 _____ the dentist last year?

~~have~~
go
eat
drink
take
see
have
go

14 Now write and ask questions about your friend's week.

Did you walk to school last week?

OBJECTIVES: By the end of the lesson, pupils will be able to identify and say the sounds /b/, /f/ and /v/ in common words and they will have practised saying the sounds /b/, /f/ and /v/. They will also have completed a communication activity.

- **TARGET LANGUAGE**

Key language: words with the phonemes /b/, /f/ and /v/ (e.g. *beach, frog, very*)
Revision: illnesses, adjectives, sports and activities, past simple, *take some medicine, see the dentist, have a temperature / a cough*

- **MATERIALS REQUIRED**

Optional: *Kid's Box Interactive DVD 4: The living room* 'Body facts' episode

Warmer

- Write words with the sounds /f/ and /v/ on the board, underlining the key sounds (e.g. *Friday, love, afraid, frog, very, Vicky, phone, never*). Show pupils how to put their fingers to their throats to feel the sounds (/v/ causes the vocal chords to vibrate, /f/ doesn't). Say the words on the board with the /f/ sound. Pupils repeat. Do the same with the /v/ words.
- Write *bag* on the board, underlining the letter *b*. Ask if the sound is like /f/ or /v/. Elicit that /b/ is similar to /f/ – the vocal chords don't vibrate. Tell pupils they will be practising the three sounds /f/, /v/ and /b/ in this lesson.

PB32. ACTIVITY 12. *Stella's phonics*

- Tell pupils to open their Pupil's Book at page 32. Elicit what they can see (a frog, a phone, a volleyball, a beach). Play the CD. Pupils listen and point. Play the CD again. Pupils join in. Check pupils are saying the sounds correctly. Pupils repeat the sentence quickly and then in groups. Point out to your pupils that another spelling for /f/ is *ph* (e.g. *phone, elephant, alphabet*).

CD 1, 36

STELLA: Hi, I'm Stella! Repeat after me!
/f/, /f/, frog
/v/, /v/, very
/b/, /b/, ball
A frog with a phone.
A frog with a phone.
A very small volleyball.
A very small volleyball.
The frog and her friends are playing volleyball at the beach.
The frog and her friends are playing volleyball at the beach.

PB32. ACTIVITY 13. *Ask and answer.*

- Focus pupils on Activity 13. A pupil reads out the question in the speech bubble and elicits answers from pupils (*Yes, I did* or *No, I didn't*). Pupils work in pairs and complete each question with a verb from the box. Check with the class before they ask and answer. Pupils take turns to ask and answer in pairs and to record their answers. Check with the class.

Key: 2 Did you go to hospital last year? 3 Did you drink milk for breakfast? 4 Did you have a cough last year? 5 Did you eat an apple yesterday? 6 Did you go to bed early last night?

7 Did you take any medicine last week? 8 Did you see the dentist last year? Answers: pupils' own.

PB32. ACTIVITY 14. *Now write and ask questions about your friend's week.*

- Focus pupils on Activity 14 and on the activity instruction. Brainstorm more ideas for questions with pupils, e.g. *Did you watch TV yesterday? Did you play in the park last weekend? Did you clean your teeth this morning?*
- Advise pupils only to use short answers for these verbs, as they have not yet seen regular verbs in their full forms. Alternatively, pupils can use use the irregular past verbs they've seen and used in the unit.
- Pupils write at least six questions. Make new pairs. Pupils ask and answer.

AB32. ACTIVITY 10. *Write. Listen, check and say.*

- Tell pupils to open their Activity Book at page 32. Check pupils know the meaning of all the words in the box. Point out the example. Pupils work individually to complete the sentences. They compare answers in pairs.
- Play the CD for pupils to listen and check. Check with the class. Play the CD again for pupils to listen and repeat.

Key: 2 football, 3 vegetables, 4 Vicky, 5 boy, 6 very, 7 village, 8 photo, 9 balloon, 10 beautiful

CD 1, 37

1. Let's go fishing. It's lots of fun!
2. Fred's very fast. He's a good football player, too.
3. You must eat lots of fruit and vegetables.
4. Vicky plays volleyball with her best friend.
5. Ben's a big boy. He's very tall, too!
6. Basketball's a very fast game.
7. Vera visits her grandmother's village on Fridays.
8. Bill took a photo of his father playing baseball.
9. Look at the baby with the big blue balloon!
10. Oh! Look at those beautiful flowers!

AB32. ACTIVITY 11. *Make sentences.*

- Focus pupils on Activity 11. Elicit what they have to do (make sentences using the table). Elicit a few examples. In pairs, pupils take turns to make sentences. Monitor and check / help where necessary.

Key: 2 Jim didn't go to the doctor. 3 Zoe saw the dentist last week. 4 Did Sally take her medicine? 5 There were a lot of people at the hospital.

Joke box

- Focus pupils on the Joke box. Pupils guess / find the answer. Explain the joke if necessary.

Extra activities: see page T112 (if time)

Optional activity

- 'Body facts' episode from *Kid's Box Interactive DVD 4* (*The living room* section). See pages 12–15 of the Teacher's Booklet for the Interactive DVD.

Ending the lesson

- Pupils say the long sound sentence as a tongue twister.

OBJECTIVES: By the end of the lesson, pupils will have read a story and reviewed language from the unit.

- **TARGET LANGUAGE**
Key language: language in the story
Revision: language from the unit, *have got*, physical descriptions

- **MATERIALS REQUIRED**
Health matters word cards from *Kid's Box Teacher's Resource Book 4* page 82 (irregular past forms)
Extra activity 1: A large piece of paper for each group of three pupils
Optional: *Kid's Box Teacher's Resource Book 4* Unit 3 Extension worksheet 2 (page 33) and / or animated version of the Unit 3 story from *Kid's Box Interactive DVD 4* (*Suzy's room* section)

Warmer
- Review the *Lock and Key* story with pupils. Ask what happened in the last episode, e.g. *Where did Lock and Key go? What day was it?* Pupils reply, using the past. (They went to the swimming club. It was the day of the competition.)

Story
PB33. LOCK AND KEY.
- Tell pupils to open their Pupil's Book at page 33. Focus pupils on the first frame, elicit who they can see (Lock and Key) and tell them who is on the screen (Nick Motors). Tell pupils that he's a car thief. Set the gist questions: *Why did Key go to the hospital? Who did he see there? Did they catch him? What did Nick Motors do?* Play the CD. Pupils listen and read for what happened. They check in pairs. Check with the class (to see his aunt; Nick Motors / a doctor; no; he took their motorbike). Focus pupils on frame 5 and elicit who this is (a doctor) and that Key made a mistake.
- Play the CD again. Pause after each frame for pupils to repeat. Check general comprehension by asking, e.g. *Where did Key see 'Nick Motors'? What did Lock and Key decide to do? What did the doctor look like? Did he have black hair and a big nose?*

CD 1, 38
As in Pupil's Book

AB33. DO YOU REMEMBER?
- Write *The past* in the centre of the board. Brainstorm past forms from the unit and write them as a mind map or stick the Unit 3 word cards on the board.
- Tell pupils to open their Activity Books at page 33. Check pupils have read the activity instructions and know what to do. They study the words on the right in silence. Then they fold the page down the middle so that they can see only the words on the left and the lines to write the words on. Without looking, they write the words in pencil. They check in pairs, asking, e.g. *What's this one? How do you spell 'drank'?* They don't look at the words on the right. When pupils have finished, they can either correct their own work or swap books and check their partner's.

AB33. CAN DO.
- Focus pupils on the *Can do* section of the page. Say *Let's read the sentences together.* Read the first sentence. Elicit what this means with examples and elicit / remind pupils of the activities they did in this unit when they talked about health. Review what the three faces mean (not very well / OK / very well). Remind pupils they circle the one they think is true for them. Repeat for the second sentence, reminding pupils of activities they did when they talked about the past. Repeat for the third sentence, eliciting / reminding pupils about the communication activity as well as other activities when they asked questions about the past. Pupils circle the appropriate face.
- Say *Now show and tell your friends.* Pupils work in groups of three and take turns to show their work for / talk about each one.

Extra activities: see page T112 (if time)

Optional activity
- Unit 3 Extension worksheet 2 from *Teacher's Resource Book 4* (pages 29 and 33).
- The animated version of the story from *Kid's Box Interactive DVD 4* (*Suzy's room* section). See pages 38–45 of the Teacher's Booklet for the Interactive DVD.

Ending the lesson
- Ask pupils which chant / song they'd like to do again from the unit. Do it together to end the lesson.

LOCK & KEY

Music | Body percussion

Fact
The quickest person in the world can clap 12 times a second.

1 🎧 39 CD1 **Listen and say the letter.**

A percussion instrument is a musical instrument that makes a sound when we hit it. We can use different kinds of instruments or other things to make percussion music.

2 🎧 40 CD1 **Listen and match. Which part of the body are they using to make the sound?**

The human body is also a great percussion instrument. There are different kinds of dance and music which use parts of the body.

OBJECTIVES: By the end of the lesson, pupils will have read and learnt about percussion and musical notation.

• TARGET LANGUAGE
Key language: *percussion, the human body*
Additional language: *click his / her fingers, tap his / her face, rhythm*
Revision: *instrument, sound, hit, parts of the body, stamp his / her feet, clap his / her hands*

• MATERIALS REQUIRED
Examples of percussion instruments (if available), e.g. triangles, drums, cymbals, xylophones
Some sheet music

Warmer
- Show pupils some percussion instruments and elicit the names in L1 or English. Ask what they all have in common. Review / teach the word *percussion*. Write it on the board. Review *hit* and *make a sound* by hitting one of the instruments and saying *I hit it and it makes a sound*.

PB34. FACT
- Tell pupils to open their Pupil's Book at page 34. Read the lesson title and ask pupils what they think *Body percussion* means. Explain that they are going to learn more about body percussion in the next two lessons.
- Read the Fact box aloud and check pupils know what *clap* means.

PB34. ACTIVITY 1. *Listen and say the letter.*
- Focus pupils on Activity 1. Direct them to the text first. Ask two volunteers to read a sentence each. Give pupils time to read the paragraph again individually. Check comprehension of *make a sound* and *hit* again.
- Ask pupils to read the activity instruction and check they know what to do. Tell them to look carefully at the pictures. Play the CD. Pause after each sound. Pupils whisper the letter. Play the CD again. Pause after each and elicit the letter. Talk about what is making the sound in each case.

Key: 1 d, 2 f, 3 e, 4 a, 5 b, 6 c

CD 1, 39
1. [sound of someone crashing metal bin lids together]
2. [sound of a cymbal]
3. [sound of a cabasa instrument]
4. [sound of someone playing the spoons]
5. [sound of a bass drum]
6. [sound of someone sweeping]

PB34. ACTIVITY 2. *Listen and match. Which part of the body are they using to make the sound?*
- Focus pupils on Activity 2. Direct them to the text first. Ask two volunteers to read a sentence each. Give pupils time to read the paragraph again individually. Check comprehension of *human body* and *parts of the body*.
- Read the activity instructions. Direct pupils to the photographs and ask them to think about what sounds they will hear. Play the CD. Pause after each sound for pupils to do the matching in pairs. They note down their answers. Play the CD again for pupils to check. This time they write down the parts of the body used to make each sound. Elicit answers / ideas. Make sure pupils know how to say *stamp his / her feet, click his / her fingers, tap his / her face* and *clap his / her hands*.

Key: 1 f (hands, mouth), 2 b (fingers), 3 a (feet, hands), 4 c (mouth), 5 d (feet), 6 e (hands, knees)

CD 1, 40
1. [sound of mouth 'popping']
2. [sound of clicking fingers]
3. [sound of flamenco hand clapping and feet stamping]
4. [sound of beatbox]
5. [sound of Irish dancing]
6. [sound of someone hitting their knees]

AB34. ACTIVITY 1. *Listen and tick. Read and correct.*
- Review parts of the body (including *feet, fingers, mouth, knees, hands*).
- Tell pupils to open their Activity Book at page 34. Read the activity instructions, play the first item on the CD and go through the example answer. Tell pupils to listen and tick first. Play the rest of the CD for pupils to listen and tick. They check their answers in pairs. They do the second part of the activity (*Read and correct*) individually. Check with the class.

Key: 2 c No, he isn't. He's stamping his feet. 3 c No, she isn't. She's clapping her hands. 4 b No, he isn't. He's tapping his face.

CD 1, 41
1. [sound of clicking fingers]
2. [sound of stamping feet]
3. [sound of hands clapping]
4. [sound of mouth percussion]

AB34. ACTIVITY 2. *Read and complete.*
- Focus pupils on the activity instruction and check understanding. Pupils complete the text. They compare answers in pairs. Check with the class.

Key: 2 instrument, 3 singing, 4 different, 5 clap, 6 feet, 7 music, 8 percussion

Extra activities: see page T112 (if time)

Ending the lesson
- Review with pupils what they learnt about in today's lesson.

> **OBJECTIVES:** By the end of the lesson, pupils will have read and learnt about body percussion and completed a project.
>
> ● **TARGET LANGUAGE**
> **Key language:** *note* (music), *musician, whole, half, quarter, eighth*
> **Additional language:** *elastic band, edge, pop your mouth*
> **Revision:** parts of the body, adjectives (*long, short, quick, slow*), *clap your hands, stamp your feet, click your fingers, hit your knees, rhythm*
>
> ● **MATERIALS REQUIRED**
> Percussion instruments (including drums of various sizes)
> Project: balloon, plastic cup, elastic band, pencil (one of each per pupil, plus one set of materials for you to make an example), CD of music with a strong rhythm
> Optional: *Kid's Box Teacher's Resource Book 4* Unit 3 Topic worksheet (page 35)

Warmer

- Review parts of the body. Say, e.g. *Point to your arm.* Include *arm, head, leg, mouth, finger, foot / feet, hands, knees.* Repeat for each word.
- Pupils stand up. Give instructions, speeding up, e.g. *Wave your arms. Shake your body. Show me one hand. Stand on one leg. Touch your mouth.*

PB35. ACTIVITY 3 *Listen to these notes. Answer the questions.*

- Show the sheet music or draw some musical notes on the board. Ask *What's this?* Elicit / explain that this is written music. Teach *note* and *musician*. Ask if anyone in the class knows how to read music.
- Focus pupils on Activity 3. Direct them to the text. Pupils read individually and then discuss in pairs. Check comprehension of *whole, half, quarter* and *eighth* by drawing a circle on the board and dividing it into parts.
- Focus on the activity instructions. Make sure pupils realise that the numbers 1 to 4 refer to the musical notes on the right. Play the CD. Pupils compare the length of the notes. They check answers in pairs. Play the CD again. Check with the class.

Key: 1 Note 1 is longer. 2 Note 2 is longer. 3 Note 2 is shorter. 4 Note 4 is shorter.

`CD 1, 42`

1. [sound of breve (four beats)]
2. [sound of semi-breve (two beats)]
3. [sound of crotchet (one beat)]
4. [sound of quaver (half a beat)]

PB35. ACTIVITY 4. *Listen and make rhythms.*

- Tell pupils they are going to practise some body percussion. Focus them on Activity 4. Check comprehension of *rhythm.* Pupils stand up. Say some instructions from the CD (e.g. *Click your fingers. 'Pop' your mouth. Hit your knees. Stamp your feet.*)
- Play the CD. Pupils listen and follow the instructions.

`CD 1, 43`

Listen to these rhythms.
Clap your hands then click your fingers. [sound effects]
Click your fingers then tap your face. [sound effects]
Tap your face then hit your knees. [sound effects]
Hit your knees then stamp your feet. [sound effects]
Stamp your feet then clap your hands. [sound effects]
Now put all the sounds together. [sound effects]
And again more quickly. And now really quickly.

PB35. PROJECT. *Make a drum.*

- Show the drums. Elicit *drum* and let pupils practise playing them.
- Focus on the project. Show pupils how to make a drum, reading the instructions aloud. Give out the materials. Pupils make their drum, referring to the instructions. Monitor and help.
- Play some music with a distinct beat. Pupils beat time on their drums.

AB35. ACTIVITY 3. MOVERS Listening, Part 2
Listen and write. There is one example. [M] *towards*

- Tell pupils to open their Activity Book at page 35. Focus them on the activity instructions. Play the example. Tell pupils they need to write one, two or three words or a number for each answer. Check comprehension of the rest of the questions and headings. Play the CD. Pupils write notes. Check with the class.

Key: 1 stomach-ache, 2 cake or biscuits, 3 in hospital, 4 39, 5 sleep a lot

`CD 1, 44`

Hi, Ann. Where were you yesterday?
Yesterday … er, I was at the doctor's.
Can you see the answer? Now you listen and write.

1. Really, you were at the doctor's! What was the matter with you?
   I had a stomach-ache.
   Oh dear. I'm sorry about that. I hope you're better now.
   Yes, I'm OK today.
2. So, what did you have to do?
   I had to take some medicine.
   … And what did the doctor say?
   She said I can't eat any cake or biscuits this week.
   Ha ha. Oh dear.
3. Are the other people in your family OK?
   Well, my aunt was in hospital on Friday.
   Your aunt! Which one?
   My Aunt Lily, the teacher.
   Oh dear.
4. Why was she there?
   She was there because she had a temperature.
   Oh no. Was it bad?
   Yes, it was 39!
   39? That is bad.
5. Is she OK now?
   Yes, she's OK, but the doctor says she has to sleep a lot.
   That's a good idea.

Extra activities: see page T112 (if time)

Optional activity

- Unit 3 Topic worksheet from *Teacher's Resource Book 4* (pages 29 and 35).

Ending the lesson

- Give instructions for pupils to follow, using language from the lesson, e.g. *Stamp your feet. Click your fingers. Clap your hands.*

The language of music tells musicians what notes to play and how to play them. They can be long or short, loud or quiet, quick or slow. Rhythm tells us how long the notes are. They can be whole notes (1), half notes ($1/2$), quarter notes ($1/4$) or eighth notes ($1/8$). Rhythm is very important in percussion music.

3 Listen to these notes. Answer the questions.

1. Which is longer, 1 or 4?
2. Which is longer, 2 or 3?
3. Which is shorter, 1 or 2?
4. Which is shorter, 3 or 4?

4 Listen and make rhythms.

Project Make a drum.

You need:
- a plastic cup
- a balloon
- an elastic band

1. Take a piece of the balloon and put it over the top of the cup.
2. Use the elastic band to keep it in place. Now you've got a drum.

Try to make different sounds. Hit it with your hand or with a pencil. Hit it in the middle or on the edge. Try different rhythms. Play your drum to music.

4 After school club

1 Look, think and answer.

1. Where did the children go yesterday afternoon?
2. Which teacher was there?
3. Who did Stella play chess with?
4. Who wasn't good at dancing?

2 Listen and check.

3 Listen and say 'yes' or 'no'.

1 The children helped Mr Star.

No.

LOOK

help	→	help**ed**
dance	→	danc**ed**
stop	→	stop**ped**
carry	→	carr**ied**

OBJECTIVES: By the end of the lesson, pupils will have talked about activities in the past and learnt spelling rules for -ed endings in the past tense.

● **TARGET LANGUAGE**
Key language: past simple regular verbs, spelling of -ed endings, *After school club, hall, play chess, school show, musical* (n)
Additional language: *kids, start to do something, vowel, consonant*
Revision: *clean, carry, help, can / can't, have to, want, sing, dance, hop, skip, jump, laugh*

● **MATERIALS REQUIRED**
Flashcard 'play chess' (39)
Optional: *Kid's Box Teacher's Resource Book 4* Unit 4 Reinforcement worksheet 1 (page 37), *Kid's Box 4 Language Portfolio* page 9

Warmer
- Write *After school clubs* on the board and elicit / explain what the phrase means. Elicit examples of activities pupils do / would like to do at an After school club. Teach / review *play chess* using the flashcard.

PB36. ACTIVITY 1. *Look, think and answer.*
- Tell pupils to open their Pupil's Book at page 36. Elicit what / who they can see. Check pupils have read the activity instruction. They read the questions in pairs and discuss them together, using the information in the pictures.

PB36. ACTIVITY 2. *Listen and check.*
- Focus pupils on Activity 2. Play the CD for pupils to listen and check. Elicit complete sentences. Play the CD again and ask checking questions, e.g. *What did Alex and Simon do? What did Stella do? Did Simon dance? What did he do?* Check understanding of *school show* and *a musical*.

Key: 1 They went to the After school club. 2 Mr Burke was there. 3 She played chess with Meera. 4 Simon wasn't good at dancing.

CD 2, 02
Mr Star: What did you do yesterday afternoon at the After school club, kids?
Simon: Well, first we helped Mr Burke. Alex and I cleaned the chairs and then we carried them into the hall.
Mr Star: And what did you do, Stella?
Stella: I played chess with Meera and then we all started to think about our school show.
Simon: Yes, Mr Burke wanted us to do a musical. We had to sing. And we danced!
Mrs Star: Did you dance, Simon?
Simon: Well, I didn't dance, but I hopped, skipped and jumped to the music ... and Meera and Stella laughed a lot.
Stella: Well, Simon, you were funny. Mr Burke watched us dancing and listened to us singing, but then he stopped us!
Mr Star: So what now?
Stella: Mr Burke doesn't want us to do a musical this year.
Simon: It's great! I don't have to sing and dance.

PB36. ACTIVITY 3. *Listen and say 'yes' or 'no'.*
- Focus pupils on Activity 3. Read the sentences and check comprehension. Play the CD. They say *yes* or *no* to their friend the first time. Play the CD again. Check with the class. Elicit correct information for the 'no' answers.

Key: 2 yes, 3 no, 4 no, 5 yes, 6 yes, 7 yes, 8 no

CD 2, 03
1. The children helped Mr Star.
2. Simon and Alex cleaned the chairs.
3. Stella played chess with Simon.
4. They started to play table tennis.
5. Mr Burke wanted them to do a musical.
6. Simon hopped, skipped and jumped to the music.
7. Meera and Stella laughed a lot.
8. Mr Burke watched them playing.

Look box
- Focus pupils on the Look box. Ask if these verbs talk about the present, the future or the past. Make four columns on the board. Write a word at the top of each column, each in a different colour, as follows: 1 *helped*; 2 *danced*; 3 *stopped*; 4 *carried*. Explain the rule for each column: 1 ends in two consonants, add -ed; 2 ends in e, add -d; 3 ends in consonant + vowel + consonant, double the consonant and add -ed; 4 ends in consonant + y, change y to i and add -ed.
- Write other verbs on the board for pupils to assign to the correct columns, e.g. *laugh* (1), *hop* (3), *walk* (1), *hurry* (4), *like* (2), *skip* (3).

AB36. ACTIVITY 1. *Complete the text. Use the past of the verbs.*
- Tell pupils to open their Activity Book at page 36. They complete the text in pairs. Check with the class. Ask, e.g. *What did they do on Saturday afternoon?*

Key: 2 sailed, 3 climbed, 4 cooked, 5 talked, 6 laughed, 7 walked, 8 planted, 9 helped, 10 played, 11 wanted, 12 needed

AB36. ACTIVITY 2. *Read and write 'yes' or 'no'.* [M] towards
- Pupils re-read the text in Activity 1 and write the answers. They check in pairs. Check with the class. Elicit the correct versions for 'no' responses.

Key: 2 yes, 3 no, 4 no, 5 yes, 6 no, 7 no

Extra activities: see page T112 (if time)

Optional activity
- Unit 4 Reinforcement worksheet 1 from *Teacher's Resource Book 4* (pages 36–37).

Language Portfolio
- Pupils complete page 9 of *Kid's Box 4 Language Portfolio* (*Our club*).

Ending the lesson
- Dictate some of the verbs from the lesson as infinitives. Pupils write the past simple. Write the past forms on the board for pupils to check.

OBJECTIVES: By the end of the lesson, pupils will have had further practice talking and asking about activities in the past.

- **TARGET LANGUAGE**

Key language: past simple affirmative and questions, regular verbs
Additional language: *playground, playtime*
Revision: *hats, scarves, snow,* activities and actions

- **MATERIALS REQUIRED**

Extra activity 1: Write one or more of the texts from Pupil's Book Activity 4 on a large piece of paper, with gaps, e.g. *Tod lived in the _____ . He loved sport and he _____ and _____ every weekend. When it rained he _____ his friend, Fred, and they played _____ inside.*

Warmer

- You need space for this activity. Pupils spread out. Say *Listen and mime.* Then say, e.g. *These are some of the things you did on your last holiday. You skated on the lake in the park. You played basketball. You swam in the swimming pool. You danced at a party. You climbed a tree and looked for pirates.* Pupils mime the actions as you say them.

PB37. ACTIVITY 4. *Read and match.*

- Tell pupils to open their Pupil's Book at page 37. Focus them on the text and the pictures. Check they have read and understand the activity instruction. They read the texts quickly (looking for key words) and match them with the pictures. They check in pairs. Check with the class. Pupils take turns to read each text aloud around the class. Check understanding. Pupils read the texts again and underline all the past verbs. Elicit to check.

Key: 1 c, 2 a, 3 b

PB37. ACTIVITY 5. *Listen and say 'a', 'b' or 'c'.*

- Focus pupils on the activity instruction and elicit what they are going to do (work out which text the sentences they hear refer to). Play the first one and point out the example answer. Play the rest of the CD. Pupils write the letter on paper the first time they listen and whisper it to their partner. Play the CD again. Check with the class. Elicit the sentence they heard each time.

Key: 2 c, 3 a, 4 c, 5 a, 6 b, 7 c, 8 b, 9 c, 10 a, 11 b, 12 a

CD 2, 04

1. It started to snow.
2. The children ate it at lunchtime.
3. He climbed and sailed every weekend.
4. They loved her pancakes.
5. He lived in the countryside.
6. They needed hats and scarves.
7. She made all the food in the morning.
8. He pointed and shouted.
9. She was the cook.
10. They played badminton inside.
11. He ice skated on the lake.
12. He loved sport.

PB37. ACTIVITY 6. *Ask and answer.*

- Focus pupils on Activity 6. Ask two pupils to read question 1 and the example answer aloud. Focus pupils on the use of *did* and the simple infinitive in the question, and the past simple in the answer. Highlight it on the board if necessary.
- Pupils work in pairs, taking turns to ask and answer the questions. Check, using open pairs.

Key: 2 She cooked in the morning. 3 The children loved her pancakes. 4 Tod lived in the countryside. 5 He loved sport. 6 They played badminton. 7 He invited (his friend) Sid. 8 He pointed and shouted because Sid wasn't careful.

AB37. ACTIVITY 3. *Put the words in groups.*

- Tell pupils to open their Activity Book at page 37. Check they have read and understand the instruction. In pairs, pupils assign the words to the columns in the table. Pairs check with pairs. Check with the class.

Key: +ed: played, jumped, shouted, climbed; +d: invited, roller skated, closed, danced; +ped: dropped, shopped, skipped, hopped; y+ied: cried, carried

AB37. ACTIVITY 4. *Write the secret message.*

- Tell pupils to look at Activity 4 and elicit who the message is about (Nick Motors). Individually, pupils decode the message and write it in their books. They check in pairs. Check with the class.

Key: I tried to catch Nick Motors. He was outside the supermarket. I pointed at him and shouted, but he laughed and jumped on our motorbike!

Extra activities: see pages T112–113 (if time)

Ending the lesson

- Review with pupils what they did last Saturday and Sunday, morning, afternoon and evening.

4 Read and match.

1. When Pat worked at a school, she was the cook. She made all the food in the morning. The children liked eating her pancakes! After lunch, Pat helped the children as they hopped, skipped and jumped in the playground.

2. Tod lived in the countryside. He loved sport and he climbed and sailed every weekend. When it rained he called his friend, Fred, and they played badminton inside.

3. Yesterday David invited his friend Sid to go ice skating. It was very cold so they needed hats and scarves. It started to snow, but Sid ice skated on the lake. David pointed and shouted because Sid wasn't careful.

5   Listen and say 'a', 'b' or 'c'.

1 It started to snow.   b

6 Ask and answer.    She worked at a school.
1 Where did Pat work?
2 When did Pat cook?
3 Who loved Pat's pancakes?
4 Where did Tod live?
5 What did Tod love?
6 What did Tod and Fred play?
7 Who did David invite?
8 Why did David point and shout?

7 Look, think and answer.

1. Which friend are the children visiting?
2. Where is Alex's flat?
3. Who loves climbing?
4. Why must they walk up the stairs?

8 Listen and check.

9 Answer the questions.

1. What's the third letter of the alphabet? *c*
2. What's the ninth letter?
3. What's the twelfth letter?
4. What's the sixteenth letter?
5. What's the twentieth letter?

10 Write more questions to ask your friend.

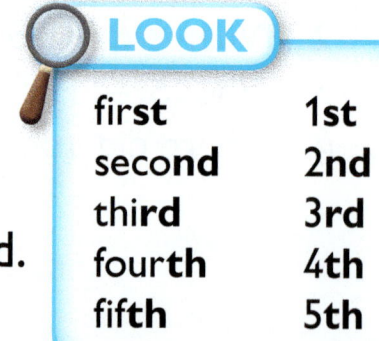

LOOK

first	1st
second	2nd
third	3rd
fourth	4th
fifth	5th

OBJECTIVES: By the end of the lesson, pupils will have described a sequence using ordinal numbers.

● TARGET LANGUAGE
Key language: ordinal numbers *first–twentieth*, the alphabet, consonant clusters, present simple
Additional language: *out of order, repairman, out of breath*
Revision: houses and flats, adjectives, *floor, lift, stairs*

● MATERIALS REQUIRED
After school club word cards from *Kid's Box Teacher's Resource Book 4* page 83 (ordinal numbers)
Extra activity 1: Ten questions containing ordinal numbers, e.g. *What's the third lesson on Mondays? What's the seventh day of the week? What's the fifth letter of my name? What's the eighteenth letter of the alphabet?*
Ending the lesson: Three or four ordinal numbers written as individual letters on fairly large pieces of paper, e.g. *fourth*: six pieces of paper (*f–o–u–r–t–h*)
Optional: *Kid's Box Teacher's Resource Book 4* Unit 4 Reinforcement worksheet 2 (page 38)

Warmer
- Ask pupils whether they live in a house or a flat. Ask *Who lives in a very tall building? Who lives on the highest floor?*

PB38. ACTIVITY 7. *Look, think and answer.*
- Tell pupils to open their Pupil's Book at page 38. Elicit who / what they can see in the pictures. Pupils discuss their predicted answers in pairs.

PB38. ACTIVITY 8. *Listen and check.*
- Play the CD for pupils to listen and check. Play the CD again and ask other checking questions, e.g. *Which floor does Alex live on? Where does Alex's uncle live?* to focus on ordinals.
Key: 1 They are visiting Alex. 2 His flat is on the fifth floor. 3 Lenny and Simon love climbing. 4 They must walk up the stairs because the lift isn't working.

CD 2, 05
NARRATOR: It's Saturday morning and the children are going to Alex's new flat.
LENNY: Which floor does Alex live on?
STELLA: I think he lives on the fifteenth floor.
SIMON: Wow, the fifteenth floor. That's exciting!
MEERA: Yeah, he says he can see the city from his bedroom window. Oh, no! The lift isn't working!
LENNY: That's OK. There are some stairs. We can walk up.
STELLA: Lenny, we have to walk up to the fifteenth floor!
SIMON: That's no problem. Lenny and I love climbing. Come on, Lenny. Let's see who gets there first!
LENNY: Yeah!
STELLA: First floor, second floor, third floor, fourth floor, fifth floor … I'm so tired!
ALEX: Hello. What's the matter?
EVERYONE ELSE: The lift isn't working.
ALEX: But it's only the fifth floor!
LENNY: Yeah, but we went up to the fifteenth floor.

PB38. ACTIVITY 9. *Answer the questions.*
- Present the ordinal numbers using the Look box and the word cards from *Teacher's Resource Book 4* (page 83). Say each one for pupils to repeat. Focus in particular on the consonant clusters.
- Focus pupils on Activity 9 and the activity instruction. Check understanding using the example answer. Pupils work out and say the answers in pairs. Check with the class.
Key: 2 i, 3 l, 4 p, 5 t

PB38. ACTIVITY 10. *Write more questions to ask your friend.*
- Pupils use the model in Activity 9 to write other questions. Suggest other things to ask about, e.g. the fifth letter in *Sunday*, the third letter in their name. Pupils each write six questions. Remind them to check the Look box for spelling. They swap questions in pairs and answer each other's.

AB38. ACTIVITY 5. *Match and write.*
- Tell pupils to open their Activity Book at page 38. They complete the activity individually and then check in pairs. Check as a class.
Key: third – 3rd, second – 2nd, ninth – 9th, first – 1st, twelfth – 12th, twentieth – 20th, eighth – 8th

AB38. ACTIVITY 6. *Find the letter. Write three words starting with that letter.*
- Focus pupils on Activity 6. Check they know what to do, using the example answer. They can ask their friends for help if they can't think of three words. Monitor and help / support. They check in pairs. Check as a class.
Possible answers: 2 l: lake, love, last, 3 g: green, guitar, got, 4 s: sing, scarf, sad, 5 d: dance, drink, dog, 6 e: elephant, English, easily, 7 n: nose, new, never, 8 c: cough, car, carried

Extra activities: see page T113 (if time)

Optional activity
- Unit 4 Reinforcement worksheet 2 from *Teacher's Resource Book 4* (pages 36 and 38).

Ending the lesson
- Choose one of the sets of letters you have prepared (spelling an ordinal number). Mix up the letters. Invite enough pupils to the front to be able to give them a letter each (e.g. for the word *fourth* you need six pupils). Give each pupil a letter. They organise themselves into the correct spelling. They spell out their word, each pupil saying a letter in turn. The class calls out the ordinal number (e.g. *fourth*). Repeat.

OBJECTIVES: By the end of the lesson, pupils will have had further practice with ordinal numbers and sung a song.

- **TARGET LANGUAGE**
Key language: ordinal numbers
Additional language: *in line, get past, league*
Revision: sports and activities, *team, competition*

- **MATERIALS REQUIRED**
After school club word cards from *Kid's Box Teacher's Resource Book 4* page 83 (ordinal numbers)
Optional: *Kid's Box Teacher's Resource Book 4* Unit 4 Song worksheet and dice (one per pupil) (page 41)

Warmer
- Write ordinal numbers as words with gaps for some letters on the board, e.g. _if_h (fifth). Pupils work in pairs to complete the words. Check with the class by asking pupils to come to the board and write in the missing letters or use the word cards from *Kid's Box Teacher's Resource Book 4* (page 83) to show the correct spelling.

PB39. ACTIVITY 11. *Listen and complete the song.*
- Tell pupils to open their Pupil's Book at page 39. Focus them on the picture and on the song. Give them time to read the song before they listen. In pairs, they can try to predict what the missing words are. Play the CD. Pupils listen and check / complete. Play the CD a second time and then check with the class (make sure pupils have spelt the words correctly). Check understanding of new vocabulary.

Key: Fifth, eighth, Ninth, twelfth, good, first

`CD 2, 06`
As in Pupil's Book and Key

PB39. ACTIVITY 12. *Sing the song.*
- Play the CD again. Pupils join in and follow in their books. Repeat in sections until pupils are confident with the song. They stand and sing as a class, counting out the numbers on their fingers.

`CD 2, 06`
As in Pupil's Book

`CD 2, 07`
Now sing the song again. (Karaoke version)

PB39. ACTIVITY 13. *Ask and answer.*
- Focus pupils on Activity 13 and on the speech bubbles. Elicit / explain the meaning of *league table*. Demonstrate the activity with the class, eliciting other questions to check they remember to use the ordinal numbers. Pupils work in pairs and take turns to ask and answer about the teams. Monitor and help with pronunciation. Check, using open pairs.

AB39. ACTIVITY 7. *Read and answer.*
- Tell pupils to open their Activity Book at page 39. Focus them on Activity 7. Check they have read the activity instruction and know what to do. They read and write the letters. They check in pairs. Check with the class.

Key: scarf, dream

AB39. ACTIVITY 8. *Read and complete the table.*
- Focus pupils on Activity 8. Read one or two of the clues with the class and help them to work out some of the missing information. Make sure they know what to write in each column of the table: name, position (an ordinal number between first and fourth) and activity. Pupils work in pairs to complete the table. Check with the class. Draw the table on the board and call volunteers to fill in the blank cells.

Key:

Name	Position	Activity
Daisy	first	jumped
Fred	second	danced
Jim	third	played table tennis
Vicky	fourth	ice skated

Extra activities: see page T113 (if time)

Optional activity
- Pupils complete the Unit 4 Song worksheet from *Teacher's Resource Book 4* (pages 36 and 41).

Ending the lesson
- Do a quick class quiz. Ask, e.g. *What's the third letter in my name? What's the first letter in (pupil)'s name? ...*

11   Listen and complete the song.

Dancing is good, dancing is fine,
Dancing is great!
Come on, children! Dance in line!

First, second , third and fourth
Dance, dance across the floor.
_____ , sixth, seventh, _____
Jump, kick, don't come in late.
_____ , tenth, eleventh, _____
Dancing is _____ for your health.

Dancing's good, dancing's fine,
Come on, children! Dance in line!

Number five's _____ ,
And number ten's last.
He can't hop and skip,
He can't get past.

Dancing is good, dancing is fine,
Dancing is great!
Come on, children! Dance in line!

12 Sing the song.

13 Ask and answer.

Which team was first last week?

Kids United.

FOOTBALL LEAGUE TABLE

1. Kids United
2. Star Athletic
3. Heart Club
4. All Sports
5. Fit City
6. Box Runners
7. Sporting
8. Sports Kids
9. Quick Kickers
10. Dream Team
11. Great Movers
12. Cambridge Flyers
13. The Non Starters
14. Dirty Players
15. Walking Legs
16. The Hungry Sharks
17. The Goal Monsters
18. Naughty Monkeys
19. The Terrible Tigers
20. Feet First

14 **Stella's phonics**

Yesterday, Sam and Pam play**ed** football.

Sam got the ball and kick**ed** it to Pam.

Oh no! They need**ed** that goal!

15 Make questions. Ask and answer.

Did you dance to music last week?

Did you watch TV in your room last week?

Yes, I did.

No, I didn't.

walk play listen	~~to music~~ to the radio to school
help ~~watch~~ take	your mum a photo your homework
~~dance~~ do practise	table tennis ~~TV in your room~~ roller skating

Find two people who … last week		name 1	name 2
… dance to music	Did you dance to music last week?		
… watch TV in your room	Did you watch TV in your room last week?		

OBJECTIVES: By the end of the lesson, pupils will be able to identify and say -ed endings in the past tense forms they have learnt (pronouncing the letters ed as /d/, /t/ or /ɪd/). They will also have completed a communication activity.

- **TARGET LANGUAGE**
Key language: past tense forms
Revision: actions and activities, past simple: questions and short answers

- **MATERIALS REQUIRED**
Warmer: Flashcards 'help my friend' (41), 'start snowing' (42) and 'climb the stairs' (43)
Optional: *Kid's Box Teacher's Resource Book 4* Unit 4 Extension worksheet 1 (page 39)

Warmer

- Stick the flashcards 'help my friend', 'start snowing' and 'climb the stairs' on the board. Elicit the phrases and say a sentence in the past with each, e.g. *Yesterday I helped my sister tidy her room. We were walking when it started snowing. They climbed the stairs because the lift wasn't working.* Say the past verbs (*helped, started, climbed*). Pupils repeat. Help them to notice the three different ways of pronouncing ed.

PB40. ACTIVITY 14. *Stella's phonics*

- Tell pupils to open their Pupil's Book at page 40. Elicit what they can see. Ask them to listen only the first time. Play the CD. Pupils point and follow the sentences. Play the CD again for pupils to repeat. Pupils practise saying the words and sentences. Monitor and check pronunciation.

Note: Repetition and practice are required before pupils will automatically use the correct pronunciation for -ed endings. Encourage your pupils to recognise that there is a pattern at this stage.

CD 2, 08

STELLA: Hi, I'm Stella! Repeat after me!
/d/, /d/, played
/t/, /t/, kicked
/ɪd/, /ɪd/, needed
Yesterday, Sam and Pam played football.
Yesterday, Sam and Pam played football.
Sam got the ball and kicked it to Pam.
Sam got the ball and kicked it to Pam.
Oh no! They needed that goal!
Oh no! They needed that goal!
Yesterday, Sam and Pam played football.
Sam got the ball and kicked it to Pam.
Oh no! They needed that goal!

PB40. ACTIVITY 15. *Make questions. Ask and answer.*

- Focus pupils on the words in the box and on the questions and answers. Review past simple questions. Pupils match the verbs and the activities and write six more questions. Check around the class. Pupils copy the table into their notebooks and write the questions as shown. They ask two friends and note their answers in the table. Make sure pupils ask two different people and that they ask the full question each time.
- Discuss what pupils found out, eliciting full sentences, e.g. *Sara danced to music last week.* Check for change of *your* to *his / her*. Elicit and provide written prompts for sentence combinations,

e.g. *Sara danced to music last week, but she didn't help her mum. Paul danced to music last week and he played table tennis.*

AB40. ACTIVITY 9. *Write. Listen, check and say.*

- Tell pupils to open their Activity Book at page 40. Check pupils know the meaning of all the verbs in the box. Point out the letters and words at the top of each column of the table. Say the words, emphasising the -ed endings. Pupils repeat. Draw attention to the example answer. Elicit an example for the other two columns if necessary. Tell pupils to complete the activity in pencil. Pupils work individually to put the words into the three columns. Tell them to say the words aloud again to help. Give them time to think about the final sound before the letters *ed* in each past form, and how this helps them choose the correct pronunciation of *ed*.
- Focus on the second part of the instruction (*Listen, check and say*). Play the CD for pupils to listen and check. Pupils compare answers in pairs. Check with the class. Play the CD again for pupils to listen and repeat.

Key:

'd' – played	't' – walked	'id' – needed
called	stopped	started
sailed	kicked	invited
rained	helped	wanted
snowed	danced	decided

CD 2, 09

/d/
called, sailed, rained, snowed
/t/
stopped, kicked, helped, danced
/ɪd/
started, invited, wanted, decided

AB40. ACTIVITY 10. *Choose the right answers and complete the text.*

- Focus pupils on Activity 10. Write *Last Wednesday* on the board. Elicit if the text is now, in the past or in the future (the past). Pupils do the activity in pairs. Make groups of four (two pairs). Pupils check their answers. Check with the class. Discuss gaps that caused problems and elicit the reason(s) for the correct answers. Pupils complete the text.
- **Key:** 2 us, 3 Saturday, 4 talk, 5 climbed, 6 fifteenth, 7 cooked, 8 watched

Joke box

- Focus pupils on the Joke box. They guess / find the answer. If pupils don't get the joke the first time, tell it again. Explain the joke if necessary.

Extra activities: see page T113 (if time)

Optional activity

- Unit 4 Extension worksheet 1 from *Teacher's Resource Book 4* (pages 36 and 39).

Ending the lesson

- Pupils repeat the sentences from the beginning of the lesson. Divide the class into three groups. They each take a line. They say their sentences in turn, concentrating on pronouncing the -ed endings correctly.

OBJECTIVES: By the end of the lesson, pupils will have read a story and reviewed language from the unit.

- **TARGET LANGUAGE**
  Key language: language in the story
  Revision: language from the unit

- **MATERIALS REQUIRED**
  After school club word cards from *Kid's Box Teacher's Resource Book 4* page 83 (ordinal numbers)
  Optional: *Kid's Box Teacher's Resource Book 4* Unit 4 Extension worksheet 2 (page 40) and / or animated version of the Unit 4 story from *Kid's Box Interactive DVD 4* (*Suzy's room* section), *Kid's Box Interactive DVD 4: The living room* 'Rehearsing for a play' episode

Warmer
- Write *Peter* and *Nick Motors* on the board. Elicit what pupils remember about them from earlier *Lock and Key* episodes. Build two mind maps.

Story

PB41. LOCK AND KEY.
- Tell pupils to open their Pupil's Book at page 41. Focus pupils on the first frame and elicit who they can see (Lock, Key and Peter) and what Peter's saying. Set the gist questions: *What's the name of the school show? Who does Lock think the pirate is? Who is it really?*
- Play the CD. Pupils listen and read for what happened. They check in pairs. Check with the class (Peter Pan; Nick Motors; Peter's dad).
- Play the CD again. Pause after each frame for pupils to repeat. Check general comprehension, by asking, e.g. *Where are Lock and Key sitting? What drinks do they have? What does Lock try to do? Has Peter's dad got a real beard?*

CD 2, 10
As in Pupil's Book

AB41. DO YOU REMEMBER?
- Write an ordinal number, e.g. *13th,* in the centre of the board. Brainstorm the other ordinals from *1st* to *20th*. You could also use the After school club Unit 4 word cards from *Teacher's Resource Book 4.*
- Tell pupils to open their Activity Books at page 41. Check they have read the activity instructions and know what to do. They study the spellings on the right in silence, using the numerals to help. Then they fold the page down the middle so that they can see only the numerals and the lines to write the words. Without looking, they write the words in pencil, using the numerals to help. They check in pairs, asking, e.g. *What's this one? How do you spell 'tenth'?* They don't look at the words on the right. When pupils have finished, they can either correct their own work or swap books with their friend.

AB41. CAN DO.
- Focus pupils on the *Can do* section of the page. Say *Let's read the sentences together.* Read the first sentence. Elicit what this means with examples and elicit / remind pupils of the activities they did in this unit when they practised the ordinal numbers. Review what the three faces mean (not very well / OK / very well). Remind pupils they circle the one they think is true for them. Repeat for the second sentence, eliciting / reminding them about the communication activity, as well as other activities when they talked about the past. Pupils circle the appropriate face. Repeat for the third sentence, eliciting / reminding them about when they asked questions about last week.
- Say *Now show and tell your friends.* Pupils work in groups of three and take turns to show their work for / talk about each one.

Extra activities: see page T113 (if time)

Optional activities
- Unit 4 Extension worksheet 2 from *Teacher's Resource Book 4* (pages 36 and 40).
- The animated version of the story from *Kid's Box Interactive DVD 4* (*Suzy's room* section). See pages 38–45 of the Teacher's Booklet for the Interactive DVD.
- The 'Rehearsing for a play' episode from *Kid's Box Interactive DVD 4* (*The living room* section). See pages 16–19 of the Teacher's Booklet for the Interactive DVD.

Ending the lesson
- Ask pupils which chant / song they'd like to do again from the unit. Do it together to end the lesson.

LOCK & KEY

English literature — Poems, plays and novels

1 Read and match.

Fact
The biggest book in the world is an atlas in the British Museum. It's 1.8 m high!

a

b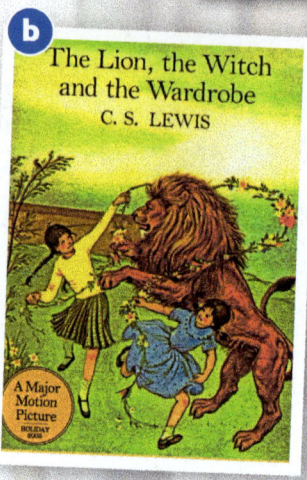

c

There are lots of different kinds of literature. What do you like reading?

1 Poems
The Owl and the Pussycat is a children's poem by Edward Lear.

> The Owl and the Pussycat went to sea
> In a beautiful pea-green boat,
> They took some honey, and plenty of money,
> Wrapped up in a five pound note.

2 Plays
We go to a theatre to see plays. *Peter Pan* by J. M. Barrie is a famous children's play about the adventures of Peter Pan, Wendy and her brothers John and Michael. They learn to fly and go to the island of Neverland, where they fight Captain Hook and his pirates.

3 Novels
C. S. Lewis is the author of *The Chronicles of Narnia*. There are seven books in *The Chronicles of Narnia*. The first is *The Lion, the Witch and the Wardrobe*. It is about the adventures of the Pevensie children in the country of Narnia.

2 Answer the questions.
1 What colour was the Owl and the Pussycat's boat?
2 Where does Peter Pan fight Captain Hook?
3 How many books are there in *The Chronicles of Narnia*?

OBJECTIVES: By the end of the lesson, pupils will have been introduced to different genres of literature and completed a poem.

- **TARGET LANGUAGE**

Key language: *atlas, literature, poem, novel, play, famous, author, theatre, actor*

Additional language: *owl, pussycat, pea-green, honey, plenty, money, wrapped up, five pound note, adventures, fight, witch, wardrobe*

Revision: *actions, adjectives, animals, food, clothes, metre, centimetre, island, pirate*

- **MATERIALS REQUIRED**

Warmer: Novels, plays and poems (to hand around the class)
An atlas and a tape measure
Photocopiable 4 (page T99), one copy for each pair of pupils (cut into parts A and B) (Optional: the text from Photocopiable 4 completed, one for each pair of pupils – see page T92)
Optional: *Kid's Box 4 Language Portfolio* page 10

Warmer

- Brainstorm with pupils which books they have read recently in L1. Show some examples of novels and teach the word *novel* in English. Ask if they know the names of other kinds of fiction, show examples of plays and poems and present the English words *play* and *poem*.

PB42. FACT

- Tell pupils to open their Pupil's Books at page 42. Focus them on the title of the lesson and check comprehension of *English literature*. Ask a pupil to read the fact to the class. Show / tell pupils what an atlas is and use your height / your arms' width or a tape measure to demonstrate the size of the largest atlas.

PB42. ACTIVITY 1. *Read and match.*

- Focus pupils on Activity 1. Remind them of the three words from the Warmer: *novel, play, poem*. Tell pupils they're going to read about three famous examples of these different kinds of writing. A pupil reads the introduction aloud to the class. Discuss their answers to the question: *What do you like reading?* Answer the questions yourself, too.
- Pupils read the texts silently to match each one with a picture. They check in pairs. Check with the class. Read the titles of the works and check comprehension. Ask if pupils have heard of any of the works or seen film versions. If they have seen films, ask what they thought (elicit adjectives in English).

Key: 1 c, 2 a, 3 b

PB42. ACTIVITY 2. *Answer the questions.*

- Focus pupils on the Activity 2 instruction. Check understanding of the questions. Pupils answer in their notebooks. Discuss answers with the class and explain any key vocabulary (but do not spend too long teaching all of the new words).

- Focus on the poem *The Owl and the Pussycat*. Elicit / explain that poetry is similar to music (both usually have rhyme, rhythm and are written to be performed). Read the poem aloud for your pupils. Write *pea-green* on the board and check comprehension. Elicit how this makes the colour more vivid. Provide one or two other examples made up of known words, e.g. *sky-blue, leaf-green, blood-red*.

Key: 1 Pea-green. 2 On the island of Neverland. 3 Seven.

Photocopiable 4 (see pages T90, T92 and T99)

AB42. ACTIVITY 1. *Read and think. Write 'play', 'poem' or 'novel'.*

- Tell pupils to open their Activity Book at page 42. They discuss and then choose the genre in groups of four. Check and discuss vocabulary with the class. Give examples where necessary.

Key: 2 novel, 3 poem, 4 novel, 5 play

AB42. ACTIVITY 2. *Choose your poem.*

- Focus pupils on Activity 2. Check they have read the activity instruction. Discuss what they have to do. Remind them that they can choose the words to: a) make sense, and b) rhyme. Ask them to find the rhyming words (in line 3) in pairs first, to raise awareness. Pupils work individually and circle the words they choose. Monitor and check, making suggestions where appropriate. After you have checked their work, pupils write the poem in their notebooks and illustrate it. Volunteers read out their poems to the class.

Extra activity: see page T113 (if time)

Language Portfolio

- Pupils complete page 10 of *Kid's Box 4 Language Portfolio* (*A short story*).

Ending the lesson

- Review with pupils what they learnt about in today's lesson.
- Tell pupils to bring a book by their favourite author and some information about him / her to the next lesson.

OBJECTIVES: By the end of the lesson, pupils will have practised ordering a text and completed a project.

- **TARGET LANGUAGE**
  Key language: *king, queen, ground, touch, boring*
  Revision: past simple, prepositions, house and home, weather, descriptions

- **MATERIALS REQUIRED**
  Project: A large piece of paper, reference materials, story books, class readers, glue, scissors, colours
  Optional: *Kid's Box Teacher's Resource Book 4* Unit 4 Topic worksheet (page 42)

Warmer
- Review with pupils what they read about in the previous lesson (poems, plays, novels). Tell pupils they are going to read more about *The Lion, the Witch and the Wardrobe* and *The Chronicles of Narnia*. If they did Photocopiable 4, review the names of the children in the story.

PB43. ACTIVITY 3. *Read and order the text.*
- Tell pupils to open their Pupil's Book at page 43. Pupils take turns to read sentences of the text aloud around the class. Don't make any comments about the order of the paragraphs. Pupils then work in threes to work out the order. Check with the class. Focus pupils on key words / phrases for textual organisation, e.g. *Lucy / she*. Check comprehension by asking, e.g. *Where was the big house? What was in one of the rooms?*
- Pupils take turns to read the text aloud in the correct order.

Key: 2 a, 3 c, 4 b

PB43. PROJECT. *Make a 'My favourite book' poster.*
- Ask pupils which are their favourite books. They can mention books they have read in their L1. They show any books they have brought to class.
- Focus pupils on the project and on the model text. Pupils make posters with the title *My favourite book*. They use the text in the Pupil's Book to help them. Monitor and help with new vocabulary.
- Put pupils into pairs. They take turns to talk about the book they wrote about. The other pupil can ask questions. Display the posters.

AB43. ACTIVITY 3. MOVERS Listening, Part 4
Listen and tick (✓) the box. There is one example.
M towards
- Tell pupils to open their Activity Book at page 43. Focus on the activity instruction. Play the example and point out the example tick. Make sure pupils know they only need to tick one box each time. Give pupils time to read the rest of the questions and look at the pictures. Play the rest of the CD. Pupils tick. They check in pairs. Play the CD again. Check with the class. Note that in the live Movers test each item is a separate scenario.

Key: 1 A, 2 A, 3 A, 4 C, 5 C

CD 2, 11
Look at the pictures. Listen and look. There is one example.

What did Daisy do on Saturday?
Hello, Daisy. Did you have a good weekend?
It was really good, thanks. I had a great day on Saturday.
Aah. What did you do?
I went to the park and we had a great time.
Oh, that's nice.

Can you see the tick? Now you listen and tick the box.

1. Who did Daisy go to the park with?
   Did you go with your family?
   No, I went with two friends, Jim and Sally.
   And was there a grown-up too?
   Oh yes, my mum was with us.
   I see.

2. What time did they go to the park?
   Did you go in the morning?
   Yes, but it was late. We had breakfast at ten o'clock.
   Did you go to the park then?
   No, we went later. We went there at 11 o'clock.

3. What did Daisy and her friends do first?
   What did you do in the park?
   We did lots of different things. We played with our kites and we played badminton.
   Did you fly your kites first?
   Er, no, we didn't … We played badminton first. I love badminton.
   So do I.

4. What did they have for lunch?
   Did you have lunch in the park?
   Yes, we did. Mum wanted to go to the café, but we decided to have a picnic.
   That was a good idea. What did you have?
   We ate some chicken and bread, and drank orange juice. It was lovely.
   Good.

5. How did Daisy and her friends go home?
   Did you go home by bus?
   No, we didn't. We were tired, but we live near the park so we walked home.
   That's good.
   Yes, it's very quick.

Extra activities: see page T113 (if time)

Optional activity
- Unit 4 Topic worksheet from *Teacher's Resource Book 4* (pages 36 and 42).

Ending the lesson
- Review with pupils what they did in today's lesson and which activities they liked best from this and the previous day's lesson and why.

3 Read and order the text. 1 – d

The Lion, the Witch and the Wardrobe

a One of the rooms had nothing inside it except a big old cupboard for clothes – a wardrobe. Lucy went inside and she saw a lot of coats. She walked to the back of the wardrobe.

b Lucy went back to Narnia with the other children. They helped the king, a lion, to make Narnia a happy place. Later, Peter, Susan, Edmund and Lucy were kings and queens of Narnia.

c Then there was snow on the ground and trees touched her face. Lucy was cold. She was in a forest at night.

The wardrobe was behind her. Lucy was in Narnia, where animals can talk. One of them told Lucy that a bad white witch lived in Narnia and it was always winter. All the animals were sad.

d Four children went to stay in a big house in the country. Their names were Peter, Susan, Edmund and Lucy. One day it was very rainy outside, so they played inside. It was boring, but the house had a lot of rooms to look in.

Project

Make a 'My favourite book' poster.

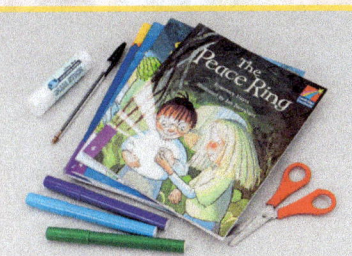

My favourite book
My favourite book is called ………… .
The author's name is ………… .
The story is about ………… .
The characters are called ………… .
I like it because ………… .

Review Units 3 and 4

1 Play the game.

Instructions

Before you play, decide which actions are good and which are bad.
Good actions: Go forward 2 spaces.
Bad actions: Go back 2 spaces.

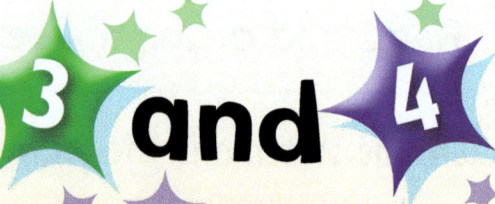

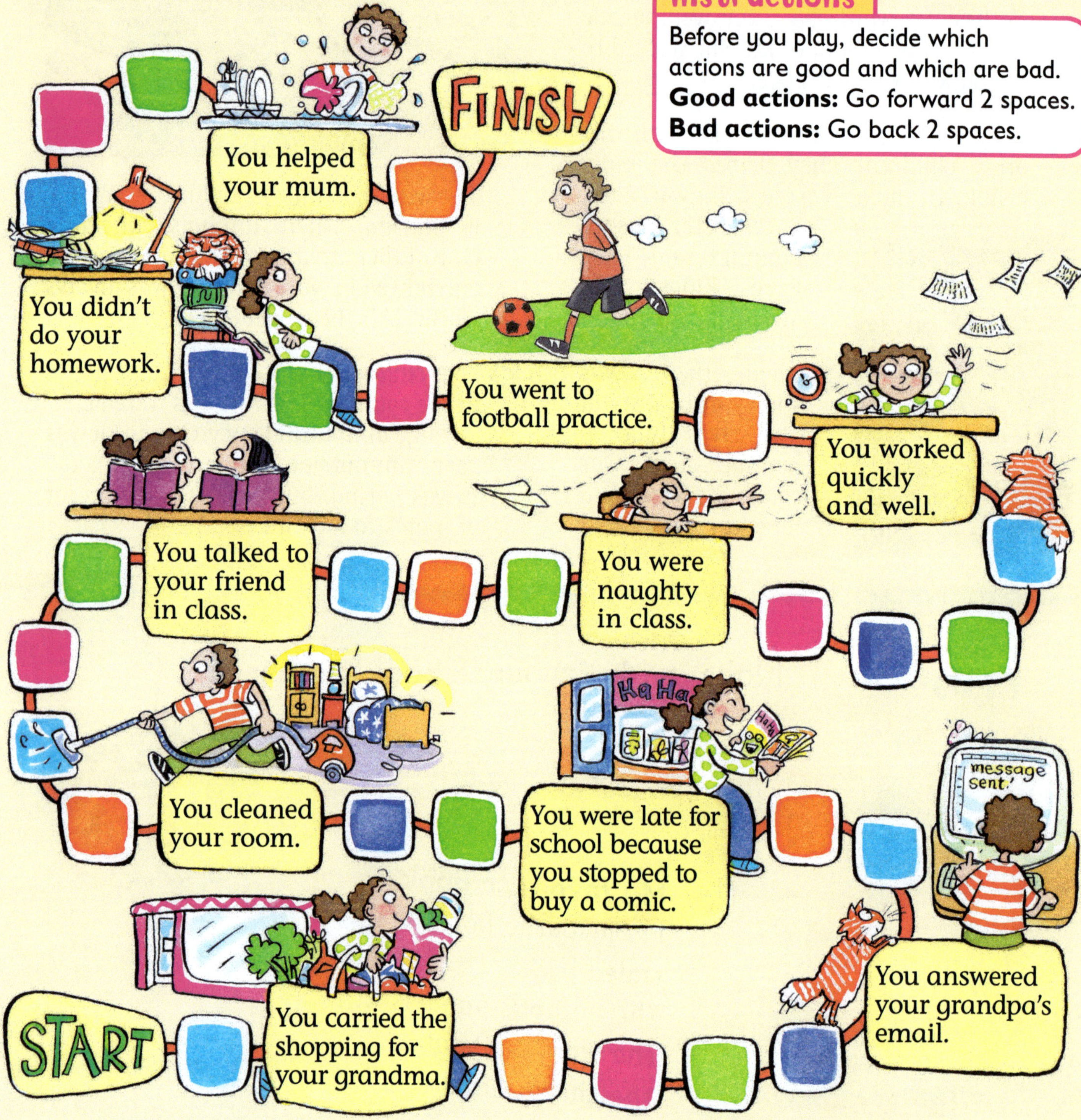

OBJECTIVES: By the end of the lesson, pupils will have reviewed language from Units 3 and 4 and played a game.

- **TARGET LANGUAGE**

Key language: vocabulary and language from Units 3 and 4
Revision: language for games, *forward, back*

- **MATERIALS REQUIRED**

Warmer: Key words and phrases from Units 3 and 4, each written on a small piece of paper (or, if you have a class of 20 or fewer, Flashcards 34–53)
Dice and four different coloured counters for each group of four pupils
Photocopiable Review 3 and 4 (page T100), copied so that each pupil has half of one page (part A or part B)

Warmer

- Make groups of five or six. Hand out a piece of paper with a word or phrase on it, or a flashcard, to each pupil. Pupils in each group take turns to say what their word is and then to make a sentence using their word. The other pupils in the group decide if it's correct or not. Monitor and help as necessary. If time, make new groups and repeat.

PB44. ACTIVITY 1. *Play the game.*

- Pupils open their Pupil's Book at page 44. Elicit what they can see (a board game). Ask volunteers to read the sentences on the squares aloud in turn and elicit if each one is a good thing to do or a bad thing to do. Focus pupils on the instructions for the game and elicit what they do for good things and for bad things (review / present *forward* and *back*). Remind pupils of the language for games before they start, e.g. *It's your turn. It's my turn. Pass the dice. I'm blue.*
- Pupils play the game in groups of three or four. When they land on a space with text, they have to read it aloud and decide if it's good or bad and how to move. The player who reaches the Finish first is the winner.

Photocopiable Review 3 and 4 (see pages T90 and T100)

AB44. ACTIVITY 1. *Find the past of the verbs.*

- Tell pupils to open their Activity Book at page 44. Check they have read and understand the activity instruction. Demonstrate by eliciting the past for one or two verbs. Pupils work individually and find the words in the wordsearch. They check in pairs. Check with the class.

Key:

s	k	a	t	e	d	w	s	f	l	m
w	w	t	s	g	d	a	y	i	i	h
e	t	w	b	a	d	s	h	s	k	a
n	s	o	r	v	w	a	s	h	e	d
t	h	c	o	e	t	r	i	e	d	n
d	r	a	n	k	g	e	o	d	o	a
e	o	w	e	r	e	p	t	a	t	e

AB44. ACTIVITY 2. *Complete the sentences with words from Activity 1.*

- Focus pupils on Activity 2 and on the activity instruction. Check understanding. They write some of the words from Activity 1 in the gaps in pencil. They check in pairs by taking turns to read the whole sentence. Check with the class, again eliciting each complete sentence.

Key: 2 drank, 3 was, saw, 4 had, took, 5 were, ate, 6 gave

AB44. ACTIVITY 3. *Read and answer. Write 'Yes, I did' or 'No, I didn't'.*

- Check comprehension of the activity instructions. Pupils answer the questions individually. They ask and answer the questions in pairs. Encourage them to ask their partner for more detail about the 'Yes' answers (e.g. *What film did you see? What time did you get up? Did you win?*). Elicit feedback in the third person, e.g. *Mariano didn't go to the cinema last Saturday.*

Extra activities: see page T114 (if time)

Ending the lesson

- Write *good* on one side of the board and *bad* on the other. Elicit the good and bad actions from the board game. Ask pupils for other ideas for good and bad actions.

OBJECTIVES: By the end of the lesson, pupils will have reviewed language from Units 3 and 4 and practised listening.

● **TARGET LANGUAGE**
Key language: vocabulary and language from Units 3 and 4
Revision: days of the week, word families

● **MATERIALS REQUIRED**
Flashcards 44–63 (ordinal numbers)
After school club word cards from *Kid's Box Teacher's Resource Book 4* page 83 (ordinal numbers)
The completed crossword for Activity Book page 45, Activity 5, written on a large piece of paper
Optional: *Kid's Box Interactive DVD 4: Stella's room* Quiz 2, Test Units 1–4 *Kid's Box Teacher's Resource Book 4* (pages 90–112), *Kid's Box 4 Language Portfolio* page 4

Warmer

- Review ordinal numbers using the flashcards. Write eight of the ordinal numbers as words on the board. Make a spelling mistake in each one. In pairs, pupils correct them. Ask pairs to take turns to come and write the correct words on the board. Use the Unit 4 word cards to check spelling.

PB45. ACTIVITY 2. *Listen and write a letter in each box. There is one example. How did Mary go to each place?* [M] towards

- Tell pupils to open their Pupil's Book at page 45. Give pupils time to look at the pictures and the text before they listen. Make sure they realise there are two extra pictures. Play the CD and go through the example. Play the rest of the CD twice. Check with the class.

Key: 1 bus C, 2 boat F, 3 bike A, 4 walking D, 5 car G

CD 2, 12

How did Mary go to these places?
Listen and write a letter in each box. There is one example.
I went to lots of different places last week.
Did you, Mary? Where did you go?
I went to the big new shopping centre. It's really cool. I went with my friends on the new train to get there.
Wow! That was exciting.
Can you see the letter H? Now you listen and write the letter in the box.

1. I went to see my new baby cousin too. I'm very happy because it's a girl.
   Fantastic! Did you go to the hospital to see her?
   Yes. But not the one in this town. Another one. We went there on the bus.
   What's your new cousin's name?
   Eva.
2. The weather was very hot last week. Did you go swimming?
   Yes. We went by boat to the island. The beach there is very nice.
   Oh yes. Much nicer than going to the sports centre.
   Yes. We had a really good day.
3. I went on a long bike ride with my friends.
   Where did you go?
   We went around the lake. And we had a picnic there.
   Very nice.
4. I saw you near the park last Friday. I waved but you didn't see me!
   Oh yes. I was there last Friday. My piano teacher lives near there. I always walk to her house.
   That's a nice place to live.
   Yes. I like going to her house.
5. My dad bought a new car last week.
   Is it nice?
   Yes, it's very cool. It's bigger than our old one. He took us to the funfair in it.
   What fun!
   Now listen again.

AB45. ACTIVITY 4. *Circle the odd one out.* [M] towards

- Tell pupils to open their Activity Book at page 45. Pupils complete the activity and then check in pairs. Check with the class.

Key: 2 phoned, 3 awake, 4 worse, 5 kick, 6 closed, 7 hurt, 8 sailed, 9 danced, 10 writes, 11 twentieth, 12 tired

AB45. ACTIVITY 5. *Now complete the crossword. Write the message.*

- Focus pupils on Activity 5. Pupils use the words from Activity 4 to complete the crossword and then write the message, using the letters from the shaded squares (nice work!).

Key:

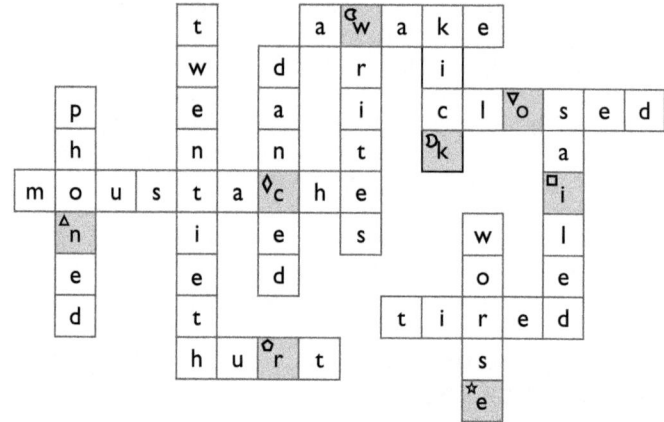

Extra activities: see page T114 (if time)

Optional evaluations

- Quiz 2 from *Kid's Box Interactive DVD 4* (*Stella's room* section). This quiz can be done as a whole-class activity or as a team competition. See pages 36 and 37 of the Teacher's Booklet for the Interactive DVD.
- The test for Units 1–4 from *Teacher's Resource Book 4* (pages 90–112)

Language Portfolio

- Pupils complete page 4 of *Kid's Box 4 Language Portfolio* (*I can ... Units 3–4*).

Ending the lesson

- Pupils work in groups of four. Two pupils (A) cover the Do you remember? words from Unit 3. The other two pupils (B) take turns to say what each word is and spell it. 'A's check. They reverse roles for Unit 4.

2 How did Mary go to these places?
Listen and write a letter in each box. There is one example.

 train H

 car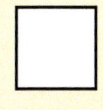

 walking

 bus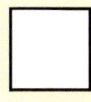

 bike

 boat

5 Exploring our world

1 Look at Simon's homework. Think and answer.
1. Who did Simon show his homework to?
2. Who did Simon write about?
3. Who was Shackleton?
4. How did Shackleton go to Antarctica?

A famous explorer, Sir Ernest Shackleton, wanted to cross Antarctica. In 1914 he started the expedition but ice closed round the ship. They took smaller boats and made a camp on the snow. They lost their ship when it went down under the ice and water.

They couldn't move because the weather was terrible. They caught fish and drank water which they got from snow. Later, they had to eat their dogs.

Shackleton and some of his men climbed over mountains of ice, found help and went back for the other men. Everybody came home two years after the start of their expedition. They didn't cross Antarctica.

Ernest Shackleton

2 Read and check.

3 Find the past of these verbs in the text.

find   catch   take   go   make
get   can't   lose   have to   come

OBJECTIVES: By the end of the lesson, pupils will have read and talked about actions and events in the past.

● TARGET LANGUAGE

Key language: *could / couldn't*: ability, past simple irregular, *catch, have (to), find, get, take, go, make, can, lose, come home, explorer, expedition, British, cross, ice, open sea, save, continent*

Additional language: *Antarctica*

Revision: actions, weather, animals, adjectives, prepositions, connectors, numbers (years)

● MATERIALS REQUIRED

Warmer: Map of the world to show the Antarctic continent
Note: Check if your school or local resource centre has a copy of the video / DVD *South* or download the film from the internet (check that you can do this legally). *South* was made at the time of the Shackleton expedition and shows Shackleton and his men, his ship The Endurance, the small boats and the sea creatures. You could show parts of it at the end of the lessons or at the end of the unit.
Flashcards 64–67 ('continents', 'Antarctica', 'expedition' and 'explorer')
Optional: *Kid's Box Teacher's Resource Book 4* Unit 5 Reinforcement worksheet 1 (page 44)

Warmer

- Show the map of the world and elicit how many continents there are and their names. Use the flashcards to teach *continent, Antarctica, expedition* and *explorer*. Ask pupils what they know about the Antarctic continent. Ask pupils if they know the names of any explorers, past or present.

PB46. ACTIVITY 1. *Look at Simon's homework. Think and answer.*

- Tell pupils to open their Pupil's Book at page 46. Focus them on the photograph and the text and elicit / tell pupils that this is part of Simon's project on explorers. Check pupils have read the activity instructions and know what to do. They read the questions in pairs and discuss them together, using the information in the pictures.

PB46. ACTIVITY 2. *Read and check.*

- Pupils read the text. Elicit complete sentences for the answers to the four questions. Read the text again and ask further checking questions, e.g. *What did Shackleton want to do? Why did they camp on the snow? What was the weather like? How did they get water to drink? What did they eat? Did everybody come home? Shackleton didn't cross Antarctica, but was he a hero?* Check understanding of *couldn't*.

Key: 1 He showed his homework to his dad. 2 He wrote about Sir Ernest Shackleton. 3 Shackleton was an explorer. 4 He went to Antarctica by ship.

PB46. ACTIVITY 3. *Find the past of these verbs in the text.*

- Focus pupils on the Activity 3 instruction and check understanding. They work in pairs and underline the past of the verbs in the text. Pairs check with pairs. Check with the class, focusing on pronunciation as well as spelling. Elicit that these are irregular verbs. Pupils write a list of the new verbs (simple infinitive and past simple) in their notebooks.

Key: found, caught, took, went, made, got, couldn't, lost, had to, came

AB46. ACTIVITY 1. *Make sentences.*

- Tell pupils to open their Activity Book at page 46. Check they have read and understand the activity instruction using the example. They work in pairs to make sentences. Check with the class.

Key: 2 f, 3 e, 4 a, 5 c, 6 b, 7 h, 8 j, 9 d, 10 g

AB46. ACTIVITY 2. *Make a wordsearch.*

- Focus pupils on the Activity 2 instructions. Tell them to use the past simple of the new verbs (from the Pupil's Book page). They write the past in the wordsearch and the simple infinitives down the side. They fill in the other boxes in the wordsearch with random letters.

AB46. ACTIVITY 3. *Now look at your friend's wordsearch and find the words.*

- Make new pairs. Pupils swap their books and find the words. They check in their pairs.

Extra activities: see page T114 (if time)

Optional activity

- Unit 5 Reinforcement worksheet 1 from *Teacher's Resource Book 4* (pages 43–44).

Ending the lesson

- Review the content of the lesson with pupils. Elicit if they think Shackleton's expedition was exciting and why / why not.

OBJECTIVES: By the end of the lesson, pupils will have talked more about past ability using *could / couldn't* and practised connecting clauses with *so*.

● **TARGET LANGUAGE**
Key language: *could / couldn't* + short answers, *exhibition, diary,* connector: *so, school trip*
Revision: *museum, explorers, Antarctic, , polar bear,* actions, prepositions, adjectives, *first, before, after, then*

● **MATERIALS REQUIRED**
Flashcards 68–70 ('exhibition', 'museum' and 'school trip')
Photocopiable 5 (page T101), one copy for each pupil. One large piece of paper.
Optional: *Kid's Box Teacher's Resource Book 4* Unit 5 Reinforcement worksheet 2 (page 45)

Warmer

- Elicit places pupils like to visit in their town / city. Review *museum* using the flashcard. Talk about the museums and galleries in nearby cities. Write their names on the board. Elicit what types of museums there are and what people can see inside. Ask pupils which is the best museum they've visited.

PB47. ACTIVITY 4. *Read and say the letter.*

- Tell pupils to open their Pupil's Book at page 47. Explain that the boy is called David and that he's on a school trip. Use the flashcard to check *school trip*. Present *exhibition* using the flashcard. Check pupils have read and understand the activity instruction and the example answer. They read the text quickly to match the numbers with the pictures. They check in pairs.

Key: 2 e, 3 d, 4 a, 5 g, 6 h, 7 c, 8 b

PB47. ACTIVITY 5. *Listen and answer the questions.*

- Focus pupils on the Activity 5 instruction and speech bubbles. Play the CD. Pause after each question for pupils to find the answer and to say it to a partner. Play the CD again, pausing after each one again to elicit answers. Review irregular past tense forms using the Unit 5 word cards, if time.

Key: 2 First they walked round an exhibition about explorers. 3 They made a poster about famous explorers. 4 They went to the museum shop after lunch. 5 He got a toy polar bear for his sister. 6 In the afternoon they went to an exhibition about sea animals. 7 David took a photograph of his friends. 8 They caught the bus at three o'clock.

CD 2, 13

1. When did David's class go to a museum?
2. What did they do first?
3. What did they make?
4. When did they go to the museum shop?
5. Who did David get a toy polar bear for?
6. Where did they go in the afternoon?
7. Who did David take a photograph of?
8. What time did they catch the bus?

PB47. ACTIVITY 6. *Make sentences.*

- Focus pupils on the Activity 6 instruction and on the example. Check understanding of *so*. Pupils work individually and make sentences. They check in pairs. Check with the class.

Key: 2 They didn't take water with them so they were thirsty. 3 The exhibition was really good so they had a great time. 4 It was his sister's birthday so he got a toy from the shop. 5 The children had to wait for the bus so they came home late. 6 They lost their map so they couldn't find the museum.

AB47. ACTIVITY 4. *Ask and answer.*

- Review *could.* Ask, e.g. *Could you walk / talk / swim when you were two?* Ask about other pupils, e.g. *Could (name) run when he was two?* to check *Yes, he / she could* and *No, he / she couldn't.*
- Tell pupils to open their Activity Books at page 47. Focus them on Activity 4. Pupils read the examples aloud. They work in pairs, taking it in turns to ask and answer about Vicky. Check, using open pairs.

AB47. ACTIVITY 5. *Ask your friends and tick or cross the boxes.*

- Introduce / check short answers *Yes, I could* and *No, I couldn't.*
- Focus pupils on Activity 5. Make groups of four. Each pupil writes the names of three friends on the left. They take turns to ask each other the questions and tick or cross in the boxes. Finally, they answer about themselves.

Photocopiable 5 (see pages T91 and T101)

AB47. ACTIVITY 6. *Match and say.*

- Focus pupils on the Activity 6 instruction and example. Pupils match the sentences individually. Check with the class.

Key: 2 e, 3 f, 4 b, 5 a, 6 c

Extra activity: see page T114 (if time)

Optional activity

- Unit 5 Reinforcement worksheet 2 from *Teacher's Resource Book 4* (pages 43 and 45).

Ending the lesson

- Say and clap *Could you swim when you were three?* The pupils that could, say *Yes, I could.* (Clap, clap, clap). The pupils that couldn't, say *No, I couldn't.* (Clap, clap, clap, clap). Repeat for other skills / actions. More confident pupils can take turns to ask the questions.

4 Read and say the letter. 1 – f

1 Last week David's class went to a museum.
2 First they walked round an exhibition about explorers.
3 They could read explorers' diaries, so it was really exciting.
4 Before lunch they made a poster about famous explorers.
5 After lunch they found the museum shop and David got a toy polar bear for his sister.
6 In the afternoon they went to an exhibition about sea animals.
7 Before they came home, David took a photograph of his friends.
8 At three o'clock they caught the bus home.

5 Listen and answer the questions.

1 When did David's class go to a museum?

They went to a museum last week.

6 Make sentences. They were hungry so they ate sandwiches.

1 They were hungry		they couldn't find the museum.
2 They didn't take water with them		he got a toy from the shop.
3 The exhibition was really good	so	they ate sandwiches.
4 It was his sister's birthday		they came home late.
5 The children had to wait for the bus		they had a great time.
6 They lost their map		they were thirsty.

7 Look, think and answer.

1 Which explorers are Simon and Alex talking about?
2 What was Cousteau's ship called?
3 Who did Alex write about?
4 What did Cousteau explore?

8 🔊 Listen and check.

9 Complete the text.

Alex thinks that Shackleton's adventures were more difficult _____ Cousteau's, but Cousteau is _____ famous for his work. Cousteau said we have to be _____ careful with the sea. Stella thinks Simon's homework was _____ interesting _____ hers. Lenny was happy because he did his homework _____ quickly than Simon and Alex.

> **LOOK**
> Cousteau is **more famous** for his work.
> Our homework was **easier than** theirs.
> Shackleton sailed **more slowly than** Cousteau.

> **OBJECTIVES:** By the end of the lesson, pupils will have used comparative adjectives to talk about different explorers.
>
> ● **TARGET LANGUAGE**
> **Key language:** comparative of two- and three-syllable adjectives and adverbs
> **Revision:** explorers, adjectives, past simple, actions and activities, question forms, *Why … ?, because, so*
>
> ● **MATERIALS REQUIRED**
> Optional: *Kid's Box Teacher's Resource Book 4* Unit 5 Extension worksheet 1 (page 46)

Warmer
- Draw two faces on the board, one smiling, one sad. Elicit names for each person. Elicit, e.g. *Victor is happier than Harry.* Using classroom objects, elicit other sentences to review comparative of one- and two-syllable adjectives, e.g. *This ruler's longer than that one. This book's thinner than that one.* Elicit the name of the structure and write it on the board (comparatives).

Presentation
- Provide sentences using known adjectives with more than one syllable and *more*, e.g. *Watching TV is more exciting than doing homework. Maths is more difficult than English. (Actor) is more famous than (actor).* Repeat the sentences and write them on the board. Underline the comparative sections, e.g. *more interesting than,* and elicit how these are different from adjectives like *easier than.* Help pupils notice the number of syllables (two or more) and that adjectives ending in *-y* (e.g. *happy*) have *-ier*.

PB48. Activity 7. *Look, think and answer.*
- Tell pupils to open their Pupil's Book at page 48 and focus on Activity 7. Pupils take turns to read the questions aloud. Ask who / what they think Cousteau is. In pairs, pupils discuss / predict the answers to the questions.

PB48. Activity 8. *Listen and check.*
- Pupils listen and check. Check with the class. Play the CD again and check comprehension by asking, e.g. *What nationality was Cousteau? According to Alex, whose adventures were more difficult? Whose work is more famous? Whose life was more exciting? Whose homework was more boring?*
- Focus pupils on the Look box to remind them of the comparative adjectives. Elicit other examples from pupils using these adjectives.

Key: 1 They are talking about Shackleton and Cousteau. 2 His ship was called the Calypso. 3 Alex wrote about Jacques Cousteau. 4 Cousteau explored sea life.

CD 2, 14
Alex: Hi, Simon. Did you finish your homework yesterday?
Simon: Yeah, I wrote about Shackleton. Who did you write about?
Alex: Jacques Cousteau. He was a French explorer. Shackleton's adventures were more difficult than Cousteau's, but I think Cousteau is more famous.
Simon: Really? What did he do?
Alex: He sailed in his ship, the Calypso, and explored sea life.
Simon: But Shackleton's life was more exciting. Why was Cousteau famous?
Alex: Because he helped us to understand our world. He made 120 TV programmes and films and he was one of the first people to tell us to be more careful with the sea.
Simon: Yeah, that's true. We have to look after our world.
Stella: Huh, our homework was more boring than theirs.
Lenny: Yes, but ours was easier than theirs, so I had time to watch TV after I finished mine.
Stella: Yeah!

PB48. Activity 9. *Complete the text.*
- Focus pupils on the Activity 9 instruction and check understanding using the example. Pupils work individually. They check and compare in pairs. Check with the class by asking pupils to take turns to read sentences aloud.

Key: than, more, more, more, than, more

AB48. Activity 7. *Read and complete.*
- Tell pupils to open their Activity Book at page 48. Focus them on Activity 7. Make sure pupils understand that they need to find the opposites, and then write the connecting word spelt out by the letters running vertically. Pupils solve the crossword individually, and then compare answers in pairs. Check with the class.

Key: 2 easy, 3 bad, 4 curly, 5 dirty, 6 right, 7 first, 8 loud, 9 old
The secret word is *beautiful*.

AB48. Activity 8. *Read and match.*
- Focus pupils on Activity 8. Pupils match the pictures with the text. They check in pairs. Check with the class. Pupils read the sentences aloud.

Key: 2 a, 3 f, 4 b, 5 c, 6 d

Extra activities: see page T114 (if time)

Optional activity
- Unit 5 Extension worksheet 1 from *Teacher's Resource Book 4* (pages 43 and 46).

Ending the lesson
- Play the CD from Pupil's Book Activity 8. Elicit some of the things that Alex and Simon said about Cousteau and Shackleton, to review comparatives.

OBJECTIVES: By the end of the lesson, pupils will have had further practice with comparative adjectives and given their opinions.

- **TARGET LANGUAGE**
Key language: comparative adjectives
Revision: adjectives, exploration, days of the week

- **MATERIALS REQUIRED**
Extra activity 2: Large piece of paper for each group of four pupils and materials for making a poster about a school trip (e.g. photographs of places to cut out, glue, scissors, coloured pencils or crayons)

Warmer
- Provide prompts for pupils to make comparative sentences, e.g. *famous* / (name of footballer / name of teacher). Include -y ending, one-, two- and three-syllable adjectives from the previous lesson.

PB49. ACTIVITY 10. *Order the words.*
- Tell pupils to open their Pupil's Book at page 49 and focus on Activity 10. Check they have read the activity instruction and know what to do. In pairs, they order the words and write the sentences correctly in their notebooks. To check, pupils come to the board and write the sentences in the correct order.

Key: 1 My book on explorers is more interesting than yours. 2 Shackleton's adventures were more difficult than Jacques Cousteau's. 3 Crossing Antarctica is more difficult than climbing trees. 4 Christopher Columbus is more famous than Jacques Cousteau. 5 Simon writes more carefully than Suzy. 6 Sailing is more exciting than walking.

PB49. ACTIVITY 11. *What do you think? Make sentences.*
- Focus pupils on Activity 11 and on the pictures. Elicit what they can see in each one. Check they have read the activity instructions and know what to do. Demonstrate, using the example. Pupils work in pairs and take turns to make sentences about the pictures, as in the example. Monitor and help / prompt / support. Check by eliciting sentences from different pairs and responding to the content of what they say (as well as the grammar). Personalise the discussion in preparation for the next activity, e.g. ask pupils which sport they think is more exciting than table tennis.

PB49. ACTIVITY 12. *Now write sentences.*
- Focus pupils on the Activity 12 instruction and check understanding. They write at least six sentences in their notebooks, using the model from Activity 11. They write about their own opinions. Monitor and support, e.g. with spelling. Make groups of four. Pupils take turns to read the sentences to the other members of the group and find out if their friends have similar opinions.

AB49. ACTIVITY 9. *Make sentences.*
- If pupils did Extra activity 2 in the previous lesson, refer them to their tables with the comparative forms. Tell pupils to open their Activity Book at page 49. Focus them on the pictures and the example. Check they have read and understand the activity instruction. Pupils complete the activity on their own and then check in pairs. Check with the class, eliciting the different options.

Key: 2 Mr Star's more famous than Grandma Star. 3 The dog is dirtier than the cat. 4 The horse is thirstier than the dog. 5 The monkey is happier than the panda. 6 The elephant is stronger than the dog. 7 The girl is more careful than the boy.

AB49. ACTIVITY 10. *Compare Tom's days. Choose words from the box.* [M] *towards*

- Focus pupils on Activity 10 and on the two pictures. Elicit descriptions of each picture: what pupils can see, what the weather was like, etc. Pupils spend about five minutes looking for the differences. In pairs, they then take turns to tell each other the differences they have found. Remind them to use the past tense, as in the example. Elicit differences from pupils to check.

Note: *Tired* and *bored* are exceptions to the rule, being one-syllable adjectives that take *more*.

Key: The weather was better on Sunday than on Wednesday. The weather was worse on Wednesday than on Sunday. It was sunnier on Sunday than on Wednesday. Tom was happier on Sunday than on Wednesday. Tom was more tired on Wednesday than on Sunday. The lesson was more exciting on Sunday than on Wednesday. The lesson was more boring on Wednesday than on Sunday. The lesson was more difficult on Wednesday than on Sunday.

Extra activities: see pages T114–T115 (if time)

Ending the lesson
- Make a statement, e.g. *I'm hungry*. Prompt a pupil to respond, e.g. *I'm hungrier than you!* Continue with other adjectives, letting more confident pupils make the opener with different adjectives, e.g. *I'm / We're clever*.

10 Order the words.

1 interesting / My book on explorers is / yours. / than / more
2 dangerous / more / Jacques Cousteau's. / than / Shackleton's adventures were
3 more / climbing trees. / Crossing Antarctica is / difficult / than
4 than / Jacques Cousteau. / more / Christopher Columbus is / famous
5 carefully / Suzy. / more / Simon writes / than
6 walking. / Sailing is / exciting / more / than

11 What do you think? Make sentences.

boring   exciting   dangerous   beautiful   difficult   easy

I think climbing is more dangerous than swimming.

climbing

swimming

pop music

classical music

Maths

Art

badminton

table tennis

horses

fish

photo

painting

12 Now write sentences.

I think badminton is more boring than table tennis.

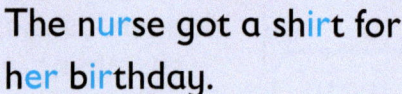 **Stella's phonics**

The n**ur**se got a sh**ir**t for h**er** b**ir**thday.

On Th**ur**sday the sh**ir**t got d**ir**ty.

The n**ur**se w**or**ked in h**er** p**ur**ple sh**ir**t.

 Complete the rap. Listen and check.

trees   green   ~~mine~~   ours   his   strong

The world isn't mine ,
The world isn't yours.
The world isn't _____,
The world isn't hers.
It's ours,
It's _____!

Our world is tired, we're making mistakes,
We need our seas, we need our lakes.
Our world is weak, we can make it _____,
It needs our help. Listen to our song.

We must look after its forests and _____,
We must look after its rivers and seas.
We can make it better, we can make it _____,
This is our world, let's keep it clean.

  Sing the song.

OBJECTIVES: By the end of the lesson, pupils will be able to identify and say the long vowel sound /ɜː/ in many common words. They will be aware of the three main spellings for the sound (er, ur and ir). They will also have performed a rap.

- **TARGET LANGUAGE**

Key language: words with the phoneme /ɜː/ (e.g. n*ur*se, sh*ir*t, w*or*k)
Additional language: make mistakes
Revision: adjectives, the world, must, need, Let's … , look after, word families

- **MATERIALS REQUIRED**

Optional: *Kid's Box Teacher's Resource Book 4* Unit 5 Song worksheet (page 48)

Warmer

- Write six words which have the vowel sound /ɜː/ on the board, e.g. *world, nurse, purple, skirt, burger, Earth*. Tell pupils to look for the sound that all the words have in common. Help by saying the words aloud, emphasising the vowel sound. Remind pupils to focus on the sound, not the spelling. Explain that they will be focusing on the sound /ɜː/ in this lesson.

PB50. ACTIVITY 13. *Stella's phonics*

- Tell pupils to open their Pupil's Book at page 50. Elicit what they can see in the pictures (a nurse, a dirty shirt, a purple shirt). Tell pupils to listen only the first time. Play the CD. Tell pupils to listen and repeat. Play the CD again for pupils to join in with the sound sentences.

Note: This can be a difficult sound for learners, as they tend to pronounce words as they are spelt, rather than recognising that there are alternative spellings for the same sound. You can help by making pupils aware of the three main alternative spellings for the sound (*er, ur* and *ir*). There are also specific words which contain the sound, which pupils will become familiar with (*Earth, world, word*).

CD 2, 15

STELLA: Hi, I'm Stella! Repeat after me!
/ɜː/, /ɜː/, nurse
/ɜː/, /ɜː/, shirt
The nurse got a shirt for her birthday.
The nurse got a shirt for her birthday.
On Thursday the shirt got dirty.
On Thursday the shirt got dirty.
The nurse worked in her purple shirt.
The nurse worked in her purple shirt.

The nurse got a shirt for her birthday.
On Thursday the shirt got dirty.
The nurse worked in her purple shirt.

PB50. ACTIVITY 14. *Complete the rap. Listen and check.*

- Focus pupils on Activity 14 and on the pictures. Review use of *my / mine*, etc., using classroom objects, e.g. pick up a pen and ask *Is it yours? Is it your pen?* The pupil responds *Yes, it's mine* or *No, it's his / hers*. Pupils read the rap before they listen and, in pairs, try to guess what goes in the gaps.

- Play the CD. Pupils listen and check / complete. Play the CD again. Check with the class. Check understanding by asking, e.g. *What's the problem with the world? What must we do?*

Key: his, ours, strong, trees, green

CD 2, 16
As in Pupil's Book

PB50. ACTIVITY 15. *Sing the song.*

- Play the rap line by line. Pupils listen and repeat.
- Pupils stand up. They perform the rap, using gesture to communicate *mine / ours*, etc. If appropriate, record pupils and let them watch their performance

CD 2, 16
As in Pupil's Book

CD 2, 17
Now sing the song again. (Karaoke version)

AB50. ACTIVITY 11. *Write. Listen, check and say.*

- Tell pupils to open their Activity Book at page 50. Focus them on the pictures and the gapped words. Explain that they all have the sound /ɜː/, but this sound is spelt using different letters. Go through the example. Pupils then work in pairs to complete the words. Check with the class. Write the correct spelling for each word on the board.
- Play the CD for pupils to listen, check and repeat.

Key: See CD script below

CD 2, 18
1 shirt, 2 person, 3 world, 4 burger, 5 nurse, 6 skirt, 7 work, 8 learn

AB50. ACTIVITY 12. *Match and colour the squares.*

- Focus pupils on Activity 12. Check they have read the activity instruction and elicit what they have to do, using the example (they colour the boxes which refer to the same person in the colour given in one of the pairs of boxes, e.g. *my / mine*). Pupils complete the activity in pairs. Check with the class. Call out a colour. Pupils provide both sentences.

Key: It's mine. – green; They're yours. – purple; It's ours. – red; They're his. – pink; They're hers. – blue

Joke box

- Focus pupils on the Joke box. Ask a pupil to read the joke to the class. If pupils don't get the joke the first time, tell it again.

Extra activities: see page T115 (if time)

Optional activities

- Pupils complete the Unit 5 Song worksheet from *Teacher's Resource Book 4* (pages 43 and 48).

Ending the lesson

- Perform the rap from the lesson again with pupils.

OBJECTIVES: By the end of the lesson, pupils will have read a story and reviewed language from the unit.

- **TARGET LANGUAGE**
Key language: language in the story, *text message, protect (the environment)*
Additional language: *adventure holiday*
Revision: language from the unit

- **MATERIALS REQUIRED**
Optional: *Kid's Box Teacher's Resource Book 4* Unit 5 Extension worksheet 2 (page 47) and / or animated version of the Unit 5 story from *Kid's Box Interactive DVD 4* (*Suzy's room* section)

Warmer
- Put pupils into groups of four, with books closed. Give them about five minutes to try to remember what happened in the last episode of *Lock and Key*? Elicit information from the groups by asking, e.g. *Where did Lock and Key go? What was the name of the play?*

Story
PB51. LOCK AND KEY.
- Tell pupils to open their Pupil's Book at page 51. Focus them on the first frame and elicit what's on the computer screen (*Explore Adventure Holidays*). Elicit some examples of adventure holidays and what kind of places people can explore. Set the gist questions: *What does it say in the brochure about places to explore? Where do Lock and Key go? Why? What text message does Lock get on his phone?* Play the CD. Pupils listen and read for what happened. They check in pairs. Check with the class (*forests, rivers and beaches; to the adventure holiday camp; because Nick Motors was there the day before; 'Look behind you!'*).
- Play the CD again. Pause after each frame for pupils to repeat. Check general comprehension by asking, e.g. *How did Nick Motors get to the adventure holiday camp? What did he do there? Can you see Nick Motors in the fourth picture? Where is he? What does Miss Rich ask them? Can you see Nick Motors in the last picture? What is he doing?*

CD 2, 19
As in Pupil's Book

AB51. DO YOU REMEMBER?
- Write *past verbs* on one side of the board and one example, e.g. *found*. Brainstorm the new past verbs (check the simple forms) from the unit. Write *comparatives* on the other side of the board and one example, e.g. *more exciting*. Brainstorm other comparatives from the unit.
- Tell pupils to open their Activity Books at page 51. Check they have read the activity instructions and know what to do. They study the spellings on the right in silence. Then they fold the page down the middle so that they can see only the words on the left and the lines to write the words on. They write the words in pencil. They check in pairs, asking, e.g. *What's this one? / How do you spell 'found'?* They don't look at the words on the right. When pupils have finished, they can either correct their own work or swap books and check their partner's.

AB51. CAN DO.
- Focus pupils on the *Can do* section of the page. Say *Let's read the sentences together.* Read the first sentence. Elicit what this means with examples and elicit / remind pupils of the activities they did in this unit when they talked about events in the past. Review what the three faces mean (*not very well / OK / very well*). Remind pupils they circle the one they think is true for them. Repeat for the second sentence, eliciting / reminding them of the activities when they made comparisons between people and things in the unit. Pupils circle the appropriate face. Repeat for the third sentence, eliciting / reminding them about when they talked about possession.
- Say *Now show and tell your friends.* Pupils work in groups of three and take turns to show their work for / talk about each one.

Extra activities: see page T115 (if time)

Optional activities
- Unit 5 Extension worksheet 2 from *Teacher's Resource Book 4* (pages 43 and 47).
- The animated version of the Unit 5 story from *Kid's Box Interactive DVD 4* (*Suzy's room* section). See pages 38–45 of the Teacher's Booklet for the Interactive DVD.

Ending the lesson
- Ask pupils which chant / song they'd like to do again from the unit. Do it together to end the lesson.

Science — Endangered animals

Fact: The name 'Arctic' comes from a Greek word meaning 'near the bear'.

 1 Look. Which animals do you think are endangered?

polar bear

kangaroo

goat

Siberian tiger

panda

 2 Read. Correct the sentences.

Lily wants to help the world. She wants to stop the Earth from getting hotter and the Arctic from getting smaller. She's in a society called the *Green Heroes*. They help endangered animals.

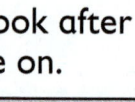

Polar bears live in the Arctic. They live on the ice and swim in the sea. They catch and eat other sea animals like seals, fish or small whales.
Polar bears have problems because the world is hotter than it was before. Oceans are hotter and the ice cap is smaller so polar bears are losing their habitat. Now it's more difficult for polar bears to fish for food or look after their babies if they haven't got ice to live on.

1 Polar bears live on mountains and swim in the lake.
2 They catch and eat other animals like lions, bats and pandas.
3 The world is colder than it was before.
4 It's easier for polar bears to fish for food.
5 It's more difficult for polar bears to look after their parents.

OBJECTIVES: By the end of the lesson, pupils will have read and talked about endangered animals.

● **TARGET LANGUAGE**
Key language: *endangered, Arctic, polar bear, society, hero(es), seal, ice cap, habitat*
Additional language: *get hotter*
Revision: animals (*kangaroo, panda, whale, tiger, goat, whale*), adjectives, comparatives, *look after, parents, body (bodies)*

● **MATERIALS REQUIRED**
Warmer: Pictures of an endangered animal not featured on Pupil's Book page 52, e.g. elephant, rhino.
Map of the world
Copies of the reordered text from Activity Book page 52, Activity 2 (see Key below)

Warmer

- Display the picture of the endangered animal. Elicit its name and what pupils know about it. Direct the discussion to species which are in danger and pre-teach *endangered*. Elicit in L1 reasons why some animals are endangered (e.g. people cutting down forests, people catching animals for body parts, global warming).

PB52. FACT

- Tell pupils to open their Pupil's Book at page 52. Focus them on the lesson heading and explain that they will be learning more about endangered animals in the next two lessons. Show the map of the world and point to the Arctic. Elicit the name in L1 and write *Arctic* on the board. Ask a pupil to read the fact to the class. Check they know the meaning of *Greek*. Elicit which kind of bears live in the Arctic (point to the photograph in Activity 1). Pre-teach *polar bear*.

PB52. ACTIVITY 1. *Look. Which animals do you think are endangered?*

- Draw attention to the photographs. Direct pupils to the activity instructions and check understanding. Pupils work in pairs. They decide if the animal in each photograph is endangered or not. Elicit ideas and confirm answers. Show the location of Siberia on the map. Focus on the polar bear and have a short discussion in L1. Ask *What kind of problems do polar bears have?* Try to touch on the fact that the world is hotter than it was before and oceans are getting bigger, so the polar bear's habitat is disappearing.

Key: The endangered animals are: polar bear, Siberian tiger, panda.

PB52. ACTIVITY 2. *Read. Correct the sentences.*

- Focus pupils on Activity 2. Read the activity instructions. Point to the photograph of the girl and explain that her name is Lily. Ask a volunteer to read aloud the text on the left. Check comprehension of *get hotter, society* and *hero* (plural *heroes*). Ask pupils if they belong to any societies.
- Go through sentences 1 to 5 and check the meaning of key language, e.g. *catch, look after, parents*. They read the text in the speech bubble individually and correct the sentences in pairs. Check answers as a class. Ask pairs to read out correct sentences. Teach *seal* and *habitat*.

Key: 1 Polar bears live on the ice and swim in the sea. 2 They catch and eat other animals like seals, fish and small whales. 3 The world is hotter than it was before. 4 It's more difficult for polar bears to fish for food. 5 It's more difficult for polar bears to look after their babies.

AB52. ACTIVITY 1. *Read and match.*

- Tell pupils to open their Activity Book at page 52. Focus them on the activity instruction and check understanding. They read the sentence halves in pairs and then try to match them. They check with another pair. Check by asking different pairs to read out complete sentences. They write the complete sentences in their notebooks.

Key: 2 a, 3 e, 4 b, 5 c

AB52. ACTIVITY 2. *Colour the boxes and put the text in order.*

- Focus pupils on the activity instruction and check understanding. Pupils reorder the text in pairs. They colour the boxes first and then follow the colours. If they are having difficulty, do the first three or four sentences together as a class. Elicit the correct order and hand out copies of the completed text if possible.

Key: 6, 4, 11, 5, 10, 13, 9, 12, 3, 7, 1, 8, 2

Complete text:
Look at what happens when we use cars. Cars make the air dirty and dirty air makes our world hotter. A hotter world changes the ice in the Arctic and Antarctic to water. Polar bears and other Arctic animals have a smaller habitat because the ice cap is smaller. The water in our seas is also hotter. Some small fish and sea animals can't live in hotter water so it's difficult for the bigger fish or sea animals to find food. We can help by using bikes or walking. What other things can we do to help?

Extra activities: see page T115 (if time)

Ending the lesson

- Review with pupils what they learnt about in today's lesson.

OBJECTIVES: By the end of the lesson, pupils will have listened to an interview about environmental issues and completed a project.

● TARGET LANGUAGE
Key language: *protect, public transport, cut down (trees)*
Additional language: *litre*
Revision: animals, comparatives, *endangered, ice cap, society, heroes, habitat*

● MATERIALS REQUIRED
Project: Large sheet of paper for each pupil, coloured pencils, photographs or pictures of endangered animals, reference materials / internet access
Optional: *Kid's Box Teacher's Resource Book 4* Unit 5 Topic worksheet (page 49)

Warmer
- Review with pupils what they remember about endangered animals. Ask if they can remember the name of the society Lily belongs to.

PB53. ACTIVITY 3. *Listen. Read and say 'yes' or 'no'.*
- Tell pupils to open their Pupil's Book at page 53. Focus them on the activity instruction and on the description of the listening text. Explain that pupils are going to listen to an interview. Give them time to read the sentences and check comprehension of *get colder* and *cut down*. Elicit / explain the meaning of *public transport*.
- Play the CD, pausing after each sentence. Pupils whisper *yes* or *no* to their partner. Play the CD again. Check with the class. Elicit correct sentences for the 'no' answers. Ask which endangered animal Lily talked about at the end (the Siberian tiger) and if pupils would like to be in a society like the Green Heroes. Elicit other ways we can protect the world.

Key: 1 yes, 2 no, 3 no, 4 no, 5 yes, 6 yes, 7 yes

CD 2, 20

PAUL: Can I ask you some questions about the Green Heroes and your project called 'Help the world'?
LILY: Yes, of course, Paul. The Green Heroes is a society for young people who want to protect endangered animals.
PAUL: Oh, good. We know now that the Earth is hotter than it was before, the weather is changing and animals are endangered. Why is this?
LILY: Well, there are a lot of answers to that question. Today more people drive cars, so the air in big cities is dirtier.
PAUL: So, is it a good idea to walk and ride bikes?
LILY: Yes, it is. We can also use public transport, like buses and trains.
PAUL: Is the problem only in cities?
LILY: No, in the forests people are cutting down trees to get more wood to make tables, chairs and paper, but the world needs trees and forests to clean the air.
PAUL: Oh, what other problems does this give us?
LILY: Well, when people cut down trees in our forests, animals like Siberian tigers lose their habitat.
PAUL: What does that mean?
LILY: Well, when forests get smaller it's more difficult for tigers to live there. It's difficult for them to get food to eat and look after their babies.
PAUL: Oh, dear. So, what can we do to help the world?
LILY: Well, we can do a lot of things. We can use less paper …

PB53. PROJECT. *Make a poster about 'endangered animals'.*
- Focus pupils on the project and on the photographs. Elicit what the poster is about (Endangered animals) and read through the instructions. Point out the key words in the boxes and explain that pupils need to write about where their animals live and why they are endangered. If they want they can also write about what we can do to help. Direct them to what Lily says on Pupil's Book page 52 as a model.
- Pupils work in pairs or small groups. They write the article in their notebooks first, using reference books or the internet to do research. Check / help as necessary. Once you have checked their work, pupils rewrite their article for the poster and add photographs or pictures. Display the posters.

AB53. ACTIVITY 3. MOVERS Reading and Writing, Part 4
Read the text. Choose the right words and write them on the lines. [M] *towards*
- Tell pupils to open their Activity Book at page 53. Focus them on the activity instructions and the example. They complete the text by choosing from the words at the bottom of the page. They check in pairs. Elicit answers. Ask pupils to explain their choices.

Key: 1 eat, 2 Their, 3 got, 4 the, 5 than

Extra activities: see page T115 (if time)

Optional activities
- Unit 5 Topic worksheet from *Teacher's Resource Book 4* (pages 43 and 49).

Ending the lesson
- Review with pupils what they did in today's lesson and what they liked best from this and the previous day's lesson and why.

3 Listen. Read and say 'yes' or 'no'.

Listen to Lily talking to a friend about the society and their work.
1. Lily's project is called 'Help the world'.
2. The Green Heroes are young people who want to protect cars.
3. The Earth is getting colder.
4. Air in big cities is cleaner now.
5. It's a good idea to ride bikes and use public transport.
6. People are cutting down trees in forests.
7. The world needs trees to clean the air.

Project Make a poster about 'endangered animals'.

- Choose three endangered animals.
  You can use whale, dolphin, panda, penguin, polar bear, tiger or elephant.
- Write an article about your animals then make a poster. Use the words in the boxes.

| in forests   in the sea   in rivers and lakes   on the ice cap |

| smaller   hotter   drier   dirtier |

6 Technology

1 Look, think and answer.
1 What's Stella talking about?
2 Who wants to learn about computers?
3 Who knows about computers?
4 Who's thinking about music?

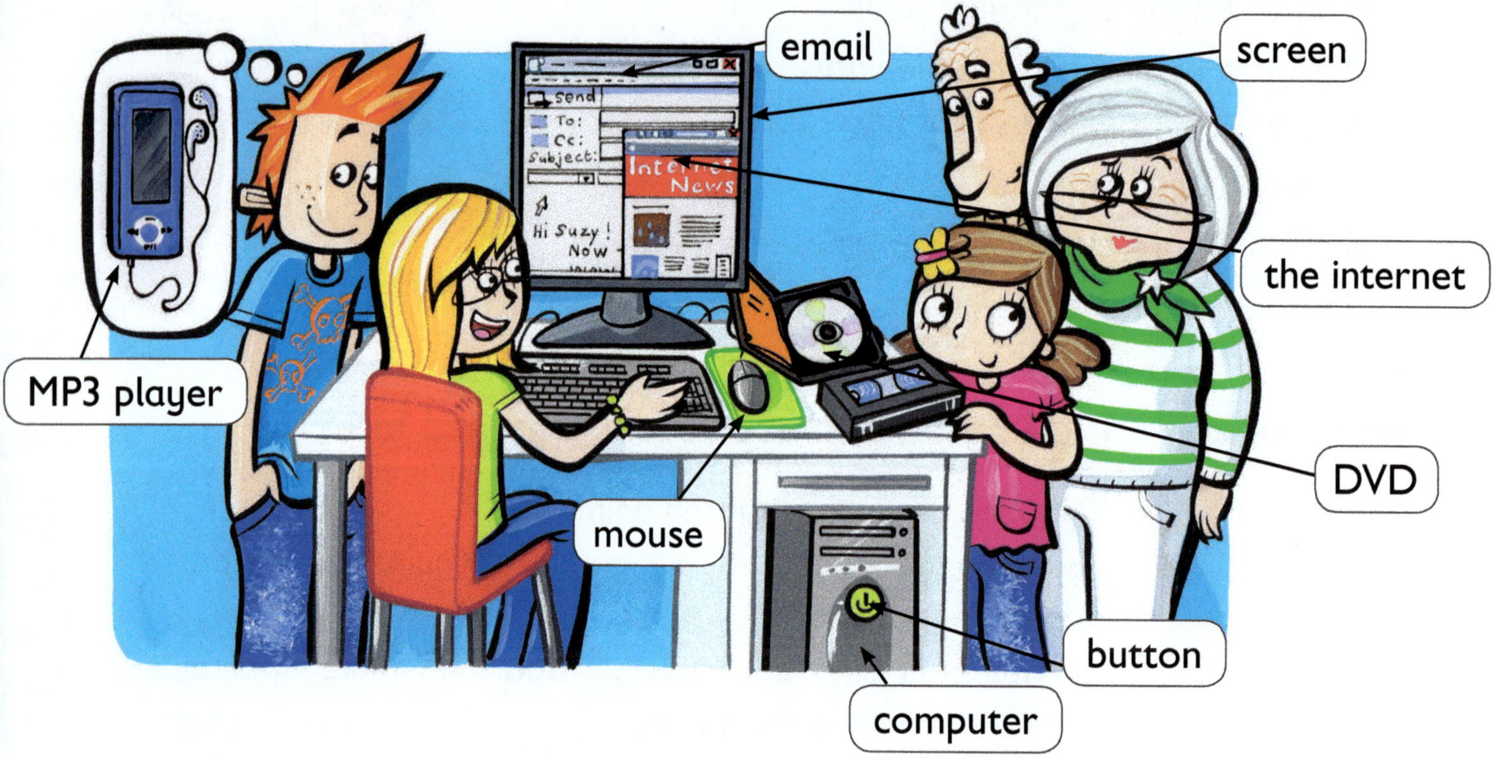

2 🎧 Listen and check.

3 🎧 Listen and repeat. Say the letter.

1 Screen — Screen – c

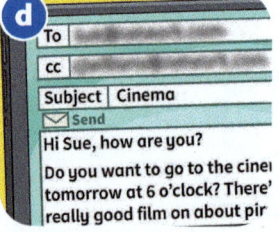
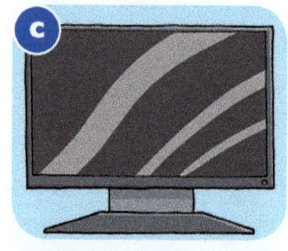

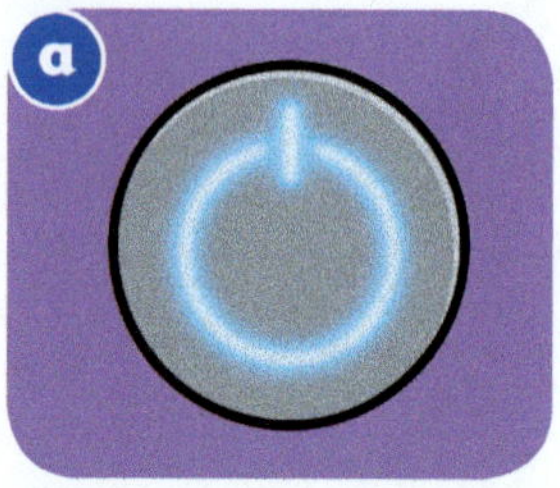

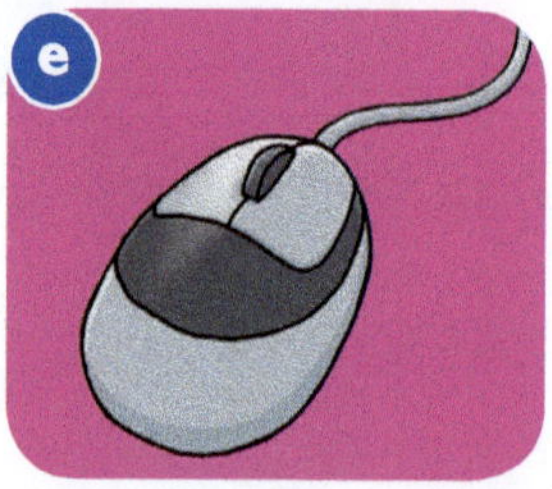

54

OBJECTIVES: By the end of the lesson, pupils will have identified and talked about modern technology.

• TARGET LANGUAGE

Key language: *technology, button, computer, MP3 player, DVD, email, mouse, program, screen, the internet, click, text, video, instructions*

Additional language: *Can you show us, please?*

Revision: *have to*, present simple, comparative adjectives, questions

• MATERIALS REQUIRED

Warmer: Realia of modern technology to show the class, e.g. DVD, MP3 player, tablet, laptop
Technology flashcards (71–81)
Optional: *Kid's Box Teacher's Resource Book 4* Unit 6 Reinforcement worksheet 1 (page 51), *Kid's Box 4 Language Portfolio* page 11

Warmer

- Using the realia you have brought to class, elicit / teach *computer, MP3 player, DVD*. Ask different pupils which devices they used yesterday and what they used them for.

PB54. ACTIVITY 1. *Look, think and answer.*

- Tell pupils to open their Pupil's Book at page 54. Focus on the unit heading and check understanding of *technology*. Elicit / teach the other key technologies from the lesson, using the pictures and the flashcards. Elicit more computer words, e.g. *website*. Check understanding of *video*, using the picture on the Pupil's Book page, and elicit different uses of *video*, e.g. *video clip, music video* and *to video*. Elicit who pupils can see in the picture. They read the questions in pairs and discuss them together, using the information from the pictures.

Note: *Video* is used for both a video cassette and a video clip.

PB54. ACTIVITY 2. *Listen and check.*

- Play the CD. Elicit complete sentences for the answers. Play the CD again and ask checking questions, e.g. *What do you have to do first to turn the computer on? Who is showing Grandma how to use the computer? What kind of DVD is Grandpa looking for? Who does Simon say needs an MP3 player? Is this true?*

Key: 1 She's talking about a computer. 2 Grandma and Grandpa Star want to learn about computers. 3 Stella knows about computers. 4 Simon's thinking about music.

CD 2, 21

GRANDMA: We want to buy a computer so we can use the internet. I'd like to email my old friend in Australia.
SUZY: Do you know how to use a computer, Grandma?
GRANDMA: No, not really. Can you show us, please?
STELLA: Yeah, first you have to turn the computer on. Push this button here. Then you have to turn on the screen. That's this button here. Now you hold the mouse in your hand and ...
GRANDMA: What mouse?
SUZY: This here, Grandma. It's called a mouse because it's got a long tail. Look.
GRANDMA: Oh, I see.
STELLA: Then you click on this program, and you can write your email.
SIMON: OK. What do you want to do, Grandpa?
GRANDPA: I want to go on the internet. I want to buy a DVD or a video about fishing.
SIMON: You don't want a video, Grandpa. A DVD's better because you can watch it on your new computer. Now, you need an MP3 player, Grandpa.
GRANDPA: No, Simon. Now I need a cup of tea.

PB54. ACTIVITY 3. *Listen and repeat. Say the letter.*

- Focus pupils on the Activity 3 instructions. Play the CD for pupils to listen and repeat. Then remind pupils to say the letter quietly to their friend first. Play the CD again. Pupils whisper the letter. Check with the class.

Key: 2 e, 3 a, 4 d, 5 f, 6 b

CD 2, 22

1 screen, 2 mouse, 3 button, 4 email, 5 DVD, 6 MP3 player

AB54. ACTIVITY 1. *Sort and write the words.*

- Tell pupils to open their Activity Book at page 54. Focus them on the activity instruction. Check understanding. Pupils first try to do the activity with their notebooks and Pupil's Books closed. They then look to check. Check with the class by eliciting the spelling of each one.

Key: 2 screen, 3 mouse, 4 button, 5 email, 6 video, 7 internet, 8 MP3 player.

AB54. ACTIVITY 2. *Read and circle the correct answer.*

- Focus pupils on Activity 2. Pupils circle the correct word(s) in each sentence and then check in pairs. Check with the class.

Key: 1 button, 2 screen (Note: Elicit from pupils that this stage is not necessary for many modern computers. Turning on the computer also turns on the screen.), 3 mouse, 4 an email, 5 internet.

Extra activities: see page T115 (if time)

Optional activity

- Unit 6 Reinforcement worksheet 1 from *Teacher's Resource Book 4* (pages 50–51).

Language Portfolio

- Pupils complete page 11 of *Kid's Box 4 Language Portfolio* (*What's the best invention?*).

Ending the lesson

- Define key words from the lesson. Pupils say the word, e.g. *This has music or films on it. You can play it on the computer or on a stereo* (CD / DVD). *This is the part of the computer you look at* (screen). Pupils can take turns to provide definitions for their classmates in the same way.

OBJECTIVES: By the end of the lesson, pupils will have had further practice talking about modern technology and sung a song.

● TARGET LANGUAGE
Key language: *music / video clip, radio, laptop, e-book*
Additional language: *I don't need any more, works perfectly well*
Revision: *technology, numbers, questions, have got*

● MATERIALS REQUIRED
Warmer: Technology flashcards (71–81)
Photocopiable 6a (page T102), one copy for each pair of pupils (Optional: the text from Photocopiable 6a completed, one for each pair of pupils – see page T92)
Extra activity: Write each line from the CD script for Activity Book Activity 3 on a different piece of paper.
Optional: *Kid's Box Teacher's Resource Book 4* Unit 6 Song worksheet (page 55) and / or extra song activities from *Kid's Box Interactive DVD 4* booklet (pages 28–33)

Warmer
- Review the vocabulary from the previous lesson using the flashcards.

PB55. ACTIVITY 4. *Listen and match.*
- Tell pupils to open their Pupil's Book at page 55. Elicit who they can see in the picture. Tell pupils that the first time they listen and match. They will sing later. Play the CD. Pupils listen and match and then check in pairs. Check with the class, eliciting what is in each picture. Check understanding of the new vocabulary, e.g. *music and video clips, plan his day, DVD player*. Check general understanding by asking, e.g. *How does Grandpa feel about all this new technology? Does he want a new phone? Why? / Why not? Is your grandpa / grandma like this with new technology?* If appropriate, draw on ideas from Unit 5 on the environment and ask pupils if it's really necessary to buy the latest technology and what happens to old mobile phones, etc.

Key: 2 a, 3 c, 4 b, 5 f, 6 d, 7 g

CD 2, 23
As in Pupil's Book

PB55. ACTIVITY 5. *Sing the song.*
- Play the CD again. Pupils join in and follow. Repeat the song in sections. When they are confident, they sing the song without the CD. Make two groups: children / Grandpa. Pupils sing their lines. Swap roles and repeat.

CD 2, 23
As in Pupil's Book

CD 2, 24
Now sing the song again. (Karaoke version)

PB55. ACTIVITY 6. *Ask and answer. Use the words in the box.*
- Focus pupils on Activity 6. Demonstrate the activity using the example speech bubbles and open pairs. Pupils do the activity in pairs. Encourage pupils to ask their friends different types of questions, using the information in the song. Elicit some questions from pairs, for other pairs to answer.

Photocopiable 6a (see pages T91, T92, and T102)

AB55. ACTIVITY 3. *Listen and write.* M *towards*
- Tell pupils to open their Activity Book at page 55. Focus them on the sheet of paper and give them time to read it. Play the CD. Pupils listen and write. They check in pairs. Play the CD again. Check with the class.

Key: 2 a new computer. 3 Jack's brother.
4 help him with his homework and to watch video clips.
5 £449.

CD 2, 25

1. Hi, Jack. Did you go shopping yesterday?
   Yes, I did. I went with my mum and my dad.

2. What did you buy?
   We bought a new computer.
   Really? That's nice.

3. Is the computer for you?
   No, it isn't.
   Who's it for?
   It's for my brother.
   I see.

4. Why does your brother need a computer, Jack?
   Well, he needs it for two things.
   What's the first?
   First, he needs the internet to help him with his homework.
   Did you say there were two things he needs a computer for?
   That's right.
   What's the second thing?
   He wants to watch video clips.
   Oh, I see.

5. Was it a lot of money?
   Yes, it was!
   How much was it?
   It was four hundred and forty-nine pounds!
   Oh, that is a lot of money!

AB55. ACTIVITY 4. *Write the sentences in order.*
- Focus pupils on Activity 4. They work individually and write the other sentences in the correct order. They check in pairs by taking turns to read their sentences aloud. Check with the class in the same way. Help pupils to notice how *we* and *you* are used impersonally in the sentences. Check understanding of *e-books*.

Key: 2 You have to turn the computer on before you can use it. 3 It's easier to text your friends than write them emails. 4 You can use a mobile phone to text your friends. 5 We can listen to music on our computers. 6 E-books are better and smaller than paper books. 7 We can use the internet on some mobile phones.

Extra activity: see page T116 (if time)

Optional activities
- Unit 6 Song worksheet from *Teacher's Resource Book 4* (pages 50 and 55).
- Extra activity for Unit 6 Song and / or karaoke worksheet. See pages 28–33 of the Teacher's Booklet for the Interactive DVD.

Ending the lesson
- Sing the song from the beginning of the lesson again.

 **Listen and match.**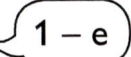

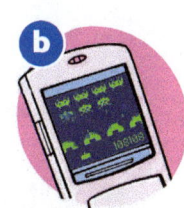

Grandpa needs a new mobile, (No, I don't!)
With an MP3. (A what?)
It's got music and (1) video clips,
And lots, lots more to see. (I don't need any more!)

Grandpa needs a new mobile, (No, I don't!)
So he can (2) text his friends. (I can talk to my friends!)
He can take lots of (3) photos,
And play (4) games at weekends. (I go fishing at weekends!)

Grandpa! (I've got a DVD player at home!)
Grandpa! (I've got a nice camera!)
Grandpa! (And my old mobile phone works perfectly well!)
Grandpa needs a new mobile. (A new mobile phone!)

Grandpa needs a new mobile, (No, I don't!)
So he can (5) plan his day. (I've got a pen and paper!)
He can listen to lots of (6) songs,
And (7) phone or even play. (I haven't got time to play! I've got a radio!
I've got a nice camera! My old mobile phone works perfectly well! Hmph!)

 **Sing the song.**

Ask and answer. Use the words in the box.

Has your grandpa got a mobile phone? No, he hasn't. Can you use a computer? Yes, I can.

computer   TV   camera   the internet
mobile phone   email   e-book   video   app

7 Look, think and answer.

1. Where did Grandma and Grandpa go yesterday?
2. What did they get?
3. What's their computer called?
4. What problem have they got?

8 🔊 Listen and check.

9 Complete the text.

> said   knew   put   ~~bought~~   thought   read   brought   chose

Grandma and Grandpa went shopping yesterday. They **bought** a computer. They chose a KBX4 because Grandma _____ about it and the man in the shop _____ it was better than the others. The man _____ it home later. He took it out of the box, _____ it on the table and _____ goodbye. He thought they _____ the KBX4 because they _____ about computers!

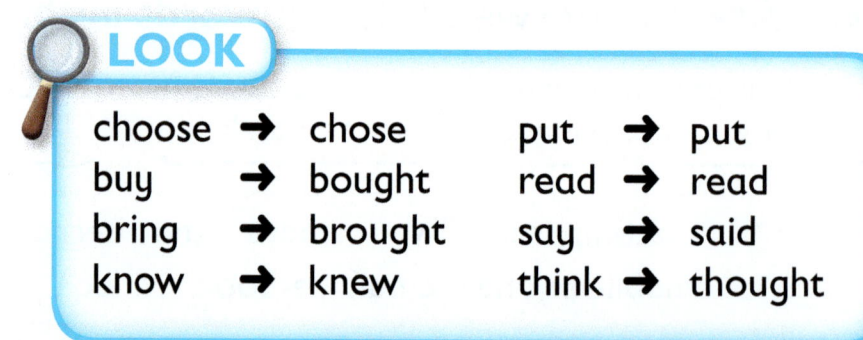

LOOK

choose	→	chose	put	→	put
buy	→	bought	read	→	read
bring	→	brought	say	→	said
know	→	knew	think	→	thought

OBJECTIVES: By the end of the lesson, pupils will have had more practice with verbs in the past simple.

● TARGET LANGUAGE
Key language: past simple, *say, know, put, buy, think, read, bring, choose, turn it on, know how to (do something)*
Additional language: *problem, really good one, How exciting!*
Revision: technology, question forms, comparatives

● MATERIALS REQUIRED
Technology flashcards (71–81)
Modern life word cards from *Kid's Box Teacher's Resource Book 4* (page 85)
Extra activity 1: The CD script from Pupil's Book Activity 8 written on a large piece of paper.
Optional: *Kid's Box Teacher's Resource Book 4* Unit 6 Reinforcement worksheet 2 (page 52)

Warmer
- Write the technology words from Lesson 1 of the unit in scrambled word order on the board. Stick the flashcards on the board in a different order. Pupils take turns to come to the board, write a word correctly and say it, pointing to the correct flashcard.

PB56. ACTIVITY 7. *Look, think and answer.*
- Tell pupils to open their Pupil's Book at page 56. Elicit what / who they can see. Check pupils have read the activity instruction and know what to do. They read the questions in pairs and discuss them together, using the information from the picture to help them guess.

PB56. ACTIVITY 8. *Listen and check.*
- Play the CD. Elicit complete sentences for the answers. Focus pupils on the Look box. Say the verbs and their past forms for pupils to repeat. Use the Unit 6 word cards to practise the past forms (show a card, pupils say the infinitive).
- Play the CD again and ask further checking questions to focus on the new past verbs, e.g. *What did they buy? What did Grandpa say about the computer? Why did they choose that computer? Did Grandpa and Grandma bring it home themselves? What did the man from the shop think? Did Grandma and Grandpa know how to turn it on?* For questions which include the new verbs, pupils repeat the whole sentence together. Check understanding of *know how to (do something)*.

Key: 1 They went shopping. 2 They got a computer. 3 Their computer's called a KBX4. 4 They don't know how to turn it on.

CD 2, 26
GRANDPA: Oh, I'm tired today. We went shopping yesterday.
SIMON: Oh, really? What did you buy?
GRANDPA: We bought a computer.
SIMON: How exciting, Grandpa! Which computer did you get?
GRANDMA: We got a really good one. It's a KBX4.
SIMON: Why did you choose that one?
GRANDPA: Well, we chose it because your grandma read about it and the man in the shop said it was a good one.
GRANDMA: Yes, he thought it was better than the others.
SIMON: Did you bring it home with you?
GRANDMA: Oooh, no. The nice man from the shop brought the computer home later.
GRANDPA: Yes, he took it out of the box, put it on the table and said goodbye.
GRANDMA: Yes, he thought that we knew something about computers, but we don't. We don't know how to turn it on.

PB56. ACTIVITY 9. *Complete the text.*
- Focus pupils on Activity 9 and on the words in the box. Elicit each one, focus on pronunciation and then elicit the simple infinitive again. Check pupils have read the activity instruction and know what to do. They work in pairs, taking turns to read the text aloud and choose the correct words. Pairs check with pairs. Check with the class by getting pupils to take turns to read the text aloud. Pupils copy the complete text into their notebooks.

Key: read, thought, brought, put, said, chose, knew

AB56. ACTIVITY 5. *Match. Write the words.*
- Tell pupils to open their Activity Book at page 56. Focus them on the activity instructions and the example answers. Pupils work in pairs to match the tags and then complete the words. Monitor and help. Check with the class by eliciting the words. Write them on the board. Note the activity focuses on spelling, not pronunciation.

Key: 2 gave, garden, 3 went, weather, 4 came, careful, 5 thought, thanks, 6 caught, cough, 7 did, dinner, 8 put, picnic, 9 knew, knee, 10 chose, chips

AB56. ACTIVITY 6. *Tick six words. Play bingo.*
- Focus pupils on the Activity 6 instructions and check understanding. Pupils have played this kind of bingo game before. They choose six words and tick them. Call out the past simple of the verbs at random. Pupils cross through the ones they hear. The first to cross all six shouts *Bingo!* Check the verbs are correct before declaring the winner.

Extra activities: see page T116 (if time)

Optional activity
- Unit 6 Reinforcement worksheet 2 from *Teacher's Resource Book 4* (pages 50 and 52).

Ending the lesson
- Play a chain game. Say, e.g. *Grandma went to the shopping mall and she bought a computer.* Pupil A says, e.g. *Grandma went to the shopping mall and she bought a computer and an MP3 player.* Vary the chains, e.g. *Grandma went shopping on the internet and she bought a computer.*

OBJECTIVES: By the end of the lesson, pupils will have talked about timed events in the past and solved some problems.

- **TARGET LANGUAGE**
Key language: past simple questions, *app, get up, get dressed, take off, put on, o'clock, potato, pop music, plant*
Revision: verbs and vocabulary describing daily routines, technology, prepositions, clothes, numbers

- **MATERIALS REQUIRED**
Optional: *Kid's Box Teacher's Resource Book 4* Extension worksheet 1 (page 53)

Warmer
- Pupils draw six circles in their notebooks. Say a time for each one, e.g. *Five o'clock*. Pupils draw it in. Check by getting pupils to come and draw the clocks on the board.

PB57. Activity 10. *Listen and correct the actions.*
- Tell pupils to open their Pupil's Book at page 57. Focus them on the pictures and elicit some of the actions they can see to review daily routines. Ask a pupil to read the activity instruction and the introductory paragraph aloud and check understanding. Play the CD. Pupils listen and correct. They look at the pictures and say the correct version. They check in pairs. Check with the class. Elicit from pupils if they have any computer games like Kid City. Elicit the names of the games and how they work.

Key: 2 At 8 o'clock Mary got dressed. 3 At 9 o'clock John went to school. 4 At 10 o'clock Jack's parents gave him a present. 5 At 11 o'clock Peter and Sue had a glass of milk. 6 At 12 o'clock Jack bought a ball. 7 At 1 o'clock Mary had lunch. 8 At 2 o'clock Mary caught a bus. 9 At 3 o'clock Sue read a book. 10 At 4 o'clock Peter took off his sweater. 11 At 5 o'clock Mary put on her shoes. 12 At 6 o'clock Peter went to the cinema.

CD 2, 27
1. At 7 o'clock John got dressed.
2. At 8 o'clock Mary got up.
3. At 9 o'clock John went to the cinema.
4. At 10 o'clock Jack's parents gave him an apple.
5. At 11 o'clock Peter and Sue had lunch.
6. At 12 o'clock Jack caught a ball.
7. At 1 o'clock Mary had breakfast.
8. At 2 o'clock Mary bought a bus.
9. At 3 o'clock Sue read a comic.
10. At 4 o'clock Peter took off his shoes.
11. At 5 o'clock Mary put on her sweater.
12. At 6 o'clock Peter went shopping.

PB57. Activity 11. *Look at the pictures. Ask and answer.*
- Focus pupils on the Activity 11 instructions and check understanding. Elicit one or two questions and answers for practice. Make pairs. One pupil asks five questions about different activities and the other answers, as in the example. Pupils change roles.

PB57. Activity 12. *Write sentences about your day yesterday. Tell your friend.*
- Focus pupils on Activity 12. Check they have read and understand the instructions. Elicit one or two sentences. Remind them to use the past simple and the time. Monitor and check / help where necessary. In pairs, pupils take turns to read their sentences. They listen for: a) activities which were the same, and b) times which were the same. Elicit from pairs.

AB57. Activity 7. *Answer the questions.*
- Tell pupils to open their Activity Book at page 57. Check they have read and understand the activity instruction. Check understanding of *delete apps*. Pupils work individually, checking in pairs if they need to. They read the texts and answer the questions (they just write the numbers). They check in pairs. Check with the class by asking pupils to read the texts aloud and then eliciting the answers from the class.

Key: 2 thirty-nine, 3 twenty-four, 4 forty

AB57. Activity 8. *Match the questions and answers.*
- Focus pupils on the Activity 8 instruction and check understanding, using the example. Pupils work individually and match the questions with the answers. They check in pairs. Check using open pairs: one pupil reads the question aloud, and another reads the answer. Elicit the strategies pupils used to do the task, e.g. looking for the same verb in the past in the answer, *when* – time, *how many* – number.

Key: 2 d, 3 g, 4 a, 5 f, 6 e, 7 b

Extra activities: see page T116 (if time)

Optional activity
- Extension worksheet 1 from *Kid's Box Teacher's Resource Book 4* (see pages 50 and 53).

Ending the lesson
- Play a clapping game to review the verbs. Say and clap, e.g. (Clap, clap) *get dressed* (clap, clap). Pupils: *Got dressed*. Continue with other verbs from this and the previous lessons. Then pupils take turns to lead.

10 Listen and correct the actions.

Jim's got a new computer game called Kid City. The people in his game do different things every day. Look at what they did yesterday.

At 7 o'clock John got dressed.

No. At 7 o'clock John got up.

yesterday

11 Look at the pictures. Ask and answer.

What time did Mary get dressed?

She got dressed at 8 o'clock.

12 Write sentences about your day yesterday. Tell your friend.

I got up at seven o'clock yesterday.

13 Stella's phonics

Paul caught a short fish.

His daughter bought a small ball.

The fish played with the ball in the water.

14 Make questions. Ask and find your partner.

OBJECTIVES: By the end of the lesson, pupils will be able to identify and say the long vowel sound /ɔː/. They will be aware of the main spellings for the sound and they will have asked and answered questions.

- **TARGET LANGUAGE**

Key language: words with the phoneme /ɔː/ (e.g. c*au*ght, sh*or*t, b*a*ll)
Revision: past simple questions and responses, sentence structure, word families

- **MATERIALS REQUIRED**

Photocopiable 6b (page T103), photocopied twice onto thin card and cut into separate cards. There must be an even number of cards so that every pupil has one card and so that pupils will be able to find their 'pair'.

Warmer

- Write the following words on the board: *door, shorts, water, ball*. Say *Look and think about the spelling and the sounds. What do they all have in common?* Give pupils time to think and discuss in pairs.
- Elicit / explain that the words all have the long vowel sound /ɔː/. Underline this sound (d*oo*r, sh*or*ts, w*a*ter, b*a*ll). Say the words. Pupils repeat.

PB58. ACTIVITY 13. *Stella's phonics*

- Tell pupils to open their Pupil's Book at page 58. Elicit what they can see (a man called Paul, his daughter, a short fish, a small ball). Tell pupils to point the first time they listen and to say the sentences quietly. Check comprehension of *caught* and *bought* (elicit the infinitives *catch* and *buy*).
- Play the CD. Pupils point and quietly repeat. Play the CD again, pausing for pupils to repeat.

Note: Sometimes the letters *or* are pronounced /ɜː/ (e.g. *work, word, world*). Rhyming words can be used as a strategy for remembering the pronunciation of words which are spelt differently but have the same sound.

CD 2, 28

STELLA: Hi, I'm Stella! Repeat after me!
/ɔː/, /ɔː/, Paul
/ɔː/, /ɔː/, daughter
Paul caught a short fish.
Paul caught a short fish.
His daughter bought a small ball.
His daughter bought a small ball.
The fish played with the ball in the water.
The fish played with the ball in the water.

Paul caught a short fish.
His daughter bought a small ball.
The fish played with the ball in the water.

Photocopiable 6b (see pages T91, T103 and the notes below)

PB58. ACTIVITY 14. *Make questions. Ask and find your partner.*

- Tell pupils today's communication activity is about things they did yesterday morning. Write examples on the board, e.g. *I got up at eight o'clock. I didn't have a shower before breakfast.* Elicit questions to check (*What time did you get up? Did you have a shower before breakfast?*).
- Hand each pupil a card from Photocopiable 6b (page T103). Tell pupils they need to walk around, asking the other pupils about the activities on their cards, to find the pupil who has exactly the same card as them. Keep pupils moving around the room and check they're talking, not looking at each other's cards. When pupils find a partner, they come to you to check and then sit down together to talk about what they actually did yesterday morning.

AB58. ACTIVITY 9. *Match the rhyming words. Listen, check and say.*

- Tell pupils to open their Activity Book at page 58. Point out the example answers. Do one or two more matches together as a class if necessary.
- Pupils work in pairs. They match the rest of the words by saying them out loud. Play the CD for pupils to check their answers. Check with the class.

Note: Words that rhyme can have the same spelling (e.g. *sport, short*) or have alternative spellings for the same phoneme (e.g. *water* rhymes with *daughter* and *bought* rhymes with *caught*).

Key: 2 e, 3 a, 4 b, 5 c, 7 j, 8 f, 9 g, 10 h

CD 2, 29

1 sport, short; 2 Paul, small; 3 daughter, water; 4 caught, bought; 5 more, floor; 6 door, four; 7 smaller, taller; 8 walked, talked; 9 call, hall; 10 taught, thought

AB58. ACTIVITY 10. *Make sentences.*

- Focus pupils on Activity 10 and on the example. Check they have read the instruction and know what to do. They work in pairs and make sentences from the grid. Monitor and help / check. Check with the class.

Key: 2 I couldn't use a laptop when I was three. 3 She loves texting her friends. 4 He bought a new computer for his mum. 5 They wanted to email their cousin in India. 6 You chose some apps on the internet.

Joke box

- Focus pupils on the Joke box. Ask a pupil to read the joke to the class. They guess / find the answer. Explain the joke if necessary.

Extra activity: see page T116 (if time)

Ending the lesson

- Make three groups. Groups take turns to say the sentences from the beginning of the lesson. Give instructions, e.g. *quiet, slow, fast, loud*.

OBJECTIVES: By the end of the lesson, pupils will have read a story and reviewed language from the unit.

- **TARGET LANGUAGE**
  Key language: language in the story
  Additional language: *CCTV, row*
  Revision: language from the unit

- **MATERIALS REQUIRED**
  Modern life word cards (irregular past forms) from *Kid's Box Teacher's Resource Book 4* page 85 (you will need to make your own card for *brought*)
  Extra activity 1: A large piece of paper for each group
  Optional: *Kid's Box Teacher's Resource Book 4* Unit 6 Extension worksheet 2 (page 54) and / or animated version of the Unit 6 story from *Kid's Box Interactive DVD 4* (*Suzy's room* section), *Kid's Box Teacher's Resource Book 4* Unit 6 Topic worksheet (page 56)

Warmer

- Review what pupils remember about Nick Motors. Elicit his description and what he did in the last episode. Elicit who else was in the previous episode (Miss Rich) and where they were (at the adventure holiday camp by the sea).

Story

PB59. LOCK AND KEY.

- Tell pupils to open their Pupil's Book at page 59. Focus them on the first picture and elicit who they can see (Lock, Key and Miss Rich) and how they are communicating with each other (via the internet). Ask pupils if they communicate like this with their friends. Set the gist questions: *What happened to Miss Rich? Who wrote the email? Can you name two things Nick Motors took?* Play the CD. Pupils listen and read for what happened. They check in pairs. Check with the class (someone took all the money from her boat; Nick Motors; the money and Lock and Key's boat).
- Play the CD again. Stop after each frame for pupils to repeat. Check general comprehension by asking, e.g. *What was the money for? Where was the money? How can Lock and Key see Nick Motors taking the money? What did Nick Motors say in the email?*

CD 2, 30

As in Pupil's Book

AB59. DO YOU REMEMBER?

- Write *Talking about the past* in the centre of the board. Brainstorm the verbs pupils have learnt in this unit. Use the word cards from the Teacher's Resource Book to review the words (you will need to make a card for *brought*). Write the infinitives on the board – pupils come to the front and choose the correct word card to stick next to each infinitive.

- Tell pupils to open their Activity Books at page 59. Check pupils have read the activity instructions and know what to do. They study the words and spellings on the right in silence. Then they fold the page down the middle so that they can only see the simple infinitives and the lines to write the words on. Without looking, they write the verbs in the past in pencil. They check in pairs, asking, e.g. *What's this one? How do you spell 'thought'?* They don't look at the words on the right. When pupils have finished, they can either correct their own work or swap books and check their partner's.

AB59. CAN DO.

- Focus pupils on the *Can do* section of the page. Say *Let's read the sentences together.* Read the first sentence. Elicit what this means with examples and elicit / remind pupils of the activities they did in this unit when they wrote 'technology' words. Repeat for the second sentence, eliciting / reminding pupils about when they learnt to talk about computers and the internet. Repeat for the third sentence, eliciting / reminding them of when they talked about the past, e.g. activities they did yesterday and the communication activity. Review what the three faces mean (not very well / OK / very well). Remind pupils they circle the one they think is true for them. Pupils circle the appropriate face.
- Say *Now show and tell your friends.* Pupils work in groups of three and take turns to show their work for / talk about each one.

Extra activities: see page T116 (if time)

Optional activities

- Unit 6 Extension worksheet 2 from *Teacher's Resource Book 4* (pages 50 and 54).
- The animated version of the story from *Kid's Box Interactive DVD 4* (*Suzy's room* section). See pages 38–45 of the Teacher's Booklet for the Interactive DVD.
- Unit 6 Topic worksheet from *Teacher's Resource Book 4* (pages 50 and 56).

Ending the lesson

- Ask pupils which chant / song they'd like to do again from the unit. Do it together to end the lesson.

Technology | Robots

> **Fact**
> The first humanoid robot was designed by Leonardo da Vinci, in 1495.

1 Read and match.

a

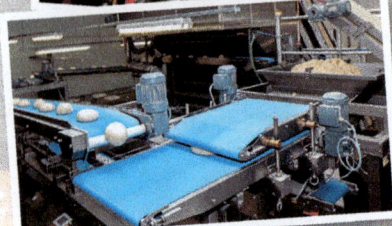

b

c

1
At home we have a lot of machines. There are machines which clean the floor, wash and dry our clothes and wash the plates. In the kitchen there are machines which can make our breakfast, lunch and dinner. Some people call these machines kitchen robots, but what is a robot?

2
A robot is a machine which makes work easier for humans. They do jobs which humans can't do because they are very difficult or dangerous. Robots can explore places where humans can't go. They can go where there are dangerous gases or high temperatures: underground, underwater or in space.

3
Robots are very important because they make, build and fix things. It's easier for robots to work in factories because they can do the same job again and again and it isn't boring for them. Robots don't need money or holidays. They are never ill or tired, but they can't think. Robots can only do what humans program them to do.

2  Listen and say 'yes' or 'no'.

OBJECTIVES: By the end of the lesson, pupils will have read and listened to facts about robots.

● TARGET LANGUAGE
Key language: *design (was designed by)*, *machine*, *gas*, *build*, *fix*, *underground*, *factories*, *again and again*, *program* (v)
Additional language: *humanoid*
Revision: *technology*, *robot*, household chores (e.g. *clean the floor*, *wash the plates*), *explore*, *temperature*, adjectives, relative clauses with *which*

● MATERIALS REQUIRED
Optional: *Kid's Box Interactive DVD 4: The living room* 'Old and new technology' episode

Warmer
- Write the word *robot* on the board and draw a simple robot with a head, body, arms and legs. Ask pupils to explain in L1 what a robot is. Ask if a robot always looks like the one in your picture (try to elicit that there are many types of robots which do different tasks). Tell pupils they will be learning more about the robots all around us in today's lesson.

PB60. FACT
- Tell pupils to open their Pupil's Book at page 60. Focus them on the title of the lesson and on the Fact box. Remind them of your drawing of a robot from the Warmer. Explain that robots which look like people are called *humanoid* robots. Ask a pupil to read the fact to the class (make sure he / she pronounces the date correctly: *Fourteen ninety-five*). Check comprehension of *design*, *build* and *fix*. Elicit other things Leonardo da Vinci is famous for (e.g. painting the Mona Lisa, designing flying machines, making sculptures) and where he was from (Italy).

PB60. ACTIVITY 1. *Read and match.*
- Focus on Activity 1 and the activity instruction. Tell pupils not to worry about new words in the texts, but just to read and match each one with the correct photograph.
- Pupils read and match individually and then compare answers in pairs. Check with the class. Read the texts again and explain / elicit the meaning of new words (e.g. *machine*, *gas*, *underground*, *factories*, *again and again*, *program*). Ask pupils *What kind of things do you think robots make?* (cars, televisions, computers, cameras, food like bread, chocolate and cakes for us to buy in the supermarket). Give / elicit examples of exploration recently carried out by robots (e.g. the NASA mission to explore Mars by robots Opportunity and Curiosity).

Key: 1 b, 2 c, 3 a

PB60. ACTIVITY 2. *Listen and say 'yes' or 'no'.*
- Focus pupils on Activity 2 and on the activity instruction. Check they understand what to do. Remind them to whisper *yes* or *no* to their partner the first time they listen. Play the first one as an example. Play the rest of the CD. Pupils listen and whisper. Play the CD again. Check after each one. Pupils correct the incorrect sentences.

Key: 1 No. 2 Yes. 3 No. 4 Yes. 5 Yes. 6 No. 7 Yes. 8 No.

CD 2, 31
1. At home we have machines which wash our hair.
2. There are machines which can dry our clothes.
3. Machines which can make our dinner are called bathroom robots.
4. A robot is a machine which makes work easier for humans.
5. Robots do jobs which are difficult or dangerous.
6. Robots get money for working in a factory.
7. Robots don't need holidays.
8. Robots can think.

AB60. ACTIVITY 1. *Read and match. Write the sentences.*
- Tell pupils to open their Activity Book at page 60. Focus them on the photographs and the sentences below. Direct them to the activity. Elicit what they have to do (label the photographs with the correct sentences). Pupils work individually. They check in pairs. Monitor and check.

Key: a 4 Robots can do jobs in the house for us. b 3 Robots can help us to explore space. c 2 Robots build things in factories. d 1 Robots can work underground.

AB60. ACTIVITY 2. *Read and correct.*
- Focus pupils on Activity 2 and on the activity instruction. Check pupils know what to do, using the example. Pupils correct the sentences and then compare answers with a partner. Check with the class, referring to the texts in the Pupil's Book.

Key: 2 Robots can do jobs which are dangerous. 3 Robots can move around the house. 4 It's easier for robots to work in factories. 5 Robots can fix things. 6 Robots are never ill or tired.

Extra activities: see page T116 (if time)

Optional activity
- 'Old and new technology' episode from *Kid's Box Interactive DVD 4* (*The living room* section). See pages 20–23 of the Teacher's Booklet for the Interactive DVD.

Ending the lesson
- Review with pupils what they learnt about in today's lesson. Ask them which things they didn't know about robots.

OBJECTIVES: By the end of the lesson, pupils will have read about how robots work and completed a project.

- **TARGET LANGUAGE**
Key language: *human, part, computer program, sensor*
Additional language: *tell* (someone) *what to do*
Revision: parts of the body, *bodies, have got, camera*

- **MATERIALS REQUIRED**
Project: One large sheet of paper per pupil, drawing and colouring materials

Warmer
- Review with pupils what they read and talked about in the previous lesson. Elicit what they remember about what robots can do.

PB61. ACTIVITY 3. *Read and match. Answer the questions.*
- Tell pupils to open their Pupil's Book at page 61. Remind them not to worry about new vocabulary, but to use key words to help them match. Pupils work individually and then compare in pairs. Check as a class and elicit translations of new vocabulary (e.g. *human, sensor*).

Key: 1 c, 2 b, 3 a

- Check comprehension of the four questions. Pupils read the texts again and answer in their notebooks. They check with a partner. Elicit answers.

Key: 1 Three. 2 The computer program. 3 Arms and legs. 4 Sensors.

PB61. PROJECT. *Design a robot.*
- Focus pupils on the photographs. Direct them to the instruction and review the meaning of *design*. Tell pupils to think about what they want their robot to do and which parts it will need.
- Pupils discuss their ideas in pairs and then design their robot individually. They draw a picture and make notes. Monitor and help with new language. Pupils write about their robot in their notebooks, using *it* (*It's called … It's got …* , etc.). Circulate and check. Pupils copy out their corrected writing and stick it below their picture. Display their work.

AB61. ACTIVITY 1. MOVERS LISTENING, PART 3
Where did Charlie go with these people? Listen and write a letter in each box. There is one example. [M] *towards*
- Tell pupils to open their Activity Book at page 61. Elicit what the boy is doing in each picture. Check that pupils know what to do. Play the CD. Pupils complete the activity individually. They compare answers in pairs. Play the CD again. Check with the class.

Key: 1 Aunt Daisy – F; 2 Grandma – D; 3 Fred – E; 4 Dad – A; 5 Lily – C

CD 2, 32

What did you do last week, Charlie?
It was a holiday and there was no school. I went to lots of different places. It was fun.
Did you go to see the new aliens film at the cinema?
Yes. I went there with my mum. It was very good but a bit scary.
Can you see the letter H? Now you listen and write the letter in the box.
1.
I went shopping with Aunt Daisy, too.
Really? What did you buy?
She bought me some new football boots.
Where did you buy them?
In the new sports shop.
2.
Did you see your Grandma last week?
Yes. She took me to the library. We got some books about animals there.
Do you like reading books about animals?
Yes. Penguins are my favourite.
I like them, too. They're funny.
3.
Did you go to the park with Fred?
No. The weather wasn't nice. We went to the swimming pool.
Did you have a nice time?
Yes. It was brilliant.
4.
I went to a farm on Saturday.
Who did you go with?
Dad. It was really cool. I played with some of the animals.
Which ones?
The puppies and the kittens. I liked them best.
5.
Where did you go with your sister Lily?
I went to the supermarket with her. We bought some nice food for lunch.
What did you buy?
We bought some noodles and meatballs. And we got a milkshake too.
Were you very hungry?
Yes, we were!
Now listen again.

Extra activities: see page T116 (if time)

Ending the lesson
- Review with pupils what they did in today's lesson and which activities they liked best from this and the previous lesson and why.

3 Read and match. Answer the questions.

  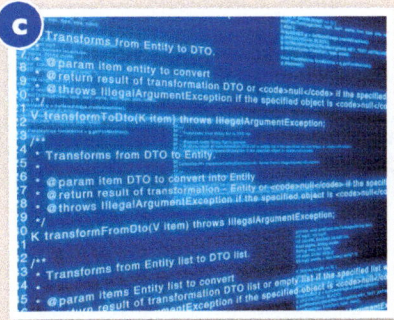

Robots aren't the same as humans. They haven't got bodies like ours, but they have got three important parts.
1. They've got a computer program. This tells the robot what to do.
2. They've sometimes got legs which can make the robot move along the floor.
3. They've got sensors. The sensors help the robot to 'see' and to know where things are. The sensors are sometimes cameras.

1. How many important parts have robots got?
2. What tells the robot what to do?
3. What can make the robot move?
4. What helps the robot know where things are?
5. Where can the robot move?

 Design a robot.

Review Units 5 and 6

1. Play the game. What did they do yesterday?

Instructions
1. Roll the dice and go around the board.
2. Say what each person did yesterday.
3. If your sentence is correct, stay where you are.
4. If your sentence is wrong, go back to where you were.

OBJECTIVES: By the end of the lesson, pupils will have reviewed language from Units 5 and 6 and played a game.

- **TARGET LANGUAGE**

Key language: vocabulary and language from Units 5 and 6, *stay where you are, go back to where you were*
Revision: language for games

- **MATERIALS REQUIRED**

Warmer: Key past tense forms from Units 5 and 6 written on pieces of paper (one for each pupil) or word cards from *Kid's Box Teacher's Resource Book 4* pages 84 and 85
Dice and four different coloured counters for each group of four pupils
Photocopiable Review 5 and 6 (page T104)

Warmer

- Hand out pieces of paper with key past tense verbs from Units 5 and 6 or use word cards (one for each pupil). Make groups of six. Pupils take turns to say what their word is and to give a sentence including their word. The other pupils in the group decide if it's correct or not. Monitor and help as necessary. Elicit an example sentence for each word.

PB62. ACTIVITY 1. *Play the game. What did they do yesterday?*

- Pupils open their Pupil's Book at page 62. Elicit what they can see (a board game). Ask pupils to read the instructions aloud in turn and check understanding of *stay where you are, go back to where you were*. Remind them of the language for games before they start, e.g. *It's your turn. It's my turn. Pass the dice. I'm blue.* Pupils play the game in groups of four. The player in each group who reaches the Finish first is the winner. If time, make new groups and pupils can play the game again.

Key: 2 She drank a glass of orange juice. 3 She made her bed. 5 She said 'Hello'. 7 He put on his shirt / got dressed. 8 He did his homework. 9 He took off his sweater. 11 He flew a kite. 13 She ate a banana. 14 She went to the cinema. 16 She bought some bread. 19 He put on his shoes. 21 She took a photo. 23 He went to the library. 25 He caught a ball. 27 He had a shower. 29 She read a book. 30 She found some money. 32 He made a cake. 34 She worked on the computer. 37 He ate / had his breakfast.

Photocopiable Review 5 and 6 (see pages T91 and T104)

AB62. ACTIVITY 1. *What can you see? Tick the boxes.*

- Tell pupils to open their Activity Book at page 62. Check they have read the activity instructions and know what to do. In pairs, they identify things in the picture, find the word and tick it. Pairs check with pairs. Check with the class.

Key: river, plant, sweater, blanket, glass, comic, beard, bottle, CD, dog, sun, picnic, rock, leaves, moustache, rabbit, grown-up, banana

AB62. ACTIVITY 2. *What can't you see? Write the words.*

- Pupils write the words of the other things they can't see in Activity 1. Monitor and check as they are working.

Key: moon, orange, cage, road, parrot, toothbrush, email

AB62. ACTIVITY 3. *Find the word. Use the first letters from Activity 2.*

- Pupils write the first letter of each word from Activity 2 to work out the new word. Check with the class.

Key: computer

Extra activities: see page T117 (if time)

Ending the lesson

- Do a spelling chant to review some of the words from the units, e.g.

Teacher:	*Give me an e*	Pupils:	e
	Give me an m		m
	Give me an a		a
	Give me an i		i
	Give me an l		l
	What does that spell?		Email!

Pupils take turns to be the callers.

OBJECTIVES: By the end of the lesson, pupils will have reviewed language from Units 5 and 6.

● **TARGET LANGUAGE**
Key language: vocabulary and language from Units 5 and 6
Revision: shopping, word families

● **MATERIALS REQUIRED**
Warmer: Two or three rolled up newspapers
Extra activity 1: Choose ten sentences / questions from Units 5 and 6 which include key vocabulary / grammar. Write each one in scrambled word order on a large piece of paper.
Optional: *Kid's Box Interactive DVD 4: Stella's room* Quiz 3, *Kid's Box 4 Language Portfolio* page 5

Warmer

- Review past simple forms from Units 5 and 6. Write the simple infinitives on the board. Make two or three teams. Pupils line up facing the board. Give a rolled up newspaper to the pupil at the front of each team. Call out the past simple of one of the verbs. The pupils run to hit the correct simple infinitive. The first to do so wins a point for their team. The pupils go to the back of the team. Hand the newspapers to the new pupils at the front and repeat.

PB63. ACTIVITY 2. *Read the story and complete the sentences. Use 1, 2 or 3 words.* [M] towards

- Tell pupils to open their Pupil's Book at page 63. Tell them to read the activity instructions and check understanding. Elicit how many words they should write. Pupils take turns to read the story aloud. In pairs, pupils complete the sentences, deciding on the words to write. Pairs check with pairs. Check with the class by eliciting the different possibilities.

Key (suggested answers): 2 a burger, 3 sister, 4 a new bike, 5 Jill's, 6 red, 7 on the bus

PB63. QUIZ!

- Say *Now let's read and remember*. Focus pupils on the questions. They look back through Units 5 and 6 to find the answers. They discuss them in groups of four. Check with the class.

Key: 1 It went down under the ice and water. 2 Cousteau is more famous. 3 The Lakeside Restaurant. 4 A mouse. 5 A KBX4. 6 An email.

AB63. ACTIVITY 4. *Circle the odd one out.* [M] towards

- Tell pupils to open their Activity Book at page 63. Direct them to the Activity 4 instruction and the example answer. Elicit why *sailed* is different (the rest are irregular past forms). Pupils work in pairs. Monitor and help / guide, but encourage them to work out the answers. Check with the class, eliciting the reasons.

Key: 2 ticket, 3 plant, 4 quickly, 5 bounced, 6 bears, 7 cave, 8 liked, 9 evening, 10 where, 11 weather, 12 know

AB63. ACTIVITY 5. *Now complete the crossword. Write the message.*

- Focus pupils on the crossword and on the activity instruction. Remind them to fit the words from Activity 4 into the crossword, depending on the length of the words and the letters in the grid. Pupils work in pairs and try to complete the crossword. Monitor to help and support.
- Focus pupils on the second part of the activity. Pupils transfer the letters in the shaded squares to find the message. Check the message with the class (*Save the world!*).

Key:

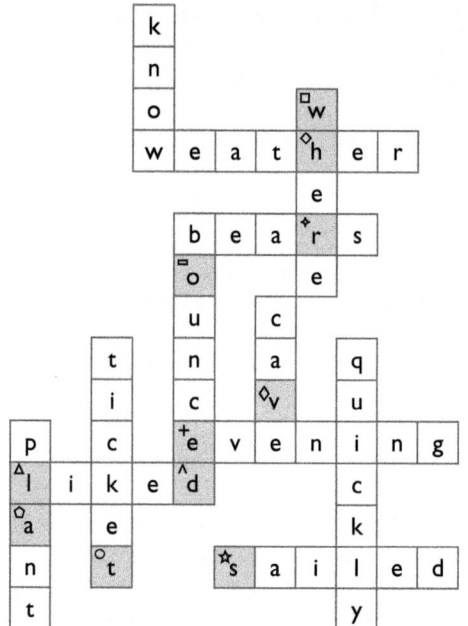

Extra activities: see page T117 (if time)

Optional evaluation

- Quiz 3 from *Kid's Box Interactive DVD 4* (*Stella's room* section). This quiz can be done as a whole-class activity or as a team competition. See pages 36 and 37 of the Teacher's Booklet for the Interactive DVD.

Language Portfolio

- Pupils complete page 5 of *Kid's Box 4 Language Portfolio* (*I can ... Units 5–6*).

Ending the lesson

- Pupils work in groups of four. They need one *Do you remember?* between three. Two pupils (A) use a book (or paper) to cover the words from Unit 5. The other two pupils (B) take turns to say what each word is and to spell the word. 'A's look and check. They reverse roles for Unit 6.
- Talk about the *Can do* statements from Units 5 and 6 with pupils and elicit examples from volunteer pupils for each one.

2 Read the story and complete the sentences. Use 1, 2 or 3 words.

Shopping trip

Last Wednesday Alex went shopping with his mother, Pat. They went to town by bus and had a burger in a café before they went to the shops. Alex's mum wanted to buy a new bike for his younger sister, Jill. It was her birthday on Friday. The name of the toyshop was Pete's Toys. They bought Jill a new red bike and took it home on the bus.

1 Alex and ___his___ ___mother___ went shopping last Wednesday.
2 They ate _____ _____ in a café.
3 Jill is Alex's _____.
4 They bought Jill _____ _____ _____.
5 On Friday it was _____ birthday.
6 Jill's bike was _____.
7 They went home _____ _____ _____.

 **Quiz!**
1 How did Shackleton and his men lose their ship?
2 Who is more famous for his work, Cousteau or Shackleton?
3 Where did Nick Motors have dinner?
4 What do you hold in your hand when you use a computer?
5 Which computer did Grandma and Grandpa buy?
6 What did Nick Motors write?

7 At the zoo

1 Look, think and answer.
1. What are Lenny and Stella doing?
2. Who's asking the questions?
3. What's the quiz about?
4. Who do you think is winning?

2 🔊 33 CD2 Listen and check.

3 🔊 34 CD2 Listen and say 'yes' or 'no'.

1 Lenny thinks the most exciting animal is the giraffe.

No.

LOOK

quick	→	the **quickest**
big	→	the **biggest**
exciting	→	the **most exciting**
beautiful	→	the **most beautiful**
good	→	the **best**

OBJECTIVES: By the end of the lesson, pupils will have read and talked about animals, using superlative adjectives.

• TARGET LANGUAGE

Key language: superlative adjectives: *the -est, the most, the best*
Additional language: *Now tell us about ... , Let's hear it ... , Five points for each fact*
Revision: animals, prepositions, adjectives, size, weight, distance, questions, family, *can / can't*

• MATERIALS REQUIRED

Extra activity 1: Reference materials with facts about wild animals
Optional: *Kid's Box Teacher's Resource Book 4* Unit 7 Reinforcement worksheet 1 (page 58)

Warmer

- Write *At the zoo* in the centre of the board and brainstorm animals you can see at a zoo.

PB64. ACTIVITY 1. *Look, think and answer.*

- Tell pupils to open their Pupil's Book at page 64. Focus on the picture. Ask if they can see any animals from the Warmer. Elicit who pupils can see and where they are. Pupils read the questions and discuss them in pairs.

PB64. ACTIVITY 2. *Listen and check.*

- Play the CD. Pupils listen and check.
- Elicit complete sentences. Play the CD again and ask checking questions with superlatives, e.g. *Which animal does Lenny think is the most exciting? Which animal does Stella think is the most beautiful?* Write the superlatives from the listening on the board in three columns: one syllable with *the + -est*, two syllables with *the + -est*, longer adjectives with *the most + adjective*. Elicit examples for each column. Focus pupils on the Look box. Also present *the heaviest* (-y ending) and *the best* (irregular).

Key: 1 They are in a quiz (at school). 2 Mr Burke is asking the questions. 3 The quiz is about animals. 4 Stella is winning.

CD 2, 33

MR BURKE: Welcome to the Kid's Box Quiz. Let's hear it for these two clever kids in today's big final: Lenny and Stella.
LENNY AND STELLA: Hello, Mr Burke.
MR BURKE: Look at the animals on the wall behind me. Lenny, which do you think is the most exciting?
LENNY: Er, I think the most exciting animal is the tiger.
MR BURKE: Great. Now tell us about tigers. You get five points for each fact.
LENNY: Well, the Siberian tiger's the biggest and the strongest animal in the cat family. It's not the quickest cat, but it can run at 55 km an hour. The heaviest Siberian tiger weighed 465 kilograms.
MR BURKE: Very good. That's 15 points. Now, Stella, which animal do you think is the most beautiful, and what can you tell us about it?
STELLA: I think the most beautiful animal is the dolphin. It's one of the cleverest animals and I also think dolphins are the best parents – they look after their young for more than three years ... Erm ... oh, yes, and do you know that dolphins can't drink sea water? They have to get water from their food.
MR BURKE: Very good, Stella. That gives you 15 points. Now, put your hands on the buttons. The quickest person to press the button and answer the question correctly gets five points. Which animal is the loudest in the world?
LENNY: Is it the elephant?
MR BURKE: Sorry, Lenny. It isn't.
STELLA: Is it the blue whale?
MR BURKE: Yes, that's right, Stella. Five points for you. The blue whale is the loudest animal in the world. And now for my next question ...

PB64. ACTIVITY 3. *Listen and say 'yes' or 'no'.*

- Focus pupils on Activity 3. Play the CD. Pupils listen and whisper the answers to a partner. Play the CD again. Check with the class.

Key: 2 Yes, 3 No, 4 Yes, 5 Yes, 6 No.

CD 2, 34

1. Lenny thinks the most exciting animal is the giraffe.
2. The Siberian tiger is the biggest animal in the cat family.
3. The Siberian tiger is the quickest cat.
4. Stella thinks the most beautiful animal is the dolphin.
5. Stella thinks the dolphin is the best parent.
6. The elephant is the loudest animal in the world.

AB64. ACTIVITY 1. *Make sentences.*

- Tell pupils to open their Activity Book at page 64. Focus them on Activity 1. Pupils write the sentences. Elicit, check and discuss with the class.

Key: 2 The dolphin can't drink sea water. 3 Penguins live in Antarctica. 4 The blue whale is the loudest animal in the world. 5 The parrot lives in the forest.

AB64. ACTIVITY 2. *Complete the text about the giraffe family.*

- Focus pupils on Activity 2 and establish that it's a giraffe family. Pupils work individually to complete the text. Pupils compare their texts in pairs.

Key: Father, Sister, grandfather, mother, Brother

Extra activities: see page T117 (if time)

Optional activity

- Unit 7 Reinforcement worksheet 1 from *Teacher's Resource Book 4* (pages 57–58).

Ending the lesson

- Call out adjectives from the lesson. Pupils provide the superlative (including *the*).

OBJECTIVES: By the end of the lesson, pupils will have had more practice talking and writing about animals, using superlative adjectives.

● TARGET LANGUAGE
Key language: superlative adjectives: *the -est* and *the most*
Additional language: *blog, kilometres an hour, the second cleverest*
Revision: wild animals, adjectives, definitions, *centimetre*

● MATERIALS REQUIRED
Photocopiable 7 (page T105). One copy for each pupil, copied onto thin card, scissors. One set of cards for demonstration.
Optional: *Kid's Box Teacher's Resource Book 4* Reinforcement worksheet 2 and / or Extension worksheet 1 (pages 59 and 60)

Warmer
- Review the comparative and superlative adjectives from the previous lesson, using a drill. Pupils stand up. Say the simple adjective, e.g. *Clever*. Pupils say in chorus *Cleverer, the cleverest*. Pupils can also take turns to call out simple adjectives.

PB65. ACTIVITY 4. *Read and correct.*
- Tell pupils to open their Pupil's Book at page 65. Focus on the blog and elicit what it is. Teach / check comprehension of *blog*. Elicit the names of the animals in the photographs. Make sure pupils know what to do. They read the text and then correct the sentences individually. They compare answers in pairs. Check with the class.

Key: 1 Blue whales are the biggest animals. 2 Blue whales are the loudest animals. 3 One of the smallest animals in the world is a lizard. 4 The quickest animal is a bird. 5 Dolphins are the second cleverest animals. 6 Fred thinks tigers are the most exciting animals.

PB65. ACTIVITY 5. *What do you think? Write sentences.*
- Focus on Activity 5 and on the pictures. Elicit the animals pupils can see and what they look like. Focus them on the example sentence to demonstrate the activity and remind them to use the words in the box in the superlative. Make sure they know they have to write about their opinions. Discuss as a class before pupils write in their notebooks. Monitor and check language. Pupils share their opinions with the class.

Photocopiable 7 (see pages T91 and T105)

AB65. ACTIVITY 3. *Which animal is it?* [M] *towards*
- Tell pupils to open their Activity Book at page 65. Focus them on the Activity 3 instruction and check understanding. Elicit that these are called *definitions*. Check pupils know what to do, using the example. They read and complete individually and then check in pairs. Check with the class.

Key: 2 elephant, 3 parrot, 4 monkey, 5 crocodile, 6 tiger

AB65. ACTIVITY 4. *Ask questions and write the answers.*
- Focus pupils on Activity 4. Check they have read the activity instruction and check understanding. Pupils move around the class, asking four friends about their family and writing the answers in the grid. They then compare their answers in groups of five. Elicit whole-sentence answers from different groups and discuss.

Extra activity: see page T117 (if time)

Optional activity
- Unit 7 Reinforcement worksheet 2 and / or Extension worksheet 1 from *Teacher's Resource Book 4* (pages 57, 59 and 60).

Ending the lesson
- Give pupils one minute to think of a definition like those in Activity Book Activity 3. They take turns to say their definitions to the class for other pupils to guess the animal.

4 Read and correct.

Animals are one of the most interesting things to watch and study. A lot of people think that elephants are the biggest animals in the world, but the biggest animals are blue whales. They're the longest, biggest and the loudest of all animals. They're louder than planes.

One of the smallest animals in the world is a lizard. It's between one and two centimetres long. The quickest animal is a bird which can fly at more than three hundred kilometres an hour.

The cleverest animals are humans, that's us! Some people think that monkeys are the second cleverest, but they aren't. Dolphins are cleverer than monkeys.

My favourite animals are tigers. I think they're the most exciting and most beautiful animals.

Fred's Blog

1 Kangaroos are the biggest animals.
2 Bears are the loudest animals.
3 One of the smallest animals in the world is a rabbit.
4 The quickest animals are lizards.
5 Monkeys are the second cleverest animals.
6 Fred thinks pandas are the most exciting animals.

5 What do you think? Write sentences.

> beautiful   exciting   boring   clever   ugly   dangerous

I think the rabbit is the most boring animal here.

6 Look, think and answer.
1 Where did the children go?
2 Who did Suzy give her picture to?
3 What animals did they feed?
4 Which animal did Simon like the best?

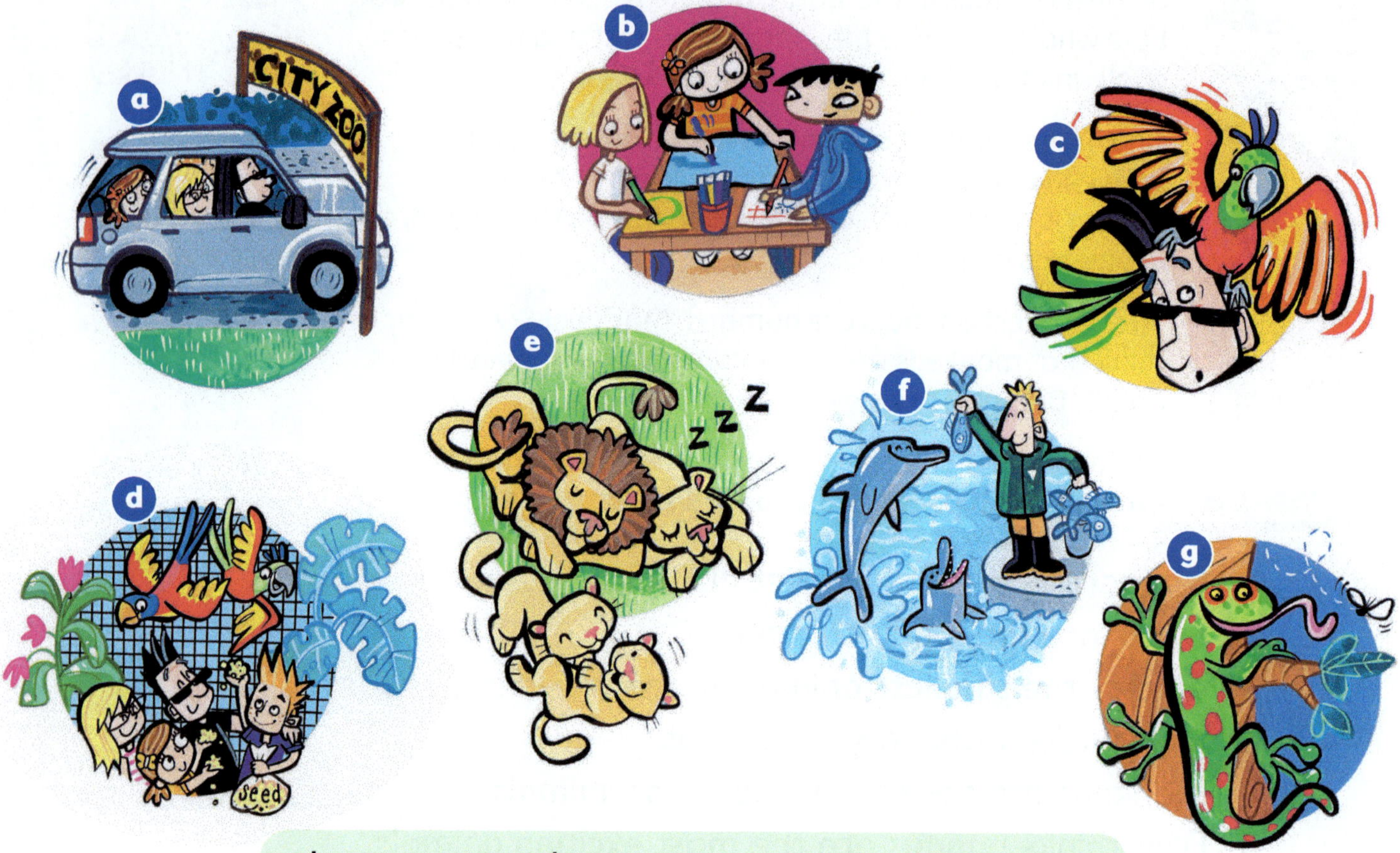

drew   came   drove   saw   swam   slept   went
flew   bought   sat   caught   ate   ran   fed

7 Listen and check.

8 Listen and say the letter.

1 Mr Star drove the children to the zoo.

a

LOOK
What **did** he **buy**?
He **bought** a toy parrot.
He **didn't buy** an ice cream.

OBJECTIVES: By the end of the lesson, pupils will have had practice using the past simple to describe events.

- **TARGET LANGUAGE**
Key language: past simple irregular: *drew, drove, ran, caught, flew, sat, slept, swam*; prepositions: *into, round, out of*; *puppies, kittens, cubs, the best*
Additional language: other baby animals
Revision: past simple, animals, *cage, after, before*

- **MATERIALS REQUIRED**
Flashcards 'round' (82), 'into' (87), 'out of' (88)
Extra activity 2: CD of line dance-style music

Warmer
- Ask *Who's got a pet? What pet have you got? How often do you feed your (cat/dog/fish)?* Explain that *feed* means *give food to*. Continue *What did you feed your dog/cat/bird yesterday?* Write *feed* and the past (*fed*) on the board. Say *Imagine a zoo. What did they feed the monkeys?* to elicit *They fed the monkeys bananas*. Continue with *lions, penguins, parrots*, etc. With books closed, tell pupils *Suzy went to the zoo*. Elicit what they think she did / saw. Write some ideas on the board.

PB66. ACTIVITY 6. *Look, think and answer.*
- Tell pupils to open their Pupil's Book at page 66. Focus them on the pictures to check ideas from the Warmer. Check they know what to do. They read the questions and discuss in pairs, using the pictures to help them.

PB66. ACTIVITY 7. *Listen and check.*
- Play the CD. Elicit complete sentences. Play the CD again and focus on the new past verbs in the box, e.g. *Where did Suzy draw the picture? When did Mr Star drive to the zoo? What did the dolphins do? What did the baby lions do? What did their parents do? What did Mr Star buy for Suzy? Why did Simon think the lizard was funny?*

Key: 1 They went to the zoo. 2 She gave her picture to her mum. 3 They saw dolphins, lions, parrots and a lizard. 4 Simon liked the lizard the best.

CD 2, 35

Suzy: Here's a picture for you, Mum. I drew it at the city zoo before we came home.
Simon: Yes, Dad drove us there this morning.
Stella: It was great. We saw the dolphins. They swam round the pool and jumped out of the water to eat fish from a man's hand.
Suzy: Look, it's here in the picture. And we saw some baby lions, Mum. They ran in a big square cage, but their parents slept all day.
Stella: After we saw the lions, we went into the parrots' cage and fed the parrots. Then they flew round our heads.
Suzy: They were the most beautiful animals. Dad bought me a toy parrot. Look, it's over there on the table.
Mrs Star: Mmm!
Simon: A parrot sat on Dad's head. It was really funny, but the lizard was the best. It caught a fly. And ate it for its lunch.

PB66. ACTIVITY 8. *Listen and say the letter.*
- Review / present *round, into* and *out of* using mime and the flashcards. Focus pupils on Activity 8 and on the instruction. Remind them to whisper the letter to their friend the first time. Play the CD. Pupils listen and whisper. Play the CD again. Check with the class.

Key: 2 d, 3 c, 4 f, 5 g, 6 e, 7 b

CD 2, 36

1. Mr Star drove the children to the zoo.
2. The children fed the parrots.
3. One of the parrots sat on Mr Star's head.
4. The dolphins swam round the pool and jumped out of the water to get the fish.
5. A lizard caught a fly.
6. The baby lions ran in their cage, but their parents slept all day.
7. Suzy drew a picture of her day.

AB66. ACTIVITY 5. *Listen and write the letter.*
- Tell pupils to open their Activity Book at page 66. Give pupils time to look at the pictures. Check / pre-teach *kittens, lift, puppies*. Review *asleep* and *awake*. Teach *kittens* and *puppies*. Point to the pictures. *Are the puppies awake or asleep? Are the kittens awake or asleep?* Play the CD. Pupils write the letters. They check in pairs. Play the CD again. Check with the class.

Key: 1 c, 2 d, 3 e, 4 h, 5 f, 6 b, (7 a), 8 g

CD 2, 37

a. The children ran round the playground.
b. The men went into the lift.
c. The kittens played in the round basket.
d. The children walked into school.
e. The old lorry drove round the mountain.
f. The children ran out of school.
g. The men came out of the lift.
h. The puppies slept in the square basket.

AB66. ACTIVITY 6. *Make a wordsearch.*
- Focus pupils on the Activity 6 instruction. Tell them to use the past simple and include new verbs. They write the past in the wordsearch and the infinitives down the side. They fill in the boxes with random letters.

AB66. ACTIVITY 7. *Now look at your friend's wordsearch and find the words. Write three sentences with the words.*
- Make new pairs. Pupils swap their books and find the words. They check in their pairs and work together to write three sentences using the verbs.

Extra activities: see page T117 (if time)

Ending the lesson
- Do a simple narrative-building activity, e.g. Teacher: *I went to the zoo yesterday. First I looked at the penguins.* Pupil 1: *I went to the zoo yesterday. First I looked at the penguins. They were funny.* Pupil 2: *I went to the zoo yesterday. First I looked at the penguins. They were funny. I gave them some fish*, etc.

OBJECTIVES: By the end of the lesson, pupils will have sung a song and written their own verses.

- **TARGET LANGUAGE**

Key language: past simple regular and irregular
Revision: prepositions, animals, adjectives, town, country, have to

- **MATERIALS REQUIRED**

Preposition flashcards (82–92)
Extra activity 1: Write the lines of the song (Pupil's Book Activity 10) on separate pieces of paper. You will need one line for each pupil. If you have more pupils than lines, copy a second set of lines on different coloured paper.
Optional: *Kid's Box Teacher's Resource Book 4* Song worksheet (page 62)

Warmer

- Review prepositions using the flashcards. Focus on the prepositions from the previous lesson (*into, round, out of*) and teach *along*. Teach the following mime to pupils:
  Out of: hands, palms together, in front of stomach rising up above head, separating at the top (like a flower coming out of the earth)
  Into: reverse action of the above. Hands above head separated, bend wrist, fingers pointing down, backs of hands coming together and hands going down towards stomach
  Round: one whole raised arm going round head in rotary movements.
  Along: hands with palms facing each other, moving forwards.

PB67. ACTIVITY 9. *Listen and do the actions.*

- Tell pupils to open their Pupil's Book at page 67. Focus them on the Look box at the bottom of the page and elicit what the dolphin is doing in each diagram and what the prepositions are.
- Focus pupils on the Activity 9 instruction and check understanding (they do the actions from the Warmer). Play the CD, one sentence at a time. They listen and mime the correct preposition. Play the CD again. Pupils mime the action. Elicit the sentence from a pupil / pupils to check.

CD 2, 38

1. The boy ran round the playground.
2. The girl jumped into the sea.
3. The children climbed out of the swimming pool.
4. The bird flew round the tree.
5. The teacher walked into the classroom.
6. The dog ran round the garden.
7. The cat jumped out of the tree.
8. The fish swam round the bowl.
9. Dad walked into the kitchen.
10. The boy jumped out of bed.

PB67. ACTIVITY 10. *Listen and sing.*

- Focus pupils on Activity 10. Play the CD several times for pupils to identify the animals and then to repeat the song in lines, verses and then as a complete song with actions: (elephants) drinking, (parrots) flying, (dolphins) swimming, (monkeys) eating, (children) drawing, (lions) sleeping, (children) seeing. Make six groups (one for each animal, and also including the children, who feature twice). The pupils all sing the song, and the 'animals' / children mime when the song is about them.

CD 2, 39

As in Pupil's Book

CD 2, 39

Now sing the song again. (Karaoke version)

PB67. ACTIVITY 11. *Write another verse for the song.*

- Focus pupils on the structure of the song, and specifically on the rhyme and the repetition, by writing a verse on the board. Look at the example together. Elicit other ideas from pupils and write them on the board. Pupils work in groups of four and write another verse. Monitor and help / support. Confident groups can perform their verses for the class.

AB67. ACTIVITY 8. *What did the animals do? Sort and write the words.*

- Tell pupils to open their Activity Book at page 67. Focus them on the activity instructions and check understanding. Pupils read the sentences and then use the anagrams and pictures to help them work out what the verb is. They check in pairs / groups. Elicit the answers from different pupils, focusing on the verbs and the prepositions.

Key: 2 ran, 3 flew, 4 swam, 5 sat, 6 slept

AB67. ACTIVITY 9. *Complete the sentences. Write 'into', 'out of', 'along' or 'round'.*

- Focus pupils on the Activity 9 instructions and check understanding. They complete the task individually and then check in pairs. Check by asking pairs to read out the sentences with the correct preposition.

Key: 2 round, 3 into, 4 out of, 5 round, 6 along

Extra activities: see page T117 (if time)

Optional activities

- Unit 7 Song worksheet from *Teacher's Resource Book 4* (pages 57 and 62).

Ending the lesson

- Sing the song from the first part of the lesson again, with groups adding the verses they have written.

9  Listen and do the actions.

10 Listen and sing.

The elephants drank, drank, drank,
The parrots flew, flew, flew,
The dolphins swam, swam, swam,
At the zoo, zoo, zoo.

The elephants drank, drank, drank,
The parrots flew, flew, flew,
The dolphins swam, swam, swam,
At the zoo, zoo, zoo.

What did you do,
What did you do,
What did you do,
When you saw, saw, saw them
At the zoo, zoo, zoo?

The monkeys ate, ate, ate,
The children drew, drew, drew,
The lions slept, slept, slept,
At the zoo, zoo, zoo.

The monkeys ate, ate, ate,
The children drew, drew, drew,
The lions slept, slept, slept,
At the zoo, zoo, zoo.

What did you do,
What did you do,
What did you do,
When you saw, saw, saw them
At the zoo, zoo, zoo?

When you saw, saw, saw them
At the zoo, zoo, zoo?

11 Write another verse for the song.

The crocodiles smiled, smiled, smiled,
The giraffes ………, ………, ………,
The tigers ………, ………, ………,
At the zoo, zoo, zoo.

crocodile   giraffe
tiger   panda
snake   bat

smile   dance
jump   laugh
climb   hop

LOOK

 out of    into    round    along

12 🔊 **Stella's phonics**

Sue's a kangaroo at the zoo.

She's looking in her cookbook.

Look! The animals at the zoo love Sue's blue juice!

13 Make questions. Ask and answer.

> Which animal is the loudest?

> I think elephants are the loudest.

| snail shark panda penguin | ugliest slowest most dangerous |
| kangaroo elephant | quickest loudest smallest |

Which animal is the … ?	name 1	name 2	name 3	name 4	name 5	name 6
loudest						
most dangerous						

OBJECTIVES: By the end of the lesson, pupils will be able to identify and say the sounds /ʊ/ and /uː/ in common words. They will recognise that these sounds are spelt in different ways and will learn to use rhyme to help them remember pronunciation. They will also have completed a communication activity.

- **TARGET LANGUAGE**
Key language: words with the phonemes /ʊ/ and /uː/ (e.g. S*ue*, z*oo*, l*ook*, c*ould*)
Additional language: cookbook, What's the past of … ?, zebra crossing
Revision: animals, superlative adjectives, question forms

- **MATERIALS REQUIRED**
Optional: *Kid's Box 4 Language Portfolio* page 12

Warmer
- Write these words on the board: *use, school, blue, shoes, new*. Say *Which sound is in all the words? Think about the sound, not the spelling*. Give pupils time to discuss together. Elicit the answer (the sound /uː/). Underline the sound /uː/ in the words. Say the sound for pupils to repeat. Explain that pupils will be practising this sound and the short vowel sound /ʊ/.

PB68. ACTIVITY 12. *Stella's phonics*
- Tell pupils to open their Pupil's Book at page 68. Elicit what they can see (Sue, a kangaroo, a book, blue juice). Present *cookbook* (a book with recipes in). Play the CD. Pupils repeat. Play the CD again for pupils to join in.
- **Note:** Help your pupils recognise the common spelling patterns for the sound /uː/ (z*oo*, bl*ue*, fl*ew*).
Rhyme is a great help with the /uː/ sound when the spelling is irregular (e.g. *who, do, you, shoe* and *through* all rhyme).

CD 2, 40
STELLA: Hi, I'm Stella! Repeat after me!
/uː/, /uː/, zoo
/ʊ/, /ʊ/, cook
Sue's a kangaroo at the zoo.
Sue's a kangaroo at the zoo.
She's looking in her cookbook.
She's looking in her cookbook.
Look! The animals at the zoo love Sue's blue juice!
Look! The animals at the zoo love Sue's blue juice!

Sue's a kangaroo at the zoo.
She's looking in her cookbook.
Look! The animals at the zoo love Sue's blue juice!

PB68. ACTIVITY 13. *Make questions. Ask and answer.*
- Focus pupils on the animal names, the superlative adjectives and the example question and answer. Remind them to choose their answers from the animals given. Pupils draw a survey sheet in their notebooks, with enough space for answers from six friends (as in the Pupil's Book) and for the six adjectives on the left. They move around, asking their friends and noting the answers. When pupils have finished, make new groups. Pupils discuss and compare their answers. Discuss as a class.

AB68. ACTIVITY 10. *Match the rhyming words. Listen, check and say.*
- Tell pupils to open their Activity Book at page 68. Make sure they understand they need to match the rhyming words which are in columns next to each other. Do one or two more matches together if necessary.
- Pupils work in pairs. They match the rest of the words by saying them out loud. Play the CD for pupils to check their answers. Check with the class.
- **Note:** The two phonemes share a spelling pattern: *oo* as in *book* /bʊk/ and in *room* /ruːm/. The /uː/ sound also has other spelling patterns (*ue* as in *blue*; *ew* as in *flew*), as well as many irregular spellings.

Key: 2 e, 3 b, 4 a, 5 c, 7 j, 8 f, 9 h, 10 g

CD 2, 41
1 school, pool; 2 choose, shoes; 3 zoo, two; 4 took, look; 5 good, could; 6 use, lose; 7 foot, put; 8 flew, blue; 9 moon, balloon; 10 cook, book

AB68. ACTIVITY 11. *Match the questions and answers.*
- Focus pupils on Activity 11. Direct them to the example. Pupils work in pairs. Check with the class in open pairs.

Key: 2 g, 3 e, 4 a, 5 b, 6 f, 7 h, 8 d

AB68. ACTIVITY 12. *Ask and answer.*
- Write the irregular verbs from this and the previous lesson on the board: *see, drink, eat, draw, do, sleep, swim, be, drive, fly*. Ask, e.g. *What's the past of see?* Pupils reply in chorus. Repeat for the other verbs. Practise the question. Pupils then ask and answer in pairs. Monitor and listen for the correct past forms.

Joke box
- Focus pupils on the Joke box. Ask a pupil to read the joke to the class. Translate / define *zebra crossing*. Explain the joke if necessary.

Extra activities: see page T117 (if time)

Language Portfolio
- Pupils complete page 12 of *Kid's Box 4 Language Portfolio* (*A place I like*). Help with new language as necessary.

Ending the lesson
- Pupils repeat the sound sentences from the beginning of the lesson. In pairs, they take turns to say the third sentence (*Look! The animals at the zoo love Sue's blue juice!*) as quickly as they can.

OBJECTIVES: By the end of the lesson, pupils will have read a story and reviewed language from the unit.

● TARGET LANGUAGE
Key language: language in the story
Additional language: *the most wanted*
Revision: language from the unit

● MATERIALS REQUIRED
Preposition flashcards (82–92)
At the zoo word cards from *Kid's Box Teacher's Resource Book 4* page 86 (prepositions)
Optional: *Kid's Box Teacher's Resource Book 4* Unit 7 Extension worksheet 2 (page 61) and / or animated version of the Unit 7 story from *Kid's Box Interactive DVD 4* (*Suzy's room* section)

Warmer
- Write *Nick Motors, Lock, Key* on the board. Ask pupils to give you sentences comparing the characters, using the superlative, e.g. *Nick Motors is the cleverest and the most dangerous.*

Story

PB69. LOCK AND KEY.
- Tell pupils to open their Pupil's Book at page 69. Focus them on the first frame and elicit who's in the poster (Nick Motors). Ask pupils: *What's running round Key's legs?* (a dog) *Whose dog is it?* (Miss Rich's). Ask a pupil to read the first speech bubble aloud and check understanding of *the most wanted*. Set the gist questions: *What did the person from the City Zoo say? What did the man take? Who was the man? What was inside the lorry?*
- Play the CD. Pupils listen and read for what happened. They check in pairs. Check with the class ('Please come quickly. We need your help'; he took one of their lorries; Nick Motors; there was a tiger inside).
- Play the CD again. Pause after each frame for pupils to repeat. Check general comprehension by asking, e.g. *Did Miss Rich have a cat? Where was the lorry when Nick Motors took it? How did Nick Motors get into the zoo? Whose motorbike was it? Did Nick Motors find the tiger? Was he frightened?*

`CD 2, 42`
As in Pupil's Book

AB69. DO YOU REMEMBER?
- Write *Prepositions* in the centre of the board. Elicit the prepositions pupils have learnt / reviewed in this unit using the flashcards and the word cards. Review the meaning of each one, using mime.
- Tell pupils to open their Activity Books at page 69. Check pupils have read the activity instructions and know what to do. They study the words and spellings on the right in silence. Then they fold the page down the middle so that they can only see the pictures and the lines to write the words on. They write the words in pencil. They check in pairs, asking, e.g. *What's this one? How do you spell 'between'?* They don't look at the words on the right. When pupils have finished, they can either correct their own work or swap books and check their partner's.

AB69. CAN DO.
- Focus pupils on the *Can do* section of the page. Say *Let's read the sentences together*. Read the first sentence. Elicit what this means with examples and elicit / remind pupils of the activities they did in this unit when they talked about the past, e.g. the visit to the zoo. Review what the three faces mean (not very well / OK / very well). Remind pupils they circle the one they think is true for them. Repeat for the second sentence, eliciting / reminding them about the prepositions they used to describe where the animals were at the zoo. Pupils circle the appropriate face. Repeat for the third sentence, eliciting / reminding them about the superlatives they used to talk about the animals and about their classmates. Pupils circle the appropriate face.
- Say *Now show and tell your friends*. Pupils work in groups of three and take turns to show their work for / talk about each one.

Extra activities: see pages T117–T118 (if time)

Optional activities
- Unit 7 Extension worksheet 2 from *Teacher's Resource Book 4* (pages 57 and 61).
- The animated version of the Unit 7 story from *Kid's Box Interactive DVD 4* (*Suzy's room* section). See pages 38–45 of the Teacher's Booklet for the Interactive DVD.

Ending the lesson
- Ask pupils which chant / song they'd like to do again from the unit. Do it together to end the lesson.

Science | Skeletons

Fact
Instead of bones, sharks have a skeleton made from cartilage.

1 Look and read. Correct the sentences.

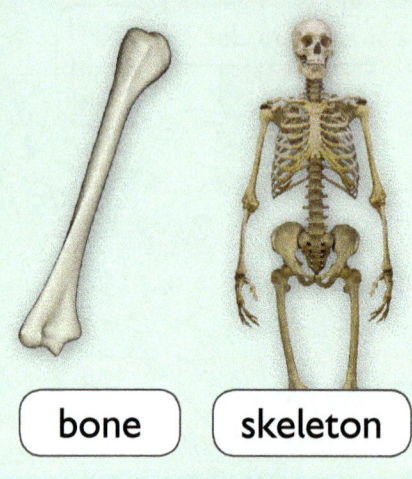

bone | skeleton

There are 206 bones in the human body. More than half of these are in the hands and feet. Bones are about 22 per cent water. The smallest bone in the body is in the ear and the longest bone is in the leg. Most bones have calcium in them. Human skeletons aren't very different from the skeletons of other animals. A human has got the same number of neck bones as a giraffe!

1 There are two hundred bones in the human body.
2 All our bones are in our hands and feet.
3 The smallest bone in our body is in the arm.
4 The shortest bone is in the leg.
5 A human has got the same number of feet bones as a giraffe.

2 Look at the four skeletons. Which animals are they from?

a    b 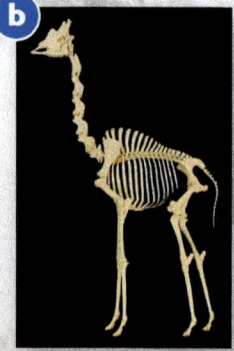   c 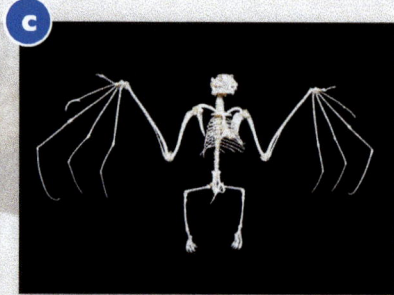   d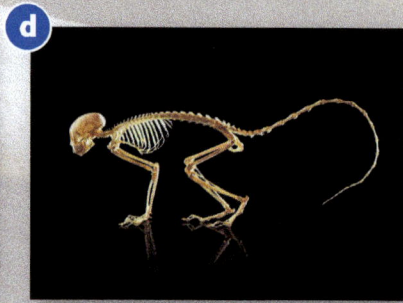

3 Read and match the animals to the skeletons.
1 This animal's got very long, strong wings to help it fly quickly.
2 This animal's got long arms and legs to climb trees in the jungle.
3 This animal's got a very long tail to help it stand up.
4 This animal's got very long neck bones to eat leaves from high trees.

OBJECTIVES: By the end of the lesson, pupils will have read about animal and human skeletons.

● TARGET LANGUAGE
Key language: *skeleton, bone, per cent, calcium*
Additional language: *cartilage*
Revision: parts of the body, animals, numbers, superlative adjectives, *human, half*

● MATERIALS REQUIRED
Pictures of wild animals including a kangaroo, a giraffe, a bat and a monkey

Warmer
- Review parts of the body, including those featured in the lesson (*hands, feet, ear, leg, neck, arm*). Give instructions for pupils to follow, e.g. *Show me your hands. Shake your head. Point to your neck. Stamp your feet.*
- Tell pupils to open their Pupil's Book at page 70. Focus on the lesson title and use the photographs in Activity 1 to teach *bone* and *skeleton*. Tell pupils they will learn about human and animal skeletons in this lesson. Ask what they already know about skeletons. Pupils reply in L1. Do not confirm ideas at this stage.

PB70. FACT
- Focus pupils on the Fact box. Ask a pupil to read the fact to the class. Check comprehension of *cartilage*. Elicit in L1 why it might be useful for a shark to have cartilage instead of bone (the cartilage is lighter than bone and it helps them to control their position in the water).

PB70. ACTIVITY 1. *Look and read. Correct the sentences.*
- Focus pupils on Activity 1. Read the activity instructions. Go through sentences 1 to 5 and make sure pupils know the meaning of key language, such as *human*. They read the text individually and correct the sentences in pairs. Check answers as a class and ask pairs to read out their correct sentences. Explain / elicit the meaning of *half, per cent* and *calcium*. Ask pupils which is the most surprising thing they learnt from the text.

Key: 1 There are two hundred and six bones in the human body. 2 More than half of our bones are in our hands and feet. 3 The smallest bone in our body is in the ear. 4 The longest bone is in the leg. 5 A human has got the same number of neck bones as a giraffe.

PB70. ACTIVITY 2. *Look at the four skeletons. Which animals are they from?*
- Focus pupils on Activity 2 and on the photographs. Stick the pictures of wild animals you have brought to class on the board. Pupils work in pairs. They try to identify each animal skeleton by choosing one of the animals on the board. Check with the class.

Key: a kangaroo, b giraffe, c bat, d monkey

PB70. ACTIVITY 3. *Read and match the animals to the skeletons.*
- Focus pupils on Activity 3. Tell them that each sentence is about one of the animals in Activity 2. Pupils work in pairs. They read the sentences and match them with the photographs. Pairs check with pairs. Check with the class. Check understanding of *tail* and *jungle*.

Key: 1 bat (c), 2 monkey (d), 3 kangaroo (a), 4 giraffe (b)

AB70. ACTIVITY 1. *Match. Write the word.*
- Tell pupils to open their Activity Book at page 70. Focus them on the activity instruction and the example answer. Pupils work individually and write the words in pencil. They check in pairs. Check around the class.

Key: 2 whale, 3 bear, 4 horse, 5 rabbit, 6 bat

AB70. ACTIVITY 2. *Write the sentences in order.*
- Focus pupils on Activity 2. Check they understand what to do, using the example. They work individually and write the other sentences in the correct order. They check in pairs by taking turns to read their sentences aloud to each other. Check with the class in the same way.

Key: 2 Some monkeys have got long arms and legs. 3 A crocodile's strong tail helps it to swim. 4 A skeleton is all an animal's bones together. 5 Crocodiles have got big eyes on the top of their heads. 6 The longest bone in the human skeleton is in the leg.

Extra activities: see page T118 (if time)

Ending the lesson
- Review and discuss with pupils what they learnt about in today's lesson.

OBJECTIVES: By the end of the lesson, pupils will have read about the adaptation of animals to their habitats and completed a project.

● TARGET LANGUAGE
Key language: body parts
Additional language: *run away, the rest of*
Revision: action verbs, parts of the body, *body, habitat, have to, have got, skeleton, bones*

● MATERIALS REQUIRED
Warmer: Four pieces of paper, each with the name of an animal habitat written on it: *jungle, savannah, mountain, sea*. Picture of each habitat (if possible)
Project: A piece of paper for each pupil, coloured pencils, reference materials / internet access

Warmer
- Display the large pieces of paper with habitat words, together with the pictures, on four different walls in the classroom. Check comprehension of the words and elicit that they are all types of habitat. Say a wild animal which lives in one of the habitats. Pupils point to / move to the correct habitat word (e.g. sea). Example animals: jungle – *monkey, crocodile, snake, parrot*; savannah – *lion, giraffe, zebra, rhino*; mountain – *panda, goat*; sea – *shark, whale, fish, dolphin*.

PB71. ACTIVITY 4. *Read and complete.*
- Tell pupils to open their Pupil's Book at page 71. Remind them of the meaning of *habitat*. Read the activity instruction and make sure pupils realise they need to use the words in the box. Pupils read and complete the text individually and then compare answers in pairs. Check with the class. Go through any new vocabulary.

Key: skeletons, Crocodiles, tail, giraffes, long, Monkeys

PB71. ACTIVITY 5. *Listen and say 'yes' or 'no'.*
- Focus pupils on Activity 5 and on the activity instruction. Check they understand what to do. Remind them to whisper *yes* or *no* to their partner the first time they listen. Play the first one as an example. Play the rest of the CD. Pupils listen and whisper. Play the CD again. Check after each one. Pupils correct the incorrect sentences.

Key: 1 no, 2 no, 3 no, 4 yes, 5 no

CD 3, 02
1. All animals have the same kind of skeleton.
2. Giraffes have got long, strong tail bones.
3. Crocodiles don't eat animals.
4. Crocodiles have got big eyes on the top of their heads.
5. Giraffes need long neck bones to eat leaves from small plants.

PB71. PROJECT. *Make a class comic of 'Super Animals'.*
- Focus pupils on the project and on the photograph. Read through the instructions and check pupils know what to do. Provide them with appropriate reference materials. Give them time to collect their information and help them if necessary. Hand out the paper. Pupils make their page for the comic. They write about their Super Animal in their notebooks first. When you have checked their work, they write their text on the page. If you aren't going to do Extra activity 1, collect the comic pages and make them into a book for display.

AB71. ACTIVITY 3. MOVERS Reading and Writing, Part 2
Read the text and choose the best answer. Sally is talking to her friend Jack. **M** *towards*
- Tell pupils to open their Activity Book at page 71. Direct them to the activity instructions and check understanding. Go through the example. Pupils work in pairs. They read the first line of each dialogue and circle the letter of the correct response. Monitor pupils as they work. Check with the class. Ask pupils how they worked out the correct answer.

Key: 1 C, 2 B, 3 A, 4 A, 5 C, 6 A

Extra activities: see page T118 (if time)

Ending the lesson
- Review with pupils what they did in today's lesson and which activities they liked best from this and the previous lesson and why.

Read and complete.

> giraffes   tail   Monkeys   long   Crocodiles   skeletons

Different animals have got different _____. This is because they live in different habitats and they have to do different things to live. Some animals fly, some swim, some run, some jump and some climb. _____ have got long, strong _____ bones. These help them to move quickly when they catch animals to eat. They've also got big eyes on the top of their heads. These stay out of the water looking for food when the rest of its body is under water. The leaves which _____ eat are at the top of high trees, so they need very _____ neck bones to get them. _____ have often got long arms, legs and tails. These help them to climb and to move more quickly from tree to tree. They sometimes need to run away from other bigger, hungrier animals!

  Listen and say 'yes' or 'no'.

Project   Make a class comic of 'Super Animals'.

- Think of two or three different animals and their skeletons.
- What can they do with their different bones and body parts?
- What's your Super Animal called?
- What body parts has it got?
- What can it do?

8 Let's party!

1 Look, think and answer.
1. Whose birthday is it today?
2. What are the grown-ups doing?
3. What kind of sandwiches are there?
4. Who's thirsty?

2 Listen and check.

3 Listen and say the letter.

1 A bowl of salad.  a

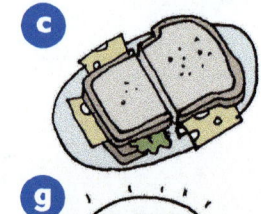 
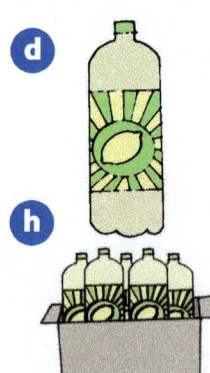

OBJECTIVES: By the end of the lesson, pupils will have read and talked about food and parties.

● TARGET LANGUAGE

Key language: food: *salad, pasta, sandwich(es), soup*; containers: *a bowl of, a bottle of, a cup of, a glass of*; *want someone to (do something)*
Additional language: *fancy dress party, Can you pass / take … ? Could you put … ?*
Revision: food and drink, *birthday, present, balloon, card, decorations, grown-ups, Would you like … ?*

● MATERIALS REQUIRED

Warmer: Birthday card, balloons and decorations
Container and food flashcards (93–103)
Extra activity 1: Copy of the CD script from Pupil's Book Activity 2 on a large piece of paper for display, paper, colours, scissors
Optional: *Kid's Box Teacher's Resource Book 4* Unit 8 Reinforcement worksheet 1 (page 65)

Warmer

- Display the birthday card and the balloons and elicit *birthday*. Elicit from pupils what happens on their birthdays. Develop a mind map on the board to include: *party, presents, balloons, food, cake, decorations.*

PB72. ACTIVITY 1. *Look, think and answer.*

- Tell pupils to open their Pupil's Book at page 72. Focus them on the pictures and elicit who / what they can see. Elicit that this is a *fancy dress party*. Ask: *What can they see?* Ensure that you teach both *tea* and *coffee*, with *cup*. Using the artwork for Mrs Star's tray. Ask *What's this hot drink? Is it tea or coffee?* (it's tea). Write *tea* and *coffee* on the board. Check pupils have read the activity instruction and know what to do. They read the questions in pairs and discuss them together, using the information from the pictures to help.

PB72. ACTIVITY 2. *Listen and check.*

- Play the CD. Elicit sentences for the answers. Set further questions, e.g. *Can you name the foods they are making? Who wants a glass of lemonade? Where are the bottles of lemonade? Does Grandpa want a cheese sandwich? What does he want to eat?* Play the CD again and pause to elicit answers.
- Show the flashcards and say, e.g. *a bowl of salad*. Pupils repeat. Call out the containers. Pupils say the food / drink, e.g. *A bottle of …* (lemonade).

Note: The 'd' in *sandwich* can be pronounced or silent – both are acceptable.

Key: 1 It's Simon's birthday. 2 They're making food for the party. 3 Cheese sandwiches. 4 Grandpa is thirsty.

CD 3, 03

NARRATOR: It's Simon's birthday. The grown-ups are making food for his party.
MR STAR: Angelina, can you take a bowl of salad to the table, please?
MRS STAR: Yes. Can you pass me a bowl of cold pasta, too, please?
GRANDMA: What do you want me to do?
MR STAR: Er, could you put these cheese sandwiches on the table please, Mum?
GRANDPA: Where's the lemonade, son?
MR STAR: There are some bottles in that box next to the door.
MRS STAR: Who'd like a cup of tea?
GRANDPA: Ooph, no, thank you. But I am thirsty. I need a glass of lemonade!
GRANDMA: Do you want a cheese sandwich too?
GRANDPA: Oh, no, thank you. I don't like party food. Bruce made some nice vegetable soup yesterday. I can have some of that later.
GRANDMA: Hmm. Vegetable soup. Oh, no, dear. We had it for dinner last night. We finished it all when you were out with your friends. It was lovely. Now, would you like a cheese sandwich?
GRANDPA: Ooohhh … yes, please.

PB72. ACTIVITY 3. *Listen and say the letter.*

- Focus pupils on Activity 3. Check they understand what to do. Remind them to whisper the answer to their partner the first time they listen. Play the first one as an example. Play the rest of the CD. Pupils listen and whisper. Play the CD again. Check with the class.

Key: 2 g, 3 h, 4 e, 5 b, 6 f, 7 c, 8 d

CD 3, 04

1 A bowl of salad, 2 A bowl of vegetable soup, 3 A box of bottles, 4 A cup of tea, 5 A bowl of pasta, 6 A glass of lemonade, 7 A cheese sandwich, 8 A bottle of lemonade

AB72. ACTIVITY 1. *Circle the odd one out.* [M] *towards*

- Tell pupils to open their Activity Book at page 72. Demonstrate, using the example. Pupils complete the activity in pairs. Check with the class.

Key: 2 water, 3 orange juice, 4 apples, 5 pears, 6 chicken

AB72. ACTIVITY 2. *Sort and write the words.*

- Focus pupils on Activity 2. Using the picture to help, they unscramble the words and write them. Pupils check in pairs. Check with the class.

Key: 2 cup of coffee, 3 glass of milk, 4 bag of pears, 5 bottle of water, 6 bowl of fruit, 7 box of oranges

Extra activities: see page T118 (if time)

Optional activity

- Unit 8 Reinforcement worksheet 1 from *Teacher's Resource Book 4* (pages 64–65).

Ending the lesson

- Write a word snake of words from the lesson on the board, e.g. *Bottleggsglassorangesaladcupearsandwichesoupbox*. Pupils copy it in their notebooks and circle the words. Point out that some words overlap. Check with the class.
- Call out a food item and ask pupils to say what different containers they can go with e.g. *lemonade – a glass of lemonade, a bottle of lemonade*. Continue with *milkshake, oranges, noodles, eggs, pasta, soup, salad*, etc.

OBJECTIVES: By the end of the lesson, pupils will have had more practice talking about food and parties and using *want someone to (do something)*.

● TARGET LANGUAGE
Key language: *want someone to (do something), in front of*
Revision: polite requests, food and drink, containers, parties, colours

● MATERIALS REQUIRED
Container and food flashcards (93–103)
Let's party! word cards from *Kid's Box Teacher's Resource Book 4* page 87 (food, drink and containers)
Optional: *Kid's Box Teacher's Resource Book 4* Unit 8 Reinforcement worksheet 2 and Extension worksheet 1 (pages 66 and 67)

Warmer
- Review the container and food words using the flashcards and word cards. Play a chain game. Say, e.g. *On the table I saw a bag of sweets.* Pupil 1: *On the table I saw a bag of sweets and a bottle of lemonade.* Continue around the class. When it gets to six or seven items, start another chain.

PB73. ACTIVITY 4. *Listen and say the letter.*
- Tell pupils to open their Pupil's Book at page 73. Focus pupils on the Activity 4 instruction and the example. Remind pupils to whisper the letter to their partner. Play the CD. Pupils listen and whisper. Play the CD again. Check with the class. Introduce *want someone to (do something)* in the checking phase, e.g. *1 What does she want the children to do? She wants …* (pupils complete the sentence).

Key: 2 e, 3 f, 4 c, 5 a, 6 d

CD 3, 05
1. Can you take these dirty cups to the kitchen, please, children?
2. Can you open this bottle of lemonade for us, please?
3. Can you put these glasses on the table, please, kids?
4. Can you pass me the bowl of salad, please?
5. Can you make me a cheese sandwich, please, Mum?
6. Bill, can you hold my glass, please?

PB73. ACTIVITY 5. *Read and correct.*
- Focus pupils on Activity 5 and on the picture. Tell them that the children are called Paul, Vicky and Jack. Ask how the people in the picture are feeling.
- Check comprehension of sentences 1 to 6. Pupils read the text and write correct sentences individually. They check in pairs. Check with the class.

Key: 1 Paul wants his brother and sister to help him. 2 He wants Vicky to make a bowl of salad. 3 He wants her to make a bowl of soup. 4 Paul wants Jack to take a plate of sandwiches to the table. 5 He wants him to make a cup of coffee for their parents. 6 Jack and Vicky want Paul to help (them).

AB73. ACTIVITY 3. *Write sentences.*
- Tell pupils to open their Activity Book at page 73. Focus them on the pictures and on the example. Pupils work in pairs, doing the activity orally first. Then they write the sentences. Check with the class.

Key: 2 Grandma wants Grandpa to text Simon. 3 Mrs Star wants Mr Star to make some coffee. 4 Stella wants Suzy to clean the table. 5 The teacher wants the children to sit down. 6 Grandpa wants Grandma to turn on the computer.

AB73. ACTIVITY 4. *Listen, colour and write.* 🄼 *towards*
- Focus pupils on the Activity 4 instruction. There is one example. Check understanding and tell them to put their coloured pencils on their desks. Play the CD. Pupils follow the instructions. They check in pairs. Play the CD again. Check with the class.

CD 3, 06
Look at the picture. Listen and look. There is one example.
Can you colour this kitchen picture?
Yes, I think it is breakfast time in this house.
That's right. The table in this kitchen is round. Can you colour it?
OK.
Make it grey.
Can you see the grey table? This is an example. Now you listen and colour and write.

1. Now, I want you to colour some of the things in the picture. OK? / OK. Where do we start? / Can you see the box of eggs below the clock? / Yes. / Colour the box brown, please.

2. Good. Now I want you to write something. Can you see the bottle next to the eggs? / Yes. / Write the word water on it, please. / All right.

3. Would you like to colour something now? / Yes, please. / Can you see the cup of tea on the table? Would you like to colour the cup blue, please? / OK.

4. Now I want you to colour some fruit. Can you see the bowl of fruit on the table? / Oh, yes. It's got bananas and apples in it. / Good. Well, I want you to colour the two apples red, please. / OK.

5. And now I want you to colour a banana yellow. / Which banana? The one in the bowl or the one in front of it? / Colour the banana in front of the bowl, please. / There you are. Finished. / Well done!

Extra activities: see page T118 (if time)

Optional activity
- Unit 8 Reinforcement worksheet 2 and Extension worksheet 1 from *Teacher's Resource Book 4* (pages 64, 66 and 67).

Ending the lesson
- Give instructions for the end of the lesson, e.g. *Can you clean the board? Can you close your books?* Elicit sentences with *want*, e.g. *You want us to clean the board / close our books.*

Listen and say the letter.

1 Can you take these dirty cups to the kitchen please, children?

b

a — He wants her to make a cheese sandwich.

b — She wants them to take the cups to the kitchen.

c — He wants him to pass the bowl of salad.

d — She wants him to hold the glass.

e — They want her to open the bottle of lemonade.

f — He wants them to put the glasses on the table.

 Read and correct.

Paul wants to make lunch for his mum and dad. He wants his brother and sister to help him. He wants Vicky to make a bowl of salad and then he wants her to make a bowl of soup. He wants Jack to take a plate of sandwiches and a bottle of lemonade to the table. After lunch he wants him to make a cup of coffee for their parents.
Paul wants to sit down and watch TV with a glass of apple juice. His brother and sister aren't happy, they're angry. They want Paul to help them.

1 Paul wants his mum and dad to help him.
2 He wants Vicky to make a box of noodles.
3 He wants her to make a cup of soup.
4 Paul wants Jack to take a plate of pancakes to the table.
5 He wants him to make a cup of coffee for their aunt and uncle.

6 Look, think and answer.
1 What are the children doing?
2 Who's first?
3 Who's last?
4 Who's walking?

7 🎧 07 CD3 Listen and check.

8 🎧 08 CD3 Listen and say the name.

1 He's jumping the most quickly.

Alex.

LOOK

quickly	➡	the **most quickly**
slowly	➡	the **most slowly**
well	➡	the **best**
badly	➡	the **worst**

OBJECTIVES: By the end of the lesson, pupils will have used superlative adverbs to talk about pictures and party events.

- **TARGET LANGUAGE**
  Key language: superlative adverbs, e.g. *the most quickly / carefully, the best, the worst, the most; well, sack race*
  Additional language: *third place*
  Revision: adverbs, adjectives, present continuous, *fancy dress, clown, pirate, robot, explorer, artist, doctor, pop star, model*

- **MATERIALS REQUIRED**
  Optional: *Kid's Box 4 Language Portfolio* page 13

Warmer

- Revise known adverbs. Ask a pupil to come to the front. Whisper an action and an adverb, e.g. *Walk slowly*. The pupil mimes the action and the adverb. The class guesses, e.g. *He's walking slowly*. Repeat.
- Ask: *Is Mr Star a pop star?* (yes) *Is Mrs Star a pop star?* (no) *Is Mrs Star a model?* (no) *What's Mrs Star's job? She's an actor.* Ask pupils to correct these sentences:
  Mr Star's a model.
  Mrs Star's a farmer.
  Uncle Fred's an actor.
  Aunt May's a dentist.
  Lock and Key are pop stars.

PB74. ACTIVITY 6. *Look, think and answer.*

- Tell pupils to open their Pupil's Book at page 74. Elicit what / who they can see. Present *sack race* and review *fancy dress, doctor, pirate, explorer, clown, robot* and *artist*. Check pupils have read the activity instruction and know what to do. They read the questions in pairs and discuss them together, using the information from the pictures to help them guess.

PB74. ACTIVITY 7. *Listen and check.*

- Play the CD. Elicit complete sentences for the answers. Elicit who each of the 'characters' is. Play the CD again and ask further checking questions to focus on the superlative adverbs, e.g. *How's the clown jumping? How's the doctor jumping? Why?*

Key: 1 They are having a sack race. 2 The explorer's first. 3 The artist's last. 4 The artist's walking.

CD 3, 07

GRANDPA: And here we are at the Star House Birthday Race. The explorer's first at the moment. He's jumping the best. The clown's jumping the most quickly, but not the most carefully. Oh, he's got problems. I think he's falling.

MR STAR: Oh, dear! He's going down!

GRANDPA: And the pirate and the robot are both trying to get third place. Ooh, this is very exciting. And the doctor's jumping the worst, but she's laughing the most. The artist is jumping the most slowly, but she's doing very well.

MR STAR: Er, she isn't jumping, Dad. She's walking.

GRANDPA: Hmph! She's doing very well. She **has** got the shortest legs.

PB74. ACTIVITY 8. *Listen and say the name.*

- Focus pupils on the Activity 8 instruction and check understanding. Remind pupils to whisper the name the first time. Play the CD. Pupils listen and whisper the name to their partner. Play the CD again. Check with the class.

Key: 2 Simon, 3 Alex, 4 Stella, 5 Lenny, 6 Suzy, 7 Suzy, 8 Meera

CD 3, 08

1. He's jumping the most quickly.
2. He's the pirate.
3. He's the clown.
4. She's jumping the worst.
5. He's jumping the best.
6. She's the artist.
7. She's jumping the most slowly.
8. She's the robot.

Look box

- Focus pupils on the Look box. They take turns to read the examples aloud. Elicit other examples of superlative adverbs from the previous activities.

AB74. ACTIVITY 5. *Choose your party.*

- Tell pupils to open their Activity Books at page 74. Focus them on the Activity 5 instruction and check understanding, doing an example for practice. They circle the words to complete the text and then write the text in their notebooks. Pupils make groups of six. They take turns to read sentences from their texts, saying *Same* or *Different* as they listen to the others' choices.

AB74. ACTIVITY 6. *Look at the picture. Write 'yes' or 'no'.*

- Focus pupils on the Activity 6 instructions and check understanding. They work in pairs and write their one-word answers next to the statements. Pairs check with pairs. Check with the class.

Key: 2 no, 3 yes, 4 yes, 5 yes, 6 yes

Extra activities: see page T118 (if time)

Language Portfolio

- Pupils complete page 13 of *Kid's Box 4 Language Portfolio* (*A special event*). Help with new language as necessary.

Ending the lesson

- Tell pupils to put their books away and prepare for the end of the lesson. As they are doing it, make comments, e.g. *Paula's putting her books away the most carefully. Danny's packing his bag the most quickly. Oh, and Jenny's the first!*

OBJECTIVES: By the end of the lesson, pupils will have had more practice talking about parties and sung a song.

- **TARGET LANGUAGE**
Key language: past simple, rhyming words
Additional language: *It's time to fly, The party's over.*
Revision: party food and drink, containers

- **MATERIALS REQUIRED**
Container and food flashcards (93–103)
Optional: *Kid's Box Teacher's Resource Book 4* Unit 8 Song worksheet (page 69)

Warmer
- In pairs, pupils brainstorm their ideal party. Elicit their ideas and review party food, decorations and party games. Use the flashcards to review food and containers.

PB75. ACTIVITY 9. *Look at the pictures. Find the differences.*
M towards

- Tell pupils to open their Pupil's Book at page 75. Focus them on Activity 9 and on the pictures. Elicit that they are different. Check they have read the activity instructions and know what to do. Demonstrate with an example. Tell them there are eight differences. In pairs, pupils look for the differences in the pictures. They talk about the differences in the same way. Check with the class.

Key:
A: The clown's eating a cake. B: The clown's drinking orange juice.
A: There is a plate of chicken. B: There is no plate of chicken.
A: There is a bottle of lemonade. B: There is a carton of orange juice.
A: There is a bowl of salad. B: There is a bowl of pasta.
A: The pirate has a beard and no moustache. B: The pirate has a moustache and no beard.
A: The doctor has black shoes. B: The doctor has red shoes.
A: There's a (mobile) phone on the chair. B: There's a book on the chair.
A: The clown has got a flower. B: The clown hasn't got a flower.

PB75. ACTIVITY 10. *Complete the song. Listen and check.*

- Focus pupils on the picture for Activity 10 and elicit some of the things they can see on the table. Ask them what kind of party it was. Check they have read the activity instructions and know what to do. Remind them to think of the rhymes and to use the picture to help them. They read the song first in pairs and try to fit the words in the gaps. Pairs check with pairs.
- Make sure pupils are ready to listen. Play the CD. They listen and check their words.

Key: gave, made, wore, danced, was, drank, ate

CD 3, 09
As in Pupil's Book

PB75. ACTIVITY 11. *Sing the song.*
- Play the CD in sections. Pupils repeat. When pupils are confident with the song, make six groups. Groups take turns to sing one of the verses / the chorus. Change groups and repeat.

CD 3, 09
As in Pupil's Book

CD 3, 10
Now sing the song again. (Karaoke version)

AB75. ACTIVITY 7. *Read and complete the table.*
- Tell pupils to open their Activity Book at page 75. Focus them on Activity 7 and on the instruction. Check they understand what to do. Pupils read the text and complete the table. They check in pairs. Check with the class by reproducing the table on the board for pupils to come up and complete. They answer the three questions, saying who dressed up as what at the party.

Key:

Name	trousers	dress	hat	nose	beard
Susan	white		big black		black
Peter	red		orange	big red	
Vicky		white	little white		

Clown: Peter; pirate: Susan; nurse: Vicky

AB75. ACTIVITY 8. *Find three words from the same group.*
- Focus pupils on the Activity 8 instruction and check understanding. Using the example, elicit what links the three words (parts of speech). Pupils work in pairs to join words in the other squares. Check with the class, discussing the reasons each time. Say, *Tell me the names of famous pop stars/ models.*

Key: 2 best, tallest, longest; 3 ate, drank, went; 4 pirate, clown, pop star

Extra activities: see page T119 (if time)

Optional activity
- Pupils complete the Unit 8 Song worksheet from *Teacher's Resource Book 4* (pages 64 and 69).

Ending the lesson
- Sing the song from earlier in the lesson again.

9 Look at the pictures. Find the differences.

In picture B the clown's drinking a milkshake.

10   Complete the song. Listen and check.

made   ate   wore   ~~said~~   drank   danced   gave   was

We had soup, we had pasta,
We had salads and cheese.
We all wanted more,
We all _said_ 'please'.
We _____ presents,
And cards which we _____ .
We _____ fancy dress,
We _____ and we played …

The party was good,
The party _____ great.
And now it's time to fly.
The party was good,
The party was great.

We'll see you soon, goodbye.

The drinks we _____ ,
The food we _____ .
The party was good,
The party was great.

We gave presents …
Now the party's over,
Now it's time to fly.
See you soon, goodbye.

11   Sing the song.

 ## Stella's phonics

Say **soup** and **blue**,
And **think**, **thought** and **flew**.
Say **wa**ter, **pas**ta and **cle**ver,
And **par**ty, **bot**tle and **wea**ther.
Another syllable will make it three,
Say **beau**tiful, **el**ephant and **care**fully!

 Choose a picture. Play the game.

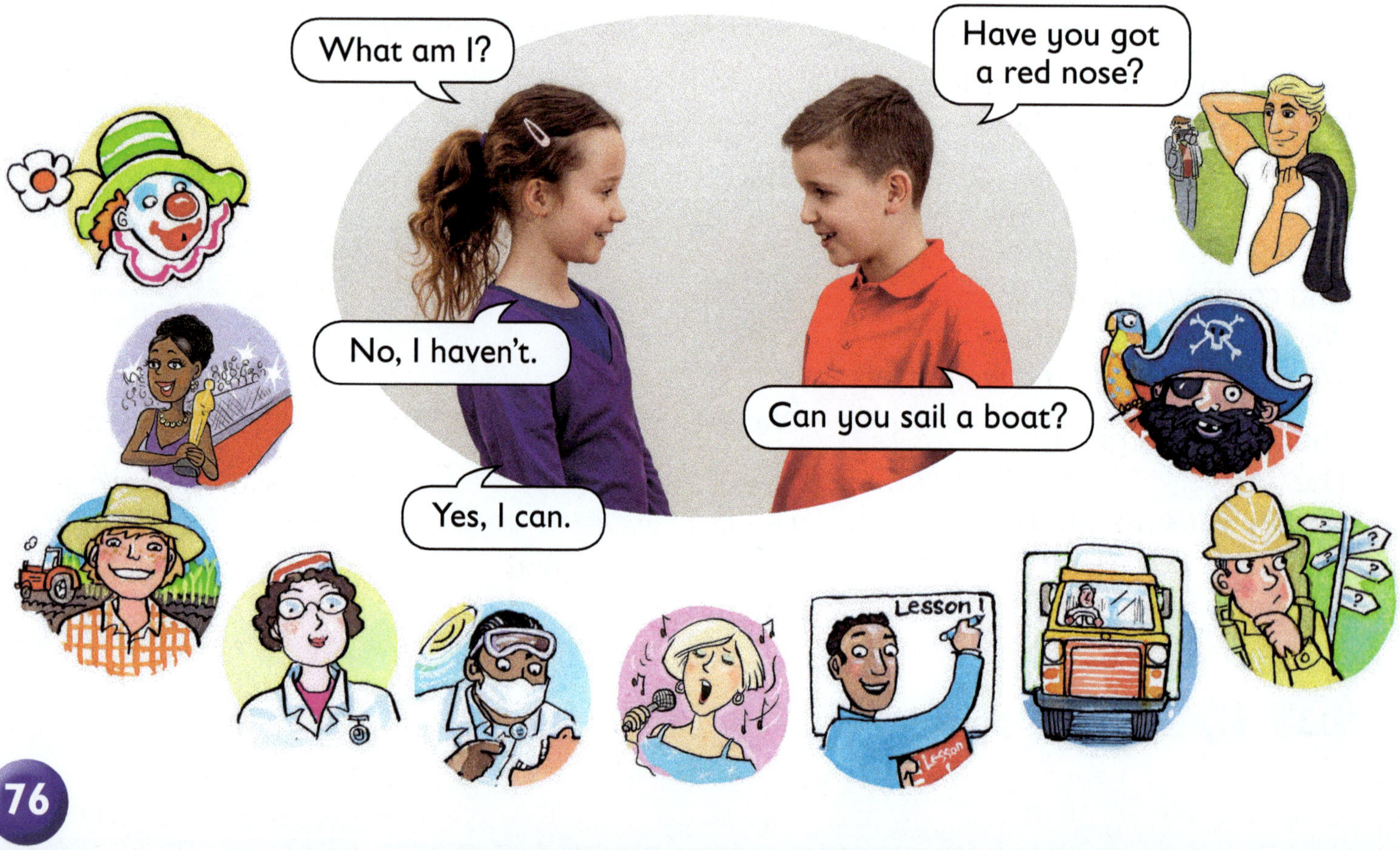

What am I?

Have you got a red nose?

No, I haven't.

Can you sail a boat?

Yes, I can.

OBJECTIVES: By the end of the lesson, pupils will be able to identify the number of syllables in a word and will be aware that some syllables within a word are stressed while others are not. They will have matched words which sound the same (homophones).

- **TARGET LANGUAGE**
Key language: *syllable*, words with one, two or three syllables
Revision: question forms, jobs (including *pop star* and *model*)

- **MATERIALS REQUIRED**
Photocopiable 8 (page T106), photocopied onto card and cut in half so there is half a page for each pair in the class

Warmer
- Write one- and two- syllable food words on the board, e.g. *soup, pasta, salad, cup, bowl, bottle, sandwich, cheese*. Clap once and say *soup*. Clap twice and say *pasta*. Point to the next word in the list and ask pupils if you need to clap once or twice. Tell them to think about the sound. Tell pupils that the 'beats' in a word are called *syllables*. *Soup* has one syllable. *Pasta* has two syllables. Pupils work in pairs to sort the words into two groups (one syllable or two syllables).

PB76. ACTIVITY 12. *Stella's phonics*
- Tell pupils to open their Pupil's Book at page 76. Elicit what they can see. Tell pupils to point the first time they listen and to say the sentences quietly. Play the CD. Pupils point and quietly repeat. Play the CD again, pausing for pupils to repeat. Point out that only the stressed syllables in the poem are highlighted in bold to help with the rhythm.

Note: Teaching the number of syllables in a word includes showing pupils where the stress falls.

CD 3, 11
STELLA: Hi, I'm Stella! Repeat after me!
Say soup and blue,
And think, thought and flew.
Say water, pasta and clever,
And party, bottle and weather.
Another syllable will make it three,
Say beautiful, elephant and carefully!

Say soup and blue,
And think, thought and flew.
Say water, pasta and clever,
And party, bottle and weather.
Another syllable will make it three,
Say beautiful, elephant and carefully!
(repeat)

PB76. ACTIVITY 13. *Choose a picture. Play the game.*
- Focus pupils on Activity 13. Elicit the names of the jobs in the pictures and write them on the board. Choose a job (without telling pupils). They ask yes / no questions to guess. They can ask ten questions. Write prompts for the questions if necessary, e.g. *Can you ... ? Do you ... ? Have you ... ? Are you ... ?*
- Pupils then play the game in pairs, taking turns to choose a job from the ones in the pictures.

Photocopiable 8 (see pages T91 and T106)
AB76. ACTIVITY 9. *Write. Listen, check and say.*
- Tell pupils to open their Activity Book at page 76. Check they know the meaning of all the words in the box. Point out the words at the top of each column of the table. Say the words, emphasising the syllables in the two- and three-syllable words. Pupils repeat. Draw attention to the examples. Pupils work individually to put the words into the three columns. Tell them to say the words aloud to help.
- Focus on the second part of the instruction (*Listen, check and say*). Play the CD for pupils to listen and check. Pupils compare answers in pairs. Check with the class. Play the CD again for pupils to listen and repeat.

Key:

one syllable	two syllables	three syllables
eggs	sandwich	vegetables
good	wanted	terrible
flew	quickly	computer
caught	easy	basketball
came	enjoy	holiday

CD 3, 12
one syllable
eggs, good, flew, caught, came

two syllables
sandwich, wanted, quickly, easy, enjoy

three syllables
vegetables, terrible, computer, basketball, holiday

AB76. ACTIVITY 10. *Listen and tick the box.*
- Focus pupils on the Activity 10 instruction and check understanding. Give pupils time to look at the pictures. Play the CD. Pupils tick the box. They check in pairs. Play the CD again. Check with the class. Elicit what the people in the other pictures are doing.

Key: 2 a, 3 c, 4 b

CD 3, 13
1. Sarah's having a jacket potato with cheese and a salad for dinner. She's got apple juice to drink.
2. It's cold and windy outside so Jim's got a bowl of hot vegetable soup for lunch.
3. Mrs Smith had a cup of tea at 11 o'clock. She has a cup of tea at the same time every day.
4. Jack was really hungry so he ate his sandwich at playtime.

Joke box
- Focus pupils on the Joke box. They guess / find the answer. Explain the joke if necessary.

Extra activity: see page T119 (if time)

Ending the lesson
- Pupils repeat the poem from the beginning of the lesson.

OBJECTIVES: By the end of the lesson, pupils will have read a story and reviewed language from the unit.

• TARGET LANGUAGE
Key language: language in the story
Additional language: *take me away*
Revision: language from the unit, *heroes*

• MATERIALS REQUIRED
Container and food flashcards (93–103)
Extra activity 1: A large piece of paper for each group of four
Optional: *Kid's Box Teacher's Resource Book 4* Unit 8 Extension worksheet 2 (page 68) and / or animated version of the Unit 8 story from *Kid's Box Interactive DVD 4* (*Suzy's room* section)

Warmer
- Review with pupils how the Unit 7 *Lock and Key* episode in the Pupil's Book ended and what their predictions are for what happens next. Tell pupils that this is the last episode of the story in *Kid's Box 4*. Take a vote as to whether pupils think the police / Lock and Key will catch Nick Motors or not.

Story

PB77. LOCK AND KEY.
- Tell pupils to open their Pupil's Book at page 77. Pupils quickly read the story to check their predictions from the Warmer. Discuss with the class. Set the gist questions: *What food / drink does Nick Motors give to the tiger? Which does the tiger eat / drink? Who are the heroes? Do you agree?* Play the CD. Pupils listen and read. They check in pairs. Check with the class (A bag of parrot food, a bottle of water, a box of fruit; nothing; Lock and Key).
- Play the CD again. Pause after each frame for pupils to repeat. Check general comprehension by asking, e.g. *Did Nick Motors like the tiger? Who saw the lorry first? Why did Nick Motors say 'Thank you' to Lock and Key?*

`CD 3, 14`

As in Pupil's Book

AB77. DO YOU REMEMBER?
- Review the food and container words using the flashcards. Stick the flashcards on the board. Ask pupils to come and label the flashcards (the class can help with the spelling). Accept other words from the unit and add them to the board.
- Tell pupils to open their Activity Book at page 77. Clean the board. Check pupils have read the activity instructions and know what to do. They study the words and spellings on the right in silence. Then they fold the page down the middle so that they can only see the pictures and the lines to write the words on. Without looking, they write the words in pencil, using the pictures to help. They check in pairs, asking, e.g. *What's this one? How do you spell 'vegetables'?* They don't look at the words on the right. When pupils have finished, they can either correct their own work or swap books and check their partner's.

AB77. CAN DO.
- Focus pupils on the *Can do* section of the page. Say *Let's read the sentences together.* Read the first sentence. Elicit what this means with examples and elicit / remind pupils of the activities they did in this unit when they talked about food, e.g. Simon's party. Review what the three faces mean (not very well / OK / very well). Remind pupils they circle the one they think is true for them. Repeat for the second sentence, eliciting / reminding them about the activity where they gave / followed instructions and reported on what they wanted the person to do. Pupils circle the appropriate face. Repeat for the third sentence, eliciting / reminding them about the party words they used in the lessons. Pupils circle the appropriate face.
- Say *Now show and tell your friends.* Pupils work in groups of three and take turns to show their work for / talk about each one.

Extra activities: see page T119 (if time)

Optional activities
- Unit 8 Extension worksheet 2 from *Teacher's Resource Book 4* (pages 64 and 68).
- The animated version of the story from *Kid's Box Interactive DVD 4* (*Suzy's room* section). See pages 38–45 of the Teacher's Booklet for the Interactive DVD.

Ending the lesson
- Ask pupils which chant / song they'd like to do again from the unit. Do it together to end the lesson.

Science — Food

> **Fact**
> A 60 gram bar of milk chocolate has seven teaspoons of sugar in it.

1 Look at the food plate.
How often do you think you need to eat food from each group?

2 Read and answer.

For a healthy body we need to eat different kinds of food. There are five important groups of food: carbohydrates; dairy products; fats and sugar; protein; fruit and vegetables.

Carbohydrates give us energy. (1) What kinds of food are carbohydrates?

Dairy products make our bones and teeth strong because they contain calcium. We get calcium from milk and food which comes from milk, like yoghurt. (2) Do you know another food which comes from milk?

Fats and sugar also give us energy, but a lot of fat and sugar is not good for our bodies. (3) What kinds of food have sugar? (4) What kinds of food have got fat?

Protein is important because it is good for our muscles and it makes them strong. Protein comes from animals or some vegetables, like beans. (5) What other foods do you think give us protein?

Fruit and vegetables have a lot of vitamins and minerals. (6) Can you say the names of five different fruits? (7) Can you name three different vegetables?

OBJECTIVES: By the end of the lesson, pupils will have learnt and talked about food and nutrients and written about what people should eat.

● TARGET LANGUAGE
Key language: *carbohydrates, proteins, dairy products, fat, sugars, energy, vitamins, minerals, muscles*
Additional language: *gram, teaspoon*
Revision: *food, bones, teeth, calcium, have to, need, should, must*

● MATERIALS REQUIRED
Extra activity 2: Empty food packets and cartons which list the carbohydrates, fats, sugars in certain foods, e.g. cereal boxes, biscuit packets, yoghurt pots (plain and fruit), energy bars, soft drink cans or cartons
Optional: *Kid's Box Teacher's Resource Book 4* Unit 8 Topic worksheet (page 70)

Warmer
- Ask pupils what they ate the previous day. Write the foods on the board, using different colours for the five food groups: protein, fats and sugar, dairy products, carbohydrates, fruit and vegetables. Don't tell pupils what the colours mean yet. Leave the words on the board.

PB78. FACT
- Tell pupils to open their Pupil's Books at page 78. Ask a pupil to read the fact to the class. Check comprehension of *gram* and *teaspoon*. Ask how big a 60 gram bar of chocolate is (it's small) and if pupils think that's a lot of sugar. Ask if they think lots of sugar is good for them.

PB78. ACTIVITY 1. *Look at the food plate. How often do you think you need to eat food from each group?*
- Focus on the picture of the plate. Elicit the names of some of the foods pupils can see in each group. Check understanding of the five food groups. Elicit what they are in L1. Point at the foods from the Warmer on the board and elicit what the colours mean / which colour is which food group.
- Read the second part of the activity instruction and check comprehension. Pupils discuss the question in pairs. Ask them which of the foods they think they have to eat at every meal, which they need to eat every day and which they need to eat less often (e.g. once or twice a week). Encourage them to give reasons. Monitor and help with new language as necessary. Have a short class discussion and explain / elicit that the size of the 'sections' of the plate represent the proportion of each group of food we should eat (around a third of the diet should be carbohydrates, a third fruit and vegetables, one third dairy products, protein, fats and sugar).

PB78. ACTIVITY 2. *Read and answer.*
- Focus pupils on Activity 2 and on the text. Pupils take turns to read the introduction aloud around the class.
- Tell pupils to read the Activity 2 instruction and make sure they realise the questions are in the text. Read the text aloud for each food group. After reading as a class, pupils work in pairs to answer the questions, using the picture in Activity 1 to help. Pairs check with pairs. Check with the class.

Key: Possible answers: 1 bread, pasta, potatoes, rice; 2 cheese; 3 chocolate, sweets; 4 crisps, chips, cake; 5 fish, eggs; 6 grapes, apples, bananas, pineapples, oranges, lemons; 7 aubergines, broccoli, peppers, carrots, lettuce, celery, mushrooms, cucumber

AB78. ACTIVITY 1. *Put the words in groups.*
- Clean the Warmer activity off the board. Tell pupils to open their Activity Book at page 78. Focus them on Activity 1 and check understanding. They have to think and decide. They can use the food plate in the Pupil's Book to help. Pupils complete the table in pairs. Check and discuss with the class.

Key:

carbo-hydrates	protein	fruit and vegetables	dairy products	fats and sugar
rice	chicken	grapes	milk	cake
pasta	fish	bananas	yoghurt	chocolate
bread	eggs	apples		sweets
	beans	peas		
		carrots		

AB78. ACTIVITY 2. *Read and write.*
- Focus pupils on Activity 2 and on the example. Elicit / check understanding of the use of *have to, can* and *must*. Tell them to consider what the people do, their problems and general health, before deciding what advice to offer. Pupils discuss their ideas in groups of four. Elicit ideas from the class.
- Individually, pupils write their advice in their Activity Books.

Possible answers: 2 He can eat fruit. 3 He must eat rice, pasta, potatoes and bread. 4 She must eat oranges. 5 He must eat yoghurt and drink milk.

Extra activities: see page T119 (if time)

Optional activity
- Unit 8 Topic worksheet from *Teacher's Resource Book 4* (pages 64 and 70).

Ending the lesson
- Review with pupils what they learnt about in today's lesson.

OBJECTIVES: By the end of the lesson, pupils will have talked more about food and nutrients and completed a project.

- **TARGET LANGUAGE**
  Key language: *recipe, oil, preparation, mix, piece*
  Revision: food and nutrients, weights and measures, sequencing, relative clauses, describing people, sports and activities, superlative adjectives, present continuous, past tense

- **MATERIALS REQUIRED**
  Project: Recipe books, a large piece of paper for each group of four pupils

Warmer
- Review the previous lesson. Elicit what pupils remember about the five nutrient groups and examples of each one.

PB79. ACTIVITY 3. *Read and match.*
- Tell pupils to open their Pupil's Book at page 79 and focus on the first photograph. Elicit what they can see (a bowl of pasta salad). Check they have read the activity instruction and know what to do. Elicit / teach *recipe* and *ingredients*. Pupils read the ingredients and match them with the pictures. They check in pairs. Check with the class.

Key: 2 c, 3 f, 4 b, 5 a, 6 d

PB79. ACTIVITY 4. *Read and order the sentences.*
- Focus pupils on the Activity 4 instructions. Elicit that these are the instructions (the *preparation* stage) for making the pasta salad. Read the instructions around the class in the order on the page. Pupils work in pairs and order the recipe by writing letters. Pairs check with pairs. Check with the class. Focus on sequencing words, e.g. *first, then, now, next, last*, as well as new words, e.g. *mix*.
- Ask who likes to cook and what kinds of things they can cook.

Key: 2 d, 3 c, 4 a, 5 g, 6 e, 7 b

PB79. PROJECT. *Write a recipe for your favourite lunch.*
- Focus pupils on the project. Brainstorm some general ideas, e.g. *sandwiches, omelette and salad, spaghetti, soup, chicken salad*, and talk about what might go into each dish. Show pictures from recipe books to help with ideas.
- Pupils work in groups of four. They decide on their recipe, discuss what's in it and then what the preparation stages are. Remind them to use the sequencing words from Activity 4: *First, Second, Next, Then, Last*. Monitor groups closely and provide any help they need. Groups draw a picture of their dish on the large piece of paper and write its name, the ingredients and the preparation stages.
- Groups display their recipes. One representative of each group stays with their poster. The other pupils look at the other posters. They stop at each poster while the pupil there talks about it (why it's good for lunch and what nutrients it contains).

AB79. ACTIVITY 3. MOVERS *Listening, Part 1*
Listen and draw lines. There is one example. [M] *towards*
- Tell pupils to open their Activity Book at page 79. Elicit what they can see and what the children are doing. Check comprehension of *cup* as a prize (e.g. *sports cup*). Read the activity instructions and the seven names. Remind pupils that there is an example on the CD and point to the example line from Jack to the boy playing the piano. Tell them that there is one name they won't need to use.
- Play the CD. Pupils complete the activity individually. They compare answers in pairs. Play the CD again. Check with the class.

CD 3, 15

Hello. What's everyone doing here?
We're having a school party. It's the last day.
That's nice. Who's the boy that's playing the piano?
The one wearing the grey T-shirt?
Yes.
That's Jack. He's my best friend.

Can you see the line? This is an example.
Now you listen and draw lines.
1.
Look over there! The teacher is giving them cups.
That's right. They're sports cups. They're for running.
Who came first? Was it the girl with the long blonde hair?
Yes, that's Jane. She ran the quickest.
2.
Did the class do any other sports?
Yes. We jumped and swam, too.
Who jumped the best?
Bill did. He's very good at jumping.
Which boy is he?
He's the one with glasses. He's eating a cheese sandwich.
3.
Who's the girl with short, curly hair? The one with the puppy on her T-shirt.
That's my friend May.
Did she get a sports cup?
No, she didn't. She got a cup for drawing a picture.
Does she like Art?
Yes. She loves it!
4.
What about the girl standing next to the piano? The one who's singing. What's her name?
That's Kim. She couldn't run, jump or swim because she hurt her leg.
Oh! I'm sorry!
No, it's OK, she got a cup for singing. Listen! She sings beautifully.
5.
So, who got the prize for swimming?
Paul did. He swam really quickly. He's over there. He's got a glass of lemonade in his hand.
Oh, yes! I can see him. He's got short fair hair.
Yes. That's right.

Extra activities: see page T119 (if time)

Ending the lesson
- Review with pupils what they talked about in today's lesson and which activities they liked best from this and the previous lesson and why.

3 Read and match. 1 – e

Pasta salad

You need:
1. 2 tomatoes
2. 250 g pasta
3. 100 g cheese
4. 200 g chicken
5. 2 carrots
6. some lemon juice and oil

a

b

c

d

e

f

4 Read and order the sentences. 1 – f

Preparation:

a. Then cut the cheese into pieces and mix it in a big bowl with the tomatoes and carrots.

b. Now you can eat your pasta salad.

c. Next, cut the tomatoes and carrots into small pieces.

d. Second, cook the chicken. When it's cold, cut it into small pieces.

e. Last, put some oil and lemon juice over the salad.

f. First, cook the pasta in a lot of water.

g. Put the pasta and chicken into the bowl with the tomato, carrots and cheese.

Project Write a recipe for your favourite lunch.

79

Review Units 7 and 8

1 Play the game.

Instructions

1. Groups of three or four.
2. Move and answer the questions. You only have 30 seconds.
- Right answer: stay.
- Wrong answer: go back one space.

START

1. Which animal lives in Antarctica?
2. Name five animals you can see at the zoo.
3. What's the fifteenth letter of the alphabet?
4. Say five 'clothes' words.
5. What's the opposite of 'dirtiest'?
6. Say five 'food' words.
7. How much is fifty-eight plus thirteen?
8. What's the past of 'think'?
9. What's the opposite of 'into'?
10. Say five 'job' words.
11. What's the past of 'choose'?
12. Say five 'school' words.
13. Which is the tallest animal?
14. What kind of animals can fly?
15. What's the past of 'know'?
16. Say five 'transport' words.
17. How much is forty-three and eighteen?
18. What's the opposite of 'outside'?
19. What's the past of 'drive'?
20. Say five 'technology' words.

FINISH!

OBJECTIVES: By the end of the lesson, pupils will have reviewed language from Units 7 and 8 and played a game.

- **TARGET LANGUAGE**
Key language: vocabulary and language from Units 1 to 8
Revision: language for games

- **MATERIALS REQUIRED**
Warmer: Key vocabulary from Units 1 to 8, each word / phrase written on a small piece of paper OR word cards from *Kid's Box Teacher's Resource Book 4* (pages 80–87)
Dice and four different coloured counters for each group of four pupils, (optional: stop watches, one for each group)
Photocopiable Review 7 and 8 (page T107). One copy cut in half for each pair of pupils. (Optional: the text from Photocopiable Review 7 and 8 completed, one for each pair of pupils – see page T92)

Warmer

- Make groups of six. Hand out a piece of paper with a word or phrase or a word card to each pupil. They take turns to say what their word / phrase is and then to make a sentence or give a definition. The other pupils decide if the sentence / definition is correct or not. Monitor and help as necessary. If time, regroup pupils and repeat.

PB80. ACTIVITY 1. *Play the game.*

- Pupils open their Pupil's Book at page 80. Elicit what they can see (a board game). Ask pupils to read the instructions aloud in turn and check understanding. Tell them not to look back in their Pupil's Books for the answers yet. Pupils play the game in groups of four. Hand out the dice, counters and, if available, the stop watches. The player in each group who reaches the Finish first is the winner. If time, make new groups and pupils play the game again.
- Monitor the game, referring to the answers below. Tell the correct answers to groups if necessary.

Note: As this game comes at the end of the book, it revises content from the whole book, not just from Units 7 and 8.

Possible answers: 1 The whale 2 Answers may vary, e.g. elephants, monkeys, lions and pandas. 3 'O' 4 jacket, skirt, gloves, trousers, T-shirt, 5 cleanest, 6 cheese, fish, bread, tomatoes, bananas, 7 Seventy-one, 8 thought, 9 out of, 10 nurse, explorer, teacher, dentist, farmer, 11 chose, 12 desk, chair, bag, shelf, pen, 13 the giraffe, 14 birds, bats, insects, 15 knew, 16 bus, train, plane, boat, bicycle, 17 Sixty-one, 18 inside, 19 drove, 20 MP3 player, the internet, mouse, screen, DVD

Photocopiable Review 7 and 8 (see pages T91, T92 and T107)

AB80. ACTIVITY 1. *Find the past of the verbs.*

- Tell pupils to open their Activity Book at page 80. Focus them on the activity instruction and on the wordsearch and check they know what to do. Pupils work in pairs. They work out the past of each verb and then look for it in the wordsearch. Pairs can check with other pairs. Check with the class, focusing on pronunciation of the past forms.

Key:

w	d	o	f	a	s	r	a	t	o	o	k
a	i	d	l	g	a	v	e	h	i	n	o
s	d	r	e	w	i	d	t	o	m	s	o
b	f	a	w	e	d	r	p	u	a	a	c
g	e	n	i	n	b	o	u	g	h	t	f
c	a	k	e	t	o	v	t	h	a	m	o
a	t	e	r	s	l	e	p	t	d	o	u
u	k	n	e	w	a	t	s	r	a	n
g	o	t	s	a	l	c	h	o	s	e	d
h	n	c	a	m	e	a	t	d	a	t	i
t	o	o	w	r	e	a	d	t	n	n	t
w	e	r	e	h	r	o	d	e	g	a	c

AB80. ACTIVITY 2. *Read and choose the picture.*

- Focus pupils on the Activity 2 instruction and on the first two sentences of the text. Pupils work individually, read the text and find the right bag. Check with the class.

Key: Picture c

AB80. ACTIVITY 3. *Now describe what's in one of the other bags to your friend.*

- Pupils play a guessing game in pairs. Pupil A describes what's in one of the other bags in Activity 2 and Pupil B guesses which one it is. They swap and repeat.

Extra activity: see page T119 (if time)

Ending the lesson

- Pupils look back through *Kid's Box 4* to find their favourite activity and / or topic. In groups or as a class, they tell their friends what it is and why.

OBJECTIVES: By the end of the lesson, pupils will have reviewed language from Units 7 and 8.

- **TARGET LANGUAGE**
Key language: vocabulary and language from Units 7 and 8
Revision: vocabulary and language from Units 1 to 6

- **MATERIALS REQUIRED**
Warmer: Ten pieces of paper with action words, e.g. *open your books, close the door, clean your shoes, write a word*, and ten pieces of paper with adverbs, e.g. *quickly, carefully, slowly*
Extra activity 1: Choose ten sentences / questions from Units 1 to 8 which include key vocabulary / grammar from *Kid's Box 4*. Write each one in scrambled word order on a large piece of paper.
Optional: *Kid's Box Interactive DVD 4: Stella's room* Quiz 4, Test Units 5–8 from *Kid's Box Teacher's Resource Book 4* (pages 113–135), *Kid's Box 4 Language Portfolio* page 6

Warmer

- Invite three pupils to come to the front. They pick one action word card and one adverb. They all mime the action, but one of them does it in the extreme, e.g. the most slowly. The class guesses the action and the adverb and then says who is doing it the most, e.g. slowly. Repeat.

PB81. ACTIVITY 2. *Tell the story.* [M] towards

- Tell pupils to open their Pupil's Book at page 81 and to look at the pictures. Elicit one or two things they can see, but don't elicit the story. Check they have read the activity instruction and know what to do. They tell the story in the past. Pupils work in groups of four and create their story. They don't write their stories. This is an oral activity. Monitor and help / advise. If the stories are quite similar, elicit the story from the class in sections, different groups telling different parts. If the stories are quite different, elicit complete stories from each group and discuss the differences.

PB81. ACTIVITY 3. *Now write the story.*

- Pupils work individually. They write their story from Activity 2, paying attention to the correct use of past forms. Monitor and encourage pupils to use linking words (e.g. *and, but*) and sequencing words (e.g. *next, then*).

PB81. QUIZ!

- Say *Now let's do a quiz*. Focus pupils on the questions. Pupils look back through Units 7 and 8 and find the answers. They discuss them in groups of four. Check with the class.
- Pupils write two more questions of their own to help them remember the language and / or vocabulary from the units. They write the questions in their notebooks. Pupils close their Pupil's Books. Volunteers ask the class one of their revision questions.

Key: 1 Lenny and Stella. 2 They flew. 3 A lorry. 4 Cheese sandwiches, salad, pasta and chocolate cake. 5 Suzy. 6 A tiger, parrot food, a bottle of water and a box of fruit.

AB81. ACTIVITY 4. *Circle the odd one out.* [M] towards

- Tell pupils to open their Activity Book at page 81. Focus them on the activity. Elicit what they are going to do (they have done this type of activity before). They find and circle the odd one out in each line. Pupils work in pairs. Check the odd ones out with the class.

Key: 2 climbed, 3 twelve, 4 hungry, 5 vegetable, 6 lift, 7 sweater, 8 were, 9 ate, 10 through, 11 beard, 12 sang

AB81. ACTIVITY 5. *Now complete the crossword. Write the message.*

- Pupils use the words from Activity 4 to complete the crossword and then the message (Bye! Time to fly!).
- They check in pairs. Check with the class.

Key:

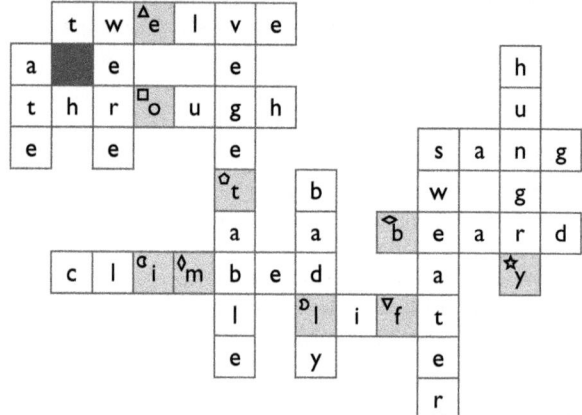

Extra activities: see page T119 (if time)

Optional evaluations

- Quiz 4 from *Kid's Box Interactive DVD 4* (*Stella's room* section). This quiz can be done as a whole-class activity or as a team competition. See pages 36 and 37 of the Teacher's Booklet for the Interactive DVD.
- The test for Units 5–8 from *Teacher's Resource Book 4* (pages 113–135).

Language Portfolio

- Pupils complete page 6 of *Kid's Box 4 Language Portfolio* (*I can … Units 7–8*).

Ending the lesson

- Pupils work in groups of four. They need one *Do you remember?* between three. Two pupils (A) use a book (or paper) to cover the words from Unit 7. The other two pupils (B) take turns to say what each picture is and to spell the word. 'A's look and check. They reverse roles for Unit 8.
- Talk about the *Can do* statements from Units 7 and 8 with pupils and elicit examples from volunteers for each one.
- Ask pupils which lessons, topics and / or activities were their favourites. If this is your last class, say *Goodbye. See you next year!*

2 Tell the story.

> Peter got up. He was sad. He wanted to play football outside, but the weather was terrible …

3 Now write the story.

> Peter got up. He was sad. He wanted to play football outside, but the weather was terrible …

Quiz!

1 Who was in the Kid's Box Quiz Final?
2 What did the parrots do at the zoo?
3 What did Nick Motors take from the zoo?
4 What was there to eat at Simon's party?
5 Who jumped the most slowly in the sack race?
6 What did Nick Motors find inside the lorry?

Units 1 & 2 — Values: Value others

1 Look and think. Say 'yes' or 'no'.
1 When our friends help us at school, we say 'sorry'.
2 We can give flowers to people when we want to say thank you.
3 We say thank you to people when they help us.
4 When our parents give us a party, we say 'goodbye'.

2 Listen and check.

3 Read and complete in pairs.

> our teacher. them a letter. and smile at them.
> ~~they help us.~~ say thank you. give them a picture.

We say thank you to people when …   *they help us.*

1 We say thank you to people when …
2 We can give someone a present to …
3 When people help us, we can say thank you …
4 When we enjoy a school lesson we can say thank you to …
5 When we want to say thank you to people, we can …
6 To say thank you to someone we can sometimes write …

OBJECTIVES: By the end of the lesson, pupils will have read and talked about valuing others.

● **TARGET LANGUAGE**
Key language: value (v), others
Revision: say thank you / sorry / goodbye, enjoy, give, smile (v)

● **MATERIALS REQUIRED**
Extra activity 1: A piece of paper per pupil, coloured pencils or crayons
Extra activity 2: Pairs of phrases forming dialogues using language from the lesson, e.g. *Thank you, Elena. / That's all right. / These flowers are for you. / Thank you, they're beautiful.* One phrase per pupil, written on a separate piece of paper.

Warmer
- Ask a pupil to pass you a book, pen or pencil. Take the item without speaking. Ask the class what you should say. Elicit *Thank you*. Ask pupils about the last time they said 'Thank you'.

PB82. ACTIVITY 1. *Look and think. Say 'yes' or 'no'.*
- Tell pupils to open their Pupil's Book at page 82. Focus on the title and explain *value others*. Elicit *lunch box, balloons, teacher, present, flowers*, etc. Pupils work in pairs. Do not confirm answers.

PB82. ACTIVITY 2. *Listen and check.*
- Play the CD. Pupils listen and check their answers to Activity 1. Check with the class. Play the CD again and check comprehension. Ask, e.g. *What's the matter with Peter? How does Jim help? Who's Mr Brown? Who is the woman in number 3? How did she help the children? What did the man think of the party? What does Mary say?* Talk briefly in L1 about valuing others. Ask if pupils have ever given a friend, teacher or relative a 'thank you' present.

Key: 1 No, 2 Yes, 3 Yes, 4 No

CD 3, 16
1.
PETER: Oh, I haven't got my fruit today and I'm hungry.
JIM: That's not a problem. I've got an apple and a banana. Which do you want, Peter?
PETER: Really, can I have one? Thanks, Jim. You're a great friend.
JIM: That's all right, Peter. That's what friends are for.
2.
JACK: Here you are, Aunt Sally. These flowers are for you.
AUNT SALLY: Thank you, Jack! They're beautiful. Why are you giving me flowers?
GIRL: When our mum was in hospital you were at home. You were there to help us.
JACK: We want to say thank you.
AUNT SALLY: Aw. Thank *you*, children.
3.
GIRL: Mr Brown. This is for you. It's from all the class.
MR BROWN: Ooh. For me? Thank you very much, children.
GIRL: We want to say goodbye and thank you.
PUPILS: Thank you, Mr Brown!
MR BROWN: That's nice. Thank you all very much. You're a very good class.

4.
DAD: Well, that was a good party.
MARY: No, Dad. It was a really good party. It was great! Thank you very much. I'm really happy.
DAD: I'm really happy that you're happy, Mary.
MARY: You're my super dad!

PB82. ACTIVITY 3. *Read and complete in pairs.*
- Pupils work in pairs. Write the sentence halves on the board. Elicit the endings.

Key: 2 say thank you. 3 and smile at them. 4 our teacher. 5 give them a picture. 6 them a letter.

AB82. ACTIVITY 1. *Listen and number.*
- Tell pupils to open their Activity Book at page 82. Play the CD. Pupils write numbers in pencil. They compare in pairs. Play the CD again. Check answers.

Key: a 5, c 3, d 6, e 2, f 4

CD 3, 17
1.
BOY: That was a great lesson, Mr Green.
MR GREEN: Thank you. I'm happy you enjoy my lessons.
GIRL: I want to learn lots of Maths with you.
2.
JACK: Thanks for helping me, Grandpa. Here's a picture for you.
GRANDPA: For me! Thank you, Jack. I love your pictures. It's beautiful.
JACK: And I love you, Grandpa. You're great!
3.
VICKY: Would you like one of my oranges, Jane?
JANE: Ooh, thanks, Vicky. You're a good friend.
4.
JOHN: Goodbye, Doctor Read. Thank you very much for helping me to get better.
DR READ: That's all right, John. I'm happy to see you're well again.
JOHN: You're a very good doctor.
DR READ: And you're a very good boy, John. Take care!
5.
BOY: Hey! Your book's on the ground, behind you.
GIRL: Oh, yes, it is. Thank you very much.
6.
WOMAN: Here's your fish and chips. Enjoy your lunch.
GIRL: Ooh, that's nice. Thank you very much.

AB82. ACTIVITY 2. *Read and choose.*
- Focus pupils on Activity 2. Go through the questions and the example. Pupils choose their answers individually and then compare in pairs. Elicit answers. Encourage pupils to give reasons.

Key: 2 a, 3 b, 4 c

Extra activities: see page T119 (if time)

Ending the lesson
- Write anagrams on the board of ways to say 'Thank you' from the lesson, e.g. *flowers, picture, letter, smile*. Pupils solve the anagrams in pairs.

OBJECTIVES: By the end of the lesson, pupils will have talked about being kind and practised helping others.

● TARGET LANGUAGE

Key language: *kind* (adj), *seat*, *Would you like to … ? Shall I … ? Can you help me, please? have a turn / give someone a turn*
Additional language: *Excuse me, carry, You're welcome, No problem, That's all right, Are you sure?*
Revision: *children, What's the matter?*

● MATERIALS REQUIRED

Extra activity 2: Large piece of paper per group of three or four pupils

Warmer

- Write the words *Be kind* on the board. Check comprehension. Elicit examples of kind things we can do. If pupils answer in L1, recast their ideas into English.

PB83. ACTIVITY 1. *Look and think. Say 'yes' or 'no'.*

- Tell pupils to open their Pupil's Book at page 83. Direct them to the four pictures. Elicit what they can see (e.g. *bus, park, supermarket, shopping bags, swings*). Read the activity instruction aloud and choose pupils to read the sentences. Check comprehension. Pupils work in pairs to talk about the sentences. Monitor and encourage them to speak in English but do not confirm answers.

PB83. ACTIVITY 2. *Listen and check.*

- Tell pupils to listen carefully. Play the CD. Pupils listen and check their answers to Activity 1. Check with the class. Play the CD again and elicit the useful phrases for being kind and saying 'thank you'. Write them on the board in two columns (e.g. Column 1: *Excuse me. Would you like to sit down? Can I help you? I can get it for you. No problem. Shall I carry your bags for you? Do you want to have a turn?*; Column 2: *That's good of you. Thank you (very much). That is kind of you. That's great, thanks.*
- Talk briefly in L1 about being kind to others. Ask pupils if they have been in any of the situations in the pictures or seen others being kind in this way. Ask how they feel if someone helps them.

Key: 1 Yes, 2 Yes, 3 No, 4 No

CD 3, 18

1.
GIRL: Excuse me, would you like to sit down?
WOMAN: Oh, thank you very much, my dear. That's good of you. I'm very tired.
GIRL: That's all right. I can stand here. That's fine.

2.
BOY 1: Hello. What's the matter? Can I help you?
BOY 2: Oh no! My kite's in the tree. I can't get it. It's very high.
BOY 1: I can get it for you. Look, here you are. No problem.
BOY 2: Oh, thank you very much.

3.
BOY: Excuse me! Shall I carry your bags for you?
WOMAN: Oh, yes, please. Would you take them to my car for me, please?
BOY: Yes, of course. That's no problem.
WOMAN: It's over there, in the car park. That is kind of you. Thank you very much, young man.
BOY: You're welcome.

4.
GIRL 1: Hello. Do you want to have a turn?
GIRL 2: Oh, great! Are you sure?
GIRL 1: Yes, here you are.
GIRL 2: Thanks.
GIRL 1: No problem, but remember to give the other children a turn too.
GIRL 2: Yes, of course.

PB83. ACTIVITY 3. *Read and match.*

- Focus pupils on Activity 3. Read the activity instruction and do an example with the class. Pupils work in pairs to match the rest of the sentence halves. Check with the class.

Key: 1 d, 2 c, 3 a, 4 b

AB83. ACTIVITY 1. *Read and complete.*

- Tell pupils to open their Activity Book at page 83. Focus on Activity 1. Check comprehension of the phrases in the box. Pupils work individually to copy the phrases in the correct speech bubbles. Tell them to write in pencil. They compare answers in pairs. Check with the class.

Key: a Would you like to sit down? b Can you help me, please? c What's the matter? d Shall I carry your shopping?

AB83. ACTIVITY 2. *Read and choose.*

- Focus on Activity 2. Pupils work in pairs to complete the activity. They circle the correct word in pencil. Elicit answers and check comprehension.

Key: 2 helps, 3 carries, 4 shares, 5 'Thank you'

Extra activities: see pages T119–T120 (if time)

Ending the lesson

- Mime one of the problems from Activity 1 (e.g. carrying heavy bags). Pupils put up their hands when they know what to say. Elicit appropriate sentences for offering help (e.g. *Can I carry your bags for you?*). Repeat with a different mime (standing on a bus looking tired / trying to reach something high up / playing on a swing).

Be kind | **Values** | **Units 3 & 4**

1 Look and think. Say 'yes' or 'no'.

1 We can give our seat to older people on the bus.
2 It's good to help younger children with a problem.
3 We can ask old people to carry our bags.
4 We can stay on the toys in the park when other children are waiting to use them.

2 Listen and check. (18 CD3)

3 Read and match.

1 If we see old people on a bus or train, we can …
2 If we see small children with problems, we can …
3 If we see an older person with a shopping bag, we can …
4 When other children want the same thing as us, …

a carry it for them.
b we can take turns.
c try to help them.
d stand up and give them our seat.

Units 5 & 6 — Values: Be safe

1 Look and think. Say 'yes' or 'no'.
1. You can play near busy roads.
2. You can cross the road between cars.
3. You must stop, look and listen before you cross the road.
4. You must wear a helmet when you ride a bike.

2 Listen and check.

3 Read and complete in pairs.

> use it to cross the road.   can't see you.   busy roads.
> ~~ride a bike.~~   before you cross the road.

1. Remember to put on a helmet when you …
2. Don't stand between cars when you cross the road. Drivers …
3. Don't play next to …
4. Remember to stop, look and listen …
5. When there is a zebra crossing always …

OBJECTIVES: By the end of the lesson, pupils will have talked about road safety.

● **TARGET LANGUAGE**
Key language: *safe, dangerous, busy road, cross the street / road, 'stop, look and listen', helmet*
Additional language: *Be careful, traffic light, driver, zebra crossing, bright (red)*
Revision: *wear, ride a bike, can, must, always,* imperatives, prepositions: *near, next to, between*

● **MATERIALS REQUIRED**
Warmer: Coloured card or paper in red, yellow and green
Extra activity 2: White chalk or white tape (for making stripes on the floor / ground), red and green card

Warmer
- Show a piece of red paper and elicit *Stop / Danger*. Repeat with the green paper to elicit *Go*. Show the red, yellow and green paper. Teach / review *traffic light*.

PB84. ACTIVITY 1. *Look and think. Say 'yes' or 'no'.*
- Tell pupils to open their Pupil's Book at page 84. Focus on the lesson title and check comprehension of *safe*. Elicit *dangerous*. Elicit the things pupils can see in the pictures (e.g. cars, ball, bike). Teach / review *helmet*.
- Review *busy*. Elicit the answer for sentence 1 from the class (no). Pupils talk about the rest of the sentences in pairs. Do not confirm answers.

PB84. ACTIVITY 2. *Listen and check.*
- Play the CD. Pupils listen and check. Check with the class.
- Play the CD again and check comprehension. Review *zebra crossing* (see if pupils remember it from the joke on page 68 of the Activity Book). Pre-teach *bright*. Talk about road safety (including what to do when riding a bike) in L1 and how zebra crossings work in your country. Elicit any slogans used in L1 to teach road safety (e.g. *Stop, look, listen*).

Key: 1 No, 2 No, 3 Yes, 4 Yes

CD 3, 19

1.
PAUL: Here. Catch the ball.
GIRL: Whoops!
MAN: Be careful! You mustn't play with your ball near a busy road. It's very dangerous.
GIRL: Yes, you're right. I'm very sorry. Come on, Paul! Let's go and play in the park.
PAUL: Yes, that's a better idea. It's safer there.

2.
TOM: Oooh!
BOY: Tom! Be careful. You mustn't stand between cars to cross the road. The drivers can't see you.
TOM: Oh, yes, you're right. I didn't think.
BOY: Don't worry. Look, there's a zebra crossing over there. We can cross the road safely there.
TOM: OK. That's a good idea.

3.
GRACE: Be careful, Jim. You can't cross now.
JIM: Why not, Grace? It's a zebra crossing. It's safe.
GRACE: It's a zebra crossing, but it isn't safe at the moment. Can you see the traffic light? You can't cross when the man's red. You must always wait for the green man.
JIM: OK. But there isn't always a traffic light.
GRACE: No, you're right. That's why you must always remember to stop, look and listen before you cross the road.
JIM: Yes.

4.
JANE: Hi, Lily.
LILY: Hi, Jane. Are you ready for school?
JANE: Yes, I'm just getting on my bike.
LILY: Where's your helmet?
JANE: Oops! It's inside … with my bright green jacket. Can you wait one moment? I need to get it.
LILY: Yes, you do. You must always wear a helmet when you ride your bike.

PB84. ACTIVITY 3. *Read and complete in pairs.*
- Go through the example. Pupils work in pairs. Elicit the complete sentences or ask pupils to complete them on the board.

Key: 2 can't see you. 3 busy roads. 4 before you cross the road. 5 use it to cross the road.

AB84. ACTIVITY 1. *Look and write. What dangerous things can you see?*
- Tell pupils to open their Activity Book at page 84. Focus on Activity 1. Review *traffic light* and *zebra crossing*. Read the activity instruction and make sure pupils know what to do. Pupils write four more sentences in pairs. Check with the class.

Key: (in any order) 2 The boy is crossing the road between cars. 3 The girl on the bicycle isn't wearing a helmet. 4 The boy is skating on the road. 5 The boys are playing football next to the road.

AB84. ACTIVITY 2. *Put the words in order.*
- Focus pupils on Activity 2. Pupils work in pairs to reorder the rest of the words. Check with the class.

Key: 2 You mustn't cross the road between cars. 3 You must cross the road at a zebra crossing. 4 You mustn't play near busy roads. 5 Wear bright colours and a helmet on your bike.

Extra activities: see page T120 (if time)

Ending the lesson
- With books closed, say, e.g. *You mustn't play near busy ….* Pupils write the last word (e.g. *roads*). Repeat with different sentences, e.g. *When you ride a bicycle wear a (helmet). Don't cross the road between (cars). Always use a zebra (crossing).* Pupils compare their answers in pairs. Elicit answers.

OBJECTIVES: By the end of the lesson, pupils will have talked about recycling.

● TARGET LANGUAGE
Key language: *recycle, reuse, recycling bins*
Additional language: *right, wrong, recycled glass, can* (n)
Revision: *must / mustn't, can / can't, bottle, bowl, glass, clothes,* materials: *plastic, glass, paper, colours*

● MATERIALS REQUIRED
Warmer and Ending the lesson: Items which can be recycled, made from different materials (e.g. empty glass jar, plastic bottles, empty drinks can, old newspapers / magazines, cardboard boxes)
Extra activity 2: Very large piece of paper or display board for a class poster

Warmer
- Show the items you have brought to class and ask what they have in common. Elicit (in L1) that they can all be recycled. Write *Recycling* on the board and check comprehension.

PB85. ACTIVITY 1. *Look and think. Say 'yes' or 'no'.*
- Tell pupils to open their Pupil's Book at page 85. Focus on the lesson title and review the meaning of the verb *recycle*. Check pupils know the difference between *recycle* and *reuse*. Elicit what pupils can see in the pictures and pre-teach *recycling bin*. Read the activity instruction and the sentences aloud. Check comprehension. Elicit the answer for sentence 1 (yes). Pupils work in pairs to talk about the rest of the sentences.

PB85. ACTIVITY 2. *Listen and check.*
- Play the CD. Pupils listen and check their answers to Activity 1. Check with the class. Play the CD again and check comprehension. Elicit what the granddad is doing to the bottle (he's squashing it) and ask why people should do this before putting plastic bottles in recycling bins (to make them smaller). Talk in L1 about the importance of recycling and ask pupils what they recycle at home, what colour the recycling bins are in their town, etc.

Key: 1 Yes, 2 No, 3 Yes, 4 No

CD 3, 20
1.
GRANDDAD: Can you put this bottle in that bin, please, Jack?
JACK: OK, Granddad, but we can't put it in this one. We need to put it into the yellow bin over there.
GRANDDAD: Oh, really? What's the difference?
JACK: The yellow bin is for plastic, the green bin is for glass, the blue bin is for paper and the red bin is for cans.
GRANDDAD: I see! So now we can put these boxes in the blue bin.
JACK: Yes, Granddad. It's good to recycle.

2.
BOY: Hello, Lucy. Where are you going?
LUCY: I'm taking this bag of glass bottles and things to the recycling bin over there.
BOY: Yes, at home we recycle glass. I love throwing the glass into the bin. Can I help you?
LUCY: If you want. Thanks.

3.
GIRL: Sally, look at these handbags. They're interesting.
SALLY: Yes, they are, and each one is different.
GIRL: Hey! They're made from recycled clothes.
MUM: Yes, they're made from old jeans. That's really clever.
GIRL: I think they're beautiful! Can I have one please, Mum?

4.
GIRL: Mum, what are you doing with those clothes?
MUM: I'm putting them in this bag, ready to take to the clothes recycling bin.
GIRL: Can't we give them to someone?
MUM: No, these clothes are very old. No-one can use them.
GIRL: Ah. I see, so when we can't reuse something we can still recycle it.
MUM: That's right.

PB85. ACTIVITY 3. *Read and match.*
- Focus pupils on Activity 3. Read the activity instruction and do the first one together. Check comprehension of *make smaller*. Pupils work in pairs to match the rest of the sentence halves. Check with the class.

Key: 1 d, 2 c, 3 b, 4 a

AB85. ACTIVITY 1. *Read and match.*
- Tell pupils to open their Activity Book at page 85. Focus on the pictures in Activity 1. Pre-teach / review *wrong*.
- Go through the example. Pupils work in pairs to match the rest of the pictures. They number them in pencil. Check with the class.

Key: 2 e, 3 a, 4 f, 5 b, 6 d

AB85. ACTIVITY 2. *Look and write. What good things are the people doing?*
- Focus on Activity 2. Read the activity instructions and the example. Make sure pupils know what to do. They write three more sentences in pairs. Check with the class.

Key: (in any order) 2 The boy is making plastic bottles smaller. 3 The man is putting a can in the right bin / The man is recycling a can. 4 The woman is reusing clothes. / The woman is making new clothes from old clothes.

Extra activities: see page T120 (if time)

Ending the lesson
- Show the items you have brought to class again. Ask pupils what material each one is made from (in English if possible) and whether it is possible to recycle the item at school or in the pupils' town. Ask which colour bin each item should go in.

Recycle | Values | Units 7 & 8

1 Look and think. Say 'yes' or 'no'.
1 We must put plastic and paper into special bins.
2 We mustn't recycle glass.
3 We can make things from old clothes.
4 We mustn't recycle clothes.

2 Listen and check.

3 Read and match.
1 When we can't reuse things, we …   a from old clothes.
2 Make plastic bottles smaller …   b into the right recycling bins.
3 Always put paper, glass, plastic and cans …   c before you recycle them.
4 We can make new things …   d can sometimes recycle them.

Grammar reference

Pupil's Book

Grandpa Star's **older than** Mr Star.
The dog's **bigger than** the cat.
Uncle Fred's **funnier than** Aunt May.

He **sometimes** has to get up at 5 o'clock.
She **always** has to work at the weekend.
He **never** has to do his homework on Saturday.

1 He's / She's the teacher **who's** wearing a red sweater.
They're the girls **who are** skipping.

2 What can I **learn to do**?
You can **learn to sing**.
What do you / they want to **learn to do**?
I / We / They want to **learn to paint**.
I / We / They don't want to **learn to roller skate**.
What does he / she want to **learn to do**?
He / She wants to **learn to dance**.
He / She doesn't want to **learn to ride** a horse.

What's the Activity Centre?
It's a place **where** you can learn to swim.

3 I / You / He / She / It / We / They **had / didn't have** lunch at school.
Did you **see** the dentist last year?
Yes, I **did**. / No, I **didn't**.
Did he / she **eat** chocolate cake?
Yes, he / she **did**. / No, he / she **didn't**.
How many ice creams **did** you **have**?
I **had** two ice creams. / I **didn't have** an ice cream.

Her mum gave her medicine **because** she had a headache.
I had a drink **because** I was hot.
They ate a sandwich **because** they were hungry.

4 What **did** Alex **need**?
Alex **needed** a hat and a scarf.
Where **did** she **live**?
She **lived** in a big town.
Who **did** Mr Burke **stop**?
Mr Burke **stopped** Simon.
What **did** Simon **carry**?
Simon **carried** the boxes.

5 They were hungry **so** they ate an apple.
It was cold **so** they had a hot drink.
I couldn't find my map **so** I got lost.

interesting ⟶ more interesting
This film is **more interesting** than that one.
famous ⟶ more famous
She is **more famous** than him.
difficult ⟶ more difficult
Maths homework is **more difficult** than English homework.

My bike goes **more slowly** than yours.
He rides his bike **more carefully** than her.

6 What **did** you **buy**?
I **bought / didn't buy** a new laptop.
Where **did** he **put** the DVD?
He **put / didn't put** it on the table.
What **did** they **think**?
They **thought / didn't think** the internet was slow.
What **did** she **know**?
She **knew / didn't know** the song on the radio.

7 quick ⟶ quicker ⟶ the quickest
It's **the quickest** lizard in the world.
beautiful ⟶ more beautiful ⟶ the most beautiful
Blue whales are **the most beautiful** animals.
good ⟶ better ⟶ the best
I think rabbits are **the best** pets.

What **did** you **eat**?
I **ate / didn't eat** the cake.
What **did** he / she **see**?
He / She **saw / didn't see** a dolphin.
Where **did** they / we **swim**?
They / We **swam / didn't swim** in the sea.

8 slowly ⟶ more slowly ⟶ the most slowly
The woman's walking **the most slowly**.
carefully ⟶ more carefully ⟶ the most carefully
The boys are riding **the most carefully**.

Grammar reference

Activity Book

ANSWER KEY

AB86. ACTIVITY. *Read and complete.*
Key: 1 easier, 2 younger, 3 thinner, 4 shorter

AB86. ACTIVITY 1. *Look and complete.*
Key: 1 's, 2 are, 3 who, 4 singing

AB86. ACTIVITY 2. *Read and order the words. Make sentences.*
Key: 1 You can learn to dance. 2 He wants to learn to swim. 3 It's a place where you can learn to sail. 4 They don't want to learn to skate.

AB86. ACTIVITY 3. *Look and complete.*
Key: eat, Yes, did, ate, didn't

AB87. ACTIVITY 4. *Read and circle the correct answer.*
Key: 1 danced, 2 tried, 3 dropped, 4 laughed

AB87. ACTIVITY 5. *Read and circle the correct answer.*
Key: 1 slowly, 2 carefully, 3 better, 4 loudly

AB87. ACTIVITY 6. *Read and complete.*
Key: 1 bought, 2 put, 3 caught, 4 went, 5 said, 6 brought

AB87. ACTIVITY 7. *Match the sentences.*
Key: 1 b, 2 c, 3 a

AB87. ACTIVITY 8. *Look and complete.*
Key: 1 most carefully, 2 worst, 3 most loudly, 4 the best

Movers practice test audioscript

CD 3, 21 Pupil's Book. Movers test. Pages 88–103. Listening. Part 1.

Look at Part 1. Look at the picture. Listen and look. There is one example.

Here's my favourite café, Aunt Sue. Some people from my school are here.
Oh. Tell me about them.
OK. That's Peter there.
Is he the boy with the fair hair who's looking at his watch?
Yes. He's waiting for a friend, I think.

Can you see the line? This is an example.

Now you listen and draw lines.

1 Look! There's my friend, Daisy!
  Which one is she?
  She's sitting there, at a round table.
  What's she doing?
  She's eating a sandwich.
  Oh, yes.
2 I'm thirsty.
  Well, we can have a drink here.
  Yes. Jim's having a cup of coffee.
  Which boy is he?
  The one in the white sweater.
3 That boy can't go inside the café. He's got a puppy with him.
  Oh, that's Paul.
  Is he in your class?
  Yes. He got that puppy last week.
4 Can you see the girl who's carrying some glasses?
  Yes. Does she work here?
  Only at weekends. I know her. Her name's Mary.
  She's got a lot of glasses!
  Yes. Be careful! Don't drop them!
5 There's my sister!
  Oh! Where?
  There! She's sitting at that square table.
  Oh, yes. That's Vicky! What's she doing?
  She's doing her homework in the café. She is naughty!

CD 3, 21 Now listen to Part 1 again.

[Repeat audioscript]

CD 3, 22 Part 2.

Listen and look. There is one example.

Dad, you know that village?
Yes. You went there with your class.
Yes. Well, I've got to write about it. Can you help me?
OK. When did you go there?
Was it last Friday?
Friday. That's right.

Can you see the answer? Now you listen and write.

1 Who did you talk to in the village?
  We talked to a farmer.
  And was the farmer nice to your class?
  Yes. He showed us all his animals.
2 Which were the biggest animals on the farm?
  I don't know. Oh, the goats, I think.
  Did you see any cows?
  Oh, yes! The brown and white cows were the biggest animals.
3 And what do they eat?
  I don't know.
  Well, where did you see them?
  In a field.
  Was there any grass in that field?
  Oh, now I know! They eat grass!
4 What's the name of the village?
  Upton.
  Can you spell it?
  Yes. It's U-P-T-O-N.
  Good.
5 One last thing. How many people live there?
  Sixty, I think.
  It's a very small place.
  It is small, but I made a mistake. There are seventy people in the village.
  Seventy?
  That's right.

CD 3, 22 Now listen to Part 2 again.

[Repeat audioscript]

CD 3, 23 Part 3.

What sport does Peter do in these places?

Listen and write a letter in these box. There is one example.

Do you like doing different sports, Peter?
Yes. I love doing different sports. Last week I did a very long run for the first time.
Where did you do that?
At school. We all had to do it. We were very tired after it.

Can you see the letter H? Now you listen and write the letter in the box.

1 What's your favourite sport?
  Ummm. Horse riding, I think. It's really exciting.
  Where do you do that?
  There's a riding school near the lake. I go there for a lesson every Saturday.
2 I love climbing too.
  Do you do that in the mountains?
  No. That's too dangerous for me now. I do it at the sports centre. They have a wall you can climb on.
  Is it difficult?
  Yes but it's fun.
3 What about bike riding? Do you like that?
  Yes. I do that a lot with my friends. We go to the park and ride there.
  That's good. It's safe there because there are no cars.
  Yes. That's what Mum says too.
4 I went fishing with Dad last weekend.
  Did you catch one?
  No. It was boring. But Dad loved it.
  Ha ha. Did you go on a boat on the lake?
  No. We were in a field by the river.
5 What other sports do you do?
  Swimming. When it's hot I love going to the beach.
  Me too. But only when the water is warm!
  Yes and I never go in when there are jellyfish.
  Oh no! I'm frightened of them too.

CD 3, 23 Now listen to Part 3 again.

[Repeat audioscript]

CD 3, 24 Part 4.

Look at the pictures. Listen and look.

There is one example.

What was the weather like last weekend?

What did you do last weekend?
Oh, we went to the beach, but we couldn't swim.
Why not? Did it rain?
No, but it was very cold and windy. We flew our kites.

Can you see the tick? Now you listen and tick the box.

1 Where did Alex go after school?
   I didn't see you at the library after school yesterday, Alex.
   No. I didn't go to the library.
   Oh. Did you go to the cinema? There's a good film on this week.
   No, I had to go to the hospital to see my uncle.
2 What did they do at the party?
   Did you enjoy Sam's birthday party?
   Yes. It was great.
   What did you do? Did you play games and have some birthday cake?
   Mum! That's for babies. We played music and danced.
3 What did the man buy?
   What did you buy at the shops?
   Well, I found a great new coat.
   Good! You needed one. Did you get some shoes, too?
   No, but I got this scarf.
   Very nice!
4 Where do the aliens live?
   I wrote a story about some aliens at school today, Dad.
   Tell me all about it. Do they live on the moon?
   No, they live in this world.
   Where? In the forest?
   No, in the ground, under rocks. It's an exciting story!
5 Which zoo animals did the girl like?
   The zoo was so good. I loved the pandas.
   Yes, I liked them, too. And the dolphins. They're so funny!
   And the big strong lions were great!
   Oh, no! I was afraid of them.

CD 3, 24 Now listen to Part 4 again.
[Repeat audioscript]

CD 3, 25 Part 5.
Look at the picture. Listen and look.
There is one example.

Hello! Can you colour this picture for me?
OK. What is it?
It's a bathroom with a bath and shower.
Oh, yes. There's lots of water!
Well, colour the water in the bath.
Right. Let's make it blue.

Can you see the blue water in the bath?
This is an example.
Now you listen and colour and write.

1 Can you see the toothbrush?
  Which one? There are two.
  The toothbrush in the boy's hand. He's cleaning his teeth with it.
  OK. Can I colour it red?
  Yes. I like that colour.
  So do I.
2 There are some towels on the floor.
  Yes. They're all wet.
  One towel isn't wet. It's on the chair.
  Yes. Colour that one. You can choose the colour.
  OK. I'm colouring it purple.
3 Would you like to write something now?
  All right.
  Can you see the bowl?
  Yes.
  Well, write the name Tom on the bowl.
  OK, I'm writing it. He's the boy in the picture, I think.
4 Next, look at the bottles.
  Right. There are three of them.
  Yes. Find the smallest bottle …
  OK.
  … and colour it green.
  Easy!
5 This is the last thing.
  OK.
  Colour one of the toy ducks.
  Which one?
  The one next to the boy's foot.
  Right. I'm colouring that duck yellow.
  Good! The picture looks great now!

CD 3, 25 Now listen to Part 5 again.
[Repeat audioscript]

Movers practice test key

LISTENING
Part 1 – 5 marks
1 Daisy at round table, eating sandwich
2 Jim in white sweater, with cup of coffee
3 Paul with puppy on lead
4 Mary carrying tray of glasses
5 Vicky sitting at square table, doing homework

Part 2 – 5 marks
1 (a / the) farmer; 2 (the) brown and white cows; 3 (the) grass; 4 Upton; 5 70 / seventy

Part 3 – 5 marks
1 horse riding F; 2 climbing C; 3 riding a bike B; 4 fishing G; 5 swimming E

Part 4 – 5 marks
1 a; 2 b; 3 b; 4 a; 5 c

Part 5 – 5 marks
1 Colour toothbrush in boy's hand – red
2 Colour towel on chair – purple
3 Write Tom on bowl
4 Colour smallest bottle – green
5 Colour toy duck by boy's foot – yellow

READING AND WRITING
Part 1 – 6 marks
1 a stomach; 2 penguins; 3 a neck; 4 a nose; 5 rabbits

Part 2 – 6 marks
1 B; 2 A; 3 C; 4 B; 5 B; 6 A

Part 3 – 6 marks
1 map; 2 angry; 3 water; 4 parrots; 5 ate; 6 The hungry pirates

Part 4 – 5 marks
1 of; 2 eat; 3 their; 4 moving; 5 are

Part 5 – 7 marks
1 idea; 2 car; 3 a market; 4 a big bag; 5 the balcony; 6 salad; 7 funny

Part 6 – 6 marks
1 is playing
2 on a blanket (on the grass)
3 (The cat is sitting) in/on the tree.
4 (They're wearing) roller skates.
5 and 6 e.g.
The dog is bigger than the small girl., There are three children in the playground., The sky is blue., The boy who is playing football is wearing a blue T-shirt.

Movers practice test   Listening

Part 1   5 questions

 Listen and draw lines. There is one example.

Vicky   Peter   Mary   Paul

Daisy   Jim   Fred

Part 2 5 questions

 Listen and write. There is one example.

The village

	When?	Friday
1	Talked to	
2	Biggest animals	
3	Animals' food	
4	Name of village	
5	Number of people in village	

Part 3 5 questions

23 CD3 What sport does Peter do in these places?
Listen and write a letter in each box. There is one example.

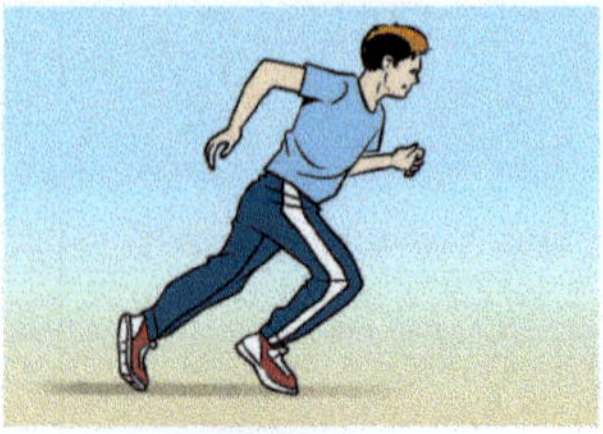

running [H]

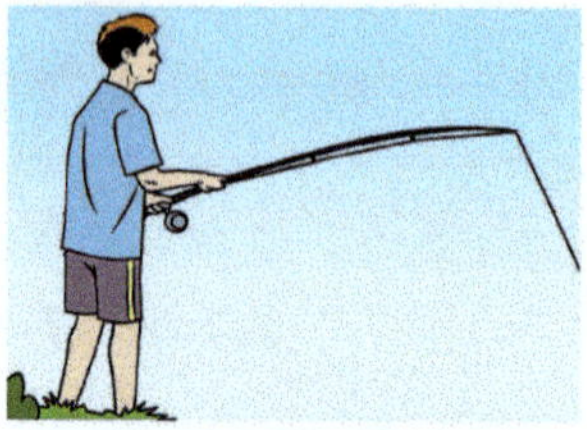

fishing [ ]

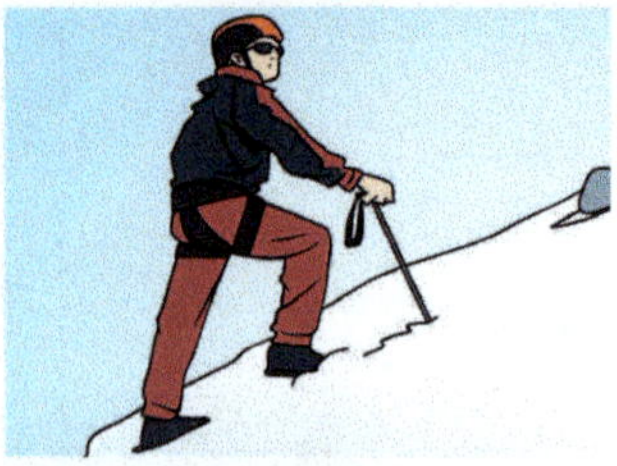

climbing [ ]

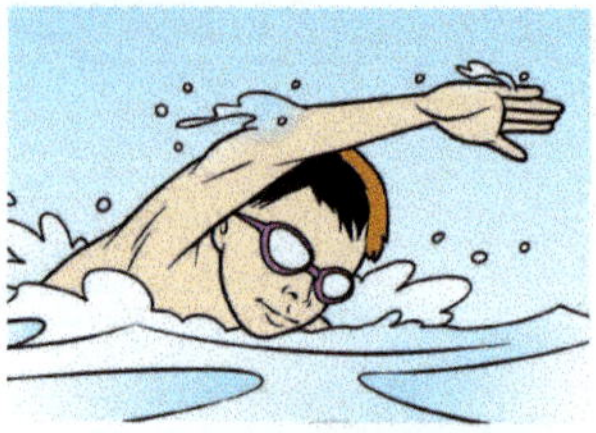

swimming [ ]

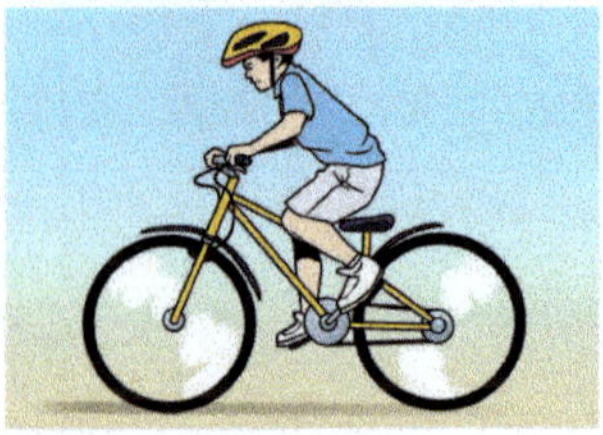

riding a bike [ ]

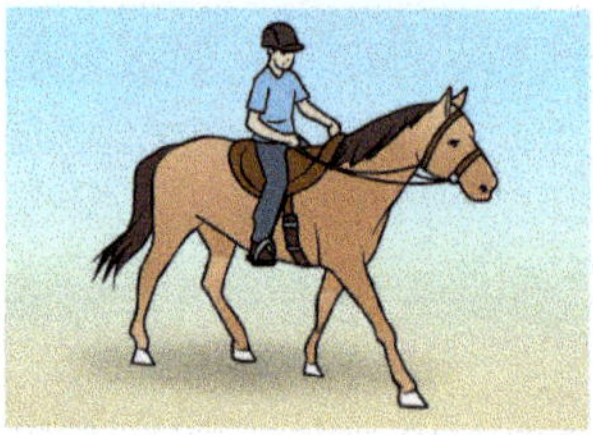

horse riding [ ]

A

B

C

D
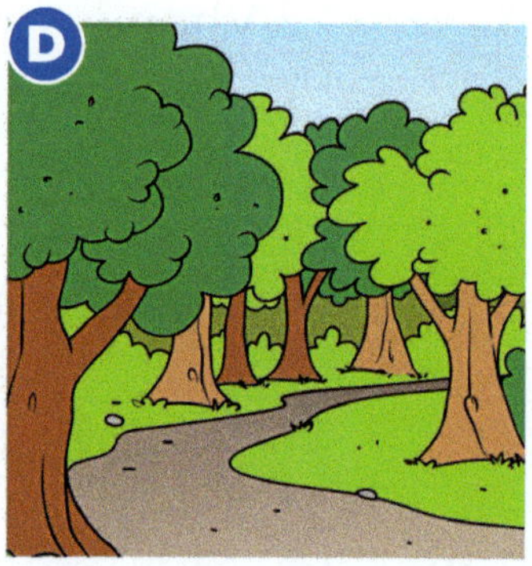

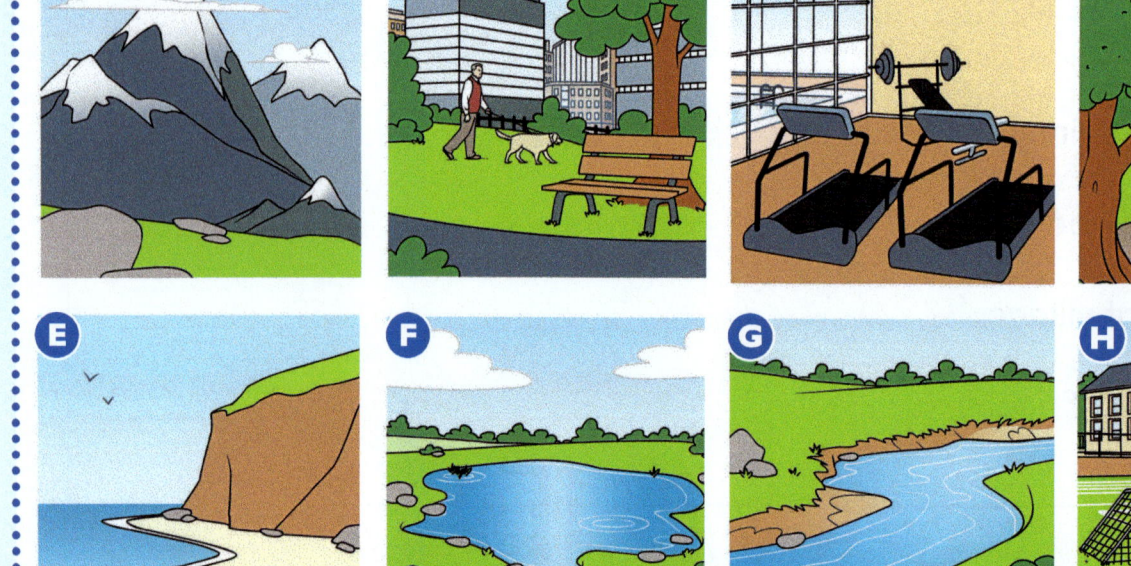

E

F

G

H
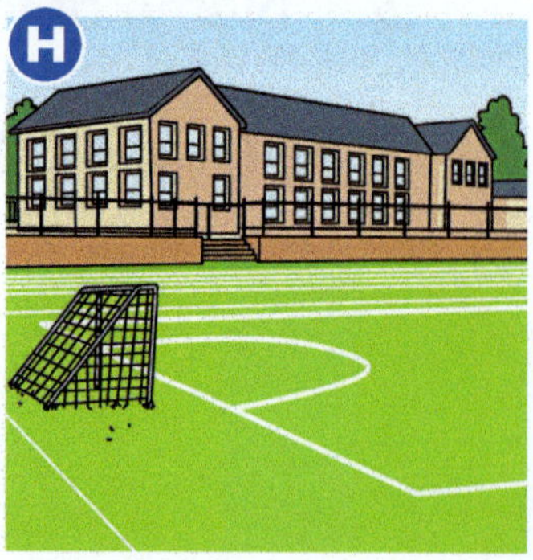

Part 4 5 questions

 Listen and tick (✓) the box. There is one example.

What was the weather like last weekend?

1 Where did Alex go after school?

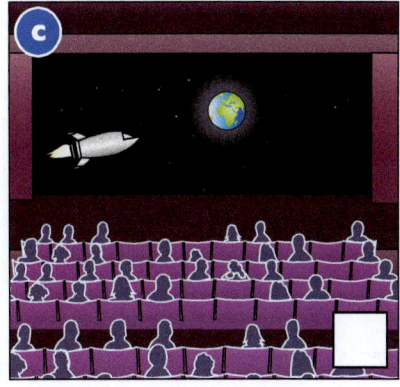

2 What did they do at the party?

3 What did the man buy?

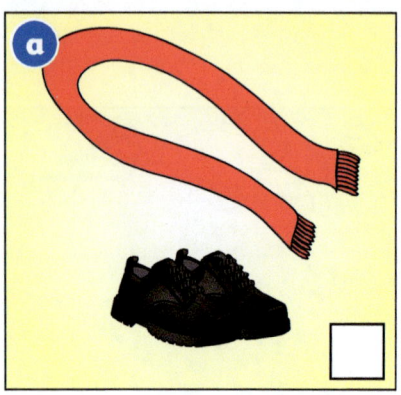 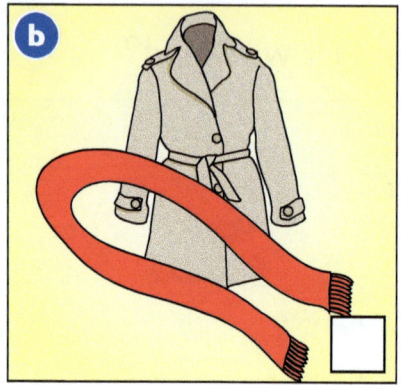 

4 Where do the aliens live?

5 Which zoo animals did the girl like?

Part 5 5 questions

25 Listen and colour and write. There is one example.

Movers practice test — Reading & Writing

Part **5 questions**

Look and read. Choose the correct words and write them on the lines. There is one example.

a neck

penguins

kittens

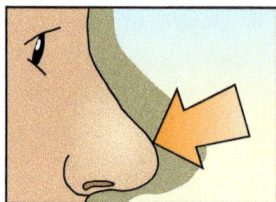
a nose

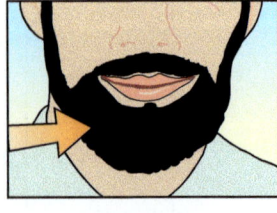
a beard

rabbits

mice

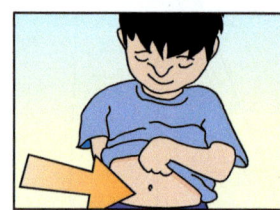
a stomach

Example

These pet animals are baby cats.   ___kittens___

Questions

1 When you eat, your food and drink goes here.   _____
2 These animals can swim.   _____
3 This is between your head and your shoulders.   _____
4 This is on your face, between your eyes and your mouth.   _____
5 These animals have big ears. They eat grass.   _____

Part 2 6 questions

Read the text and choose the best answer.

Example

Miss Grey: Hello, Jack. Why are you sitting there?
Jack: A I can't walk home.
 B It doesn't work.
 C I'm not walking.

Questions

1 **Miss Grey:** Oh dear! What's the matter?
 Jack: A It doesn't matter.
 B I hurt my foot.
 C It hurt me.

2 **Miss Grey:** When did you do that?
 Jack: A After school this afternoon.
 B I didn't do it.
 C I'm sorry.

3 Miss Grey: Don't cry! I can help you. Where do you live?
Jack:
   A It's a big house.
   B At home.
   C In Bath Street.

4 Miss Grey: Is there a bus to your house?
Jack:
   A No, I haven't got a ticket.
   B No, we always walk.
   C No, but I like going by bus.

5 Miss Grey: Have you got your phone with you?
Jack:
   A No. He hasn't got one.
   B No. I lost it yesterday.
   C No. There isn't a phone.

6 Miss Grey: Well, do you want to phone your mum?
Jack:
   A Yes, please!
   B Yes, you do.
   C Yes, it would.

Part 3 6 questions

Read the story. Choose a word from the box.
Write the correct word next to numbers 1–5.
There is one example.

The Flying Shark was a very famous pirate ship. Everyone was afraid of the pirates from this ship. But one day they got lost. They ____sailed____ to an island to look for treasure. They looked and looked but they couldn't find any because there was a mistake on their **(1)** _____ . They were on the wrong island! The pirates were very **(2)** _____. In the morning it was very hot but there was nothing to eat or drink. Now they didn't want treasure. They wanted food and **(3)** _____. Then they heard someone calling to them from the trees. It said, 'Coconuts and bananas. Coconuts and bananas.' The pirates ran to see who it was. But it wasn't a person, it was some **(4)** _____. There were lots of coconuts and bananas in the trees. They **(5)** _____ the bananas and drank milk from the coconuts.
'This is better than treasure,' they said.

Example

sailed • beach • water
map • read • angry
happy • parrots • ate

(6) Now choose the best name for the story.
Tick one box.

The beautiful treasure ☐

The terrible weather ☐

The hungry pirates ☐

Part 4 5 questions

Read the text. Choose the right words and write them on the lines.

Sharks

Example Sharks are fish. They ____don't____ like cold water.

1 They live in the sea in hot parts _____ the world.

They catch smaller fish and sea animals, which they

2 _____ with their strong teeth.

Some people say that sharks never fall asleep, but this is

3 wrong. They sleep, but _____ eyes are always

4 open and they never stop _____ .

There are many different kinds of sharks. The biggest

5 ones are white. People _____ afraid of them,

but most sharks are small and they can't hurt you.

Example	doesn't	don't	didn't
1	on	at	of
2	ate	eat	eaten
3	her	its	their
4	moving	moves	move
5	is	are	be

Part 5 7 questions

Look at the pictures and read the story.
Write some words to complete the sentences about the story. You can use 1, 2 or 3 words.

A nice Saturday

'What can I do?' Jane asked her mum on Saturday morning.
'Let's go to the supermarket!' Mum said. 'We can do the shopping and then make lunch.' 'I hate shopping,' Jane said. 'It's boring.'

'OK,' Mum said, 'I've got a better idea.' She phoned Jane's grandma. 'Bring Jane to me,' Grandma said. 'I love having her here.'

They got in the car and drove to Grandma's flat. Grandma opened the door and said, 'Come on, Jane, we must go shopping. Let's buy some nice food.'

Examples

Mum wanted to go to the supermarket on ____Saturday morning____.

Jane didn't want to go ____shopping____ with her mum.

Questions

1 Mum had a good _____ and she phoned Jane's grandma.

2 Mum took Jane to Grandma's flat by _____.

Grandma took Jane to a market in the street near her flat. They bought lots of good things – vegetables, pasta, bread and a bottle of juice. Jane carried it all in a big bag. She took it upstairs carefully.

3 Jane and Grandma bought lots of nice things to eat at _____.

4 They put all the food in _____ and carried it to Grandma's flat.

Grandma cooked the pasta. Jane made a salad. 'It's sunny today,' Grandma said. 'Let's eat on the balcony.' They sat and enjoyed their lunch. 'I like your salad, Jane,' Grandma said. 'It's very good.' Then Mum phoned. 'I'm having a great day,' Jane told her. 'We went shopping and made lunch.' Mum laughed. 'Oh, Jane, you are funny!' she said.

5 Jane and Grandma had lunch on _____ .

6 The _____ which Jane made was very good.

7 Mum thought it was _____ when Jane said, 'I'm having a great day'.

Part 6 6 questions

Look and read and write.

Examples

The woman has got <u>curly black</u> hair.
What is the small girl playing with? <u>two toy cars</u>

Complete the sentences.

1 The man _____ football with a boy.
2 The woman and the girl are sitting _____ .

Answer the questions.

3 Where is the cat? _____
4 What are the girl and boy with blond hair wearing on their feet?

_____

Now write two sentences about the picture.

5 _____
6 _____

Teaching notes for Photocopiables

Photocopiable 1 (Unit 1 page 17)
- Check understanding of *plus* and *minus*. Elicit the questions pupils will need to get the answers, e.g. *What's 4 across?* Pupils work in pairs. Plan the pairings carefully (e.g. weak pupils with strong pupils). Tell pupils who is A and who is B. Hand out pages A and B from Photocopiable 1 (see pages T93 and T94). Make sure pupils don't look at each other's crosswords.
- Pairs ask and answer. Reveal the answers or hand out copies of the completed crossword so pupils can check their work.

Photocopiable 2a (Unit 2 page 22)
- Tell pupils they are going to get a card with activities on it. They must keep the card hidden and move around asking questions until they find the pupil whose card has the same activities as theirs. Ask two pupils to read out the speech bubbles on Pupil's Book page 22. Practise the questions with the class.
- Hand a card from Photocopiable 2a (see page T95) to each pupil. They move around the class and ask and answer (e.g. A: *What do you want to do?* B: *I want to go climbing and skating*). When they find someone with a matching card they stand together.
- If time, make groups of six from three pairs of pupils. Each pupil reads their card and then says if it's something they want to do or not, e.g. *I don't want to go swimming and climbing this weekend. I want to go dancing and shopping.* Monitor and help. When all six pupils have said what they want to do, pupils write the true information in their notebooks.

Photocopiable 2b (Unit 2 page 25)
- Demonstrate how the activity works. Pupils work in pairs to dictate to each other. Pupil A starts reading (slowly and clearly) while Pupil B writes. When Pupil A has a gap, Pupil B takes over reading. They continue in this way until the end. They don't look at each other's texts. Go through the language on page T96 (*Can you repeat that, please? How do you spell ... , please?*). Check / review key vocabulary: *swimming pool, swimmer, race*.
- Hand out copies of Photocopiable 2b (see page T96), part A to one half of the class and part B to the other half. Make pairs (one pupil with part A, one with part B). Monitor and remind pupils to read loudly and clearly.
- At the end, reveal the completed text or hand out copies for pupils to check (see page T92). Ask questions to check understanding of the whole text.

Photocopiable Review 1 & 2 (page 26)
- Pupils work in groups of three or four. Hand out a set of cards from Photocopiable Review 1 & 2 (see page T97) to each group. The pupils put the cards face down, with the grey cards and the white cards in two separate piles.
- The group decides who will go first. This pupil takes a card from each pile and looks at them, without showing anyone else (e.g. *running* and *slowly*). He / she stands up and acts out the verb and adverb. The rest of the group guess by asking, e.g. *Are you running badly? Are you walking slowly?* The pupil who guesses correctly scores a point. The cards are placed back at the bottom of the two piles. The next pupil in the group then takes a card from each pile and mimes.

Photocopiable 3 (Unit 3 page 29)
- Hand out a copy of Photocopiable 3 (see page T98) to each pupil. The pupils cut the cards out and keep the grey cards and the white cards in two separate piles.
- Pupils work in pairs. They put their sets of cards together (10 grey cards and 20 white cards in total). They put the two piles of cards face down. Pupil A turns over a grey card and a white card. If the two cards make a sentence with *because*, he / she says it, e.g. *The doctor gave me some medicine because I was ill.* Pupil A scores two points. If the cards make a sentence but Pupil A doesn't realise, then Pupil B says the sentence and scores one point. These cards are then moved to the bottom of the piles and each pile is mixed up. If the two cards don't make a sentence, Pupil A just moves the cards to the bottom of the piles (without mixing them) and it is Pupil B's turn.
- Play continues in this way until you stop the game, or until one pupil in the pair reaches eight points. Monitor carefully. Check pupils are using *because* and that their sentences make sense. They could write down their sentences for you to check.

Photocopiable 4 (Unit 4 page 42)
- Make pairs, A and B. Hand out Photocopiable 4 (see page T99), part A to Pupil A and part B to Pupil B. Remind pupils how to do the activity (see instructions for Photocopiable 2b, above).
- Reveal or hand out copies of the completed text for pupils to check (see page T92). Elicit who the text is about (the children in *The Chronicles of Narnia*). Elicit the children's names and other information, to check comprehension.

Photocopiable Review 3 & 4 (page 44)
- Make pairs, A and B. Hand out Photocopiable Review 3 & 4 (see page T100), part A to Pupil A and part B to Pupil B. Demonstrate how to do the activity. Pupils ask questions to complete the gaps in their paragraph. They use the question word in brackets and make a question with the verb in the sentence, e.g. to complete the gap in sentence 1 'On Saturday morning Simon went (Where?) _____ _____ _____ _____ by bus', Pupil B asks *Where did Simon go?* Do one or two examples with the class before they begin. Pupil B asks questions first and then pupils swap over. Monitor and check that they are not comparing texts.
- When they have finished, they compare the completed paragraphs.

Photocopiable 5 (Unit 5 page 47)
- This is an extension of Activity Book page 47 Activity 5. Pupils work in the same groups of four. Hand out a copy of Photocopiable 5 (see page T101) to each pupil. Pupils discuss what they can write for each sentence in Activity 1. Elicit a few examples before pupils write.
- Show pupils how to complete the bar chart on the board if necessary. Pupils then transfer the information from the sentences onto the bar chart. Monitor and help. Elicit the information from the groups to make a class bar chart for display.

Photocopiable 6a (Unit 6 page 55)
- Pre-teach / check understanding of key words from the text before handing it out to pupils: *robot, machine, bored*. Hand out a copy of Photocopiable 6a (see page T102) to each pair of pupils, part A to Pupil A and part B to Pupil B. Review with pupils how they do pairwork dictations (see instructions for Photocopiable 2b on page T90).
- At the end, reveal the completed text for pupils to check or hand out copies (see page T92). Check understanding by asking questions, e.g. *Do robots get bored? What do robots look like?*

Photocopiable 6b (Unit 6 page 58)
- Tell pupils this communication activity is about things they did yesterday morning. Write example sentences on the board, e.g. *I got up at eight o'clock. I didn't have a shower before breakfast.* Elicit the questions needed to check this information (*What time did you get up? Did you have a shower before breakfast?*).
- Hand each pupil a card from Photocopiable 6b (page T103). Tell pupils they need to walk around asking questions until they find someone who has exactly the same card as them. Remind them not to look at each other's cards. Keep pupils moving around the room and check they're talking, not comparing cards. When pupils find a partner they come to you to check. Then they sit together and talk about what they actually did yesterday morning.

Photocopiable Review 5 & 6 (page 62)
- This activity is good practice of the skills needed for the storytelling task in the Movers test, although there there are 4 pictures not 8. Pupils work in pairs. Hand out copies of the pictures on page T104, one to each pair. Pupils look at the pictures, give the girl a name and work out a story. They write notes, including a verb for each picture in the past tense. If you wish, write some phrases with infinitives on the board (in random order) to give pupils ideas (e.g. *go home, find, get up, go into the park, call the number, come, give back, open the bag*). Pupils practise telling their story to each other in their pairs. Monitor and listen for correct use of the past tense.
- Make groups of four from two pairs (A, B, A, B). The two Pupil As sit together and tell each other their story. Pupil Bs do the same. Elicit some of the best stories.
  Optional: Cut out the pictures before handing the copies out. Pupils have to put them in order to make a story and then tell it in the past tense, as above.

Photocopiable 7 (Unit 7 page 65)
- Show pupils your set of cards. Write the categories from the cards on the board: *Height, Weight, Length, Speed* and elicit the corresponding adjectives (*tall, heavy, long, fast*). Tell pupils that in this game they will be trying to get the card with the tallest animal, the heaviest animal, the longest animal, the best swimmer and so on.
- Hand out a copy of Photocopiable 7 (see page T105) to each pupil. They cut out the cards and make a small mark in one corner of each card, so they know which set is theirs.
- Pupils play the game in groups of four. Demonstrate first, using a group of pupils. Mix the cards and deal them out to the pupils in the group. Each pupil holds his / her cards so that the others can't see them and he / she can only see the card on the top. The first pupil selects a category from his / her top card and reads it out, e.g. *Length: 10 metres*. The other pupils then read out their Length information in turn. The pupil with the highest number says, e.g. *My animal is the longest*. He / She wins this round, and takes the other players' cards and puts them at the bottom of his / her pile. If there is a draw, pupils put the four cards on the desk and the same pupil chooses a new category from his / her next card. The winner of that round also gets the other four cards.
- Play continues around the group. Monitor and check. Encourage pupils to make sentences with the superlative.

Photocopiable 8 (Unit 8 page 76)
- Hand out half of a copy of Photocopiable 8 (see page T106) to each pair. They cut along the dotted lines to make playing cards. Demonstrate using two cards. Put two words together which have the same sound, e.g. *wear–where*.
- Pupils work in their pairs to arrange the cards so that words with the same sounds are touching (making squares). Pairs check other pairs' answers. Monitor pupils as they do the activity and review any problem areas at the end.

Key: wear–where; eye–I; bye–buy; read–red; nose–knows; eight–ate; aren't–aunt; write–right; no–know; for–four

Photocopiable Review 7 & 8 (page 80)
- Review key vocabulary: *expedition, South Pole, Antarctica*. Hand out a copy of Photocopiable Review 7 & 8 (see page T107) to each pair of pupils, part A to Pupil A and part B to Pupil B. Review with pupils how they do pairwork dictations (see instructions for Photocopiable 2b on page T90).
- At the end, reveal the completed text for pupils to check or hand out copies (see page T92). Check understanding by asking about Scott's past expeditions, the last expedition and whether he reached the South Pole first.

Texts for Photocopiables 2b, 4, 6a and Review 7 & 8

Photocopiable 2b (page T96)

Swimming

An Olympic swimming pool is 50 metres long and 25 metres wide. There are a lot of different races. Races can be from 50 metres to 10 kilometres long and swimmers can swim on their stomachs or on their backs. There are eight swimmers in a race. At the end of the race, the swimmer who touches the wall first is the winner.

Photocopiable 4 (page T99)

The Pevensie children

There are four children in 'The Chronicles of Narnia'. They are the Pevensies, two boys and two girls. The boys are called Peter and Edmund and the girls are called Susan and Lucy.
Peter is older than all the other children. He is bigger than the others, and is also stronger. Edmund is younger than Susan, but older than Lucy.
Lucy is younger than her brothers and sister. She is the one who finds Narnia.

Photocopiable 6a (page T102)

Robots

A robot is a machine which can do some jobs like a person. Robots can do a lot of difficult things, but they never get tired or bored, thirsty or hungry. They can look different from men or women, but some of them have arms, legs, hands or feet.
All robots are different because they need to do different things. They can't think like us, but they have a computer inside them which tells them what they must do.

Photocopiable Review 7 & 8 (page T107)

Scott and Amundsen

Robert Scott was an explorer. Scott went on two expeditions to the South Pole, but he and his men didn't come back from the terrible second expedition.
Scott went on his first British Antarctic expedition in 1901. On this adventure, he was the first person to fly a hot air balloon on Antarctica.
Scott left for Antarctica again in 1910. He was racing Roald Amundsen to be the first man to the South Pole. Amundsen got there first, fourteen days before Scott and his men.

Photocopiable 1a

Unit 1, page 17
Name: _____

Numbers crossword

A

Ask your partner questions.

Example:
A: What's 4 across?
B: It's thirty-nine minus nineteen.

Give these clues to your partner.

Across →
5 Eleven plus nineteen
10 Eighty-six plus fourteen

Down ↓
3 Fifteen minus three
6 Seventy-four minus sixty-one
7 Fifty-six minus sixteen
8 Thirty-nine plus eleven
9 Sixty-eight plus twelve

Photocopiable 1b

Unit 1, page 17

Name: _____

Numbers crossword

B

Ask your partner questions.

Example:

B: What's 5 across?

A: It's eleven plus nineteen.

Give these clues to your partner.

Across →
- 4 Thirty-nine minus nineteen
- 7 Twelve plus three
- 11 Forty-four plus twenty-six
- 12 Twenty-six minus fifteen

Down ↓
- 1 Thirty-eight plus fifty-two
- 2 Twenty-three plus thirty-seven

Photocopiable 2a

Unit 2, page 22
Name: _____

I want to go swimming and climbing.	I want to go climbing and skating.	I want to go skating and fishing.
I want to go swimming and skating.	I want to go climbing and sailing.	I want to go skating and dancing.
I want to go swimming and sailing.	I want to go climbing and fishing.	I want to go sailing and fishing.
I want to go swimming and fishing.	I want to go climbing and dancing.	I want to go sailing and dancing.
I want to go swimming and cycling.	I want to go skating and sailing.	I want to go fishing and dancing.

PHOTOCOPIABLE © Cambridge University Press 2017

Photocopiable 2b

Unit 2, page 25
Name: _____

A Swimming

An Olympic _____ _____ is 50 metres long _____ _____ _____ _____ . There are a lot _____ _____ _____ _____ . Races can be _____ _____ _____ to 10 kilometres _____ _____ _____ can swim on _____ _____ _____ on their backs. There _____ _____ _____ in a race. _____ _____ _____ of the race, _____ _____ _____ touches the wall _____ _____ _____ _____ .

> Can you repeat that, please?
> How do you spell ****, please?

- - - ✂ -

B Swimming

_____ _____ swimming pool _____ _____ _____ _____ and 25 metres wide. _____ _____ _____ _____ of different races. _____ _____ _____ from 50 metres _____ _____ _____ long and swimmers _____ _____ _____ their stomachs or _____ _____ _____ . _____ are eight swimmers _____ _____ _____ . At the end _____ _____ _____ , the swimmer who _____ _____ _____ first is the winner.

> Can you repeat that, please?
> How do you spell ****, please?

Photocopiable Review 1 and 2

Review 1 & 2, page 26

Name: _____

| happily | quickly | slowly |
| quietly | loudly | |

Photocopiable 3

Unit 3, page 29

Name: _____

I ate a cheese sandwich	I had a temperature.	I had a toothache.
The doctor gave me some medicine	I was thirsty.	I was tired.
I drank some juice	I wanted to.	I like cheese a lot.
I saw the dentist	I was ill.	I don't like milk.
I went to bed early	my tooth was worse.	I was hungry.

Photocopiable 4

Unit 4, page 42
Name: _____

A

The Pevensie children

There are four _____ _____ '_____ _____ of Narnia'. They are _____ _____ , _____ _____ and two girls. The _____ _____ _____ Peter and Edmund _____ _____ _____ are called _____ _____ _____ .

Peter is older _____ _____ the other children. _____ _____ _____ _____ the others, and _____ _____ _____ . Edmund is younger than _____ , _____ _____ _____ Lucy.
_____ _____ _____ than _____ _____ and sister. _____ _____ _____ _____ who finds _____ .

B

The Pevensie children

_____ _____ _____ children in 'The Chronicles _____ _____ ', _____ _____ the Pevensies, two boys _____ _____ _____ . _____ boys are called _____ _____ _____ and the girls _____ _____ Susan and Lucy.
_____ _____ _____ than all _____ _____ _____ . He is bigger than _____ _____ , _____ is also stronger. _____ _____ _____ _____ _____ Susan, but older than _____ .
Lucy is younger _____ her brothers _____ _____ .
She is the one _____ _____ Narnia.

Photocopiable Review 3 and 4

Review 3 & 4, page 44
Name: _____

A

Simon's Saturday
On Saturday morning Simon went to the city centre by bus. He saw his friend Alex at the bus station. They ate lunch at a restaurant. Then they went to the cinema. They watched a very funny film. They laughed a lot. Simon went home at four o'clock.

Stella's Saturday
On Saturday morning Stella went (Where?) _____ _____ _____ _____ . Uncle Fred was (Where?) _____ _____ _____ . Stella helped Uncle Fred (How?) _____ _____ the sheep. Then she ate lunch (Where?) _____ _____ _____ . After lunch Stella and Uncle Fred (What?) _____ _____ _____ _____ . They played with Uncle Fred's dog. Stella went home at (What time?) _____ _____ .

B

Simon's Saturday
On Saturday morning Simon went (Where?) _____ _____ _____ _____ by bus. He saw his friend (Who?) _____ at the bus station. They ate lunch (Where?) _____ _____ _____ . Then they went (Where?) _____ _____ _____ . They watched (What?) _____ _____ _____ _____ . They laughed a lot. Simon went home at (What time?) _____ _____ .

Stella's Saturday
On Saturday morning Stella went to Uncle Fred's farm. Uncle Fred was in the field. Stella helped Uncle Fred to feed the sheep. Then she ate lunch in the farmhouse. After lunch Stella and Uncle Fred walked in the fields. They played with Uncle Fred's dog. Stella went home at three o'clock.

Photocopiable 5

Unit 5, page 47
Name: _____

1 Complete the sentences.

In my group _____ of us could walk when we were 1.
In my group _____ of us could _____
In my group _____ of us _____
In my group _____
In my group _____
In my group _____

2 Complete the chart.

	Could walk at 1	Could talk at 2	Could write at 4	Could swim at 5	Could read at 6	Could ride a bike at 8
4						
3						
2						
1						
	yellow	blue	purple	green	red	orange

Photocopiable 6a

Unit 6, page 55
Name: _____

A Robots

A robot is _____ _____ _____ can do some jobs like _____ _____ _____ . _____ can do a _____ _____ _____ things, but they _____ _____ _____ or bored, thirsty _____ _____ _____ . _____ can look different _____ _____ _____ women, but some _____ _____ _____ arms, legs, hands _____ _____ . _____ _____ are different because _____ _____ _____ do different things. _____ _____ _____ like us, but _____ _____ _____ computer inside them _____ _____ _____ what they must _____ .

✂ -

B Robots

_____ _____ _____ a machine which _____ _____ _____ _____ a person. Robots _____ _____ _____ lot of difficult _____ , _____ _____ never get tired _____ _____ , _____ or hungry. They _____ _____ _____ from men or _____ , _____ _____ of them have _____ , _____ , _____ or feet. All robots _____ _____ _____ they need to _____ _____ _____ . They can't think _____ _____ , _____ they have a _____ _____ _____ which tells them _____ _____ _____ do.

Photocopiable 6b

Unit 6, page 58
Name: _____

I got up at eight o'clock. I didn't have a shower before breakfast.	I got up at eight o'clock. I bought a comic after breakfast.	I got up at seven o'clock. I read a book after breakfast.
I got up at seven o'clock. I had a shower after I got up.	I bought a comic after breakfast. I didn't have a shower before breakfast.	I had a shower after I got up. I read a book after breakfast.
I got up at seven o'clock. I didn't have a shower before breakfast.	I bought a comic after breakfast. I went to school with my sister.	I didn't have a shower before breakfast. I read a book after breakfast.

PHOTOCOPIABLE © Cambridge University Press 2017

Photocopiable Review 5 and 6

Review 5 & 6, page 62

Name: _____

Photocopiable 7

Unit 7, page 65

Name: _____

Animal fact cards

Animal: Bengal tiger  Height: 1 metre Weight: 250 kg Length: 3 metres Beautiful: ***** Good swimmer: *** Speed: 60 km/h	**Animal: Blue whale** 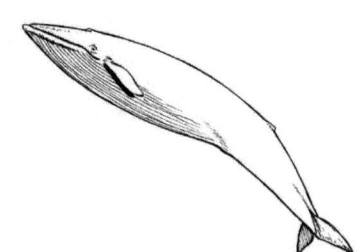 Height: 4 metres Weight: 181,000 kg Length: 21 metres Beautiful: *** Good swimmer: ***** Speed: 45 km/h	**Animal: Python**  Height: 20 cm Weight: 110 kg Length: 10 metres Beautiful: ** Good swimmer: *** Speed: 10 km/h
Animal: African elephant  Height: 4 metres Weight: 7,000 kg Length: 9 metres Beautiful: ** Good swimmer: *** Speed: 25 km/h	**Animal: Crocodile**  Height: 40 cm Weight: 1,200 kg Length: 6 metres Beautiful: * Good swimmer: *** Speed: 15 km/h	**Animal: Giraffe**  Height: 5 metres Weight: 1,300 kg Length: 3 metres Beautiful: *** Good swimmer: ** Speed: 50 km/h

Photocopiable 8

Unit 8, page 76
Name: _____

Homophones jigsaw

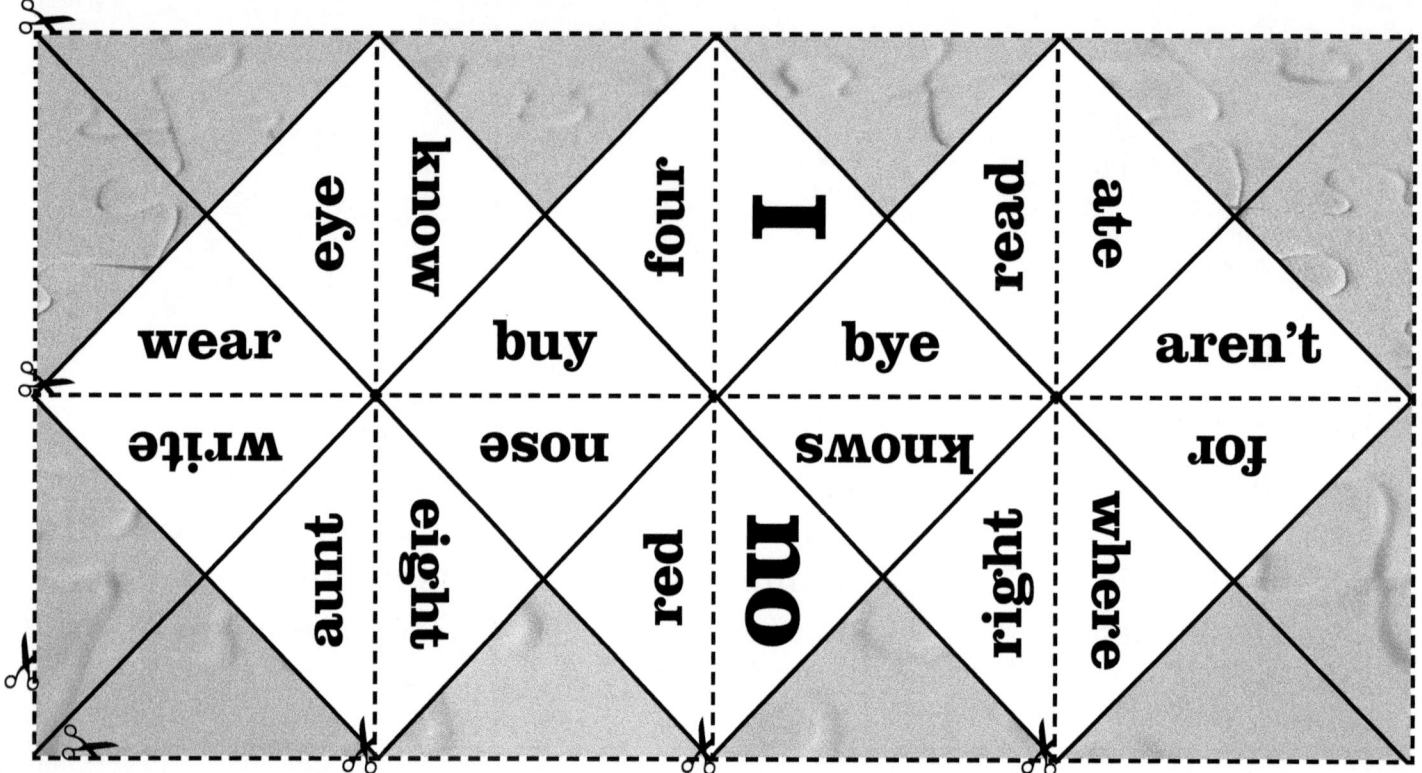

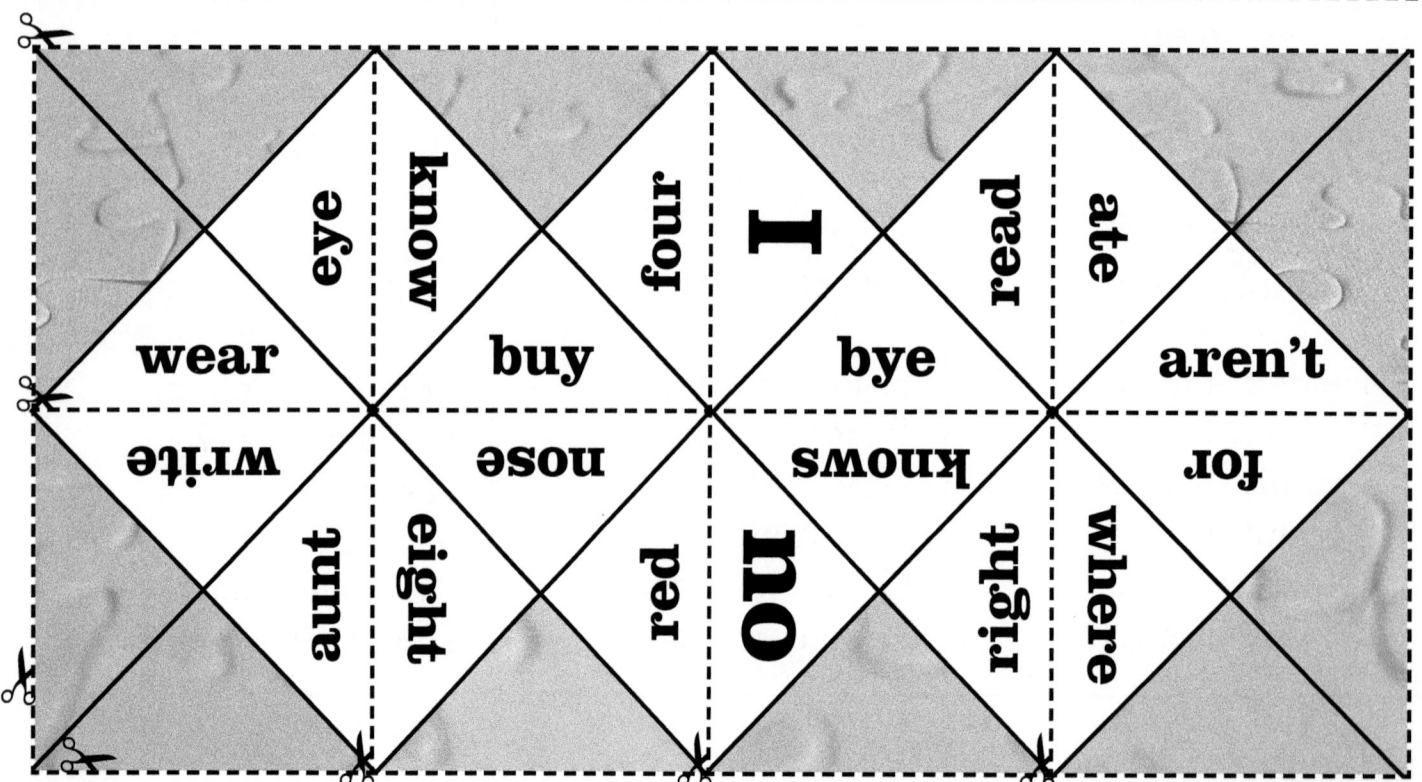

Photocopiable Review 7 and 8

Review 7 & 8, page 80
Name: _____

A Scott and Amundsen

Robert Scott was _____ _____ . _____ went on two _____ _____ _____ _____ Pole, but he and _____ _____ _____ _____ back from the _____ _____ _____ .

Scott went on _____ _____ _____ Antarctic expedition in _____ . On this _____ , _____ _____ the first person _____ _____ _____ _____ air balloon on Antarctica.

_____ _____ _____ _____ again in 1910. He _____ _____ _____ _____ to be the first _____ _____ _____ _____ Pole. Amundsen got _____ _____ _____ , _____ days before Scott _____ _____ _____ .

- -

B Scott and Amundsen

_____ _____ _____ an explorer. Scott _____ _____ _____ expeditions to the South _____ , _____ _____ _____ his men didn't come _____ _____ _____ terrible second expedition. _____ _____ _____ his first British _____ _____ _____ 1901. _____ _____ adventure, he was _____ _____ _____ to fly a hot _____ _____ _____ _____ .

Scott left for Antarctica _____ _____ _____ . _____ was racing Roald Amundsen _____ _____ _____ _____ man to the South _____ . _____ _____ there first, fourteen _____ _____ _____ and his men.

Extra activities

Hello there!

Page 4
- **Extra activity 1: Information exchange**
Display the large piece of paper with the scrambled questions. Pupils work in pairs. They unscramble the questions and write them in their notebooks. They take turns to interview each other using the questions. They don't write the answers. Pupils can report about their partner to the class.
- **Extra activity 2: What do you want to do?**
You will need space for this activity. Write the sports and hobbies from Activity Book page 4 Activity 2 on the board. Make a sentence with one of the activities and *want to*, e.g. *I want to go cycling*. Ask individual pupils to make sentences in the same way.
Play the CD of quiet music. Pupils move around the space. Pause the CD. Pupils make pairs. They tell each other what they want to do. If they say the same thing, encourage them to say *Me too!* Play the CD again. Pupils swap partners. Continue until pupils have spoken to five or six different classmates.

Page 5
- **Extra activity 1: Mime the adjective**
Place the cards with the adjectives on them face down on your desk. Twelve pupils come to the front. They take it in turns to mime each adjective. The rest of the class don't speak: they write down the adjectives. Pupils swap their lists of words with a neighbour and check each other's. If time, repeat with 12 more pupils miming. Make sure the adjectives are in a different order this time.
- **Extra activity 2: What does it mean?**
You will need space for this activity. Pupils choose one piece of information from their fact file and write it on a piece of paper, e.g. *blue / Adriana, Biagio and Milena / playing computer games*. They pin or stick the paper to their front. Play the CD of quiet music. Pupils move around the space. Pause the CD. Pupils make pairs. They look at each other's papers and think of / ask the question which has this response, e.g. for the label *blue* the question might be *What colour are your eyes?* They take turns to ask questions. They can each ask two questions. Start the music again. Pupils move on. Repeat.

Page 6
- **Extra activity 1: Daily routines**
Display the 15 pieces of paper with the phrases on at random on the board. Write a number between *1* and *15* under each one. In groups of four, pupils decide on the order for the activities in a typical day. They don't have to include all of them. They then (secretly if possible) prepare a mime of the activities in sequence for the other groups to guess. After groups have done their mimes, compare the sequences as a class and put the pieces of paper in an agreed class sequence down the side of the board. Check how often some of the things happen, e.g. *Do you always go to the park after school?*
- **Extra activity 2: Bingo**
Write the phrases *get up, wake up, get dressed, have a shower, have breakfast, go to school, do homework, have lunch, play in the playground, come home, have supper, watch TV, go to bed, go to the park, go to sleep* on the board. Tell pupils you are going to play Bingo. Pupils draw a 2 x 2 Bingo card and choose a phrase from the list to write in each square. Call out the phrases at random. Make a list of the phrases you say. Pupils cross out the phrases on their Bingo card when they hear them. The first pupil to cross out all four words on his / her card shouts *Bingo!* Elicit the phrases on the winner's card to check. Repeat.

Page 7
- **Extra activity 1: Clothes race**
Set a time limit. Pupils close their Pupil's Books. In pairs, they write a list of all the clothes they can remember from the pictures on the Pupil's Book page. Pupils swap lists with other pairs. They open their books and check.
- **Extra activity 2: Play the game**
Write the head words for all the word families from Activity Book Activity 9 on the board (jobs, homes, in the city, animals, in the country, plants, family, weather, clothes, comparing). Pupils copy the head words in their notebooks. They work in pairs to add as many words to each family as they can. Set a time limit of ten minutes. They swap notebooks with another pair. Correct as a class. Award pupils 2 points for each correct word with correct spelling, 1 point for a correct word with incorrect spelling. The winners are the pair with the most points.

Page 8
- **Extra activity 1: About my friend**
Pupils use the information from Pupil's Book Activity 13 to write a short paragraph about their friend. Tell them to think about how to organise and sequence the information: they can choose. Tell them also to think about using linking words, e.g. *and, but*. Pupils write a draft of their texts and then give it to their partner for him / her to check language and content. Pupils then write a final version of their text for display. They can illustrate the text, if time.
- **Extra activity 2: Notice the spellings**
Write on the board the three head words from the table in Activity Book Activity 10, which show examples of the different 'a' sounds from the lesson. Make three groups. Give each group a piece of paper and assign each group a word, e.g. *sad*. Each group finds all the words in the lesson with the appropriate 'a' sound (they look back at the Pupil's Book and the Activity Book pages). They list the different spellings of this sound on their paper for display.

Page 9
- **Extra activity 1: Role play**
Make groups of five (Lock, Key, Peter, Peter's aunt, the man in the park). Pupils practise and then role play the story. More confident groups can perform their role plays for the class. Encourage them to do the role plays without their books; they should speak, not read. If time, pupils can make a 'Wanted' poster for a picnic thief, to be displayed in the park.
- **Extra activity 2: Play a game**
Pupils vote for a game from the unit to play again.

Unit 1

Page 10

- **Extra activity 1: Mime game**
With books closed, make four teams. A pupil from one of the teams comes to the front. Whisper an adjective to the pupil. He / she mimes the adjective for the class to guess. The pupil who guesses has to spell it correctly without help from his / her team to win a point. Repeat with a pupil from the next team, and so on.

- **Extra activity 2: Make a wordsearch**
Brainstorm school subjects with pupils, or use the list from the Warmer, adding any others that came up in the lesson. Pupils draw a 10 x 10 grid in their notebooks (or hand out squared paper). They choose six subjects, place them in the wordsearch and then fill the wordsearch with letters. They draw / write clues for their subjects under the wordsearch. Pupils swap with a partner, find the subjects and write them next to the pictures / clues.

Page 11

- **Extra activity 1: Our teachers**
Pupils make groups of eight. They each write a list of the adjectives from the lesson. They take it in turns to read their texts about the teacher aloud to their groups. Pupils listen to hear how many times each adjective is used. They also note the teacher and the subject. Elicit information from the groups about what they learnt. Pupils display their texts in the classroom.

- **Extra activity 2: Comparing answers**
Pupils make new groups of four (not with their partners). They tally the information they have found about the subjects in the Activity Book questionnaire, e.g. *Music lessons: boring x 1, easy x 5, exciting x 3.* They prepare a poster with the information. For each subject, they draw a small illustration at the side. They display the posters on the wall. Discuss the results with the class and compare them with the results from the Warmer. Remind them that 'easy' is not always good.

Page 12

- **Extra activity 1: In our class**
Describe a pupil in the class using a relative clause with *who*, e.g. *She's the pupil who's got a purple bag. He's the pupil who's got blonde, curly hair.* Pupils put up their hands to guess. The first pupil to guess correctly describes a classmate in the same way for the others to guess.

- **Extra activity 2: Word race**
Give pupils one minute to write down as many objects as they can which they can see in the classroom. Pupils swap their lists. Elicit all the objects to check they are correct. The pupil who has written the most is the winner.

Page 13

- **Extra activity 1: Playground games**
Pupils do a class survey of the playground games / activities their friends do. Elicit playground games / activities and write them on the board, e.g. *skipping, chatting, looking at comics, races.* Pupils prepare a survey sheet in their notebooks (7 rows x 5 columns). They write the six activities down the left-hand side. At the top of the four columns they write *Me* and then the names of three friends. Practise the questions, e.g. *Do you like skipping in the playground?* They ask and answer in groups of four and note their friends' answers. Find out which are the most / least popular playground games / activities and if these are different for boys and girls.

- **Extra activity 2: Hobbies**
Brainstorm at least 12 hobbies and write them on the board (some the pupils do, some they don't). Make groups of four. Hand out the 12 pieces of paper / card to each group. Pupils in the group write a hobby on each one. They place them face down on the desk. They take turns to turn one over and say as much as they can about it in 30 seconds, e.g. *I like playing tennis. I play with my sister on Saturdays. I have got a new racquet. We play at the sports centre.* The player keeps the card. At the end of the game, pupils write about the hobby they found it easiest to talk about in their notebooks.

Page 14

- **Extra activity 1: About my friends**
Pupils use the information from the communication activity to write a short paragraph about their two friends. They also add information about themselves. Remind them about linking words, e.g. *and, but.*

- **Extra activity 2: Notice the spellings**
In their notebooks, pupils write all the words from the lesson which had the /i:/ sound. They put them in three columns according to spelling: *e, ee, ea.*

Page 15

- **Extra activity 1: Role play**
Make groups of five. Elicit from pupils who the five characters are (Lock, Key, teacher, boy, Peter). Pupils decide roles in their groups. Play the CD again. Pause after each frame. Pupils repeat their section in role. Stop after frame 4 (when they're having lunch). In their groups, pupils decide on a different ending for the episode. They practise the new role play in their groups. Confident pupils can perform their role plays for the class.

- **Extra activity 2: What I can do**
You will need space for this activity. Pupils each choose one of the *Can do* sentences from Activity Book page 15. They walk around the room without touching anyone else. Clap your hands. Pupils make pairs. They take turns to say their sentence and to demonstrate it, e.g. *I can describe things. I think Art is exciting because we can paint and it's not difficult. I don't like Maths. It's difficult and I'm terrible at it. I love English. It's always fun.* Clap your hands. Pupils move on to a different partner. Repeat four or five times.
OR
Pupils look back through their work for this unit and select an example which provides evidence for each *Can do* statement. They put the example in their portfolio. For each example, they write the full *Can do* statement at the top of a piece of paper and a short paragraph which explains why they chose each one.

Page 16

- **Extra activity 1: Measuring things**
Make groups of four or five. Ask each group to guess the lengths and heights of some famous landmarks in kilometres or metres, as follows:
1. the length of the Amazon River
2. the height of the Empire State Building in New York
3. the length of a Ferrari sports car
4. the height of pop star Kylie Minogue
5. the length of an anaconda snake
6. the height of Everest

Each group writes their guesses on a piece of paper. Groups swap papers. Reveal the answers. Groups check the figures on the piece of paper they have. The winning group are the ones whose guesses were nearest to the actual lengths and heights.

Key: 1 6,400 km, 2 381 m, 3 4.7 m, 4 1.55 m, 5 7–11 m, 6 8,848 m

- **Extra activity 2: Bingo**

Write about 16 large, decimal numbers, fractions and dates on the board, only writing those that pupils ask you to (they have to know how to say them). Pupils draw 2 x 2 bingo grids and write one number from the board in each square. They swap grids with their partner and play using their partner's board. Call out numbers quickly one after another. Pupils cross out the ones they hear. When all four numbers are crossed out, the pupil shouts *Bingo!* Check the numbers back before announcing the winner.

OR

Pupils can play the same game in groups of five, using the numbers on the board. Four draw grids; one calls the numbers. They repeat, changing the caller each time.

Page 17

- **Extra activity: CLIL vocabulary**

Elicit new words and phrases from the last two lessons. Write them on the board. Check pupils understand them and know how to say them. In their vocabulary books, pupils write the heading *Maths*. They write the new words, phrases and expressions from the lessons, either as a mind map or as a list. At the bottom of the page, they write some of the things they did in the lessons, e.g. *I measured the length of my desk.* If time, pupils can illustrate the page.

Unit 2

Page 18

- **Extra activity 1: Yes or no**

Pupils close their Pupil's Books. Tell them to write numbers *1* to *8* in their notebooks. Ask them to listen and write *Yes* or *No* next to each number. Read the sentences below. Pairs swap books to check. Pupils can repeat the game in pairs.

1 At the activity centre you can learn to sail. (yes)
2 At the activity centre you can learn to sing. (no)
3 At the activity centre you can learn to climb. (yes)
4 At the activity centre you can learn to dance. (yes)
5 At the activity centre you can learn to skate. (yes)
6 At the activity centre you can learn to draw. (no)
7 At the activity centre you can learn to use a computer. (no)
8 At the activity centre you can learn to drive a car. (no)

- **Extra activity 2: Activity centre posters**

Pupils work in groups of four and make a poster for an activity centre. They give the centre a name and write what sports there are, in sentences, e.g. *You can learn to ski.* They can add pictures and prices too. Remind pupils to check the Look box. They should write the question *What can I learn to do?* at the top of their poster. Groups present their posters to the class. Pupils ask each other about their centres, using *What can I learn to do? What water sports can I learn?* and so on. The class can vote for the best activity centre.

Page 19

- **Extra activity 1: True or false**

Say the following sentences using the names of pupils in your class. The class responds to each sentence by either sitting down (if they think the sentence is false), or standing up (if they think it's true). Elicit the equipment needed for the sports in the false sentences.

(Name) *wants to swim. She needs a towel.* (true)
(Name) *wants to climb. He needs a ball.* (false)
(Name) *wants to sail. She needs a net.* (false)
(Name) *wants to skate. He needs some skates.* (true)
(Name) *wants to swim. She needs some shoes.* (false)
(Name) *wants to fish. He needs some boots.* (false)
(Name) *wants to play basketball. She needs a racquet.* (false)
(Name) *wants to play football. He needs some shorts.* (true)
(Name) *wants to run. She needs a hat.* (false)
(Name) *wants to climb. He needs a rope.* (true)

- **Extra activity 2: Job wordsearch**

Pupils work individually. They choose at least six of the jobs from Activity Book Activity 4, draw a 10 x 10 grid and put the words into a wordsearch. They swap wordsearches with a partner and find the words.

Page 20

- **Extra activity 1: Match and mime**

Put the pieces of coloured card in two piles on your desk (actions in one pile, adverbs in another). Take a card from each pile (e.g. *get dressed, carefully*) and mime the action in the manner of the adverb. Pupils guess by asking questions, e.g. *Are you drawing a picture quickly?* When a pupil guesses correctly, put the cards back at the bottom of the piles. The pupil comes and takes two cards and mimes for the class to guess. Repeat with different pupils.

- **Extra activity 2: Compare and write**

Pupils work in pairs. They compare each other's answers for Activity Book Activity 6. Pupils write six sentences in their notebooks comparing themselves with their partner, e.g. *I play tennis well and Sally plays tennis well, too.* Provide models on the board for pupils to use when writing:
I play tennis well and Sally plays tennis well, too.
I read quickly but Sally reads slowly and carefully.

Page 21

- **Extra activity 1: Sentence race**

Write the following words at random on the board: *badly, quickly, can, swim, swims, they, he, she, dance, dances, skate, skates, Suzy, Grandpa, the children, play, plays, football, the guitar, carefully, easily.* In pairs, pupils write as many sentences as they can with these words on a piece of paper. Set a time limit. Pupils swap papers. Elicit sentences to correct. Sentences have to be grammatically and semantically correct. This could also be played as a team game.

- **Extra activity 2: Complete the sentences**

Pupils copy the full sentences from Activity Book Activity 9 into their notebooks. They then rewrite the beginnings of sentences 1, 2, 3, 4 and 6 and add other endings / reasons, starting with *because*. Pairs check each other's work.

Page 22

- **Extra activity: Spelling patterns**

Write the following selection of words with silent consonants on the board (but in random order): *knee, know, knife, scissors, science, scene, comb, climb, tomb, where, why, which.* Pupils put the words in groups according to spelling patterns. Monitor, check and help weaker pupils as necessary. Elicit the groups, write them on the board and practise pronunciation.

Page 23

- **Extra activity 1: Role play**

Make groups of four. Elicit from pupils who the characters are (Lock, Key, coach, Terry Sweep). Pupils decide their roles. Play the CD. Characters repeat in role. Pupils practise their role plays in groups. Remind them to write the note. They can use props for the magnifying glass and the cup. Groups perform their role plays for the class without their books.

- **Extra activity 2: What I can do**

You will need space for this activity. Pupils each choose one of the *Can do* sentences. They walk around the room without touching anyone else. Clap your hands. They make pairs. They take turns to say their sentence and to demonstrate it, e.g. *I can say more action verbs. I want to learn to sail and climb. I like climbing because it's exciting. I don't want to learn to skate. I don't like falling.* Clap your hands. Pupils move on. Repeat four or five times.

OR

Pupils look back through their work for this unit and select an example which provides evidence for each *Can do* statement. They put the example in their portfolio. For each example, they write the full *Can do* statement at the top of a piece of paper and a short paragraph which explains why they chose each one.

Page 24

- **Extra activity 1: Quiz**

Pupils work in pairs. They study the texts on Pupil's Book page 24 and write three more statements about the two sports. They write each statement with its answer on a strip of paper. Collect the strips and make three teams. Each team gives its team members numbers. Call a number at random for each team and read a statement. That team member answers and wins a point if it's correct. Repeat for other teams, making sure not to call on team members more than once to answer. The team with the most points is the winner.

- **Extra activity 2: One of the top five**

Pupils work in groups of four. They research one of the other top five US sports (American football, golf, hockey), using reference books and / or the internet. They find at least five facts about the sport, find out what the players and the equipment are called and, if possible, find out the rules. Groups write their information on posters in the form of bullet points or fact files (not continuous text) and illustrate them with relevant, supportive information. Groups display and then present their posters to the class.

Page 25

- **Extra activity: Playing ball**

You will need a large space such as a gymnasium for this activity. Pupils play in groups of four. They take turns to use a ball. Call out instructions for them to follow, e.g. *Put the ball behind your back. Throw the ball to the person on your left.* When they get back to the classroom, pupils write a set of rules in their notebooks for playing a game with their ball.

Review Units 1–2

Page 26

- **Extra activity 1: Songs and chants**

Sing one of the songs or do one of the chants from Units 1 and 2.

- **Extra activity 2: Write your own quiz**

Pupils use the model in Activity Book Activity 1 to write questions for their partner. They look back through Units 1 and 2 to find the new words. They have to draw the pictures too. Tell them to think of the final word (the one made up of the missing letters) before writing the quiz questions. They write and draw on a piece of paper and swap with their partners to answer.

Page 27

- **Extra activity 1: Conversations**

Pupils use lines from Pupil's Book Activity 2 to make short conversations, e.g. *Who is she? She's my Aunt Sue.* They act out their conversations for the class.

- **Extra activity 2: Games**

Play one of the games from Units 1 and 2 with the class. Let pupils choose which one to play.

Unit 3

Page 28

- **Extra activity 1: Role play**

Display the large piece of paper with the CD script from Pupil's Book Activity 2. Pupils role play the dialogue in pairs, taking turns to be Simon and Alex. More confident pupils can role play their dialogue for the class.

- **Extra activity 2: My day**

Pupils write a diary about one school day last week, using Stella's diary in Activity Book Activity 1 as a model. Remind them to use the nine verbs on the Activity Book page. Monitor and check. Pupils exchange diaries with their partner and read each other's.

Page 29

- **Extra activity 1: Giving reasons**

Pupils work in pairs. They write the first part of each sentence from Pupil's Book Activity 4 and then discuss and decide their own reason, e.g. *She went to bed early because (she was not well).* They don't have to use the information in the pictures.

- **Extra activity 2: Spelling game**

Pupils each choose ten words from this and the previous lesson. They should include adjectives, verbs and nouns. Make new pairs. In these pairs, they take turns to dictate their words to each other. If they have the same word, they move on to the next word on their list. They swap and check each other's work. Elicit the words pupils chose.

Page 30

- **Extra activity 1: Questions and answers**

Ask the following questions. Pupils individually write the answers, keeping them secret. *What did you eat for breakfast yesterday? Who did you see in the playground yesterday (one person)? What did you give your mum yesterday? What did you have in your school bag yesterday (one item)?* Write the prompt *Did you … ?* on the board. Review the responses *Yes, I did* and *No, I didn't.* Pupils make pairs. They take turns to guess what their partner has written, e.g. Pupil A says *Did you eat eggs and bread for breakfast?* B responds, e.g. *No, I didn't. I ate fruit and cereal.* Pupils say *Yes, I did* for correct guesses.

- **Extra activity 2: Scrambled sentences**

Display the large piece of paper on the board with the scrambled sentences / questions. Pupils work in pairs to unscramble them. Pairs check with pairs. Check with the class.

Page 31

- **Extra activity 1: Comparing breakfasts**

Brainstorm what pupils ate and drank for breakfast (or the previous Saturday or Sunday), writing any new words on the board. Individually, pupils write a list of what they ate and drank for breakfast. Pupils work in groups of three. Pupil A asks the others, using information from his / her list, e.g. *Did you eat eggs for breakfast?* Pupil A marks the information about Pupils B and C on his / her list.

Pupils construct a Venn diagram on a large piece of paper to show the results of their discussion: they draw three intersecting circles and label each one with the name of one pupil from the group (see below). Where the circles all overlap, they write the common foods / drinks. Where two circles overlap, they write the common foods / drinks for those two pupils. Pupils display their diagrams and talk about the results to the class.

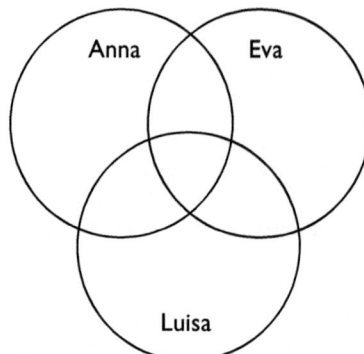

- **Extra activity 2: Meera's day**
Pupils use the information from the table in Activity Book Activity 8 to write a short text about Meera's day in their notebooks. If time, they can illustrate their texts.

Page 32
- **Extra activity 1: Things we did in the past**
Pupils work in new groups of four. They take turns to ask the rest of the group their questions from Pupil's Book Activity 14. They write down the answers. In their notebooks, they write a short paragraph about each of their three friends. Provide a model on the board if necessary.
- **Extra activity 2: Notice the spellings**
In their notebooks, pupils write all the words from the lesson which had the /f/, /b/ and the /v/ sounds, underlining the relevant letters. They put them in two columns.

Page 33
- **Extra activity 1: Role play**
Make groups of three (Lock, Key, Nick Motors). Pupils decide their roles. Play the CD again. Pause after each frame. Pupils repeat their section in role. Stop after frame 4 (when they run into the hospital). In their groups, pupils decide on a different ending for the episode to include Nick Motors. They write the new ending on the large piece of paper and practise it in their groups. Confident pupils can perform their role plays for the class and display their new endings.
- **Extra activity 2: What I can do**
You will need space for this activity. Pupils each choose one of the *Can do* sentences. They walk around the room without touching anyone else. Clap your hands. They make pairs. They take turns to say their sentence / ask their questions and to demonstrate them, e.g. *I can talk about the past. I ate fruit for breakfast yesterday and I drank milk.* Clap your hands. Pupils move on. Repeat four or five times.
OR
Pupils look back through their work for this unit and select an example which provides evidence for each *Can do* statement. They put the example in their portfolio. For each example, they write the full *Can do* statement at the top of a piece of paper and a short paragraph which explains why they chose each one.

Page 34
- **Extra activity 1: Parts of the body**
Hand out a piece of paper to each pupil. They draw an outline of the human body. They label as many parts of the body as they can, keeping their picture hidden. Pupils compare their pictures in pairs. They see who has the most words. Elicit words and write them on the board. Tell pupils to check their spelling.
- **Extra activity 2: What made the sound?**
Pupils work in pairs. Pupil A closes his / her eyes. Pupil B makes a sound, using either a part of their body (e.g. clicking fingers, clapping, popping their mouth) or an item on their desk (e.g. closing a book, tapping a pencil on the desk). Pupil B asks *What made the sound?* Pupil A has to guess by asking questions (e.g. *Was it a … ?*). Then they swap roles. Demonstrate the game with the class first (pupils close their eyes and you make a sound).

Page 35
- **Extra activity 1: Play your drum**
Pupils use their drums from the Pupil's Book project activity. Give instructions about how the pupils should play, e.g. *Play your drum slowly / quickly / loudly / softly / carefully.* Pupils respond by playing in the appropriate way. They can repeat the activity in pairs (one gives instructions, the other plays, then they swap over).
- **Extra activity 2: CLIL vocabulary**
Elicit the new words and phrases from the last two lessons and write them on the board. Check pupils understand them and know how to say them. In their vocabulary books, pupils write the heading *Body percussion*. They write the new words, phrases and expressions from the lesson, either as a mind map, or as a list. At the bottom of the page, they write some of the things they did in the lessons, e.g. *I learnt about musical notes. I made a drum.* If time, pupils can illustrate the page.

Unit 4
Page 36
- **Extra activity 1: After school clubs**
Pupils work in groups of four. Each group makes a poster to advertise an After school club. They display their posters. They imagine what they did there the day before and tell the class.
- **Extra activity 2: Spelling game**
Make two or three teams. Teams line up at the front. Give the pupils at the front of each team a board pen. Say a regular verb. Each pupil with a pen writes the past form on the board at the same time (spelling it carefully). They shouldn't look at what the pupils from the other teams are writing. Check the spellings with the class. Pupils who have spelt the past form correctly win a point for their team. Clean the board. Pupils pass the board pens to the next member of their team. Repeat with a different verb. Continue until as many pupils as possible have had a chance to write.

Page 37
- **Extra activity 1: Gapped texts**
Display the large piece of paper with the gapped text(s). Individually, pupils fill in the gaps and write their own texts. More confident pupils can make more changes to the texts. In groups of four, pupils take turns to read their texts aloud to their friends.

- **Extra activity 2: Categorising verbs**
Pupils work in pairs. They categorise the verbs from the texts in Pupil's Book Activity 4 into three groups according to spelling (+ed, double consonant +ed, +d). Provide a headword for each group (e.g. *worked, hopped, bounced*). Pupils list the other words in the correct columns. Check with the class.
Key: +ed: *helped, walked, kicked, laughed, climbed, sailed, rained, called, played, needed, started, shouted, pointed*; double consonant +ed: *skipped*; +d: *lived, loved, invited, skated*

Page 38

- **Extra activity 1: Class quiz**
Pupils close their books. They need a piece of paper and a pencil. Ask the questions you have prepared. Ask them quickly one after another, not giving pupils very long to think. Pupils swap papers. Ask the questions again and correct as a class.
- **Extra activity 2: Bingo**
Pupils draw a 2 x 2 grid in their books. They choose ordinals from *1st* to *20th* and write them in the four squares as figures, not words. Call out ordinals at random. You could use the Unit 4 word cards from *Kid's Box Teacher's Resource Book 4* to remember the words you have said. Pupils cross out the numbers on their bingo grid as they hear them. The first pupil to cross out all four numbers on his / her grid shouts *Bingo!* Elicit the numbers to check and stick the word cards on the board, if available. Repeat.

Page 39

- **Extra activity 1: Numbers game**
Make three teams. They stand in a line facing the board. Whisper a different ordinal number to the first pupil in each team. They whisper it to the back. The pupil at the back runs to the front and writes it on the board as a figure, e.g. *2nd*. This pupil now stands at the front of the line. Repeat with other numbers. The team with the most correct numbers at the end is the winner.
- **Extra activity 2: Word puzzles**
Pupils use the word puzzle in Activity Book Activity 7 as a model to write their own. They can use the model as it is, or they can make it more complex, e.g. *My first is in bed but not in bad*. Tell pupils to think of the word first and then to write the clues. They swap with their partner and complete each other's puzzles.

Page 40

- **Extra activity 1: Things my friends did last week**
Pupils use the information from the communication activity (Pupil's Book Activity 15) to write sentences in their notebooks about their friends. Check that they remember when to join sentences with *and / but* and to change *your* to *his* or *her*. Monitor and help where necessary.
- **Extra activity 2: Verb practice**
Write the past tense forms from Activity Book Activity 9 on the board, mixing up the three pronunciations. Pupils work in pairs. They write the letters *d*, *t* and *id* in their notebooks. Pupil A says one of the past tense forms, concentrating on the pronunciation of the letters *ed*. Pupil B listens carefully and points to *d*, *t* or *id* in his / her notebook, as appropriate. Then pupils swap roles. Monitor and check / support.

Page 41

- **Extra activity 1: Completing the story**
In groups of four, pupils imagine what happens next in the story and write dialogues for two more frames. They practise their dialogues in their groups. Monitor and help / advise where necessary. Groups perform the endings of their stories: play the CD first each time to give the performances more context.
- **Extra activity 2: What I can do**
You will need space for this activity. Pupils each choose one of the *Can do* sentences. They walk around the room without touching anyone else. Clap your hands. They make pairs. They take turns to say their sentence / ask their questions and to demonstrate them, e.g. *I can ask questions about last week. Did you watch TV on Friday? Did you walk to school last week?* Clap your hands. Pupils move on. Repeat four or five times.
OR
Pupils look back through their work for this unit and select an example which provides evidence for each *Can do* statement. They put the example in their portfolio. For each example, they write the full statement at the top of a piece of paper and a short paragraph which explains why they chose each one.

Page 42

- **Extra activity: Plays, poems and novels I like**
In groups of four, pupils talk about the plays, poems and novels they like reading (in their own language). If the pupils find this task challenging in small groups, do it as a class activity, writing ideas and suggestions onto the board. Provide additional vocabulary if necessary. Individually in their notebooks, pupils write about a play, novel or poem they read / saw (what it is about and why they like it).

Page 43

- **Extra activity 1: Team quiz**
Make groups of four. Tell pupils you are going to do a quiz about the text. They write the numbers 1–14 in their notebooks. Read the statements below. Pupils write *True* or *False* for each one. Do the first one as an example. After the quiz, give groups five minutes to compare their answers. Read the questions again. Groups swap their answer sheets with another group. Check as a class. The group(s) with the most correct answers is / are the winner(s).
1 The book is called *The Lion, the Witch and the Bookcase*. (false)
2 The writer's name is C.S. Luton. (false)
3 It is the first in a series called *The Chronicles of Narnia*. (true)
4 It was very rainy outside. (true)
5 The children had to play in the garden. (false)
6 Inside the room there was a wardrobe. (true)
7 Inside the wardrobe there were a lot of old sweaters. (false)
8 There were a lot of coats. (true)
9 There were leaves on the ground. (false)
10 There was snow on the ground. (true)
11 Lucy was in a forest. (true)
12 It was morning. (false)
13 In the forest it was hotter than inside the room. (false)
14 Lucy was in Narnia with Edmund. (false)
- **Extra activity 2: CLIL vocabulary**
Elicit the new key words and phrases from the last two lessons and write them on the board. Check pupils understand the words and know how to say them. In their vocabulary books, pupils write the heading *Literature*. They write the new words and phrases either as a mind map or as a list. At the bottom of the page, they write some of the things they did in the lessons, e.g. *I wrote a poem. I read part of 'The Lion, the Witch and the Wardrobe'. I made a poster about my favourite book*. If time, pupils can illustrate the page.

Review Units 3–4

Page 44
- **Extra activity 1: Songs and chants**
Sing one of the songs or do one of the chants from Units 3 and 4.
- **Extra activity 2: Write your own quiz**
Brainstorm past verb forms (regular and irregular) from Units 3 and 4. Pupils work in groups of four. Each pupil chooses two different verbs (eight per group) and writes two sentences, one for each verb. They then check each other's sentences in their groups. Monitor and help as necessary. Each group prepares a word box with the key verbs from their sentences in the infinitive, using Activity Book Activity 1 as a model (but not a wordsearch). They write the sentences under the word box with spaces where the verbs should be. They display their quizzes on the walls. Number each quiz. Pupils move around in their groups. They write the quiz number and the verbs for the gaps in their notebooks in the past form. They don't answer their own quiz.
Each group provides the answers for their quiz. Pupils check their answers. The group with the most correct answers is the winner.

Page 45
- **Extra activity 1: What did you do last week?**
Draw the table below on the board. Pupils copy it and at the top of the second and third columns they write the names of two friends (make sure everyone in the class is chosen by at least one pupil).

	[name of friend 1]	[name of friend 2]
Monday		
Tuesday		
Wednesday		
Thursday		
Friday		
Saturday and Sunday		

Pupils ask their two chosen friends about what they did each day and note the answers. Remind them to use the information from the listening (CD2 track 12) to help them. In their notebooks, they write about what their two friends did last week.
- **Extra activity 2: Games**
Play one of the games from Units 3 and 4 with the class. Let pupils choose which one to play.

Unit 5

Page 46
- **Extra activity 1: True or false**
Pupils study the text on the Pupil's Book page and, in pairs, write eight true / false statements about the text, using the new verbs. They make groups of four. They close their books. Pairs take turns to read a sentence to the other pair. They get one point for correctly guessing if the sentence is true or false and another for correcting the information if the sentence is false.
- **Extra activity 2: Make sentences**
In their notebooks, pupils write six sentences using the verbs from the wordsearch on Activity Book page 46 in the past simple. Give them a context, e.g. *last weekend / your last holidays / an expedition to the mountains / sea*.

Page 47
- **Extra activity: Pelmanism**
Pupils work in pairs. They use the sentence openers from Activity Book Activity 6, but write their own reasons, e.g. *He couldn't find his pen so he wrote a letter on his computer.* They write each sentence on a different strip of paper. Pupils then cut each sentence in half after *so*, e.g. *He couldn't find his pen so / he wrote a letter on his computer.* Pairs swap sentence papers with other pairs. They put the paper face down on their desks and take turns to turn over two pieces. They say the two sentence parts. If they match, the pupil who turned them over keeps them. If not, the pupil turns them face down again. At the end, pairs confirm with the other pair that their sentence matches are correct. The pupil with the most sentences at the end is the winner.

Page 48
- **Extra activity 1: Opposites**
Write the following adjectives on the board: *good, beautiful, straight, boring, last, quick, easy, strong, clean, quiet, wrong, tall, new,* and their opposites, at random. Give pupils two minutes to match the adjectives in pairs. Choose a word from the board. One pair of pupils make a sentence, using the adjective in the comparative. Another pair gives a sentence, using the opposite comparative adjective. Repeat until all the adjectives have been used.
- **Extra activity 2: Comparative adjectives**
Write the heading *Comparative adjectives* on the board and draw a table like this:

One syllable	Ending in 'y'	Two syllables not ending in 'y'	Three + syllables	Irregular

Pupils copy the table in their notebooks. Elicit an example for each column. They check back through the lesson to find the adjectives used and write them in the correct columns. Monitor and check. Under the table, pupils write an example sentence for each column (not for each word) as a reminder.

Page 49
- **Extra activity 1: Our own scrambled sentences**
Pupils work in pairs. They either create their own sentences using the comparative or look back through the unit to find examples. They write the sentences in scrambled word order without using a capital letter for the first word. Each pair writes at least six scrambled sentences. They swap their sentences with other pairs and write the correct version on the paper. Pairs join with the other pair to check / correct.
- **Extra activity 2: School trips**
Elicit places pupils can go for school trips, e.g. museums, art galleries, the theatre, the cinema, the zoo. In groups of four, pupils imagine a school trip they went on and make a poster about it. They draw / cut out pictures and then write text at the bottom. Provide a model on the board, e.g.
Last month we went on a school trip to _____ . It was really _____ . First we saw the _____ .

They were _____ . Then we went to visit the _____ . Our teacher told us they were very _____ because _____ . Our favourite part of the trip was when we _____ . It was a _____ day.

Pupils display and talk about their posters. Elicit comparatives from pupils about the posters / trips, e.g. *Do you think the school trip to the art gallery was more interesting than the one to the museum?* Pupils should give their reasons too, using *because*.

Page 50

- **Extra activity 1: Write a rap**

Write the two verses from the rap on the board. Erase the words, so it looks like this:

Our world is _____ , we're making mistakes,
We need our _____ , we need our lakes.
Our world is _____ , we can make it _____ ,
It needs our help. Listen to our song.
We must look after its _____ and _____ ,
We must look after its _____ and _____ .
We can make it better, we can make it _____ ,
This is our world, let's keep it clean.

Pupils work in groups of four to compose one or two more verses for the rap. Groups should try to make the lines rhyme if they can. Monitor and help / give ideas. Groups write the new verse(s) on a large piece of paper. They display the poster and perform their new verse(s). The class votes for the best new verse.

- **Extra activity 2: Find the words**

In their notebooks, pupils write all the /ɜː/ words from the lesson, underlining the letters which represent the /ɜː/ sound. They write the words in groups according to their spelling.

Page 51

- **Extra activity 1: Role play**

Make groups of five (Lock, Key, Nick Motors, Miss Rich, waiter). In their groups, pupils prepare some props: a Wanted poster of Nick Motors, and a front page for a holiday brochure. Pupils decide their roles. Play the CD again. Pause after each frame. Pupils repeat their section in role. Stop after frame 5 (when Lock gets the text message). In their groups, pupils decide on a different text message and a different ending for the episode. They write and practise their new endings in their groups. Confident pupils perform their role plays for the class. Vote for the best text message and the best new ending.

- **Extra activity 2: What I can do**

You will need space for this activity. Pupils each choose one of the *Can do* sentences. They walk around the room without touching anyone else. Clap your hands. They make pairs. They take turns to say their sentence / ask their questions and to demonstrate them, e.g. *I can compare people and things. Shackleton's expedition was more dangerous than Jacques Cousteau's, but Jacques Cousteau is more famous.* Clap your hands. Pupils move on. Repeat four or five times.
OR
Pupils look back through their work for this unit and select an example which provides evidence for each *Can do* statement. They put the example in their portfolio. For each example, they write the full *Can do* statement at the top of a piece of paper and a short paragraph which explains why they chose each one.

Page 52

- **Extra activity: Animal comparisons**

Write the names of animals you have talked about in the lesson on the board (e.g. *kangaroo, polar bear, goat, tiger, panda, whale, fish, elephant*). Pupils work in pairs to write as many comparative sentences on the board as they can, using only these animals. Write some adjectives on the board to help, if you wish (e.g. *fast, slow, beautiful, ugly, dangerous, small, big*). Set a time limit of five minutes. Elicit the sentences and write them on the board. Pairs check each other's work. The pair with the most correct sentences wins.

- **Extra activity 2: Polar bear facts**

With books closed, write the following sentences on the board:
1 Polar bears live in the _____ .
2 They live on the _____ .
3 They eat seals, fish and small _____ .
4 Polar bears are _____ their habitat.
5 It's more difficult for the bears to _____ for food.
6 They can't look _____ their babies well.

Pupils copy and complete them individually. Tell them to use only one word each time. They compare answers in pairs. Check with the class. Let pupils look back at Pupil's Book page 52 to confirm.
Key: 1 Arctic, 2 ice, 3 whales, 4 losing, 5 fish, 6 after

Page 53

- **Extra activity 1: Sharing information**

Make groups of four to six pupils, making sure there are pupils who wrote about different animals for the Pupil's Book Project. Pupils take turns to read their article about endangered animals to the rest of the group. The pupils in the group take notes about all the animals they hear about, using the following headings:
Name of animal
Where it lives
What it eats
Why it's endangered
What we must do
Monitor and ask pupils to share any interesting facts they discovered from the rest of their group with you.

- **Extra activity 2: CLIL vocabulary**

Elicit the new words and phrases from the last two lessons and write them on the board. Check pupils understand them and know how to say them. In their vocabulary books, pupils write the heading *Endangered animals*. They write the new words, phrases and expressions from the lessons, either as a mind map, or as a list. At the bottom of the page, they write some of the things they did in the lessons, e.g. *I read about endangered animals. I wrote about an endangered animal.* If time, pupils can illustrate the page.

Unit 6

Page 54

- **Extra activity 1: My desk**

In their notebooks, pupils draw a picture of an imaginary desk at home showing all the new vocabulary from the lesson. They label the items. Provide other words if pupils need them, e.g. *mobile phone, headphones*.

- **Extra activity 2: Writing instructions**

In pairs, pupils use the set of instructions in Activity Book Activity 2 as a model for writing a set of instructions for using one of the other technologies, e.g. laptop, phone or e-book. Provide vocabulary as necessary. Pairs write their set of instructions on paper for display. If time, they can illustrate their instructions / write another set for a different device.

Page 55

- **Extra activity: Ordering the dialogues**
Make five groups. Hand out the lines of one section of the dialogue from Activity Book Activity 3 to each group. They work together to put the dialogue in the correct order. Play the CD for groups to check. If time, give groups another section and repeat.

Page 56

- **Extra activity 1: Role play**
Display the CD script of the listening from Pupil's Book Activity 8. Play the CD again as pupils read the CD script. In groups of three, pupils role play the conversation. More confident pupils can role play it for the class.

- **Extra activity 2: Verbs and sentences**
Pupils write all the verbs from the Bingo game (Activity Book Activity 6) in their notebooks (simple infinitive and past simple forms). They write a sentence for each one in the past: they can choose sentences from the lesson or write their own.

Page 57

- **Extra activity 1: Game**
Make two or three teams. Teams line up facing the board. Say three words, e.g. *Jack, school, yesterday*. Give a time limit. The pupils at the front of the teams run to the board and write a sentence in the past using these prompt words, e.g. *Jack was at school yesterday. / Jack went to school yesterday*. Shout *Stop!* The pupils go to the back of their teams. Repeat with other prompts.

- **Extra activity 2: More problems!**
Pupils work in pairs. They each write another problem, using Activity Book Activity 7 as a model. Remind them to keep answers under 100. Make groups of ten (five pairs). Pairs pass their problems to the left and write the answers to each problem they receive. They write their answers silently / in secret. When they have answered all four problems in their groups, the pairs who wrote the problem read it aloud and give the answer. The other pupils mark their answers. Pupils with the most correct answers in their groups are the winners. If time, pairs can pass their problems to other groups.

Page 58

- **Extra activity: Find the rhymes**
With books closed, write some of the rhyming words from Activity Book Activity 9 on the board (e.g. *taller, bought, hall, water, floor, talked*). Pupils work in pairs. In their notebooks, they write one or more rhyming words for each one. Check with the class. The pair with the most correctly rhymed words wins.
Suggested answers: *taller – smaller; bought – caught, taught, thought, sport, short; hall – call, Paul, ball, tall; water – daughter; floor – door, four, poor, more; talked – walked*

Page 59

- **Extra activity 1: Role play**
Make groups of four (Lock, Key, Miss Rich, Nick Motors). Pupils decide their roles. Play the CD again. Pause after each frame. Pupils repeat their section in role. Stop after frame 4 (when they are rowing to Miss Rich's boat). In their groups, pupils decide on a different email and a different ending for the episode to include Nick Motors. They write the new emails and endings on the large piece of paper and practise it in their groups. Confident pupils can perform their role plays for the class and display their new emails / endings.

- **Extra activity 2: What I can do**
You will need space for this activity. Pupils each choose one of the *Can do* sentences. They walk around the room without touching anyone else. Clap your hands. They make pairs. They take turns to say their sentence / ask their questions and to demonstrate them, e.g. *I can say more verbs in the past. I got up at 9 o'clock yesterday. I went shopping with my mum and dad and I bought a new computer game.* Clap your hands. Pupils move on. Repeat four or five times.
OR
Pupils look back through their work for this unit and select an example which provides evidence for each *Can do* statement. They put the example in their portfolio. For each example, they write the full *Can do* statement at the top of a piece of paper and a short paragraph which explains why they chose each one.

Page 60

- **Extra activity 1: Boring jobs**
Write the following everyday tasks on the board: *washing plates, making my bed, cooking, cleaning the floor, taking out the rubbish, looking after pets*. Ask pupils to rank them by numbering them 1 to 6, with 1 being the most boring task and 6 the least boring. They compare answers in small groups. Have a class vote on the most boring task.

- **Extra activity 2: Robots vs people**
Make pairs. Name pupils A and B in each pair. Ask 'A' pupils to make a list of all the things robots can do which people can't do. Ask 'B' pupils to make a list of the things people can do which robots can't do. Set a time limit of five minutes. Monitor and help with ideas and new language.
Pupils compare their sentences in pairs to see who has the most. They can role play a discussion between a robot and a person, talking in the first person, e.g. Pupil A (the robot): *I can explore dangerous places like underwater or space.* Pupil B: *But you can't think. I program you.* Confident pupils can perform their role play for the class.

Page 61

- **Extra activity 1: Meet my robot**
Pupils need their picture and writing from the Pupil's Book project. They work in small groups. They take turns to show and talk about the robot they have designed. Encourage pupils to ask the people in their group about the robots. Elicit some key questions and write them on the board (e.g. *What does your robot do? What's it called? What parts does it have? Can it talk / walk?*). Each group can choose their favourite robot.

- **Extra activity 2: CLIL vocabulary**
Elicit the new words and phrases from the CLIL lessons and write them on the board. Check pupils understand them and know how to say them. In their vocabulary books, pupils write the heading *Robots*. They write the new words, phrases and expressions from the lessons, either as a mind map, or as a list. At the bottom of the page, they write some of the things they did in the lessons, e.g. *I read about robots. I designed a robot.* If time, pupils can illustrate the page.

Review Units 5–6

Page 62
- **Extra activity 1: What they did yesterday**
Allocate names to the people on the game board in the Pupil's Book. In their notebooks, pupils write the sentences from the game, using the names of the people.
- **Extra activity 2: Songs, chants and rhymes**
Sing one of the songs or say one of the chants from Units 5 and 6.

Page 63
- **Extra activity 1: Scrambled sentences**
Display the large piece of paper with the ten scrambled statements / questions. Pupils work individually to unscramble the sentences and write them correctly. Cut up each sentence. Hand the words to the same number of pupils as words. They come to the board and stick the words on the board, arranging them in the correct order.
- **Extra activity 2: Game**
Play one of the games from Units 5 and 6 with the class. Let pupils choose which one to play.

Unit 7

Page 64
- **Extra activity 1: Animal quiz**
Pupils work in groups. Give each group a reference book about animals. Each group writes three or four questions using the model from the quiz in the Pupil's Book listening, using their reference book or the internet to check facts. They write two factual questions and two personal opinion questions, e.g. Factual: *Which animal is the longest: the crocodile, the boa constrictor or the blue whale?* Personal opinion: *Which animal do you think is the most frightening?* For the factual questions, pupils provide the answer. Collect the questions.
Make three teams. Teams number their members from 1 to however many there are in the team. Ask a question of the teams in turn, calling out a number at random to decide who answers. For the opinion questions, pupils have to give two reasons using superlatives. Award 1 point for each correct answer. The team with the most points is the winner.
- **Extra activity 2: Families!**
Draw a simple family tree on the board to review family relationships, e.g. *mother, father, brother, cousin, uncle*. Brainstorm some adjectives used to describe family members and write them in simple form down one side of the board, e.g. *tall, old, young, intelligent, interesting, careful*. Pupils each write the words for the family members on small pieces of paper. In pairs, they put the pieces of paper in front of them and turn them face down on their desks. Pupil A turns over one of his / her pieces of paper and says to Pupil B, e.g. *Now tell me about your mother.* Pupil B then says a sentence using at least two superlative adjectives, e.g. *She's the tallest person in my family. She's the most beautiful person in my family.* Then it's Pupil B's turn.

Page 65
- **Extra activity 1: Draw my animals**
Pupils work individually. They draw pictures of three animals for comparison. Make pairs (make sure pupils haven't seen each other's pictures). Pupils take turns to talk about the animals, describing them using comparative and superlative adjectives so that their partner can draw them in their notebook. After both pupils have described and drawn, they look and check.

Page 66
- **Extra activity 1: A zoo picture**
Pupils draw a composite zoo picture in their notebooks. They work in groups and talk about what they did / saw at the zoo with their friends. They write sentences under the picture.
- **Extra activity 2: Following instructions**
You will need space for this activity. Pupils hold hands and make circles of five or six. Call out instructions for the groups to follow as in line dancing, e.g. *Steps to the right, one, two, three. Steps to the left, one, two, three. Move into the centre, one, two, three. Touch hands and shout. Move out of the centre, one, two, three.*

Page 67
- **Extra activity 1: Make the song**
Tell pupils they are going to listen and stand in a line in the same order as the song. Hand out the pieces of paper at random. (Tell them to form two groups of pupils with the same coloured paper, if you have more than 12 pupils.) Play the CD for Pupil's Book Activity 10. The first time, pupils listen for their line. Play the CD again. Pupils organise themselves into lines to match the sequence of the song. Play the CD again, if necessary, to check.
- **Extra activity 2: Prepositions**
Pupils look back through the lesson and find all the prepositions used. Brainstorm them and write them on the board. In their notebooks, pupils draw a simple picture to illustrate each one and write the preposition under the drawing (they should try to draw something different from the picture on the flashcard).

Page 68
- **Extra activity 1: Animal opinions**
Pairs use the information from the communication activity and write up the surveys in their notebooks. Provide language on the board, e.g. *Everyone / most / some people I talked to thought that … One person I talked to thought that … No-one I talked to thought that …* Monitor and help where necessary.
- **Extra activity 2: Find the words**
In their notebooks, pupils write all the rhyming words from the lesson, underlining the relevant parts of the words. They put them in colour columns.

Page 69
- **Extra activity 1: How did the story end?**
Make groups of four (Lock, Key, Zookeeper, Nick Motors). Pupils decide their roles. Play the CD again. Pause after each frame. Pupils repeat their section in role. In their groups, pupils decide how the story ends. On a large piece of paper, they draw two more frames to illustrate this and add the dialogue. They practise the complete dialogue (including the ending) in their groups. Confident pupils can perform their role plays for the class. All groups display their posters with their endings. The class votes for the best one.
- **Extra activity 2: What I can do**
You will need space for this activity. Pupils each choose one of the *Can do* sentences. They walk around the room without touching anyone else. Clap your hands. They make pairs. They take turns to say their sentence / ask their questions and to demonstrate them, e.g. *I can say more verbs in the past. The parrots flew round their cage. The baby lions ran in their cage. Suzy drew a picture of her visit to the zoo.* Clap your hands. Pupils move on. Repeat four or five times.

OR
Pupils look back through their work for this unit and select an example which provides evidence for each *Can do* statement. They put the example in their portfolio. For each example, they write the full *Can do* statement at the top of a piece of paper and a short paragraph which explains why they chose each one.

Page 70
- **Extra activity 1: Body facts**

Draw an outline of the human body on the board. Hand out the paper to each pupil. They copy the body outline. They label as many different parts of the body as they can (e.g. *head, arm, wrist, finger*). Monitor and check spelling and position of labels. Pupils compare their pictures in pairs. Elicit all the body parts pupils know and use them to label your picture on the board.

- **Extra activity 2: Heart beats**

You will need space for this activity. Show pupils how to feel their heart beat / pulse in their wrists. In pairs, they take turns to take each other's pulse, counting how many beats there are in a minute. They can use the second hands of their watches. Pupils stand up. They do about one minute of quite vigorous exercise by following your instructions, e.g. *Touch your head. Touch your toes. Turn around. Jump up and down.* When the minute is up, pupils work in the same pairs again. Pupil A takes Pupil B's pulse again and notes it down. Repeat the exercise and then Pupil B takes Pupil A's pulse and notes it down. Discuss the results with the class.

Page 71
- **Extra activity 1: My Super Animal**

Call on volunteers to present the Super Animal they drew and wrote about for the project. They talk about what the animal looks like and what it can do, without reading what they wrote word for word. Invite the rest of the class to ask questions, e.g. *Has it got a tail? Can it swim?*

- **Extra activity 2: CLIL vocabulary**

Elicit the new words and phrases from the CLIL lessons and write them on the board. Check pupils understand the meaning and know how to say them. In their vocabulary books, pupils write the heading *Skeleton and body*. They write the new words, phrases and expressions from the lessons, either as a mind map, or as a list. At the bottom of the page, they write some of the things they did in the lessons, e.g. *I read about animal skeletons. I made a book about Super Animals.* If time, pupils can illustrate the page.

Unit 8
Page 72
- **Extra activity 1: Role play**

Make groups of five. Elicit the food and drink that pupils heard on the CD and write the words on the board. In their groups, pupils draw and cut out pictures of each of these foods and drinks. Display the large piece of paper and play the CD one more time. Pupils work in their groups, decide on their roles and then role play the conversation, using the pictures as props. More confident groups act out their conversations for the class.

- **Extra activity 2: Word maps**

Make six groups. Give each group one of the expressions of quantity, e.g. *A box of.* They write the expression in the centre of a piece of paper and then make a word map of the food words that go with it, e.g. *a box of – bananas, oranges, eggs, apples.* Pupils present their word maps to the class.

Page 73
- **Extra activity 1: Chant**

Teach the following chant to pupils:

Hum, hum, hum, hum, hum (as if mouth full, miming actions to open the door)
Hum, hum, hum, hum, hum (as if mouth full, miming actions to open the door)
(Grandma / Grandpa-type voice) *What did you say, dear? I can't hear you!*
She wants him to open, to open, to open,
She wants him to open the door!
Hum, hum, hum, hum, hum (as if mouth full, miming actions to pass a cake)
Hum, hum, hum, hum, hum (as if mouth full, miming actions to pass a cake)
(Grandma / Grandpa-type voice) *What did you say, dear? I can't hear you!*
He wants her to pass, to pass, to pass,
He wants her to pass the cake!
Hum, hum, hum, hum, hum (as if mouth full, miming actions to make a sandwich)
Hum, hum, hum, hum, hum (as if mouth full, miming actions to make a sandwich)
(Grandma / Grandpa-type voice) *What did you say, dear? I can't hear you!*
She wants him to make, to make, to make,
She wants him to make a sandwich.

- **Extra activity 2: Party food**

Draw a rectangle on the board and tell pupils that this is a party table. Demonstrate the activity by drawing six items on the 'table', e.g. a bottle of lemonade, a plate of sandwiches, a box of chocolates, a bag of crisps. Elicit from pupils what they can see and where it is, e.g. *The box of chocolates is behind the bottle of lemonade.* Pupils work individually. They draw a 'table' in their notebooks with up to six items of party food on it. Make new pairs. They take turns to describe their tables and draw their partner's table of items in their notebooks.

Page 74
- **Extra activity 1: Make sentences**

Draw the following grid on the board. Pupils use it to make sentences about the picture on Pupil's Book page 74 and about what the children are doing. If they can't remember, tell them to put down their pens and listen while you play the CD for Activity 7 again. Then they can write their sentences.

Suzy		the best.
Meera		the most carefully.
Simon	's jumping	the most slowly.
Alex		the worst.
Lenny		the most quickly.
Stella		

- **Extra activity 2: My party**

Pupils use the model in Activity Book Activity 5 to write about the last birthday party they went to. They can make other changes too, e.g. change *Last week* to *Last December*. Monitor the planning and writing and help with ideas / vocabulary. Pupils write a draft of their text. They swap with a partner to check their work. They then write a final version in their notebooks.

Page 75
- **Extra activity 1: Describing differences**
Pupils write the differences between the two Pupil's Book pictures (page 75 Activity 9) in their notebooks.
- **Extra activity 2: Children in costumes**
In their notebooks, pupils draw the children from Activity Book Activity 7 in their costumes and write their names.

Page 76
- **Extra activity: What's for dinner, Mr Wolf?**
You'll need a large space for this activity. Demonstrate the activity. You are Mr Wolf. Stand at one end of the room, facing the wall. The pupils line up at the other end of the room. They creep forward so Mr Wolf doesn't hear. The aim is to reach Mr Wolf. Mr Wolf keeps turning round. When he does, the pupils freeze. A pupil asks *What's for dinner, Mr Wolf?* Mr Wolf responds with a one- or two-syllable word, e.g. *Soup* and turns back to the wall. One time Mr Wolf responds *Vegetables!* (the three-syllable word is the clue to run) and runs to catch one of the pupils. Repeat the game, this time tell pupils to listen for a one-syllable word as the clue that they need to run.

Page 77
- **Extra activity 1: Lock and Key's party**
Pupils work in groups of four. They plan a party for Lock and Key. They decide on food, drink, games, decorations, guests, etc. They draw a picture of the party. At the bottom they write a text about the party, e.g. *Lock and Key had a party last week because they caught Nick Motors. They had lots of yummy food. They had …*
- **Extra activity 2: What I can do**
You will need space for this activity. Pupils each choose one of the *Can do* sentences. They walk around the room without touching anyone else. Clap your hands. They make pairs. They take turns to say their sentence / ask their questions and to demonstrate them, e.g. *I can say more food and container words. At the party we had three bottles of lemonade and four bags of sweets.* Clap your hands. Pupils move on. Repeat four or five times.
OR
Pupils look back through their work for this unit and select an example which provides evidence for each *Can do* statement. They put the example in their portfolio. For each example they write the full *Can do* statement at the top of a piece of paper and a short paragraph which explains why they chose each one.

Page 78
- **Extra activity 1: Our menu**
Pupils work individually. In their notebooks, they write a list of what they ate for each meal on the previous day. Then they write one or two sentences about whether they think they ate the correct amount of each food group, and how they should change their diet (e.g. *I ate too many sweets yesterday. I need to eat more fruit and vegetables.*)
- **Extra activity 2: What's in our food?**
Make groups of four. Show pupils the packets and cartons you have brought in. Tell them they are going to look at the list of nutrients in the food and find out what is in each one. Before handing out the packets and cartons, pupils guess what the main food group in each one is. Hand out cartons and packets to groups in turn. They read the information and record it in their notebooks. After all the groups have recorded information about all the foods, discuss what they found and if there were any surprises.

Page 79
- **Extra activity 1: Food and meals**
In their notebooks, pupils write up what recipes the different groups created for the project. They briefly discuss each one in turn and say what they like about it. They summarise by saying which recipe they prefer and why.
- **Extra activity 2: CLIL vocabulary**
Elicit the new words and phrases from the CLIL / Real world lessons and write them on the board. Check pupils understand them and know how to say them. In their vocabulary books, pupils write the heading *Food and nutrients*. They write the new words, phrases and expressions from the last two lessons, either as a mind map, or as a list.
At the bottom of the page, they write some of the things they did in the lessons, e.g. *I learnt about the different food groups and how to eat a balanced diet. I wrote a recipe for a healthy lunchtime meal.* If time, pupils can illustrate the page.

Review Units 7–8
Page 80
- **Extra activity: Songs, chants and rhymes**
Sing one of the songs or do one of the chants or rhymes from *Kid's Box 4*.

Page 81
- **Extra activity 1: Scrambled sentences**
Display the large piece of paper with the ten scrambled statements / questions. Pupils work individually to unscramble the sentences and write them correctly. Cut up each sentence. Hand the words to the same number of pupils as words. They come to the board and stick the words on the board, arranging them in the correct order to make the sentences / questions.
- **Extra activity 2: Games**
Play one of the games from *Kid's Box 4* with the class. Let pupils choose which one to play.

Values 1–4
Page 82
- **Extra activity 1: A present for you**
Elicit examples of presents people can give others to say 'Thank you' and write them on the board, e.g. *fruit, flowers, a picture, a book, a letter*. Give each pupil a piece of paper. Ask them to draw one of the things from the board.
Pupils work in pairs. They make up two dialogues using the pictures they have drawn, e.g. Pupil A hands over a picture of flowers to Pupil B. He / she says *These are for you. Thank you for your help.* Pupil B: *That's nice. Thank you very much.* Monitor and help. Write useful phrases on the board, if necessary. Ask pairs to perform their favourite dialogue for the class.
- **Extra activity 2: Matching**
Give each pupil a piece of paper with a phrase from the lesson. Pupils stand up. They walk around, saying their sentence to different pupils until they find a partner who has an appropriate response. They come to you to check. Ask them to invent the rest of the dialogue / situation.

Page 83
- **Extra activity 1: Scriptwriters**
Say *Let's write a script.* Teach / check the meaning of *script*. Demonstrate the activity. Tell pupils they need to write a mini script for the characters from the first picture on Pupil's Book

page 83, Activity 1. Tell them it has to be different from the dialogue they listened to. Elicit a short dialogue between the girl and the elderly woman and write it on the board (e.g. Girl: *Are you tired?* Woman: *Yes, I am.* Girl: *Please have my seat.* Woman: *Oh, thank you. You're very kind.*). Call on volunteers to act out the dialogue. Pupils work in pairs. They choose one of the other three pictures from Activity 1 and write a mini script. Monitor and help with language. Pairs practise their scenes. Pairs work with pairs. They perform the mini dialogues.

- **Extra activity 2: Posters**

Elicit situations at school when we can be kind (e.g. lending some school equipment, taking turns in the playground, helping a younger pupil reach something, helping someone find their way). Pupils work in groups of three or four. Give each group a large piece of paper. Ask them to design a poster with the title *Be kind at school*. They draw a picture to illustrate one of the situations you talked about and write one or two phrases in English to use, e.g. *Would you like to use my pencil?* Display the finished posters in the classroom.

Page 84

- **Extra activity 1: Cycling rules**

Ask pupils how often they use their bicycles and where they usually ride them. Write the road safety rules about cycling from the lesson on the board (*Always wear a helmet when you are on your bike. Wear bright clothes when you ride your bike.*). Elicit reasons for each rule. Write more rules for safe cycling on the board, with the pupils' help (if they tell you in L1, recast them into English), e.g. *Don't cycle on the pavement when there are people walking. Cycle on the correct side of the road. Stop at traffic lights, just like cars. Don't listen to music when you are on your bike.*

- **Extra activity 2: Crossing the road**

Take your class into the school hall or out into the playground. Draw some white stripes on the ground or use white tape. Have pupils practise crossing the road safely, using the stripes as a zebra crossing. One pupil can 'be' the traffic light for pedestrians – showing a red or green piece of card at the side of the 'crossing' to make pupils stop or go.

Page 85

- **Extra activity 1: Colours in our lives**

Display pieces of paper or card in the following colours: yellow, black, white, green, blue. Tell pupils to look at each colour and think carefully about what it means to them. They write the name of the colour and then any words (in English or L1) which they think of related to the colour. They work individually, without comparing with a partner. Set a time limit of five minutes. Monitor and help with new language.
Brainstorm words for each colour and make mind maps on the board (e.g. yellow – *sun, summer, hot, happy, banana*; black – *night, dark, cat, shoes, sad*; white – *snow, winter, clean, whiteboard, paper*; green – *spring, grass, healthy, countryside, apple*; blue – *sea, cold, sky*).

- **Extra activity 2: Class poster**

Write the title *Recycling at our school* on the board. Elicit suggestions for ways to reuse or recycle things at school and write them on the board as sentences, e.g. *Use less paper. Don't throw glass or plastic away. Bring a drinking bottle from home.* Pupils work in pairs or small groups. Assign a sentence from the board to each pair / group. They draw a sign / picture to illustrate their sentence and write a reason why it is important. Monitor and help with language and ideas. Pupils write below their picture on the same piece of paper. Make a class poster with the work from each pair / group.

Extra project ideas

Unit 1 Volumes and weights

You will need:
About six empty plastic bottles / jars of different sizes, plastic cups for measuring, water, sand, lentils, polystyrene balls, a bag of paper clips, weighing scales.

A worksheet for each group.

For this project, pupils make predictions about volume and weight and then do experiments to check their predictions.

Tell pupils what the focus of the project is (predicting volume and weight and then checking their predictions through experimentation). You can use other materials for measuring weight, but make sure they are not all equally heavy / light. Write the steps of the project on the board for pupils to copy into their notebooks:

Step 1: Make groups of four.
Step 2: Read the questions on the worksheet. Look at the containers and predict the answers. Write your predictions on the worksheet.
Step 3: Do each experiment and find out the answers.
Step 4: Join with another group and compare your predictions and the results of your experiments.
Step 5: In your group of four, write about what you did and what you found out. Write a draft first. Check the writing of another group.
Step 6: Write a final version in your notebook.

Display the bottles and containers and number each experiment as on the worksheet to make the predictive phase more concrete. Monitor and guide pupils as they are working. Organise the experiment phase so that pupils don't hear the results from other groups and so that all pupils do the experiments. Groups can do the experiments in any order. Help pupils with their drafts, writing a model text on the board if appropriate. Encourage pupils to swap their work for peer correction at Step 5.

Worksheet sample

The questions you write will depend on the containers you have. There should be about six questions / experiments. Here is an example:

	Predicted outcome	Outcome of experiment
1 How many cups of water does it take to fill the bottle?		
2 Which is heavier: a cup of lentils or a cup of sand?		
3 How much liquid does the jar contain?		
4 How much does the bag of paper clips weigh?		

Unit 2 Sports and sportspeople

You will need:
Reference books, the internet, large pieces of paper, glue, coloured pencils and markers, paints, scissors, dictionaries.

For this project, pupils work in pairs or small groups to research a sportsperson and / or a local or unusual sport. They produce a poster which they display as they make their class presentation. Posters should be a mix of pictures and text (their own, not copied from the internet / reference books).

Tell pupils what the focus of the project is (a sportsperson and / or an unusual sport from their region). If you have time to make a poster of your own before the lesson, show it to them. Write the steps of the project on the board for pupils to copy into their notebooks:

Step 1: Make pairs / small groups.
Step 2: Decide which sportsperson and / or sport to do.
Step 3: Research the person and / or the sport, using the internet and reference books. Make notes about what you find out.
Step 4: Divide up the information into the number of people in your group. Each person finds pictures to illustrate their information. Plan the poster.
Step 5: Each person writes a draft of their text on paper. Swap texts in your group and check for content and grammar.
Step 6: Write final versions of the texts on paper. Stick the pictures and texts on the poster.
Step 7: Present your poster to the class.

Monitor and guide pupils as they are working, making sure they all keep on task, don't take too long on any one step and don't try to be too ambitious. Help pupils with their drafts. Provide models for texts on the board or on paper as appropriate. Encourage pupils to swap their work for peer correction at Step 5.

Each group should have time to make their presentation to the rest of the class. Leave the posters on display in the classroom. If possible, display them around the school for other pupils, teachers and parents to see.

Unit 3 Responding to music

You will need:
About six short extracts of different kinds of music, e.g. classical, rock, modern, techno; paper, coloured pencils, paints, large pieces of paper.

Note: In the previous lesson, ask pupils to bring CDs of their favourite music.

For this project, pupils work individually to create their responses to music they hear. They can draw / paint a picture or write a text, e.g. a story or a poem. They can respond in different ways to each piece of music they hear. Pupils share their responses / interpretations of the music in groups and then as a class.

Tell pupils what the focus of the project is (responding in different ways to different kinds of music). Write the steps of the project on the board for pupils to copy into their notebooks:

Step 1: Close your eyes so you are ready to listen to the music. Let your mind wander as you listen. Perhaps you will see pictures in your head. Perhaps the music will create a story or a poem for you.
Step 2: After listening, draw your picture or write your story / poem.
Step 3: Repeat Steps 1 and 2 for each piece of music your teacher plays.
Step 4: Make groups of four. Take turns to show the other pupils what you drew / wrote and to talk about how each piece of music made you feel.
Step 5: Make a chart of your group's responses to the music on a large piece of paper.
Step 6: Display your posters with examples of the pictures / texts from your group around them.
Step 7: Read the other groups' posters and discuss the similarities / differences of responses as a class.

Choose a variety of music: some that pupils know and some that they don't. Allocate the same time for pupils to write / draw their responses each time and monitor and guide pupils closely to make sure they are on task. At Step 4, provide prompts for the groups if appropriate, e.g. *How did you feel? Did you like the music? What did it make you think of?* Provide an example of a chart for groups at Step 5 so that they can note the type of response (picture / story / poem) and each person's feeling for each piece of music. After pupils have read each other's posters, discuss the different responses as a class.

Unit 4 Performing a play

You will need:
One or more titles in Level 3 or 4 of the *Cambridge Storybooks* which are designed to be read as plays OR the text of *The Owl and the Pussycat*, materials to make props, costumes and scenery.

For this project, pupils work in groups or as a class to dramatise a play / plays. All the pupils will have a role in the performance as actors, musicians, prop painters, costume makers, scene changers and so on. The final performance can be recorded on DVD and / or be performed in front of other pupils, teachers and parents.

Tell pupils what the focus of the project is (dramatisation of one or more short plays). If you are using the *Cambridge Storybooks*, choose one or two plays which are suitable and decide if the whole class work on one play, or if you divide the class to work on different plays. If you are dramatising *The Owl and the Pussycat*, decide how many pupils there will be in each group. Write the steps of the project on the board for pupils to copy into their notebooks:

Step 1: Take turns to read the play(s) / poem around the class.
Step 2: Make groups and reread your play / poem. Decide on and divide up the roles.
Step 3: Make the props and the costumes and paint the scenery. Your teacher will give you some ideas.
Step 4: Practise the performance. Think about the feelings of the people and make sure you speak loudly if you are an actor. Rehearse the play / poem so that you remember the words and don't need to read them.
Step 5: Do a dress rehearsal.
Step 6: Perform the play / poem to other pupils and / or to parents. Have someone record the performance on DVD so you can see it afterwards.
Step 7: Watch the performance(s) and discuss what you liked best when preparing for and doing the performance.

Make sure each group has a task plan, so that they know the order to do things and what they have to do when. Monitor and guide pupils closely to make sure they are on task. Remind them not to be too ambitious with the costumes / props / music. At the rehearsal stage, pupils will need to be reminded not to read their lines and to speak loudly and confidently. After the performance(s) to other pupils and parents, take time to reflect with pupils on the whole experience. It will help them if they can watch themselves on DVD.

Unit 5 Planning an expedition

> **You will need:**
> Reference books, the internet, large pieces of paper, glue, coloured pencils and markers, paints, scissors, dictionaries.

For this project, pupils work in pairs or small groups to plan their own expedition. They produce a poster which they display as they make a presentation to the class. Posters should be a mix of pictures and text (their own, not copied from the internet / reference books).

Tell pupils what the focus of the project is (planning an expedition). Write the steps of the project on the board for pupils to copy into their notebooks:

Step 1: Make small groups.
Step 2: Decide which part of the world you would like to explore.
Step 3: Research the area using the internet and reference books. Make notes about what time of year you will travel, how you will travel, what you will need to take and what you want to do / see on the expedition.
Step 4: Exchange information about the expedition in your groups. Decide how to present the information and plan the poster. Find some pictures of the place you want to visit and the equipment you need.
Step 5: Each person writes a draft of their text on paper – one can write about where the place is and what it is like, one can write about climate and weather, one about the equipment you need, etc. Swap texts in your group and check for content and grammar.
Step 6: Write final versions of the texts on paper. Stick the pictures and texts on the poster.
Step 7: Present your poster to the class. Every person in the group needs to speak.

Monitor and guide pupils as they are working, making sure they all keep on task and don't take too long on any one step. Help pupils with their drafts. Provide models for texts on the board or on paper as appropriate. Encourage pupils to swap their work for peer correction at Step 5.

Each group should have time to make their presentation to the rest of the class. Leave the posters on display in the classroom. If possible, display them around the school for other pupils, teachers and parents to see.

Unit 6 Mobile phone survey

> **You will need:**
> Paper, pens, computer and printing facilities or a photocopier.

For this project, pupils work in pairs to write a survey about mobile phones. They make a handout of their survey by typing it out on the computer and printing out four copies each. They can then ask four members of their families or friends the questions on the survey for homework.

Tell pupils what the focus of the project is (mobile phones). Explain the meaning of *survey*. Write the steps of the project on the board for pupils to copy into their notebooks:

Step 1: Make pairs.
Step 2: Think about mobile phones you or members of your family own. What can they do? How do people use them most? Are there any problems with mobile phones? Make notes about what you want to find out in your survey.
Step 3: Write six or seven questions for your survey.
Step 4: Type out the questions on a computer or copy them out neatly. Use the title 'Mobile phone survey'.
Step 5: Hand your survey to your teacher to photocopy or print it out.
Step 6: Take copies of your survey home and ask your family / friends the questions.
Step 7: Bring the completed surveys to the next class and compare answers with your partner. Do you have the same answers? Do you think the people you know use their mobile phones correctly?

Monitor and guide pupils as they are working, making sure they all keep on task and helping with new language as necessary. Before the pairwork, you may want to elicit some example questions and write them on the board, e.g. *How often do you use your mobile phone? Do you switch it off at night? Do you worry when you can't find your phone? How often do you buy a new mobile phone? Do you prefer sending people messages or speaking to them face to face?*

Encourage pairs to swap their work for peer correction at Step 3. In the next lesson, make sure you allow time for pupils to feed back about the results of their survey.

Extra project ideas

Unit 7 Muscles and bones

> **You will need:**
> Biology reference books, paper.

For this project, pupils research a part of the human body, e.g. an arm, draw it and then label the muscles and bones. The part they choose may depend on what they have done / are doing in Biology. It is a good idea for them to reinforce their L1 work in the English lesson. Pupils can display their work if that is appropriate, though there is no formal presentation phase in this project.

Tell pupils what the focus of the project is (muscles and bones in a part of the human body) and check what they have been studying in Biology. Write the steps of the project on the board for pupils to copy into their notebooks:

Step 1: Make pairs.
Step 2: Decide what part of the body to draw / research. Use reference books and Biology textbooks to find out the names of the muscles and bones. Find out what the different muscles do and try it out.
Step 3: Draw and label the part of the body on a piece of paper. Each pupil produces his / her own diagram.
Step 4: Make groups of four (two pairs). Take turns to show the other pair your work and to talk about what you learnt about the bones and the muscles.
Step 5: Display your drawing and / or stick it in your notebook.

Monitor and guide pupils as they are working, making sure they have appropriate reference materials. If they can't find the information they need, guide them to a different body part. For Step 4, prompt pupils to talk about what they learnt and to demonstrate, using, e.g. their arm / hand / foot. Depending on the time you have, pupils can exchange information with several other pairs. If appropriate, leave pupils' drawings on display in the classroom. If possible, display their work around the school for other pupils, teachers and parents to see.

Unit 8 What's in our food?

> **You will need:**
> Empty food packets and containers, large pieces of paper, glue, coloured pencils and markers, paints, scissors, dictionaries.

For this project, pupils work in pairs or small groups to find out and compare the ingredients of different common food products, e.g. soft drinks, cereal bars, yoghurts, dried pasta, ready meals. Each group produces a poster with a chart of what they found out and presents what they learnt to the class. Presentations should also include the food packets with their lists of ingredients and nutritional content.

Tell pupils what the focus of the project is (finding out and comparing the nutritional content of different common foods). You will need to tell pupils to bring in empty food packets, bottles and clean yoghurt pots before the project. Remind them to keep the food labels. You will also need to bring some empty packets in yourself. Write the steps of the project on the board for pupils to copy into their notebooks:

Step 1: Make pairs / small groups.
Step 2: Choose some empty food containers which have nutritional information on them.
Step 3: Using the information you learnt in the Pupil's Book lessons about food and nutrition, list the contents of the different foods according to fats, carbohydrates, etc. Note how many of the foods contain sugar.
Step 4: Plan a chart which compares the information about the different foods. Draw the chart on your poster.
Step 5: Prepare your talk in groups. Make notes to help you in your presentation. Include comments on what you learnt and what surprised you about any of the foods.
Step 6: Display your poster and your food containers. Deliver your presentation.
Step 7: After you have listened to all the presentations, discuss with your teacher what you have learnt about different foods and their nutritional value.

Monitor and guide pupils as they are working, making sure they all keep on task and don't take too long on any one step. Help pupils with any difficult vocabulary and make suggestions for the chart in Step 4. Pupils make notes for their presentation: they don't need to write a complete text. Allocate the same amount of time to each group for their presentation. Help pupils to draw conclusions about healthy food and eating.

Irregular verbs

Infinitive	Past tense	Past participle
be	was / were	been
be called	was / were called	been called
be going to	was / were going to	been going to
begin	began	begun
break	broke	broken
bring	brought	brought
buy	bought	bought
can	could	could
catch	caught	caught
choose	chose	chosen
come	came	come
cut	cut	cut
do	did	done
draw	drew	drawn
drink	drank	drunk
drive	drove	driven
dry	dried	dried
eat	ate	eaten
fall	fell	fallen
fall over	fell over	fallen over
feel	felt	felt
find	found	found
find out	found out	found out
fly	flew	flown
forget	forgot	forgotten
get	got	got
get (un)dressed	got (un)dressed	got (un)dressed
get (up / on / off)	got (up / on / off)	got (up / on / off)
get married	got married	got married
get to	got to	got to
give	gave	given
go	went	gone / been
go out	went out	gone / been out
go shopping	went shopping	gone / been shopping
grow	grew	grown
have	had	had
have (got) to	had (got) to	had (got) to
have got	had got	had got
hear	heard	heard
hide	hid	hidden
hit	hit	hit
hold	held	held
hurt	hurt	hurt
keep	kept	kept

Infinitive	Past tense	Past participle
know	knew	known
learn	learnt / learned	learnt / learned
leave	left	left
let	let	let
lie down	lay down	lain down
lose	lost	lost
make	made	made
make sure	made sure	made sure
mean	meant	meant
meet	met	met
must	had to	had to
put	put	put
put on	put on	put on
read	read	read
ride	rode	ridden
run	ran	run
say	said	said
see	saw	seen
sell	sold	sold
send	sent	sent
should	should	should
sing	sang	sung
sit	sat	sat
sleep	slept	slept
smell	smelt / smelled	smelt / smelled
speak	spoke	spoken
spell	spelt / spelled	spelt / spelled
spend	spent	spent
stand	stood	stood
steal	stole	stolen
swim	swam	swum
swing	swung	swung
take	took	taken
take a photo / picture	took a photo / picture	taken a photo / picture
take off	took off	taken off
teach	taught	taught
tell	told	told
think	thought	thought
throw	threw	thrown
understand	understood	understood
wake up	woke up	woken up
wear	wore	worn
win	won	won
write	wrote	written

Thanks and Acknowledgements

The authors and publishers acknowledge the following sources of copyright material and are grateful for the permissions granted. While every effort has been made, it has not always been possible to identify the sources of all the material used, or to trace all copyright holders. If any omissions are brought to our notice, we will be happy to include the appropriate acknowledgements on reprinting.

The authors and publishers would like to thank the following for permission to reproduce photographs:

p. 11: Alamy/© MBI; p. 16-17 (B/G): Shutterstock/© Yurchyks; p. 16 (T): Alamy/©jonathan tennan; p. 16 (B 1): Shutterstock/© A Periam Photography; p. 16 (B 2): Alamy/© imagebroker; p. 16 (B 3): Alamy/© Unlisted Images, Inc; p. 16 (B 4): Alamy/© AlamyCelebrity; p. 24-25 (B/G): Corbis/© Duomo; p. 24 (L): Shutterstock/© spirit of America; p. 24 (R): Alamy/© Stephen Bartholomew; p. 24 (boy): Shutterstock/© Gelpi JM; p. 24 (girl): Thinkstock/© Design Pics; p. 24 (a): iStock/© Christine Balderas; p. 24 (b): iStock/© Stefan Klein; p. 24 (c): iStock/© Nick Schlax; p. 24 (d): iStock/© archives; p. 34-35 (B/G): Shutterstock/© Mikhail Bakunovich; p. 34 (1a): Corbis/© Michael St. Maur Sheil; p. 34 (1b): Shutterstock/© discpicture; p. 34 (1c): Getty Images/© Photographer's Choice RF/Gilbert Laurie; p. 34 (1d): Alamy/© B. O'Kane; p. 34 (1e): Shutterstock/© grigiomedio; p. 34 (1f): Shutterstock/© DAArtist; p. 34 (2a): Alamy/© Efrain Padro; p. 34 (2c): Corbis/© Terry Scott/Demotix; p. 34 (2d): Press Association Images/© Andreas Lander/DPA; p. 34 (2f): Shutterstock/© sheff; p. 42-43 (B/G): Shutterstock/© Pressmaster; p. 42 (a): Alamy/© AlamyCelebrity; p. 42 (b): © Courtesy of the CS Lewis company; p. 42 (c): Alamy/© Mary Evans Picture Library; p. 46 (T): Getty Images/© Hulton Archive/Stringer; p. 46 (B): Corbis/© Hulton-Deutsch Collection; p. 49 (climbing): Alamy/© Radharc Images; p. 49 (swimming): Alamy/© Elvele Images Ltd; p. 49 (pop music): Alamy/© Radharc Images; p. 49 (classical music): Alamy/© Bob Daemmrich; p. 49 (maths): Shutterstock/© chonrawit boonprakob; p. 49 (maths): Shutterstock/© Hallgerd; p. 49 (art): Shutterstock/© Africa Studio; p. 49 (badminton): Thinkstock/© Goodshoot/Jupiterimages; p. 49 (table tennis): Shutterstock/© Denys Kurbatov; p. 49 (horses): Thinkstock/© iStock/Zuzule; p. 49 (fish): Alamy/© blickwinkel; p. 49 (photo): Alamy/© caia image; p. 49 (painting): Alamy/© Island Images; p. 52-53 (B/G): Shutterstock/© Soren Egeberg Photography; p. 52 (polar bear): Shutterstock/© Yvonne Pijnenburg-Schonewille; p. 52 (kangaroo): Alamy/© LOOK Die Bildagentur der Fotografen GmbH; p. 52 (goat): Shutterstock/© Txanbelin; p. 52 (tiger): Alamy/© imagebroker; p. 52 (panda): Shutterstock/© Hung Chung Chih; p. 52 (girl): Thinkstock/© iStock/michaeljung; p. 53 (T): Shutterstock/© tobkatrina; p. 57: Alamy/© MBI; p. 60-61 (B/G): Shutterstock/© Stefano Tinti; p. 60 (a T): Alamy/© Cultura Creative(RF); p. 60 (a C): Shutterstock/© Semen Lixodeev ; p. 60 (a B): Alamy/© Jim West; p. 60 (b T): Shutterstock/© sutsaiy; p. 60 (b C): Thinkstock/© iStock/ppart; p. 60 (b B): Shutterstock/John Kasawa; p. 60 (c T): SuperStock/NASA/Science Faction; p. 60 (c C): Alamy/© B.A.E Inc; p. 60 (c B): Alamy/© digitalunderwater; p. 61 (a): Shutterstock/© Soulart; p. 61 (b): Shutterstock/© Julien Tromeur; p. 61 (c): Shutterstock/© Ociacia; p. 65 (whale): FLPA/© Flip Nicklin/Minden Pictures; p. 65 (elephant): Thinkstock/© iStockJohan Swanepoel; p. 65 (dolphin): Thinkstock/© Fuse; p. 65 (gecko): Shutterstock/© alslutsky; p. 65 (falcon): Thinkstock/© iStock/John Pitcher; p. 65 (chimpanzee): Shutterstock/© dmvphotos; p. 65 (tiger): Alamy/© Sanjay Shrishrimal; p. 65 (shark): Thinkstock/© iStock/Cor Bosman; p. 65 (bear): Thinkstock/© Stockbyte/Comstock Images; p. 65 (kangaroo): Thinkstock/© Stockbyte/Tom Brakefield; p. 65 (rabbit): Thinkstock/© iStock/Rick Wylie; p. 70-71 (B/G): Shutterstock/Igorsky; p. 70 (bone): Corbis/© MedicalRF.com; p. 70 (skeleton): Thinkstock/© iStock/DrPAS; p. 70 (a): Getty Images/© Dorling Kindersley/Dave King; p. 70 (b): www.skullsunlimited.com; p. 70 (c): Shutterstock/© Waddell Images; p. 70 (d): Shutterstock/© Owen Smith Photography; p. 78-79 (B/G): Alamy/© amana images inc; p. 78: Thinkstock/© iStock/Okea.

Commissioned photography on pages 8, 17, 22, 25, 34 (2b), 34 (2e), 35, 43, 53 (B), 58, 61 (B), 71, 76, 79 (B) by Trevor Clifford Photography. Commissioned photography on page 79 (T) by Stephen Bond.

The authors and publishers are grateful to the following illustrators:

Adrian Barclay, c/o Beehive; Andrew Painter; Alan Rowe; Bryan Beach, c/o Advocate Art; Kelly Kennedy, c/o Sylvie Poggio; Jenny Nightingale; Trevor Metcalfe; Julian Mosedale; Ken Oliver, c/o Art Agency; Mark Ruffle, c/o Beehive; c/o Sylvie Poggio; Melanie Sharp; Lisa Smith, c/o Sylvie Poggio; Mark Turner,c/o Beehive; James Walmesley, c/o Graham-Cameron Illustration; Gwyneth Williamson; FLP; Lee Montgomery

The publishers are grateful to the following contributors:

Hilary Ratcliff: Editor
Louise Edgeworth: picture research and art direction
Wild Apple Design Ltd: page design
Blooberry: additional design
Lon Chan: cover design
John Green and Tim Woolf, TEFL Audio: audio recordings
Songs written and produced by Robert Lee, Dib Dib Dub Studios.
hyphen S.A.: editorial management